Assembling
the Architect

Assembling the Architect

The History and Theory of Professional Practice

GEORGE BARNETT JOHNSTON

BLOOMSBURY VISUAL ARTS
LONDON · NEW YORK · OXFORD · NEW DELHI · SYDNEY

BLOOMSBURY VISUAL ARTS
Bloomsbury Publishing Plc
50 Bedford Square, London, WC1B 3DP, UK
1385 Broadway, New York, NY 10018, USA

BLOOMSBURY, BLOOMSBURY VISUAL ARTS and the Diana logo
are trademarks of Bloomsbury Publishing Plc

First published in Great Britain 2020

Copyright © George Barnett Johnston, 2020

George Barnett Johnston has asserted his right under the Copyright,
Designs and Patents Act, 1988, to be identified as Author of this work.

Cover design: Eleanor Rose

All rights reserved. No part of this publication may be reproduced or transmitted
in any form or by any means, electronic or mechanical, including photocopying,
recording, or any information storage or retrieval system, without
prior permission in writing from the publishers.

Bloomsbury Publishing Plc does not have any control over, or responsibility for,
any third-party websites referred to or in this book. All internet addresses given
in this book were correct at the time of going to press. The author and publisher
regret any inconvenience caused if addresses have changed or sites have ceased
to exist, but can accept no responsibility for any such changes.

A catalogue record for this book is available from the British Library.

A catalog record for this book is available from the Library of Congress.

ISBN: HB: 978-1-3501-2682-4
       PB: 978-1-3501-2686-2
       ePDF: 978-1-3501-2685-5
       eBook: 978-1-3501-2684-8

Typeset by Integra Software Services Pvt. Ltd.
Printed and bound in India

To find out more about our authors and books visit www.bloomsbury.com
and sign up for our newsletters.

CONTENTS

List of Figures vii
Preface xvi

Introduction 1

1 Seeing Double: Histories of Architectural Practice 7
   Owners and builders, their umpires and agents 8
   Mr. Day's handbook 20
   The wisdom of Tom Thumtack 26
   Another kind of architects' handbook 33

2 The Architect's Office 35
   Pictures at an exhibition 42
   Rockwell Kent 49
   Squires & Wynkoop 51
   Ewing & Chappell 67
   The Architects' Building 71

3 Architect and Owner 93
   A collection of practices 94
   Various forms of architectural service 96
   The selection of an architect 105
   Fees, contracts, and consultants 115
   The architect–owner relationship 132

4 Architects and Builders 145
   Card games and boxing matches 146
   General contractors 151
   Architect as owner's agent 155

Builders organize 161
A new standard of care 177

5   Tools, Technology, Practice 181
    Tools of architectural practice 182
    New tools of practice 199
    A conversion 214

Notes 219
Bibliography 270
Index 292

LIST OF FIGURES

0.1 Rockwell Kent, Preface, *Architec-tonics: The Tales of Tom Thumtack, Architect* (New York: Comstock, 1914) xvi

1.1 Form of Contract Adopted by the Joint Committee of the American Institute of Architects, the Western Association of Architects, and the National Association of Builders, 1888. By permission of the American Institute of Architects Archives 16

1.2 Frank Miles Day. *Brickbuilder* 24 (1915) 21

1.3 Cover detail, *The Handbook of Architectural Practice* (Washington, DC: American Institute of Architects, 1927) 25

1.4 Rockwell Kent, Frontispiece, *Architec-tonics: The Tales of Tom Thumtack, Architect* (New York: Comstock, 1914) 27

1.5 Rockwell Kent, "Tom Thumtack AIA," *Architec-tonics: The Tales of Tom Thumtack, Architect* (New York: Comstock, 1914) 29

1.6 Frederick Squires, "an architect of to-day," *Architecture* 20 (1909) 30

1.7 Rockwell Kent, Table of Contents, *Architec-tonics: The Tales of Tom Thumtack, Architect* (New York: Comstock, 1914) 31

LIST OF FIGURES

1.8 Rockwell Kent, "The Rector's Brother," *Architec-tonics: The Tales of Tom Thumtack, Architect* (New York: Comstock, 1914) 32

2.1 Rockwell Kent, "Thumtack & Hen Partners," *Architec-tonics: The Tales of Tom Thumtack, Architect* (New York: Comstock, 1914) 36

2.2 Rockwell Kent, "Tom Thumtack, Client," *Architecture and Building* 46 (1914) 36

2.3 Floor plan, "The Business Side of an Architect's Office: The Office of Mr. Donn Barber," *The Brickbuilder* 22 (1913) 38

2.4 Reception room, "The Business Side of an Architect's Office: The Office of Mr. Donn Barber," *The Brickbuilder* 22 (1913) 39

2.5 Stenographers' room, "The Business Side of an Architect's Office: The Office of Mr. Donn Barber," *The Brickbuilder* 22 (1913) 39

2.6 Drafting room, "The Business Side of an Architect's Office: The Office of Mr. Donn Barber," *The Brickbuilder* 22 (1913) 40

2.7 Private office, "The Business Side of an Architect's Office: The Office of Mr. Donn Barber," *The Brickbuilder* 22 (1913) 40

2.8 Office record reference card, "The 'Business' of Architecture," *Architectural Review* 23 (1918) 41

2.9 Frontispiece, *Year Book of the Architectural League of New York and Catalogue of the Twenty-Fourth Annual Exhibition* (New York: Kalkhoff, 1909) 44

2.10 Contractor's advertisement, *Year Book of the Architectural League of New York and Catalogue of the Twenty-Fourth Annual Exhibition* (New York: Kalkhoff, 1909) 46

2.11 Frank Miles Day & Bro., Architects; House at Melrose, PA; *Year Book of the Architectural League of New York and Catalogue of the Twenty-Fourth Annual Exhibition* (New York: Kalkhoff, 1909) 48

2.12 Frank Miles Day & Bro., Architects; House at Melrose, PA; *The Year Book and Catalogue of the T Square Club* (Philadelphia: McLaughlin Printing Co., Ltd., 1910) 48

2.13 Squires & Wynkoop, Architects; Residence for Mr. A.B. Steen; *The Year Book and Catalogue of the T Square Club* (Philadelphia: McLaughlin Printing Co., Ltd., 1910) 49

2.14 Editorial Board of *The Columbia Jester*, 1902. Rockwell Kent and Frederick Squires appear on the back row center, left to right. Ely Jacques Kahn is seated on the floor, left. Rare Book & Manuscript Library, Columbia University in the City of New York 51

2.15 John Wynkoop, Atelier Donn Barber, A Market Cross, *The T Square Club Eleventh Annual Exhibition 1904–1905* (Philadelphia: McLaughlin Bros. Co., Ltd., 1905) 52

2.16 Squires & Wynkoop, Architects; The Gargoyle Gate at Williams College, *The Hollow-Tile House* (New York: William T. Comstock Co., 1913) 53

LIST OF FIGURES

2.17 Squires & Wynkoop, Architects; Phi Delta Theta Fraternity, Williams College, *Architectural Record* 24 (1908) 54

2.18 Squires & Wynkoop, Architects; "The First Terra Cotta House in New York," *The Hollow-Tile House* (New York: William T. Comstock Co., 1913) 55

2.19 Squires & Wynkoop, Architects; Church of St. Luke the Evangelist; Roselle, NJ; *The Hollow-Tile House* (New York: William T. Comstock Co., 1913) 56

2.20 Map of extents of Baltimore fire, *Inland Architect & News Record* 43 (1904) 58

2.21 Aftermath of Baltimore Fire, The Brickbuilder 13 (1904) 58

2.22 Squires & Wynkoop, Architects; Demonstration house in stucco-covered hollow-tile commissioned by the journal *Building Progress*; *The Hollow-Tile House* (New York: William T. Comstock Co., 1913) 60

2.23 Squires & Wynkoop, Architects; House for Mrs. J.J. Adams, construction of hollow-tile walls; *The Hollow-Tile House* (New York: William T. Comstock Co., 1913) 63

2.24 Squires & Wendehack, Architects; details of tile construction, *The Hollow-Tile House* (New York: William T. Comstock Co., 1913) 63

2.25 Floor assembly construction using hollow-tile, *The Hollow-Tile House* (New York: William T. Comstock Co., 1913) 64

LIST OF FIGURES

2.26 Ewing & Chappell, Architects; Interior, Riding Academy of Mr. Alfred G. Vanderbilt; Portsmouth, RI; *Architectural Record* 21 (1907) 68

2.27 Ewing & Chappell, Architects; House of Mrs. Rockwell Kent in Tarrytown, NY; *American Architect & Building News* 96 (1909) 69

2.28 George S. Chappell, "Charrette!" in "Paris School Days," *Architectural Record* 29 (1911) 69

2.29 Ewing & Chappell with LaFarge & Morris Architects, The Architects Building in New York City. From *left to right: Architecture and Building* 44 (1912) and *Brickbuilder* 22 (1913) 72

2.30 Plan, Office of Ewing & Chappell in the Architects' Building, *Brickbuilder* 22 (1913) 75

2.31 Reception Room, Office of Ewing & Chappell in the Architects' Building, *Brickbuilder* 22 (1913) 76

2.32 Mr. Ewing's Private Office, Office of Ewing & Chappell in the Architects' Building, *Brickbuilder* 22 (1913) 77

2.33 Drafting Room, Office of Ewing & Chappell in the Architects' Building, *Brickbuilder* 22 (1913). Rockwell Kent is likely the drafter seated on the stool in the foreground. Note drafting tables configured on trestles 78

2.34 Rockwell Kent and George S. Chappell, "The Nomenclature of the Styles: The Greek Freeze," *Brickbuilder* 24 (1915) 80

2.35 Hogarth, Jr. (Rockwell Kent) with George S. Chappell, "Th' Avenue," First published in *Vanity Fair* (January 1916) 82

2.36 Hogarth, Jr. (Rockwell Kent) with George S. Chappell, Rollo and Uncle George, *Rollo in Society: A Guide for Youth* (New York: G.P. Putnam's Sons, 1922) 83

2.37 George S. Chappell in the guise of Walter E. Traprock, F.R.S.S.E.U., *The Cruise of the Kawa* (New York: G.P. Putnam's Sons, 1921) 85

2.38 The W.E. Traprock Expedition, *The Cruise of the Kawa* (New York: G.P. Putnam's Sons, 1921). Publisher George Palmer Putnam appears standing at left in the guise of *Kawa* First Mate William Henry Thomas 85

2.39 Rockwell Kent in Eskimo guise, *My Northern Exposure: The Kawa at the Pole* (New York: G.P. Putnam's Sons, 1922) 86

2.40 Ralph Barton, "George S. Chappell Demonstrating His Outline of Censorship," *Nonsenseorship* (New York: G.P. Putnam's Sons, 1922) 87

3.1 Rockwell Kent, "Client vs. Architect: A Plea," *Architec-tonics: The Tales of Tom Thumtack, Architect* (New York: Comstock, 1914) 97

3.2 Rockwell Kent, "Tom Thumtack Detective," *Architec-tonics: The Tales of Tom Thumtack, Architect* (New York: Comstock, 1914) 100

3.3 Rockwell Kent, another mistaken identity from "The Pinch Hitter," *Architec-tonics: The Tales of Tom Thumtack, Architect* (New York: Comstock, 1914) 101

3.4 Frederick Squires, Architect; The Mercantile Building, New York City; *Architecture and Building* 44 (1912) 102

3.5	Rockwell Kent, "The Speculative Builder," *Architec-tonics: The Tales of Tom Thumtack, Architect* (New York: Comstock, 1914)	103
3.6	Rockwell Kent, "Repeal of the Tarsney Act," *Architecture and Building* 47 (1915)	111
3.7	Rockwell Kent, "Fees: A Reductio Ad Absurdum," *Architecture and Building* 46 (1914)	117
3.8	Rockwell Kent, "The Tectarch," *Architecture and Building* 47 (1915)	126
3.9	Rockwell Kent, "Advertising: Reports from the Canon of Ethics," *Architec-tonics: The Tales of Tom Thumtack, Architect* (New York: Comstock, 1914)	137
3.10	Rockwell Kent, a work horse from "Temperament," *Architecture and Building* 47 (1915)	140
3.11	Rockwell Kent, a race horse from "Temperament," *Architecture and Building* 47 (1915)	140
4.1	Rockwell Kent, the client at ringside from "Contractors," *Architec-tonics: The Tales of Tom Thumtack, Architect* (New York: Comstock, 1914)	147
4.2	Rockwell Kent, the card game from "Contractors," *Architec-tonics: The Tales of Tom Thumtack, Architect* (New York: Comstock, 1914)	147
4.3	Rockwell Kent, "Contractors," *Architec-tonics: The Tales of Tom Thumtack, Architect* (New York: Comstock, 1914)	148
4.4	Exchange Room, Master Builders Exchange, Philadelphia, *Carpentry and Building* 12 (1890)	165

4.5 Floor plan of Permanent Exhibitions Department, Master Builders Exchange, Philadelphia, *Carpentry and Building* 12 (1890) 166

4.6 Diagrams of masonry assemblies erected to illustrate materials and workmanship, Master Builders Exchange, Philadelphia, *Carpentry and Building* 12 (1890) 167

4.7 Rockwell Kent, the squared circle from "Contractors," *Architec-tonics: The Tales of Tom Thumtack, Architect* (New York: Comstock, 1914) 176

4.8 Rockwell Kent, the rearview mirror from "Contractors," *Architec-tonics: The Tales of Tom Thumtack, Architect* (New York: Comstock, 1914) 179

5.1 Rockwell Kent, "Specifications," *Architec-tonics: The Tales of Tom Thumtack, Architect* (New York: Comstock, 1914) 187

5.2 Rockwell Kent, architect on the ropes from "Contractors," *Architec-tonics: The Tales of Tom Thumtack, Architect* (New York: Comstock, 1914) 200

5.3 Organization Chart, *The Hoggson Building Method* (New York: Hoggson Brothers, 1910) 203

5.4 "A Conversion by Tom Thumtack." Artist's proof, 1914. Rockwell Kent Papers; Box 21; Squires, Frederick; Rare Book and Manuscript Library, Columbia University Library. By permission of Plattsburgh State Art Museum 215

5.5   Squires & Wynkoop, Architects; Country House for Mrs. E.L. Best; Bronxville, NY; *The Hollow-Tile House* (New York: William T. Comstock Co., 1913)   217

5.6   "Finis." Artist's proof, 1914. Rockwell Kent Papers; Box 21; Squires, Frederick; Rare Book and Manuscript Library, Columbia University Library. By permission of Plattsburgh State Art Museum   218

PREFACE

FIGURE 0.1 *Rockwell Kent, Preface,* Architec-tonics: The Tales of Tom Thumtack, Architect *(New York: Comstock, 1914).*

What is architectural theory if not reflection upon architectural practice? Yet, business and management-oriented coursework in our schools of architecture, a requisite for the preparation of competent and ethical practitioners, too often omits historical and theoretical speculation around the very topics they teach. By essentializing the profession in terms of a timeless A-O-C trinity—of Architects, Owners, and Contractors—what is gained in schematic clarity only elides more fundamental lessons about deeper processes fomenting change. Rendering a dynamic subject as a static object may convey such taxonomies of practice as can be tested on a licensing exam, but it misses a higher call to inspire architect-aspirants for roles as actors and as innovators in designing practice itself. It is the aim of this book to be a historical and theoretical supplement to otherwise inadequate rubrics of professionalism that present practice atemporally as if formed of a single synchronic slice. While not negating the explanatory value of such present-oriented approaches, *Assembling the Architect* sets instead the historical pre-texts of US architectural practice and suggests some theoretical post-scripts for future debate.

PREFACE

Among the most useful and enduring touchstones stimulating historical imagination about the profession of architecture, I have returned time and again to the collected essays in Spiro Kostof's *The Architect: Chapters in the History of a Profession*. In savoring those historical accounts, I have also been prodded into research of my own because the questions suggested there about our own contemporary circumstances confirm that there are yet so many more chapters to be written. The context of US architectural practice has been the focus of attention in this and a previous book, *Drafting Culture: A Social History of Architectural Graphic Standards*, because I have felt that assumptions about New World professions as polyglots of European tradition were inadequate to explain the particular circumstances that pertained here on the ground. This focus is not formed of a cultural chauvinism; rather, it is meant to suggest a mode of inquiry that allows practices to be reconsidered as manifestations of local tendencies as well as universalizing and colonizing trends. In my previous work, for example, I discovered that a profession with such great potential to serve as a vehicle for upward social mobility had, over time, become increasingly restrictive and closed. In the present work, it may be suggested that one unintended consequence of the quest for contractual uniformity has been to relegate potentially vital practices and diverse practitioners to the margins of professional respectability—for example in the roles of women and other historically under-represented groups.

My own approach has been to focus on particular tools of architectural practice as a means of cracking open the social relationships embedded there—specifically in tomes such as *Architectural Graphic Standards* and now *The Handbook of Architectural Practice* whereby conventions were codified and standards were spread. The fortuitous discovery of *Architectonics: The Tales of Tom Thumtack, Architect*, a satirical account of the architecture profession contemporaneous with the emergence of *The Handbook*, suggested an approach to presenting certain key structuring relationships of architectural practice in very human terms. The first pairing of those doppelgangers was posed in 2011 as part of a festschrift honoring two of my mentors at Emory University, urban historian Dana White and cultural anthropologist Ivan Karp. This larger project progressed slowly, however—too slowly in fact for Dana or Ivan to see the work come to its fruition. In admiration and appreciation for all that their lives contributed, I dedicate this book to their memories.

I have benefited greatly from opportunities to present portions of this work in its formative stages to colleagues at various scholarly gatherings. These include the "Tools of Drafting" symposium organized at the Internationales Kolleg für Kulturtechnikforschung und Medienphilosophie (IKKM) of the Bauhaus-Universität Weimar, the "Drawing Summit" organized by Volkan Alkanoglu at the Georgia Tech School of Architecture, to members of the architecture faculty at the University of Seoul, as well as annual meetings of the Association of Collegiate Schools of Architecture, the Southeast Society of

Architectural Historians, and the Construction History Society of America. Comments from anonymous reviewers as well as those face-to-face following presentations have helped sharpen my arguments and suggested additional avenues for research. Likewise, the thorough and insightful comments of the pre-publication manuscript reviewers, also anonymous, were greatly appreciated and well-received. I have tried to respond to the spirit of their suggestions and have endeavored in my revisions and refinements to always keep the reader foremost in mind. Any lapses in that regard are my own responsibility, however, and not theirs.

Thanks are due to my friends and colleagues at Georgia Tech for their support and constructive critique of this project. Professors of the Practice Stuart Romm, Ennis Parker, and Brian Bowen bring a wealth of experience to bear as they rehearse their students in lessons of leadership and collaboration across fields of design and construction. School Chair Scott Marble has leant his enthusiasm as well for how this project might support a broader vision of disciplinary change. The office corridor I share with Professors John Peponis, Sonit Bafna, and Harris Dimitropoulos has been tagged by one other as a "cemetery of intellectuals," a sobriquet we happily embrace. Our daily dialogs, musings, and debates help imbue each other's intellectual passions with a spirit of fun, generosity, and mutual respect.

The publisher and I gratefully acknowledge the permission granted to reproduce the copyrighted material in this book. I was fortunate in my research to locate key documents germane to this study in archival collections at the American Institute of Architects Archives and the Architectural Archives of the University of Pennsylvania, each of which graciously granted permission to draw upon and reproduce original textual materials found therein. Access to the collections of the Avery Architectural & Fine Arts Library at Columbia University was of great assistance to the research, and Columbia's Rare Books and Manuscript Library yielded some wonderful gems for which they provided publishable reproductions. Appreciation is extended to the Plattsburg State Art Museum at SUNY-Plattsburgh for their assistance in navigating permissions requests among the several institutions containing collections devoted to artist Rockwell Kent, especially those housed at Columbia University and the Archives of American Art of the Smithsonian Institution. Thanks are also extended to the Association of Collegiate Schools of Architecture for permission to include in this book several pieces of work previously presented at annual meetings and published in conference proceedings.

Many textual sources and most of the images reproduced here are drawn from pre-1924 professional trade journals, materials that are now in the public domain. Photographs reproduced herein are regrettably unattributed reflecting practices of the era in which many photographers' work went uncredited. Every effort has been made to trace copyright holders and to obtain their permission for the use of copyrighted material. The publisher apologizes for any errors or omissions in the above list and would be grateful if notified of any corrections that should be incorporated in future reprints or editions of this book. The third-party copyrighted material displayed in the pages of this book is done so on the basis of "fair dealing for the purposes of criticism and review" or "fair use for the purposes of teaching, criticism, scholarship or research" only in accordance with international copyright laws, and is not intended to infringe upon the ownership rights of the original owners.

The long duration of this project would have been much longer still without the timely and crucial support of two sources. First, the Hambidge Center for the Creative Arts & Sciences in Rabun County, Georgia, was generous in its award of a writing residency during Summer 2015 that provided the combination of daily solitude, mid-day hikes, and evening fellowship over meals so conducive to shaping the basic outline and themes of this work. A grant of release-time from teaching by the office of Associate Dean for Research in the Georgia Tech College of Design during Fall semester 2017 combined with research time from the preceding summer allowed six full months of focused attention to develop the outline into a full-fledged manuscript. The commissioning process for this work has been rendered a pleasure through the meticulous and thoughtful attention of James Thompson and the folks at Bloomsbury Publishers.

Finally, and most of all, I express my love and appreciation to my family for their support over the years, and especially to Denise Colette Dumais for being as unsparing with her challenging insights as she is in her affections, for her uncanny perceptiveness, and for a shared perspective that life can simultaneously and in equal portions be special, unpredictable, and routine.

Introduction

Architects in the late-nineteenth and early-twentieth centuries were assembling a new profession. They were honing their practices in consequential ways in response to modern demands. By individual and organized efforts, architects in the United States aimed to enhance social standing and to build professional prestige. The impressive commissions realized during this period, public and private edifices with all their spatial and stylistic flourishes, give ample evidence of the material, cultural, and economic success of their labors. Less apparent than these physical displays, however, are the intertwining networks of social and economic relations, the conflicts and competition among architects, their clients, and the builders who constructed the projects from architects' increasingly exacting designs. Despite their best efforts to assert authority and project control, architects' aims were often stymied by other actors' interests and intents.

A mere century ago, many of the defining traits of modern professionalism that we take for granted today were only then beginning to take shape. The architecture profession in the United States back then was a heterogeneous mix of socially positioned gentleman architects, office apprenticed drafters, business-savvy labor contractors, self-assumed designing builders, engineers, mechanics, and a small but growing number of academically polished designers often lacking adequate construction knowledge. By 1900, Illinois was the only state out of the forty-five then-existing that had adopted architect registration laws. The role of the general contractor was still a novelty, general conditions of contracts were inconsistent, competitive bidding was decried as an evil, local customs frustrated consensus about national norms, and the agency of the architect was unsettled law. Relations between and among architects, general contractors, sub-contractors, and clients were ambiguous, unclear. Construction was often shoddy, a magnet for fire; and in journals, tabloids, and novels of popular culture, the motivations of the building trades and professions were often portrayed in unflattering terms.

The increasing complexity and disputatiousness of the design and construction fields in the period from the end of the Civil War to the advent of the Great Depression were particularly noteworthy, and many substantive debates were played out in the pages of trade and professional journals. Such tensions precipitated the restructuring of basic relationships among the parties and propelled the systemization of office operating procedures out of the ad hoc local conventions that mostly prevailed. Emergent legal, business, and administrative protocols were codified in the series of standardized contractual documents originated by members of the American Institute of Architects (AIA) and their construction industry counterparts; and in the period of 1917–1920, these efforts were further extended in the drafting and publication of the AIA's very first *Handbook of Architectural Practice*.

Over a relatively short period of time, in the half-century between the Civil War and the First World War, an increasingly business-oriented and litigious society was reshaping traditional ties and expectations, and foundations were being laid for the architecture profession we recognize today. With a century of hindsight we can only now begin to understand the transformative role that *The Handbook of Architectural Practice* played in both recording and propelling the very process of professionalization. The model of practice that *The Handbook* projected—one rationalized through detailed contractual obligations, managerial controls, and instrumentalized procedures—today approaches its apotheosis in emergent modes of digitally enabled practice. Rather than being some novel formations, however, building information modeling and integrated project delivery represent the realization of programs and agendas that have been over a century in-play.

Modern professions have been ordained out of social necessity to serve as agents of the specialized knowledge essential to navigate an increasingly atomized world. Their substantive functions as well as their social meta-functions have continually shifted with the times. Their purposes and priorities have been regularly transformed and reconfigured in relation to adjacent and competing vocations. While professions have typically embraced altruistic ideals of devoted public service, they have also often been motivated by parochial interests and protectionist intents. Thus, advocacy in the public interest for governmental regulation of professions through state licensure was part of a compact to preserve the self-policing powers of professional domains as well as their prerogatives of social closure and reproduction. Likewise, just as science rescued Western medicine from the grip of quackery, each of the learned professions sought its proper legitimation through varied appeals to the arts and sciences as the basis of esoteric know-how. While the rise of a "culture of professionalism" was directly tied to the ascendancy of the modern university, it was further shaped by emergence of the American business ethos.[2] Commercial relationships increasingly structured the ground of social and economic exchange in a marketplace teeming with ideas, goods, and services.

Over the intervening century till today, *The Handbook of Architectural Practice* has expanded its scope and grown in bulk in a perennial effort to encompass the ever-growing complexity of the design and construction industry and to chart the incrementally changing norms and conventions of practice. Yet in that very first handbook from 1920, we can recognize a concerted effort to ameliorate the stresses that were even then unsettling architectural discourse and practice in a manner not unlike the so-called disruptions we are now experiencing. Like today, the forces fomenting change were not merely technological, though the technological transformation of the construction industry in the aftermath of the First World War— new materials, national standards, manufacturing processes, distribution networks—was certainly profound. Both in answer to those changes and calling them forth, a shifting order of responsibility within the construction industry was being negotiated and contested. The old social hierarchies that had set rank and status among the principle actors—owners, builders, architects—were being reshuffled by exigencies of capital and labor, production and consumption, commerce and communication, knowledge and skill. New performance expectations were being set.

The aims of this study are twofold: first, to stoke a broader awareness of architectural practice by mapping some aspects of its cultural terrain; and second, to unravel some of the knots of overlapping interest that have historically structured the field. The conflicts driving reform of architecture practice a century ago may seem like quaint relics from a receding past; yet, an effort to reconstruct some aspects of that change may be instructive for us today. The tools and technologies of architectural production—compasses, contracts, capital—are all mutable. They are implicated as both causes and effects of a whole network of social relations to which they give fleeting form. Indeed, many of the instruments designed to enhance architects' authority contributed to the very controversies they were meant to mediate or defuse. The challenge is to recognize and to better understand the unresolved and perhaps unresolvable tensions at play even now in the pursuit of some new digitally mediated disciplinary ideals.[3]

The ongoing revolution in architectural practice cannot simply be explained by the ascendancy of new design technologies. Dynamic relationships that intertwine public and private interests, academic and vocational knowledge, and dialectics of means and ends have long been at work in shaping the destiny of architecture culture. The archetypal actors on the stage of architectural production—owners, architects, builders—have ever been fluid characters, each redefining their own agency and identity with respect to all the others in the shifting political economy of building. New digital information technologies may reveal or further mask the terms of those relationships, and they may accelerate or retard their transformation; but instability in the framework of architectural practice is arguably as much a precipitating *cause* of the digital dialectic as it is a resulting *effect*.

This book, then, is a cultural history of US architectural practices from a century ago. "Practices" are not just the physical venues or changing organizational schemes of so many architects' offices, though the individual characteristics of these are always of interest. "Practices" also suggests a plurality of ways and means and forms of action, the *modi operandi* of a heterogeneous cast of actors—owners, builders, architects, all of a variety of stripes. While these avatars of culture and construction are often treated as eternal archetypes, a mere century ago those roles had not been so precisely cast. Lacking plot lines firmly fixed by either contract or convention, with new conditions emerging in both business and law, individual agents engaged each other in dealings and disputes and endeavored to perfect their practices. What resulted were the unintended consequences of their action, a kind of improvised construction that we have institutionalized, now in the singular rather than a plural sense, as architectural practice.[4]

This work draws upon scholarship addressing the history and sociology of professions, but in its effort to theorize ongoing transformations in architectural practice it shifts perspective from macro to micro scale. Instead of focusing on the determinism of an overarching structure of professionalism or on precipitating causes at its base, this study attends at the ground level to locally conditioned practices, to the efforts of individual agents to shape their roles and negotiate their working relationships face-to-face. Accounts of the contributions of professional contemporaries such as Frank Miles Day, architect-author Frederick Squires, and their overlapping circles of colleagues and acquaintances are thus meant to provide concrete examples of the means by which variable and inchoate practices, ones driving the commissioning, design, and construction of buildings, were rationalized, formalized, and contested; and they are meant to provoke speculation about how architectural practice continues to be reassembled today. Sociology teaches that practice reproduces practices as techno-political *faits accomplis*; but it also proposes that practice—in the form of social practices, architectural practices—can be shaped by individual choices and informed by shared, emergent concerns.

The field of architectural practice is a dynamic social formation, both a cause and effect of the material transformations emblematic of capitalist modernity. The social and technological transformations of building, propelling and propelled by specialization of skills, the division of labor, the particularization of new functional building types, and expanding urban milieus, introduced over time an increasing retinue of players into the process. By the middle of the nineteenth century, the role and function of the architect as an intermediary between clients and mechanics was well-established as one model, though any number of hybrid arrangements were simultaneously in play—as they still are today. Besides owners serving as their own architects, or when in the role of developer as their own builder, architects might spring forth out of the ranks of builders; or architect and builder might be one and the same. The capital interests differentiating business and the state, private profit from public trust, could ramify in a variety of associations with the laboring agents of construction and design. Likewise, the competing and overlapping motivations of owners, architects, and builders have constantly been in flux. In contemporary practice, each of these figures embodies a multitude and symbolically personifies a distillation of the respective functional and economic interests that govern their relations and those of society as a whole. The resilience of these three as archetypes is nonetheless an index of ongoing historical processes of intellectual and vocational differentiation that in the early-twentieth century grew increasingly urgent as competition for marketplace position became the primary motive of an ascendant business culture.

The tripartite differentiation of owner, architect, and builder was definitively codified in *The Handbook of Architectural Practice*. Following Day's same basic scheme, this book—*Assembling the Architect*—accounts for the inter-relationship between and among those three essential actors as issued from the late-nineteenth through the early-twentieth centuries. It must be kept in mind, however, that while this strict division of labor may be edifying as a conceptual model in architecture school or for shaping public perception, it masks the basic fluidity and the hybrids of responsibility that have historically held sway. Far from being a static formation, the design and construction field has perennially morphed into novel configurations, as it still does. It reflects the competing interests of rule-bound players but ones whose respective roles and identities are continually being redefined by chance, available tools, and emerging technologies. Rather than simply reproducing old stereotypes engendered by century-old contractual conventions, the goal is to describe instead some of the forces that have been at play in the ongoing transformation of the construction industry. Like architectural practice itself, the following chapters may be read as either the same story told five different ways or else as a mangle of intertwining narratives. The archival and anecdotal evidence of history presented here may also serve as a cautionary tale; once recognized as tragedy, or even comedy, it need not repeat as farce.

CHAPTER ONE

Seeing Double: Histories of Architectural Practice

A predominant historical assumption about the transplantation of the European concept of architecture to North America uncritically accepts an old-world/new-world dialectic about the origins of culture and the trajectory of civilizing taste. We need not subscribe to reactionary doctrines of American exceptionalism in order to counter that trope; rather, it is possible to recognize that within the mechanisms of colonialism, practices as well as theories are transformed when they travel. Their meanings and practical implications can and do change when transplanted to new soils.[1] The "break" in continuity of architecture culture and practice from the old world to the new embodied both political and ideological differences despite any apparent continuities with European formal stylistic traditions. In many respects, architectural practice had to be reinvented in the new colonial context, but it emerged in turn with its own colonizing tendencies that acted back upon the source.

Instruments of architectural practice such as contracts and change orders, shop drawings and specifications did not just spring forth from nowhere; rather, they developed over time as functional equivalents on the social plane of the material-specific tools that mediate any craft or trade. They rationalized and formalized the social and material interactions bred by increasingly complex building tasks. As such, they served as structuring mechanisms both shaped by and shaping practice, both enabling and constraining human agency. Such tools were forged in response to indigenous needs to mediate differentiated local building cultures.

Even while local conventions held sway, architectural practice in the United States became increasingly nationalized following the Civil War. Legal precedents, business tactics, and building materials and techniques migrated across state boundaries; dialog and debate about the uniform terms of contractual relations were propagated by professional organizations and trade publications; the education of architects became increasingly institutionalized. When Frank Miles Day set himself the task in 1917 of soliciting, sifting, and distilling "best practices" from professional colleagues from across the country, he hit upon a novel device that seems only in retrospect to have been an obvious or inevitable form. The drafting and ongoing revision of Day's *Handbook of Architectural Practice* made the nationalization—and rationalization—of architectural practice an explicit process. Once published, it established a baseline of shared experience and common wisdom that redounded to the standardization of previously tacit, locally differentiated practices.

Owners and builders, their umpires and agents

Before we can even begin to imagine an architect on-the-scene as owner's agent or master builder, we must first envision a relationship far more fundamental, the one that obtains between owners and builders themselves. According to a late-nineteenth-century treatise on construction law, "The relation between the builder and the owner is formed exclusively by the contract."[2] From this we might wonder, which came first, the architect or the contract? While Vitruvius posited the existence of the architect as an historical *fait accompli* already deeply embedded in Greco-Roman culture from ancient times, the *raison d'être* of the architect in America cannot be so quickly assumed. The necessity for and presence of the architect in the settlement of North America were neither functionally nor historically preordained; rather, the role of architect on this continent had to be reestablished in its own right, within an endemic culture of practice.

The logic of building practice in the United States can be best understood in terms of gradual shifts in the political economy of building which issued from colonial times and outward, advancing toward an imaginary frontier into which displaced native peoples had retreated. Over three centuries of settlement, pioneers and ostensibly self-sufficient settlers became a symbiotic society, both widely dispersed across the landscape and tightly concentrated in cities. They were composed of property owners unable to simply build for themselves; and of crafts people building for others, whether for trade or through involuntary servitude, plying their skill in wood, brick, iron, and stone. The notion of an architect could issue from either side of that equation, but each formulation carried embedded relations of class and power.[3]

On the one hand, we might imagine royally entitled owners of landed estates possessing—along with scores of enslaved individuals whose skilled labor they could direct toward ambitious building goals—some knowledge in science and mathematics, a set of fine drawing instruments, and a personal library with European architectural folios, perhaps of Palladian plates.[4] In this instance, the colonial grantee would serve in effect as both developer and their own architect following a model of English aristocracy. The gentlemanly architect supplied a vision and the necessary resources, guiding craft laborers either directly or organizing them through skilled intermediaries, in the day-to-day execution of their tasks. The second or third sons of those estates, foreclosed as legatees by the customs of primogeniture, might find for themselves a calling as building designer and adviser, an "architect" to others of their same social class.

On the other hand, and in contrast to agrarian narratives, we might envision a flourishing city, still fresh within recent memory as a mere settlement, expanding and being subdivided into land lots assigned for private, commercial, or public uses now awaiting their requisite structures. By commission on contract, or increasingly on speculation for profit, loose companies of masons and carpenters, journeymen and apprentices guided by the experience of their contracting masters—and their sometime sketches adapted from pattern books of classical detail—could infill with ample facility the surveyor's grid with a serviceable building fabric. With increasing acumen, such builders' draftsmen might provide plans as a service to their commercial or other clientele, or they might separate from their builder colleagues altogether and distinguish themselves independently with a self-anointed title, "architect." They might also strive in their dealings with clients, some with more and some with less success, to attain the social status and position of gentleman.

Then, moving into the nineteenth century, in a familiar trope of westward expansion, we might conjure up the figure of the pioneer settler, hewing shelter out of the forest or out on the prairie.[5] We imagine the triad of actors that defines the contemporary construction industry springing forth from some primary unity where the roles of owner, architect, and builder were all performed by one-and-the-same, rugged individuals fulfilling their basic dwelling needs with just the means at hand. As the scope and complexity of projects expanded, then a reservoir of labor stood ready at hand but in need of direction. The various trades—carpenters and masons, masters and apprentices—at first could construe and construct designs verbally conveyed to them by their clients, owners acting in effect if not in fact as their own architects. Over time and as the scale and complexity of building grew, enterprising builders managed, through the intermediary of drafters and their drawings, to supply to the owner ever more differentiated designs to satisfy increasingly exacting requirements.[6]

These three versions of the same story illustrate the hybrid genealogy of a nascent profession. Construction customs and building design practices migrated to North America along with embedded architectural traditions, but they adapted to local conditions. They were shaped by, and in turn shaped, the diverse interests and expectations of building instigators, all of whom operated within regionally differentiated notions of commerce and trade.[7] In the late-nineteenth and early-twentieth centuries, even as the field of architecture was being formalized within a still maturing framework of American business and law, journal editorialists and convention speakers strove to chart the degree of change in the social standing of the profession. While such accounts might vary in objectivity by virtue of the vagaries of memory, their degree of historical proximity, or polemics of progress and decline, they nonetheless present a composite narrative of an emergent idea, the American architect.

"Fifty years ago"

In his role as editor at the fledgling Boston-based journal *American Architect and Building News*, William Rotch Ware (1848–1917) reminisced from his perspective of 1876 upon the state of the profession as compared to the 1820s:

> Fifty years ago, … [t]he men who designed buildings were, ordinarily, the men who built them; and it was only in rare cases, and for structures of unusual importance, that the two or three men in the country who made a profession of designing were called upon. The position of these men was anomalous and individual: most people had nothing to do with it, knew and thought nothing about it. As towns grew, and building increased, architects became more common; but their position and influence were for a long time determined in each case only by the success and action of the individual. It was but slowly that they were accepted as a class, or that any defined usages grew up in their relations to the public or their clients.[8]

Ware was sanguine about the progress achieved in the public standing of the architecture profession in the intervening decades since the founding of the American Institute of Architects (AIA) in 1857. He argued, "… the first reason why they have gained is that they have become a body; that is to say, they are now a class of men, fulfilling a special function in a somewhat uniform way, and with more or less of common understanding among them." Ware cautioned, nonetheless, that "even now those relations and usages are far from being universally determined and recognized." Future progress in establishing architects' professional authority as "arbiters in all matters of design" still depended, he insisted, upon professional unity in the establishment of consistent standards of practice, style, and taste in order to gain broad public approbation and support.[9]

"Fifty years ago" was a recurrent frame of reference for succeeding generations of architects striving to stake their own progress against fading memories of a receding past. In a speech at the 1887 AIA convention, architect William W. Boyington (1839–1898) noted the virtual absence of the profession of architecture from Chicago at the beginning of his career in the 1850s. Addressing methods of practice that prevailed "fifty years ago," Boyington described the direct relationship that then obtained between owners and builders and the gradual emergence and recognition of the profession as he had observed over the course of his career[10]:

> Fifty years ago, and even less, architects were largely supported by contractors. Now and for years past the owners have found it for their interest to deal directly with architects. Still there are many impecunious persons who think it is so much money wasted to employ an architect except for partial service, through their contractor, although, by such a course, they, as a usual thing, indirectly pay three prices for the designs. ...
>
> When I came to Chicago, thirty-four years ago, I found the architects then in practice were recent master builders or contractors. Chicago and the West at that time could hardly be said to require the services of architects separately as such. At that time the structures were just simple buildings. But the builders soon found it would be better for them to have plans made for them, than to spend their time in making plans, so they clubbed together, and induced one of the most apt in drawing plans, to give up contracting and devote his whole time to Architecture, and guaranteed him a compensation of two dollars per day, which should be paid to him, if he did not get business enough to aggregate that amount. ... It was not uncommon to be asked in what the business of an architect consisted. This simply shows that as a profession it was not understood.[11]

Echoing each other from Boston to Chicago, these recollections suggest that the architect arose only slowly out of the ranks of master craftsmen, a situation matched in Philadelphia which, Boyington claimed, "in proportion to the number of its inhabitants, put up, in the last fifty years, more buildings without employment of architects on them, than any city in the country."[12] The changing scope and variety of building within these urbanizing milieus, the changing materials and building systems, called forth a new class of construction intermediary to satisfy dual and sometimes competing demands—accommodating and representing the interests owners; coordinating and supervising the work of builders.

Near the turn of the century, Frank E. Kidder (1859–1905), the architect and civil engineer best known as the author of an essential handbook for his respective disciplines, charted a similar vocational genealogy from the mid-nineteenth century when the field of architecture was typically recognized as being descended from the craft of building. He expressed his frustration, however, that despite the increasing technical complexity of building projects over intervening years, architects of the present seemed ever more apt to align themselves with the art of architecture. Rather than staking a claim on the science and mechanics of building, they relegated those concerns and delegated much authority to so many engineers and consultants. While never negating the importance of artistically inspired design, Kidder questioned the wisdom of this cognitive, disciplinary divorce.

> Forty years ago nearly all of those persons who were engaged in the business of preparing plans for buildings had first been carpenters, and were better educated in building than in the art of architecture. Today, the case is reversed, and, except in the smaller towns and cities, there are but few architects who have worked at the bench, and comparatively few who have had a scientific training in the mechanics of construction. ...
>
> That an architect must have considerable artistic feeling and creative ability is not only generally recognized, but it is also a requisite for securing work and consequently essential to the successful practice of the profession. How far he should be a builder and engineer is not so generally agreed, nor, the writer believes, sufficiently considered.[13]

The golden anniversary issue of the *American Architect and Building News* in 1926 provided another occasion for sharing fifty-year retrospectives about the emergence of the practice of architecture. Looking backward to the period of the national Centennial of 1876, two architects chronicled certain pervasive paradoxes in the field of architecture as it passed across the "dark veil" of the Civil War. In these accounts, the character of the architect as a "professional" was divided between those operating as artists on the principle of gentlemen's agreements and those pursuing the most avaricious sort of business dealings. Prominent Boston architect Clarence H. Blackall (1857–1942) acknowledged only the former group as being among those entitled to a professional title, but even among that group a reputation as an artist could undercut that nominal distinction:

> No, fifty years ago was not a golden period. It was a time of seed planting, of nurture and of hope, but not of fruition or harvest. The architect of those days was ... essentially a dilettante ....
>
> ... In '76 architects had a sort of feeling it was rather beneath their dignity to know much about construction. ... Then again in '76 an architect was not supposed to know anything about money; in fact, he was classified as a sort of irresponsible poet and never allowed to handle any money. ... As we look back at '76 we see how the architect was seldom really trusted, was always curbed and occasionally reprimanded. Today all architects are not good ones by any means, and there are disgraceful conditions incidental to the vast amount of building operations; still it is a fact that the profession today commands an influence with our clients such as we never dreamed of in '76 and is given powers and limitless opportunity which would then have been absolutely denied.[14]

According to New York City architect William P. Bannister, the profession-in-formation was riven in roughly equal numbers between categories of the "real architect" who was a "real gentleman" and the "underworld of architecture" which "sold itself as a miserably paid servant to the builder" of the deplorably overcrowded urban tenements that constituted the "slums of architecture." Indeed, a whole spectrum of practitioners from those times could be grouped under the rubric of architect, all in competition with each other and generally reflecting traits of character drawn more from the clientele of owners or builders they served than from some intrinsic ethical core. Because so many competing manifestations of the field could be conflated in the public imagination, distinguishing one from the other became a primary concern among the ostensibly more respectable group in the interest of enhancing collective professional esteem.[15]

Thus, at the middle of the nineteenth century, the American concept of "architect" was still fungible. Any number of permutations, called by whatever names, remained present in memory and still available as possible realities. Owners could act as their own architects or their own principle contractors assembling and paying the necessary labor; alternately, builders could provide designs to owners, or even build speculatively for themselves. The role of architect was thus a hybrid and variable arrangement, composed by parts of project originator and project executor to which was added a third part, mediator between the other two. The architect might be a superintendent on behalf of the owner, and might engage directly with the various contractors of the trades almost like a general contractor, hiring them, directing their work, and disbursing their pay. No single practice model prevailed; rather, in broad application, necessary capabilities could be variably joined and then deployed to meet the contingent needs of a situation, responsive to local customs and to whatever client motives and builder skills might pertain.

Fifty years later, however, the ambiguities of architects' social and vocational origins had been largely forgotten or elided. Instead of arising out of the building crafts to achieve mastery of artful execution, "real architects" of recent memory were assumed to have all been artists, dilettantes, and gentlemen steeped in their discipline but aloof from both the messy practicality of building and the ethical morass of business. Where these competing and complementary roles had co-existed historically under the slippery signifier of "architect," over time that name was rationalized and formalized in ever more exclusive terms. It was circumscribed within the strictures of civil society and an ever-increasing division of labor to promote a singular professional ideal.[16]

The process of professionalization—through institutional organization of architects beginning in the 1850s, formal university-based education commencing in the 1860s, and licensure implemented state by state from the 1890s—tended to favor the dominance of patrician interests over democratic values even as self-serving motives were promoted in the name of the public good.[17] Social closure of the ranks of a profession could serve as a means of market control as well as a marker of competence to bolster public trust. In essence and effect, the ethical imperatives of professionalization imposed a necessary boundary between the same and the other—between a uniform class of authoritative practitioners and all those others, pretenders and imposters; between architects and so many amateurs, owners, builders, or engineers. An unintended consequence of asserting such a broad and exclusive claim to the title of architect, however, was to entitle other groups' overlapping and competing territorial claims.

The uniform contract

In 1887, a special committee of the AIA was appointed "to confer with like committees from the Western Association of Architects, and the National Association of Builders, on the subject of Uniform Contracts, and to prepare and adapt, in such Committee of Conference, a form of contract properly protecting the interests of owner and contractor."[18] The impetus for this effort had been long-coming, but the matter became more urgent when the call came from a newly organized group of master builders to join efforts in common cause, to bring uniformity and fairness to the transactions between owners and builders.[19] By this juncture, contractors considered architects—such as those represented by their respective professional organizations—to be more "the legal representatives and agents of the owners" than they were adepts from among the builders' fold.[20] Builders therefore sought a conversation with architects, in their role as surrogates for owners, in the interest of shaping a "unity of practice," by developing uniform contractual standards that could be applied nationwide.

In a speech at the first convention of the National Association of Builders, Peter B. Wight (1838–1925) described the pervasive chaos of the contracting system then in effect, in which "each [architect] is a law unto himself. He lays down the law as to the practice in his own office and expects everyone doing business there to comply with it. He does not think of the position in which the builder is placed, often a very embarrassing one."[21] With each architect as agent promulgating their own proprietary contractual forms on behalf of their respective clients, contractors found themselves at a disadvantage and in a constant state of uncertainty with regard to the obligations they were expected to fulfill. Wight emphasized the fundamental conflict that resides at the intersection of the architect's dual roles—as agent for the owner and as impartial referee between that same owner and the builder in cases of conflict.

> There is an old theory that the architect is a sort of middle man or umpire to stand between the owner and contractor and see that both get their rights. This is only a theory. It is not the fact. It is not the law. It is not to

the discredit of the architectural profession that it is not. The architect is the agent of the owner. The courts have so decided. He is paid by him, and only by him if he is an honest man. An architect's certificate is as good in law as a bill of exchange, a draft or a promissory note. He is, therefore, doing his duty when he is looking after the owner's interests. The contractor is doing his duty to himself by looking after his own interests. If he expects the architect to do this he is very much mistaken. It is our duty as a body to look after our own interests as contractors and material men. We suffer from our own neglect.[22]

A half-century distant from the days of the American architect being identified primarily as a master builder, builders now considered architects to be agents of the owner instead. Once architects were cast into that representative role, builders challenged their credibility to serve in the mediating role of impartial judge. Wight seemed to accept the inevitability of this structural conflict in observing, "The main defect ... in contracts in which the architect is referee, has arisen from the difficulty of defining his duties as superintendent ..."; therefore, he proposed as a measure of remedy, "it is of the utmost necessity that the contracting parties agree as to the nature and extent of the referee's duties and authority." The builders' association was pressing, albeit still in congenial terms—"I have no desire to be harsh with our brethren of the architectural profession"—to circumscribe the authority of the architect within the bounds of a legal compact.[23] Builders' parallel purpose was to assert their own agency and position, one "which entitled them to be ranked as members of a profession and not merely as tradesmen and mechanics."[24]

Correspondence commenced between the architects' and builders' organizations early in 1888 focused on the task of coming to terms on the substance of a uniform contract. According to the annual report of the AIA's Committee on Uniform Contracts, much of the back and forth of negotiation was handled by that committee's chair, Oliver P. Hatfield, and the secretary of the National Association of Builders, William H. Sayward. Working primarily from a draft previously prepared by the AIA, the joint committees "continued their sessions through two days and one evening, until they had brought the form of contract sought for into a satisfactory shape, and then referred it to the Chairman and Secretary, as a sub-committee, to have it printed and again submitted to the members of the Committee for their further consideration." The final version of the contract was printed after a few more minor changes and amendments (Figure 1.1).[25]

What seems on the surface to have been a straightforward and congenial meeting of minds nonetheless belies continuing apprehensions on both sides. The terms codified in the contract cast contractors in a decidedly subordinate position in relation to the architect's assumed authority as the owner's delegatee. The first three clauses of the contract established in quick succession the architect's role as owner's agent,[26] as author of the drawings

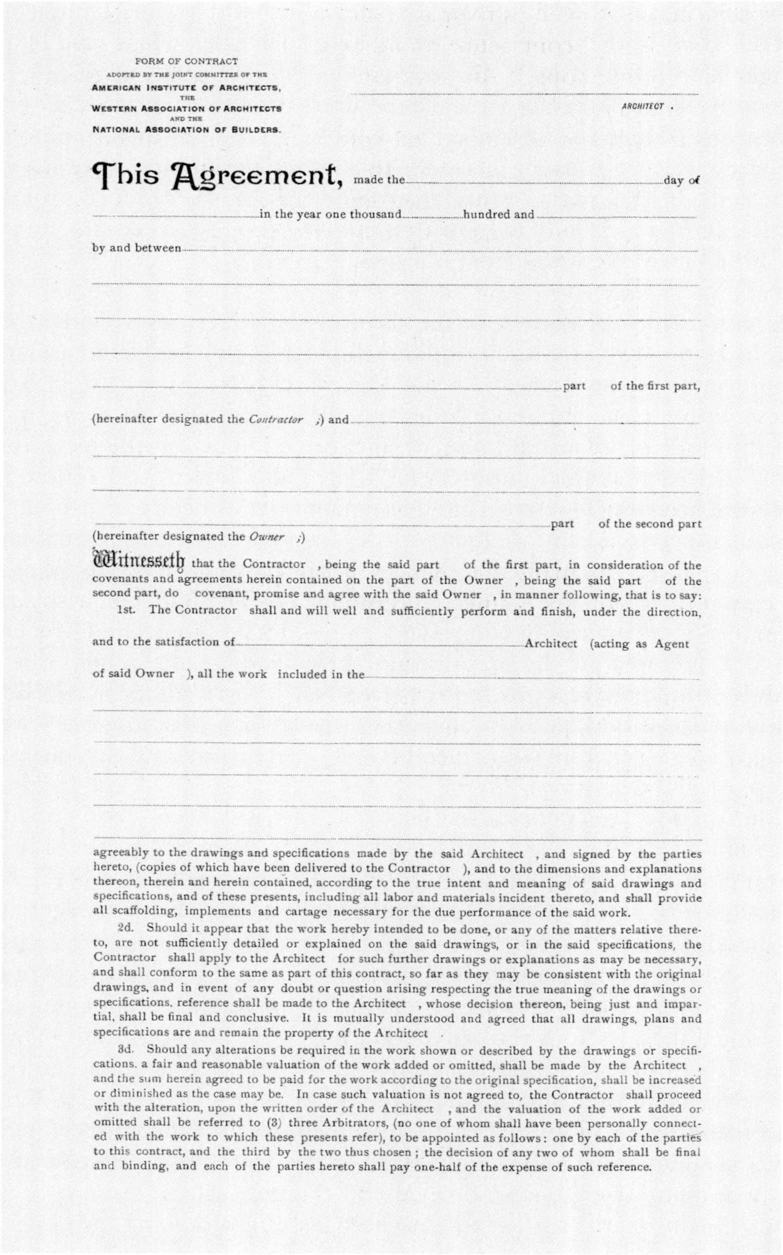

FORM OF CONTRACT
ADOPTED BY THE JOINT COMMITTEE OF THE
AMERICAN INSTITUTE OF ARCHITECTS,
THE
WESTERN ASSOCIATION OF ARCHITECTS
AND THE
NATIONAL ASSOCIATION OF BUILDERS.

ARCHITECT .

This Agreement, made the day of

in the year one thousand hundred and

by and between

part of the first part,

(hereinafter designated the *Contractor* ;) and

part of the second part

(hereinafter designated the *Owner* ;)

Witnesseth that the Contractor , being the said part of the first part, in consideration of the covenants and agreements herein contained on the part of the Owner , being the said part of the second part, do covenant, promise and agree with the said Owner , in manner following, that is to say:

1st. The Contractor shall and will well and sufficiently perform and finish, under the direction,

and to the satisfaction of Architect (acting as Agent

of said Owner), all the work included in the

agreeably to the drawings and specifications made by the said Architect , and signed by the parties hereto, (copies of which have been delivered to the Contractor), and to the dimensions and explanations thereon, therein and herein contained, according to the true intent and meaning of said drawings and specifications, and of these presents, including all labor and materials incident thereto, and shall provide all scaffolding, implements and cartage necessary for the due performance of the said work.

2d. Should it appear that the work hereby intended to be done, or any of the matters relative thereto, are not sufficiently detailed or explained on the said drawings, or in the said specifications, the Contractor shall apply to the Architect for such further drawings or explanations as may be necessary, and shall conform to the same as part of this contract, so far as they may be consistent with the original drawings, and in event of any doubt or question arising respecting the true meaning of the drawings or specifications, reference shall be made to the Architect , whose decision thereon, being just and impartial, shall be final and conclusive. It is mutually understood and agreed that all drawings, plans and specifications are and remain the property of the Architect .

3d. Should any alterations be required in the work shown or described by the drawings or specifications, a fair and reasonable valuation of the work added or omitted, shall be made by the Architect , and the sum herein agreed to be paid for the work according to the original specification, shall be increased or diminished as the case may be. In case such valuation is not agreed to, the Contractor shall proceed with the alteration, upon the written order of the Architect , and the valuation of the work added or omitted shall be referred to (3) three Arbitrators, (no one of whom shall have been personally connected with the work to which these presents refer), to be appointed as follows: one by each of the parties to this contract, and the third by the two thus chosen ; the decision of any two of whom shall be final and binding, and each of the parties hereto shall pay one-half of the expense of such reference.

FIGURE 1.1 *Form of Contract Adopted by the Joint Committee of the American Institute of Architects, the Western Association of Architects, and the National Association of Builders, 1888. By permission of the American Institute of Architects Archives.*

and specifications as well as their ultimate interpreter,[27] and as adjudicator between owner and contractor of adjustments in contract cost due to changes in project scope.[28] An additional provision allowed contractors' appeals to a board of arbitration in cases where the architect's judgment was challenged. In contrast to embedded contractual characterizations of the architect as impartial, fair, and reasonable, the contractor's modus operandi was assumed to be that of refusal, neglect, or failure.[29]

To explain why builders might have agreed to such asymmetrical terms, it must be recognized that at that time regularization of mutual contractual obligations in any form was superior to the caprices contractors then confronted. Consider the circumstances from the builder's point of view:

> One contract may have three pages of fine print, which he can hardly read without glasses, and another may have one page of coarse print; and so they may vary through all the possible changes from one to ten. In each case, it is not expected that he will demur to anything; but he is expected to sit down and affix his name.[30]

At their convention the following year, the president of the National Association of Builders admitted certain caveats about their contract negotiations with architects: "I may be pardoned here for saying that while we do not claim to have made a 'perfect contract,' yet this one is far in advance of any that has been used heretofore in establishing equitably the duties and responsibilities of owners, architects, and contractors."[31] William Sayward went a bit further in his secretary's report to convey underlying tensions that had accumulated from slights of the past as well as suggestions of builders' newfound assertiveness:

> Architectural associations have developed an interest in our proceedings unusual and encouraging. Their correspondence has been welcomed as a sign that we are to be better understood in the future; for although it is to be expected that they will not readily adjust themselves to a new *regime*, in which the builder is to do a little thinking in his own behalf, to secure a more equitable "practice" than has prevailed in the past, still there is a growing willingness, evidenced in the correspondence, to co-operate with us to the end that better conditions may prevail for all concerned.[32]

The report of the builders' Committee on Uniform Contracts sought to reassure the organization's membership that the new contract could be modified in the future to meet new challenges, that "the machinery for perfecting the [contract] form is at hand" through reconvening the joint committees. Voices arose nonetheless from the Cincinnati and Buffalo delegations with recommendations for further modifications of the contractual form. While these objections were set aside for the moment—architects' agency for owners, the assumed fairness of their judgments, the insufficiencies of the arbitration clauses—the reverberations of these conflicts would still linger.[33] As the builders became more familiar with the Uniform Contract in practice and in use, the previously acknowledged flaws became less and less palatable to them. Almost a decade later, the concerns still festered even as the builders refrained from direct confrontation for change. As one speaker at the builders' 1895 Baltimore convention seemed to rationalize:

> Business has been in a very precarious state for a year or so, there have been a great many more contractors than there has been work to be done, and everybody has been so hungry for work that the contractors in a great measure became suppliants at the architects' offices; and so we felt that this was hardly the time for us to make any further demands. Some of us on the Committee know full well the trouble we had and the labor that was performed to get the concessions that we have; and I for one was fearful that if we opened up this matter at this time, possibly we might lose some few of the things we had gained.[34]

For their part, neither did architects universally approve of all the provisions of the Uniform Contract. The Boston Society of Architects, for example, continued to promote their own "suggestive form of contract" and even engaged a young attorney and future Supreme Court Justice Louis D. Brandeis to compare its merits to those of the Uniform Contract promoted by the AIA. Brandeis found the stipulation in the Institute's form that made the architect the agent of the owner to be "objectionable" in that it "increases unreasonably the architect's responsibilities." He also found fault with the Uniform Contract's arbitration provisions and the manner by which the cost of changes was decided, echoing in substance the builders' concerns.[35] At the AIA's own convention in 1901, the committee assigned to stewardship of the contract admitted:

> It is urged by some that it is too long; that there are provisions contained in it which should be more properly put into the preliminary clauses of a specification, and by others, that although it is too long, it still omits clauses which should be found therein. ... Some object to the arbitration clauses, others highly commend them. Some object to recognizing the architect as agent of the owner. Some object to the insurance clause, and others think both clauses should remain.[36]

A year later, the committee reported back to the AIA convention on several revisions to the Uniform Contract, the results of a joint meeting with cohorts from the National Association of Builders. According to their summation, the most significant change to the contract form was the deletion of "the clause which designates the architect as agent of the owner." While seemingly final, the status of this fraught agency relationship would remain an ongoing legal and professional concern. Also clarified were the architect's ownership of the drawings and specifications as instruments of service, "and that the charges for their use and for the services of the architect are to be paid by the owner, thus condemning the unprofessional practice which has obtained in some quarters of making contractors pay for detail drawings." Finally, the arbitration clause was clarified "to make it more effective, hoping thereby to facilitate settlements out of court should disputes arise that from any cause could not be adjusted by the architect."[37] By these measures, the project hegemony that architects had been seeking gradually yielded to contractors' competing concerns.

Despite both builders' and architects' ongoing dissatisfactions with the uniform contract, its broad adoption by owners, builders, and architects effected changes in the status quo of design and building practice nationwide. As architects recognized:

> One great advantage of a uniform contract is that its long continued use establishes by that fact its reasonableness, and creates a series of requirements which are universally recognized as fair and equitable. It also creates confidence on the part of the owner that he is properly and amply protected, and on the part of the contractor that there are no hidden traps requiring a lawyer to search out and detect lest he unwittingly sign away his rights.[38]

The Uniform Contract was a new tool of practice contributing to architects' own emergent professional uniformity, and it was cast from a die mostly of their own design. In helping draft a standardized form of agreement, architects asserted a uniquely representative role for themselves in-between owners and builders. They were no longer master builders and not quite full agents on owners' behalfs, but they were originators and proprietors of their own instruments of service, the drawings and specifications where their authority increasingly resided.

By the end of the nineteenth century, architects of various stripes had emerged out of the circumstantial gaps in a myriad of improvised contracts in order to fill the necessary roles—as advisor, agent, organizer, designer, drafter, contractor, superintendent, administrator, or arbitrator of disputes. Counter to American constitutional logic, they seemingly combined executive, legislative, and judicial roles into one. Architects might embody in variable proportions and combinations the refined sensibilities of a well-informed clientele, practical wisdom distilled from the acumen of a master builder, or the insight into human nature requisite of an able leader and impartial judge. They might also reflect the more exploitative traits to which each of those cohorts was prone under the sway of increasingly predatory business concerns. At the beginning of the twentieth century, in order both to counter those commercial tendencies and to comport with their inexorable logic, architectural practice was being formalized as a profession based upon standards of a well-meaning but paternalistic code.

Even prior to the sedimentation of roles from the once fluid universe of building practice, what had mediated the relationship between an owner and a builder was some ad hoc form of agreement—a contract, whether written, oral, or implied. That gentlemanly covenant was addressed to immediate conditions that locally prevailed.[39] At the turn of the century, the division of labor in society depended upon increasingly specific contracts as part of the dual process of integration and regulation that leads to organic solidarity, to social cohesion.[40] Once the conditions of the contract were standardized and concretized, they redounded back to the modus operandi of practice. Whether the builders realized it at the time or not, when they invited the architects to confer with them on the terms of a uniform contract, they were not merely initiating an incremental challenge to the status quo; rather, they were shaping new precedents that could be tested in court. They were codifying a mechanism for change. In a manner analogous to that played by a contract mediating between opposing parties, the architect emerged as a crucial social mechanism facilitating a process of exchange between owners and builders. At the turn of the twentieth century, the architect instantiated this paradox of reciprocity, as both agent and arbitrator of exchange.[41]

Mr. Day's handbook

In 1914, Philadelphia architect and former AIA President Frank Miles Day (1861–1918) assumed the chairmanship of the AIA's Committee on Contracts and Specifications of which he had been a member since 1908 (Figure 1.2). Over preceding years, Day had been especially interested in matters pertaining to the establishment of a code of ethics; the conduct of design competitions; competitive bidding procedures; and the standardization of contracts between and among owners, architects, and builders. His aim as a progressive member of the profession's self-selecting elite was to build up the profession, to elevate the architect's status to its rightful position alongside that of doctor or lawyer.[42]

A few years later in a letter to the executive board of the AIA, Day described the changing environment of his own firm that was requiring extra measures to ensure consistency and clarity of his office affairs. In the face of an expanding practice, Day himself was finding it increasingly difficult to exercise personal control:

> Of late it has been necessary for me to delegate to others a considerable proportion of the administrative detail of this office, and I have found that many procedures which seemed to me of an elementary sort presented certain difficulties to those now in charge. I therefore thought it advisable to prepare memoranda of procedure which would state in the order of their occurrence those administrative acts which the

FIGURE 1.2 *Frank Miles Day.* Brickbuilder *24 (1915).*

architect has usually to perform, or the performing of which he must at least consider in carrying to completion any given piece of work entrusted to him. I found that such memoranda afforded an opportunity for keeping a record of the dates on which various administrative acts were performed, and I found that the work was rapidly developing into a code of good practice, in which well accepted methods for performing these acts were carefully described. The number of such acts greatly exceeded my expectation. I found that various letters in form suited for sundry occasions might well be included, and that various forms, such as applications of payment, certificates of payment, etc., naturally found their way into this work.[43]

Day inductively extended his own administrative experience into a compelling vision for a new tool of practice, one that he then magnanimously offered to the profession as a whole without any apparent concern for personal economic gain:

> At this point it occurred to me that I was engaged in writing a handbook of business administration; that it was entirely based on my personal experience, and that it would be far better if it expressed the consensus of opinion of a number of men interested in such work. After discussing the matter ..., I have determined to offer it to the Institute, since I believe that improved and extended as alone the Institute can improve and extend it, the work will be of great value to the profession. It will be of value to the young man untrained in good business methods; it will be of value to the experienced practitioner who looks after his own administrative detail, but whose work would be lightened by having forms suited to many occasions and whose memory would be refreshed by following the sequence of events set down. It would be of service to architects of large practice who have to delegate their administrative details to others, who perhaps do not always fully realize the significance of each act.[44]

Day's insight and proposal to shape a handbook of architectural practice based upon his own firm's office manual set into motion a series of discussions, deliberations, and debates nationwide that would help propel the standardization of the terms and assumptions of US architectural practice. Day's project for a "code of good practice" drew upon the network of connections and associations that he had built across the country as president of the nation's premier professional organization of architects.[45] First shaping a draft document and then distributing it widely, he invited feedback that elicited a range of regional and often parochial viewpoints. The biases and professional predispositions thus conveyed to him reveal some of the anxieties besetting practitioners in those days: the bounds of the architect's authority as owner's agent, the ascendancy of the general contractor, changes in the architect's relationship to the trades, the imprecision of specifications, the corrupting potential of the bid process, the calculation of overhead and fees, virtues of the quantity survey system, the architect's role as the final arbiter of the contract. Working alone with only intermittent support from his committee, Day received these written responses, sifted them and endeavored to synthesize them into a paper consensus.[46]

In his "Preface to the Handbook," Day gave due regard to each of these three—art, science, and business—as defining attributes of the architectural profession. Typical of the leading practitioners of his day, he extolled architecture as primarily a fine art and ranked its inspirational and imaginative values above "merely the science of building or of even building well." As conceived by Day, however, *The Handbook* was to be more narrowly focused:

The Architect, by expressing his ideas in forms and words of exact contractual significance, by controlling machinery for their embodiment, by giving just decisions between conflicting interests, by bearing himself as worthy of his high calling, gives to his art the status of a profession. It is with that aspect of the Architect's work, professional practice and its servant, business administration, that this Handbook is concerned.[47]

Day sought critical feedback to his first draft of the handbook from professional colleagues, and his effort to convey a systematic approach to both office and project administration clearly struck a nerve. Opinions from across a spectrum of fields confirmed a shared sentiment that architects' business acumen was sorely deficient and a belief that *The Handbook* would help fill this experience gap with sound advice distilled from collective professional experience. Architect John L. Hamilton wrote to Day about his concerns:

I am quite impressed with the fact that the impression prevails among leading business men and financiers that members of the architectural profession, as a class, do not possess, by training or instinct, adequate business qualifications for the administration of large projects or the expenditure of large amounts of money. I, also, am painfully of the opinion that there is large foundation for this impression, and believe that the training of architectural students, the training received as employees by a great majority of men who later are engaged in practice, provides at present no adequate preparation for the proper business conduct of an architect's office.[48]

Attorney William B. King offered Day similar observations drawn from his experience as legal counsel for the AIA:

In discussing with competent builders the relations between them and architects, they constantly impressed upon me the deficiencies which they find in architects as business men, as well as constructors. Their view is that the stress of the architects upon the artistic side of their work is so great that it has led to neglect of the craft. I do not know how true this is, but these comments have made enough of an impression on me to make me think that you are performing an extremely valuable service to the profession in preparing a book which aims at the importance of the business transactions in architects' offices.[49]

H.G. Heddinger, president of a firm serving as manufacturers' agent and building specialties dealer, concurred that the value of Day's handbook lay in helping both established and fledgling architects "put their ideas and practices on a more uniform basis and … teach them the business side of their profession and put them on their guard in protecting the interests of their clients." In addition, he offered:

> From my observation, architects, particularly the younger ones, are so much absorbed in their profession or art that they have failed to consider the business side of their duties and are therefore poorly fitted to cope with the shrewd and cold business men, whose sole idea in life is to secure riches by stretching the "fine line" that divides good business from dishonesty.[50]

In a similar vein, Warren P. Laird, Professor-in-Charge of the Department of Architecture at University of Pennsylvania, asserted the opinion:

> The highest duty to the client is not the production of good art, indispensable though that be, but a sound administration of his interests from a business standpoint. The lack of this has brought reproach on many architects and will continue to do so until the younger men universally are persuaded of its need. Even if all the schools taught it, as they do not, the great majority of architects would not be reached, being graduates of the office only and it is this majority who can be reached by the Handbook.[51]

From these several comments, we can discern a prevalent complaint emerging from attorneys, bankers, clients, contractors, manufacturers, educators, and even other architects. The argument gaining traction among these varied interests was not simply that architects lacked business acumen, but rather that an over-emphasis within the profession upon the notion of architecture as a fine art had, in effect, unbalanced the old equation of firmness, commodity, and delight. Practical deficiencies in requisite skills were less a function of the architect's professional constitution, however, as they were evidence of a struggle to adapt. Rapidly changing social, technological, and economic conditions were redefining the division of labor and the units of expertise that had constituted the architect's traditional work domain.[52]

Architects' purview over the science and business of construction had been progressively usurped by—or ceded to—structural engineers and general contractors. In the first instance, the empirical design of masonry and timber structures that architects' experience had once allowed was no longer sufficient to the challenge of skeletal steel construction. The sizing of supports and spans in steel required the structural engineer's analytical methods, an expertise based in calculable, predictive science. Likewise, the organization necessary for providing managerial and financial control for projects of expanding scope and complexity gradually overwhelmed the administrative and supervisory capacities of typical architects' bureaus. Within an increasingly business and profit-motivated culture, general contractors emerged as intermediaries between architects and trade laborers and challenged architects' dual role as both agent and arbiter of owners' contractual interests.

Under these intertwined and aggravating circumstances, and with the initiative of a relatively small number of socially influential and well-positioned individuals devoted to the academic ideal of the unity of the fine arts, the profession laid institutional claim to the art of architecture as its inviolable knowledge domain. Yet, as discourse surrounding the birth of *The Handbook of Architectural Practice* attests, architects' assertions of the ascendancy of art as the defining value of architecture did not go unchallenged from either outside or inside the profession. Indeed, *The Handbook* itself is evidence of a potent counter-claim that it was only through the primacy of "an efficient organization, constantly evolving in harmony with new methods of business management" that "the designer will be the freer to exert his creative and artistic talents."[53] A dynamic interplay of art, science, and business values thus defined the ideological terrain of a very American version of Vitruvianism. How architects in the early-twentieth century situated themselves both socially and functionally within that landscape, and from such position then negotiated the terms of engagement with other players on the field of the design and building enterprise, continues to govern the forms of architectural practice that we still enact today.

The early editions of the AIA's *Handbook of Architectural Practice* from the 1920s are thus sub-texts of the profession-in-formation (Figure 1.3).

FIGURE 1.3 *Cover detail*, The Handbook of Architectural Practice *(Washington, DC: American Institute of Architects, 1927).*

The dry prose embedded in the office procedures and contractual templates gathered there are residues of common law and convention along with emergent problems that foreshadow and resonate with contemporary concerns. Recurrent dialectics of art and science were reframed within new imperatives of business logic and economic optimization, of legal strictures and an evolving standard of care. The issues comprising the contents of "Mr. Day's Handbook" chart a map of controversies and disputes that were actively shaping the terrain of increasingly business-oriented architectural practice while the relationships between and among architects, owners, buildings, contractors, and their publics were congealing into historically understandable yet nonetheless paradoxical forms.

The wisdom of Tom Thumtack

Besides gauging the internal pressures compelling the architecture profession to standardize its procedures and to codify its practices, it is important to set Day's efforts into a broader context. The controversies shaping and surrounding architectural practice of the time are also evident in the discourses and diatribes that whetted partisan debate at professional conferences and that were recorded in the editorials and letters in architecture and construction industry trade journals of the day. Within a wider public sphere, architectural criticism and social commentary published in periodicals as well as genres of satire and literary fiction engaged new levels of popular interest.[54] While architects worried about their diminishing status and project authority, they competed against increasingly emboldened builders for public approbation and support.

One little book crystallizes these historical circumstances particularly well through its portrayal of a wily old architect whose self-deprecating persona and wry observations level withering critiques of the motivations of owners, architects, and builders alike. Based largely upon a series of essays from the New York-based professional journal *Architecture and Building*, the book *Architec-tonics: The Tales of Tom Thumtack, Architect* was published in 1914 (Figure 1.4).[55] Conceived and written in the same era and professional climate as Frank Miles Day's *Handbook of Architectural Practice, Architec-tonics* is a particularly idiosyncratic example of architecture culture on the cusp of the First World War. This little satirical tome reflects seriously nonetheless upon the prevailing practices of the day, the inter-relations between and among architects and clients and contractors, the legal instruments of practice, and the role of human foibles in shaping the character of this "noble" art. The author of the book, presented in the theatrical guise of our fictional architect, described the purpose of the book in this way:

FIGURE 1.4 *Rockwell Kent, Frontispiece,* Architec-tonics: The Tales of Tom Thumtack, Architect *(New York: Comstock, 1914).*

I'll sign my name with "Tom Thumtack," the thumbtack which held your earliest order; and then your first commission; and now your greatest competition. Many of you already know me and those who don't, know many like me. I'm old, and I have been through the mill. I've built little and I've built big. I've won out and I've lost out. I've seen good execution count for nothing and I've trapped big jobs by choosing paint for little ones. I've used influence and I've encountered it. I've drawn lines, and I've hired line-makers. I know clients, public, private, feminine, and am known by them. I know contractors, I make them and I break them. I've built with adobe and concrete, with scantling and steel, with brick and paint and silk and flowers. I've been and known and done all these and *so have you.* We know each other; blind-folded I can touch your medals and your scars, and you can mine. I know the tricks of our trade and so do you. I know her power and her eternity. I know her artifice and inconsistency. Many have sung her praises. Why has no one pricked her bubbles?[56]

Tom Thumtack managed to prick the bubbles of the profession through humorous devices highlighting social pretentions, professional stereotypes, mistaken identities, and chicaneries unmasked. In so doing, a knowingly authentic portrait of architectural practice was sketched, one that magnified the well-intentioned and good-humored fallibility that lay behind an institutional facade of self-serious professionalism. Tom Thumtack opened a crack through which we can peek at the professional identity of the modern American architect under assembly—not the social revolutionary of a contemporaneous European avant-garde, but rather the business-oriented professional seeking to cement a social standing. Whether it concerned the relationship between architect and client, the conduct and organization of the architect's office, or the dictates of a "cannon" of ethics, Tom Thumtack's essays satirized customs of architectural practice on the way to becoming standards of professional conduct, ones uncannily mirroring those to be codified in Mr. Day's *Handbook*.

The narrator's wryly self-conscious critique of the architectural profession is signaled in the book's frontispiece with Tom Thumtack's introductory portrait (Figure 1.5). There he stands at center stage. The curtains are drawn on a distant scene of ancient Greece, classical temples on an acropolis, an assemblage of actors poised upon their plinths. He stands with hands in the pockets of pants striped like fluted columns, with buttoned vest, morning coat, and bowtie: his hairline receding, his ears protruding, eyebrow arched, an Ionic scroll of drawings tucked beneath his arm, an ironic expression upon his face. This, we presume, is a portrait of the author. The book—his memoires after a fashion, a veritable theater of practice.

Behind the scenes, just out of view, other actors and contractors are at work to sustain this theatrical illusion. It is a morality play and a farce intended to expose the tensions and pretensions of our dramatis personae—architects, their clients, builders, all—as they work at odds and grudgingly together to shape the spatial and social terrains of the fledgling twentieth-century American metropolis. The book unfolds in scenes and sketches, illustrated chapters in the history of the architectural profession itself under construction where the aims of art, science, and business collide and coincide on the way to an indeterminate destination: progress.

Who was Tom Thumtack? Compared side-by-side, Thumtack's portrait bears an uncanny resemblance to a photographic portrait published in an architecture journal five years previously, that of Frederick Squires of New York (Figure 1.6). The journal designated Squires along with his then partner John Wynkoop as "Architects of To-Day." Thumtack strikes Squires's same pose: hands in pockets, jacket slightly askew, high collar shirt, and tightly buttoned vest. But while Thumtack's visage shares with Squires the same prominence of ears and brow, Squires's darkly handsome face is fresh, unfurrowed, non-ironic, but rather, serious and sincere. In fact, this image dates from an even earlier time; it is Squires's senior portrait from Columbia University.[57]

Tom Thumtack is the nom de guerre of our real protagonist, architect and author Frederick Squires. Squires's architectural training had begun at Williams College and continued at Columbia University where he earned a bachelor of arts degree in 1904, thereafter immediately launching his architectural career as a partner in the firm Squires & Wynkoop. By the time of the publication of *Architec-tonics* in 1914, Squires was ten years in practice and already an accomplished architect having built numerous residential and commercial projects in New York, city and state. Among these were two twelve-story loft buildings in Manhattan, the Mercantile Building at Seventh Avenue and 24th Street and another on East 16th Street. He had published extensively on the subject of hollow tile construction in a treatise that reviewed both the historical precedents and the technical requirements for this durable, fireproof building method.[58]

FIGURE 1.5 *Rockwell Kent, "Tom Thumtack AIA,"* Architec-tonics: The Tales of Tom Thumtack, Architect *(New York: Comstock, 1914).*

FIGURE 1.6 *Frederick Squires, "an architect of to-day,"* Architecture 20 (1909).

Squires distilled his own experience through the wizened old voice of Tom Thumtack to add gravitas to his tales. The stories conveyed a perspective at once sage and sardonic: the vanities of clients, the inanities of builders, and the comedies of the architect's own self-deceptions (Figure 1.7). Each account was accompanied by charming vignettes, illustrations that captured in pen and ink the wit of Thumtack's themes, setting the stage, so to speak, and augmenting the narratives by visualizing their tropes and double entendres. The drawings, including the introductory portrait of Tom Thumtack, were unsigned and unattributed, though we know them to be the work of Squires's architecture classmate Rockwell Kent, an emerging artist and peripatetic draftsman and architectural renderer of note.

In line with the Squires's own pseudonymous practice, we can detect in Tom Thumtack's tales an architectonic pattern of dualities, doublings,

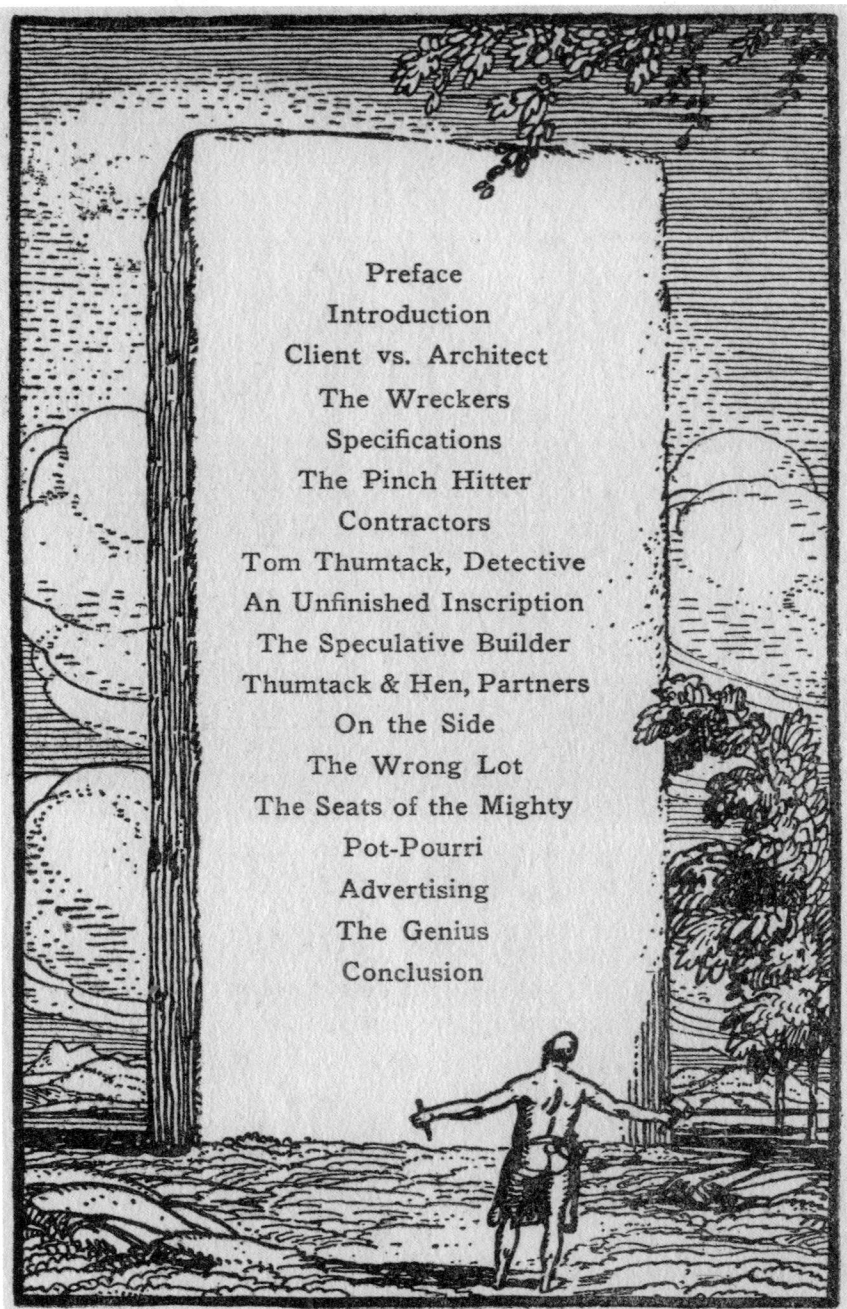

FIGURE 1.7 Rockwell Kent, *Table of Contents,* Architec-tonics: The Tales of Tom Thumtack, Architect *(New York: Comstock, 1914).*

and impersonations, of identities both veiled and mistaken. Indeed, Squires revealed his own method of disguise, of composing his stories out of his own experiences, as when he wrote, "I can take half fact and add to it but half of my own construction."[59] In his role as architect Tom Thumtack must be adept as an actor, called upon to play many parts, to improvise on a moment's notice, but he must also be a detective. He must be wary of the ploys and motivations of others, be they clients or builders or even other architects, and he must be ready to ferret out and expose their every deception.

Pursuing his inductive approach to causal relations, Tom Thumtack observes for example that "the most fascinating thing about building is demolition." He was able to read the clues revealed by the wrecker's ball

FIGURE 1.8 *Rockwell Kent, "The Rector's Brother,"* Architec-tonics: The Tales of Tom Thumtack, Architect *(New York: Comstock, 1914).*

like tea leaves, an archaeologist finding forensic evidence, for example, of substandard materials, of walls built with "lies for bricks and knavery for mortar." In one case, he describes how an incautious demolition resulted in shifting foundations on an adjacent property with collateral effects. With the owners being absent, our hero-architect-detective rushes to inspect the damage. The property consisted of two adjoining houses for a pair of brothers, identical twins. One brother was a rector and the other an actor, a study in contrasts despite their uncanny physical resemblance. Their contrasting public personae, one a saint and one a sinner, were well-reflected, Thumtack finds, in the monastic and bacchanalian décors inside their respective abodes. Detective Thumtack discovers that a crack had opened in their shared party wall to reveal a hidden door in the wainscoat of the rector's study where it connected directly to the actor's den. The "twin brothers" were thus unmasked (Figure 1.8); rector and actor were one in the same![60]

In other stories, Tom Thumtack portrays the architect and the contractor in a card game where the bid process set the stakes of their bluff and gamble. Pitched later into the boxing ring, they vie for the client's favor in a knockout match over extra charges.[61] In a courtroom, itself just another theater of practice, the architect mounts evidence to turn the tables on his client in defense of his professional honor against accusations of impracticality.[62] These vignettes, a total in all of twenty-one stories plus prefatory and concluding remarks, suggest some of the all too human qualities by which the relationships intertwining builders, clients, architects, and the buildings and spaces they create could become complicated or complicitous. And while the tales may at first seem far-fetched, a kernel of truth resides in them for they dramatize formative episodes of the American architectural profession undergoing the messy process of its assembly.

Another kind of architects' handbook

Frederick Squires wrote at a time when debates and controversies swirled in the pages of architectural journals and no doubt in the drafting rooms, ateliers, salons, and saloons of cities like Chicago, Philadelphia, Boston, and New York. In Frank Miles Day's concurrent efforts to collect the strictures of the profession into the pages of a definitive tome, some of the conflicts were leveled, some buried or suppressed, and some elevated into far greater prominence than perhaps deserved. One hundred years later, however, when so many *a priori* assumptions about the forms and frames of architectural practice are being challenged apace, contemporary experience suggests that very few of the controversies being tackled back then were settled once and for all. Despite any illusion about a profession being some pre-ordained and unchanging social category, the field of architectural practice is still very much in play. Its terms are not set in stone; rather, they are malleable and in constant state of change. Day's *Handbook of Architectural Practice* and Squires's *Architec-tonics* must be understood, like the rector and the actor in Tom Thumtack's tale, as mirror reflections of one and the same phenomenon.

Day's and Squires's respective works comprise distinct yet complementary manifestations of American architecture culture in the first quarter of the twentieth century. Each text illuminates and is illuminated by the other to suggest an intertwined web of social interactions and shared professional concerns. That network encompasses, yet extends well beyond, the stereotypical triad of owner, builder, and architect to include an entourage of legal, economic, and technological agents. The two texts taken in tandem corroborate certain historically persistent characteristics of architectural practice germane to our own contemporary concerns. They are indices of an ongoing, dynamic process of profession-formation.

Informed by Tom Thumtack's ironic ruses, the approach of the following chapters is to cast the architect in roles as both actor and detective, as both agent and critic of an unfolding process of the profession's own social production. We enter Frank Miles Day's archives of personal and official correspondence, miscellaneous procedural documents, contracts, and marked-up handbook manuscripts thus prepared to trace the overlapping circles of influence and acquaintance embedded there. Searching for clues in the literary residue of popular culture and the ephemera of architectural journalism, we can reconstruct the narrative of social ferment then shaping a national building culture. By paying close attention to an eclectic range of evidence, we gauge the insistent and resistant forces at play in the structural transformation of architects' practices. And finally, we pose the question: *Are not architects still wrestling with these same forces today?*

This study suggests the shape of another kind of architect's handbook, one organized as a critical guide to the historical practices and relationships that its very existence is meant to clarify and to interrogate. The fundamental relations of architectural practice comprise the topics of inquiry in the following chapters. How did the character of the American architecture profession unfold and by what means was the architect's social position fashioned? What interests and irritants were roiling relationships and inter-relationships among owners, architects, builders, and the changing retinues of other actors, contractors, and subs? And what key contractual and managerial tools were contrived to mediate the forces of change? Such tools, then as now, facilitated an intricate web of social and technological interactions conjoining people—their ideas, materials, capital, and labor—into any project for any purpose on any site. Like Day's originary efforts, the aim here is to provide a curated distillation of shared experience to inform future practices and procedures. But like Tom Thumtack's more ironic approach, the aim is to leaven experience with a germ of critical awareness about the self-perpetuating tendencies that architects' own practices provoke.

CHAPTER TWO

The Architect's Office

In the course of an otherwise farfetched tale, Tom Thumtack conjured an idealized model of architectural practice, one both non-adversarial and cooperative. It was an approach founded upon sound business principles, clarity of client intents, and the architect's skill and care in design and supervision. Once having retired and come into a sizable inheritance, Architect Thumtack now reversed and doubled his roles by offering advice to himself *as the client*, one seeking to commission another architect to design his new abode (Figures 2.1–2.2). Guiding himself through each phase of the project, Thumtack challenged old stereotypes ingrained by experience and anticipated new approaches to managing the relations among architect, client, and contractor.[1] He counseled himself and his family on choosing an architect, "that we decide what kind of house we wanted … and select an architect who has a good reputation …. Then go to see him, and look him over and look his organization over and see if he is apparently capable of handling not only the design, but the construction of this kind of building."[2] In Tom Thumtack's tale just as in the discursive advice offered in *The Handbook of Architectural Practice*, the architect's office was itself an index of professional competence and proof of organizational skill.

As the architect's unique role and functions became ever more clearly differentiated from those of either builder or owner, the architect receded by degrees from direct participation and labor at the building site. The immediate site of design creation might hypothetically be no more than a lone drafter at a single drafting board, but the actual space of architectural production encompassed all the extended and contingent relations that the expanding scope and complexity of modern construction required. These included accommodations for all those external actors needing to visit and interact with the office—clients, contractors, material suppliers, applicants for work; to all the internally departmentalized functions spatially ordered and bureaucratically orchestrated for optimal project execution—drafting,

FIGURE 2.1 *Rockwell Kent, "Thumtack & Hen Partners,"* Architec-tonics: The Tales of Tom Thumtack, Architect *(New York: Comstock, 1914).*

FIGURE 2.2 *Rockwell Kent, "Tom Thumtack, Client,"* Architecture and Building 46 *(1914).*

specifications, construction, and accounting. At the turn of the century, there was a growing awareness, and even self-consciousness, that the spatial organization of the architect's office manifested systems of administrative management, that those systems in turn reflected the character and priorities of the firm principals, and that taken together they constituted "the mechanism of profitable practice"[3] (Figures 2.3–2.7).

The inner office and outer office were integral to each other, but they were also juxtaposed. The inner office reflected and spatially instantiated each firm's particular methods of production. Did partners divide responsibilities or share? Were engineers accommodated in-house? How were drawings reproduced? *The Handbook* recommended that each transaction within each department be recorded in a manner consistent with its essential functions, be stamped and dated, logged on its respective form—people coming and going, drawings issued and received, correspondence in and out, accounts payable and receivable. In Tom Thumtack's account, product representatives as victims of "the caste distinction which the profession sets up against the manufacturer" were often intercepted by the "Keyboard Sadie," relegated to a separate entry, or shunted aside to the office boy.[4] The fine grain of inner-office operations, information flows, and delegated duties too subtle to show on any organizational chart could be outlined in office policy manuals laying out standards and procedures, grand compendia for new employees or those lacking experience enough to know. Indeed, *The Handbook* had been conceived as an aid for just this purpose.

The outer office was the extended threshold of the firm, where different currents of visitors were received and directed. Most significantly, contractors and the architect's clientele arriving there might converge on contract signing days or else diverge through different doors each to their separate purposes. The entry sequence, from foyer to reception room to adjoining partner's office, was orchestrated to feature the firm's design sensibilities, the backroom drafting staff carefully shielded from clients' view. The outer office was a curated exhibit of architecture and its accouterments—renderings on the walls, furnishings, objets d'art—akin to the public architectural exhibitions annually staged in the local academies of fine arts. In a culture of increasingly ubiquitous commercial displays, the architect's outer office was an experiential advertisement for a profession that otherwise frowned on advertising in print.

While offering general guidelines for the program and organization of an architect's office, *The Handbook* advised, "For the way in which the offices of sundry well-known Architects are planned and arranged, the reader should consult a series of articles by D. Everett Waid."[5] The essays chronicling offices of over two dozen New York City architects constitute a virtual ethnography of architectural practice of the early-twentieth century. They were replete with floor plans, illustrative photographs, and narratives describing significant spaces, departmental organization, workflows, and

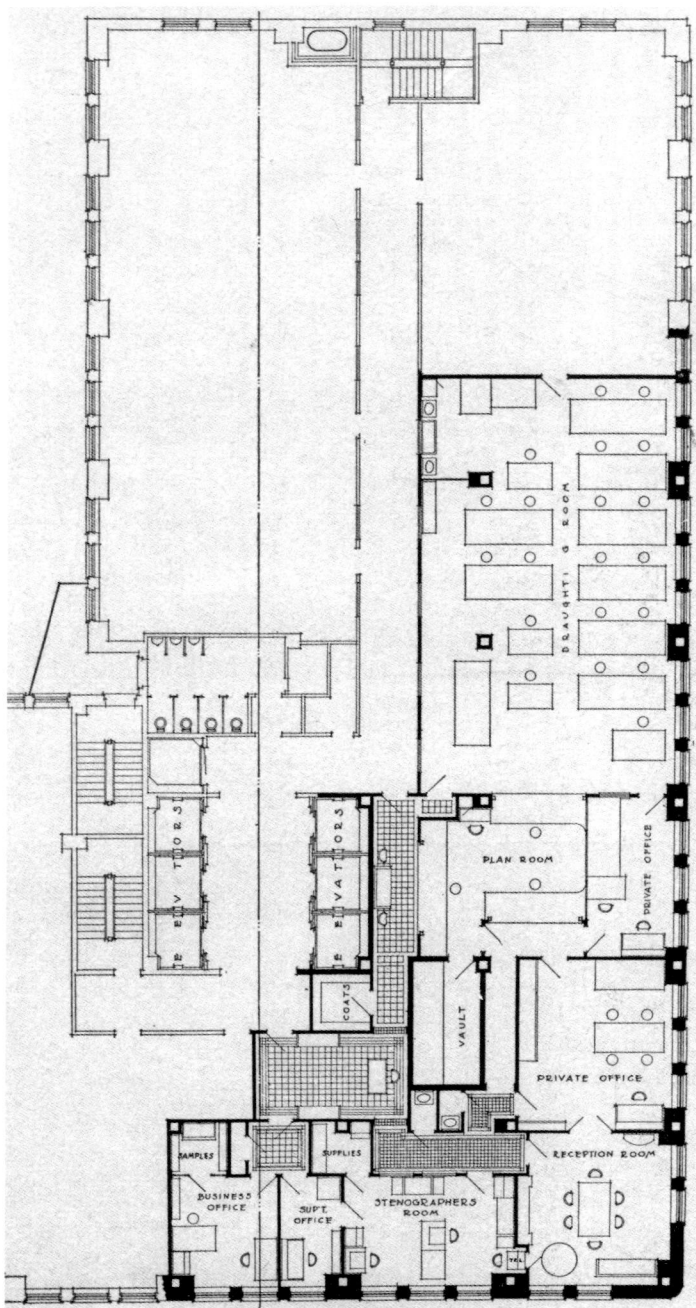

FIGURE 2.3 *Floor plan, "The Business Side of an Architect's Office: The Office of Mr. Donn Barber,"* The Brickbuilder *22 (1913).*

FIGURE 2.4 *Reception room, "The Business Side of an Architect's Office: The Office of Mr. Donn Barber,"* The Brickbuilder 22 *(1913).*

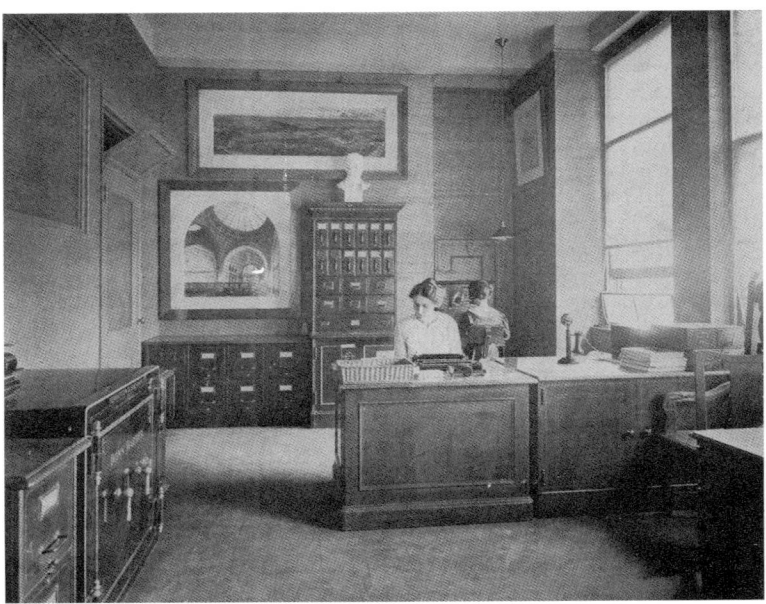

FIGURE 2.5 *Stenographers' room, "The Business Side of an Architect's Office: The Office of Mr. Donn Barber,"* The Brickbuilder 22 *(1913).*

FIGURE 2.6 *Drafting room, "The Business Side of an Architect's Office: The Office of Mr. Donn Barber,"* The Brickbuilder *22 (1913).*

FIGURE 2.7 *Private office, "The Business Side of an Architect's Office: The Office of Mr. Donn Barber,"* The Brickbuilder *22 (1913).*

even examples of standard office forms (Figure 2.8). As Waid explained the premise of his comparative methodology, "Each imaginative visitor may speculate for himself as to the influence on the plan of each office due to the personal qualities and taste of each architect, or the volume of his work, or the class of work, if he specializes, or all those factors."[6]

The first half of the case studies, published as a series between 1911 and 1912, examined the offices of notable architects such as Cass Gilbert, Donn Barber, Charles A. Platt, Carrère and Hastings, Delano and Aldrich, and Grosvenor Atterbury.[7] Waid took note of the architects' various approaches to the disposition of the basic office elements within a range of midtown Manhattan contexts, from townhouses to loft office buildings. He paid special regard to entry and reception sequences, the principals' private offices, and then the drafting rooms where he found "the dreams of the artist are taking shape in a most business-like way." He observed their quality of light and finish, aesthetic displays, pragmatic considerations, and storage strategies for the volumes of documents and forms. The photographs typically reveal the drafting rooms populated by men and the filing and stenography spaces staffed by women—with a notable exception that "one interesting feature of Mr. Atterbury's office is the presence of half a dozen skilled and efficient women draftsmen."[8] From this survey, Waid drew some interim conclusions.

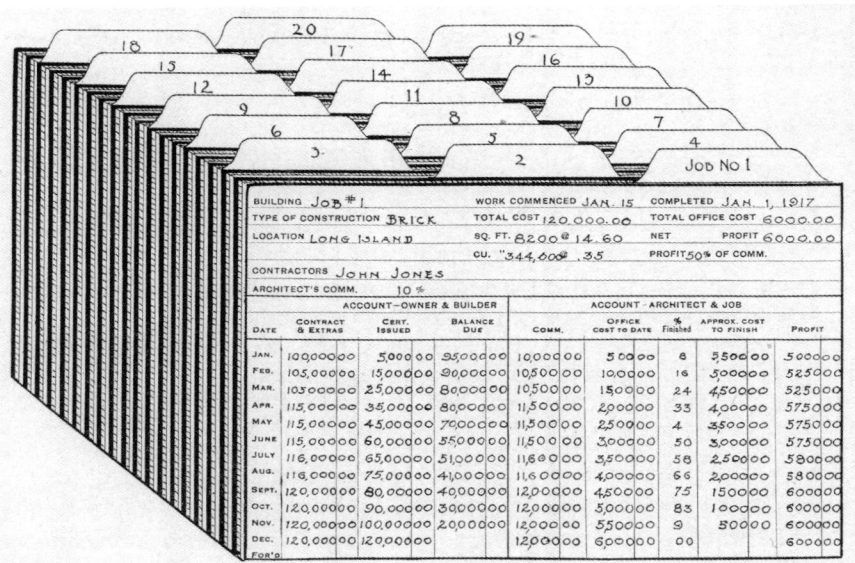

FIGURE 2.8 *Office record reference card, "The 'Business' of Architecture,"* Architectural Review *23 (1918).*

The result of such planning not only provides an atmosphere of helpfulness and inspiration to the architect himself and his co-workers, but also impresses the client with a deeper appreciation for the ability of the artist whom he has selected to design the work contemplated by him …. Since art is a product of genius and imitative qualities, the architect must necessarily surround himself with conditions both inspiring and creative. This he accomplishes by making his library a source of valuable information, his office and reception room restfully attractive, and his drafting room extremely practicable. Such an atmosphere is conducive to the broadening influences of pure architecture.[9]

Pictures at an exhibition

The importance that turn-of-the-century architects ascribed to art as the defining value of their profession is evident in the rise of architectural exhibitions that marked the era. Beginning in the late-nineteenth century, annual architectural exhibitions became a regular fixture in urban centers as an outgrowth of the exhibitionary culture spurred by an explosion of commerce as well as the great national expositions held in St. Louis in 1876 and Chicago in 1893.[10] The annual architecture reviews were often staged in conjunction with local art academies' annual exhibitions of painting, sculpture, and decorative arts, and they included a range of both public and private projects, works both completed and in-progress. Entries were drawn from near and far from established as well as rising practices; from Philadelphia, New York, Chicago and a host of smaller cities where after-hours drafters' ateliers and architecture clubs had been established as nexuses of fellowship and creative exchange; and from representatives of the increasingly influential schools of architecture. These exhibitions, chronicled in accompanying catalogs and reviewed nationally in trade and professional journals, are indicative of the networks of relationships then coalescing to shape a metropolitan professional culture.

Writing in 1905, noted architect and University of Pennsylvania professor Paul Philippe Cret offered a surprising opinion about the value of architectural exhibitions. In his critical introduction to the *Catalogue of the Eleventh Annual Architectural Exhibition* of the T Square Club of Philadelphia, the French-born Cret conveyed what he described as a typical jest found in Parisian journals about "the alleged deserted air of the rooms assigned to architectural displays in the annual Salon." He continued, "They declare that no one is found in them save those who have been choked with the dust raised by the crowds which throng through the galleries of paintings, and that even these only linger to rest themselves for a few moments upon the empty benches."[11]

Cret's anecdote about a marked lack of public enthusiasm for architectural exhibitions advanced a broader point. He suggested that rather than serving as a means of cultivating public taste and appreciation of exemplary architecture, the primary purpose of architectural exhibitions was actually to edify and inspire architects themselves about the possibilities of their own art:

> It is my own opinion—though subject to correction—that it is not the public who is really most benefited by these exhibitions. Such of the general public who attend will be ill prepared to understand what they see. Laymen should only judge architecture from the executed work. The labor of comparing the three projections of a design in order to reach a just conclusion of its merits is beyond their power; and as for those who profess to judge from the facade alone, or, more especially, from a more or less well rendered drawing of the facade—for myself, I confess I should prefer their indifference. Architectural exhibitions are of value then most of all to architects, and especially to those who are prepared to profit by them. To these they afford both aid and encouragement.[12]

Cret suggested that exhibitions could serve in lieu of "extensive travel and skilled observation of the important buildings in process of construction or just completed ... as a source of inspiration for the earnest designer." Architecture drawings on display, Cret asserted, could be "more effective ... for the advancement of art than many pages of dissertation however learned." Cret was especially critical of what he considered to be the confused state of architectural discourse of the day, where many writers "follow the now prevailing fashion of attempting to explain scientific problems by quasi-philosophical theories." He found fault with the tendency to dichotomize art and science and said of those theorists, "They especially err in thinking that the aesthetic side of their theme may be divorced from its other aspects, not perceiving that they are all fundamentally related."[13]

To open the cover of an architectural exhibition catalog from a century ago is to enter a virtual gallery as a solitary spectator, perhaps as lonely a witness to that distant spectacle as the visitors to the nearly deserted galleries that Professor Cret's anecdote suggests (Figure 2.9). As valuable a document as the catalogs are, they yet provide poor substitute for the ornate trappings and rich spatial processions that served simultaneously as both backgrounds and foregrounds for a month-long architectural display. A resonant setting such as the exhibition halls of the Pennsylvania Academy of the Fine Arts, the Chicago Art Institute, or the American Fine Arts Society in New York no doubt provided immediate confirmation (or critique) of the two-dimensional propositions being showcased there—meta-representations of a representational art of building.

Despite Cret's admonition that the aesthetic dimension of architecture must not be separated from its other aspects, the view of architecture presented on gallery walls was nonetheless fractured. For the consumption of gallery goers, both general public and experienced practitioner alike, architecture was lionized and essentialized as a *fine art*—equal parts

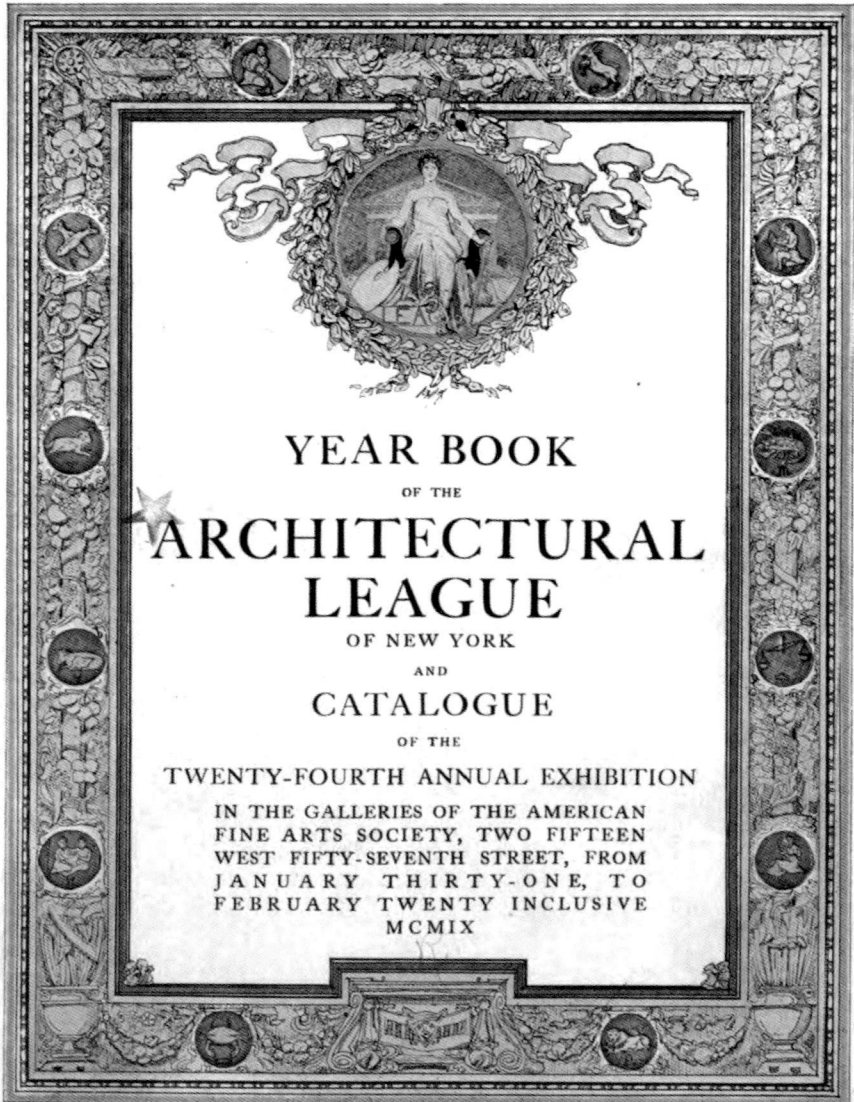

FIGURE 2.9 *Frontispiece*, Year Book of the Architectural League of New York and Catalogue of the Twenty-Fourth Annual Exhibition *(New York: Kalkhoff, 1909)*.

historical precedent, formal composition, and drafterly technique all aimed at the edification of elite culture. Social and technological developments in the science and business of building so crucial to the progress of that art were merely implicit, mostly out of view.

Beyond providing a survey of the stylistic tendencies of projects on display, the exhibition catalogs offer subtle clues about the networks of relationships that underlay ongoing advances in the state of the art. Most tellingly, many of the catalogs were evenly divided between front and back matter almost like the front-of-house and back-of-house social separation of architects' outer and inner offices.[14] On one hand, the front half of the catalog typically recorded the respective club's history, programs, and membership; the roster of exhibition participants, including locations of their practices and locations of exhibited projects; and often the names of clientele. From among hundreds of exhibited items, the catalog would include a representative sample of plans, various renderings, and staid photographs the selection of which bestowed upon those whose work was included a supplemental curatorial distinction.

The second half of the catalog, on the other hand, was typically composed of an indexed section of advertisements, an exhibition of the products and trades of manufacturers and builders, those underwriters of catalog and exhibition costs whose substantive contributions as construction collaborators would otherwise go un-credited (Figure 2.10). Such financial and formatting arrangements as supported the catalog followed the sometimes insidious practice in trade and professional journals where publishers, architects, and builders were inevitably bound in quid pro quo relationships that stretched as yet unwritten ethical bounds. As a Chicago architecture journal editorialized about one such arrangement as had been gathered from hearsay gossip, "The wily publisher sought the ducats, the architect fame, and the prosperous contractor was invited to foot the bill."[15]

Thus, in its documentation and re-presentation of an architectural exhibition, the catalog served as an index to a more extended field of production than the work foregrounded in the gallery alone suggested. The academic renderings of conspicuous architectural consumption were presumably intended at least as much for the mutual benefit of their architect-auteurs as for their appeal to either public curiosity or private vanities—of once or future clients. The means of production of the drawings and designs, a staff of anonymous drafters, were as likely to be hidden behind the scenes of the exhibition as were the agents of building production, the organizers and executors of materials and assemblies, and all the labor and finance they entailed. In a broader sense, and particularly relevant to the present study, such exhibitions and their catalogs can be seen as manifestations, from the connoisseur's privileged standpoint, of the same intertwining interests of architects, owners, and builders that Frank Miles Day's *Handbook of Architectural Practice* would strive to document and describe from a decidedly business perspective. While in the catalog, architects could project their art and themselves into the foreground of attention and at the pinnacle of a social hierarchy, in *The Handbook*, the grounds of economic and technological authority were much more contested and still subject to negotiation. The two kinds of texts, catalog and handbook, may indeed

FIGURE 2.10 *Contractor's advertisement*, Year Book of the Architectural League of New York and Catalogue of the Twenty-Fourth Annual Exhibition *(New York: Kalkhoff, 1909)*.

reflect each other, but it is as if through a distorting mirror of uncertain causes and unintended effects.

The Twenty-Fourth Annual Exhibition of the Architectural League of New York held in 1909 and the Sixteenth Annual Architectural Exhibition of the T Square Club held in Philadelphia in 1910 were typical of such events, and each was documented by its respective catalog. As the only remaining index of these temporary events, the catalogs are suggestive of the intertwining social, professional, and business networks active in the day as well as the inter-city relations and self-promoting motives joining architects, builders, and suppliers. This cross-section through architecture culture in the early decades of the twentieth century, a seemingly random selection of pictures at an exhibition, makes emblematic the range of competing forces that were tugging at the still elastic boundaries of a profession in formation.

As can be gleaned from the exhibition catalogs, work of several major protagonists in this history of *The Handbook* appeared in serendipitous proximity to each other within the exhibition galleries in both New York and Philadelphia. It is certainly within the realm of possibility that these architects rubbed elbows with each other on an opening night. As a reviewer of the 1910 T Square Club Exhibition reported:

> The man whose duty it is to visit each year the various exhibitions throughout the country, after seeing his [own work] first, will greet as old acquaintances at least half of the material hung in succeeding displays. He will find in his catalogues many repetitions of the same subjects varying in size of reproduction as representing the estimate of its importance, by catalogue committees. He will have seen much that is spectacular, and will have listened, with some amusement, to the criticisms of the lay visitor, who carried away by a blaze of color and many decorative motives, declares it is all very fine and elevating. But, he will not find an equal amount of enthusiasm in the remarks of the professional visitor, who comes to regard it as perhaps the scene of a social function, a gathering place for the dilettante, of exactly the same sort as a private view of the National Academy or of the National Sculpture Society.[16]

Work from *The Handbook* author's own long-established architectural firm, Frank Miles Day & Brother of Philadelphia, was included in both exhibitions—a grand English-style country house appearing first in renderings and the following year as photographs of a finished project. In close catalog proximity, work from the comparatively young New York City practice of Squires & Wynkoop was on display, houses of fireproof construction in picturesque style (Figures 2.11–2.13). Firm principal Frederick Squires, drawing on his own experience and keen observations of the difficulties of balancing art, business, and science, would soon be summoning the sage voice of Tom Thumtack as a witness in his satirical prosecution of the profession.

Among other architects included in both shows was work from a third and socially well-connected firm, Ewing & Chappell of New York. At the time of these two exhibitions, Ewing & Chappell had in their employment the very talented Rockwell Kent, an aspiring artist and peripatetic draftsman. Kent's tireless efforts across creative genres and fields yielded surprising overlaps of

FIGURE 2.11 *Frank Miles Day & Bro., Architects; House at Melrose, PA;* Year Book of the Architectural League of New York and Catalogue of the Twenty-Fourth Annual Exhibition *(New York: Kalkhoff, 1909)*.

FIGURE 2.12 *Frank Miles Day & Bro., Architects; House at Melrose, PA;* The Year Book and Catalogue of the T Square Club *(Philadelphia: McLaughlin Printing Co., Ltd., 1910)*.

FIGURE 2.13 *Squires & Wynkoop, Architects; Residence for Mr. A.B. Steen;* The Year Book and Catalogue of the T Square Club *(Philadelphia: McLaughlin Printing Co., Ltd., 1910).*

people, ideas, and worlds. His droll illustrations for his Columbia classmate Frederick Squires's creation, *Architec-tonics*, would in coming years help bring the tales of Tom Thumtack to life. All the while he was pursuing a serious and ultimately successful career as artist, Kent was building a reputation as a draftsman and architectural renderer. Working under the pseudonym "Hogarth, Jr.," Kent would regularly collaborate with his intermittent architect-employer George S. Chappell serving as illustrator for a number of Chappell's satirical literary ventures. Chappell, too, posed under various pseudonymous identities—as critic, social commentator, poet, playwright, and novelist—for the consumption of café society and the amusement of his friends.

Rockwell Kent

Rockwell Kent's early friendships and professional relationships, first with Frederick Squires as classmates studying architecture at Columbia University and then later with George Chappell during his employment with Ewing & Chappell, set the stage for subsequent collaborations that cast him as the lynchpin of these overlapping exhibitionary tales. It is ironic that Kent's name should not be so clearly in evidence as theirs in the exhibition catalogs of 1909 and 1910, for it is likely that architectural renderings issuing from his hand, for both his primary employer and for other firms on a freelance basis, were well in-view. The public renown he would accrue in coming decades—through his work as architectural renderer, illustrator, and artist; through his own self-fashioning travelogs and autobiographies; and through his political activism—would eventually outshine the reputations of his former associates in the field of architecture.[17] Yet Squires and especially Chappell would call upon Kent time and again to supply the clever sketches and caricatures that would illustrate their respective authorial efforts and help to visually ignite the sparks of their social satires.

Kent's second autobiography, *It's Me O Lord: The Autobiography of Rockwell Kent*, recounts his early orientation toward art and his family's pragmatic re-orientation of him toward the field of architecture at Columbia University.[18] In his recollections, Kent's early exposure to the culture of drawing and making through the manual training pedagogy of the Horace Mann School had been a critical factor in shaping an ethos of craftsmanship so crucial to his future endeavors at Columbia and beyond.[19] What seems to have drawn him and Squires together, however, was a common orientation toward humor and frivolity, a trait he claimed was widespread among his fellow architecture students.[20]

Kent described participation in such sophomoric hijinks as mounting exhibitions of cartoons mocking their professors and taking aim with pen and ink at other serious and not-so-serious subjects. In addition, Kent's and Squires's extracurricular pursuits through participation on the editorial board of the Columbia *Jester*, the student-run semi-monthly humor magazine, gave them ample opportunity to exercise a shared penchant for levity and *double entendre* through contributions of both written and graphic pieces. Joining the staff of *The Jester* in its—and his—second year, Squires and fellow architecture student Ely Jacques Kahn were among those regularly providing the little cartoons, cover art, and masthead banners that served as illustrative bon mots for satirical texts and verses such as ones supplied by Kent in following years (Figure 2.14). As chronicled in the *New York Times*, "The paper is the only one at Columbia that is illustrated, and this part of it is really one of its best features. Pictorially speaking, it really does not fall much below the standard of its more pretentious professional contemporaries."[21]

Besides their participation on staff of *The Jester*, Kent and Squires were elected members of the editorial board as art editors of *The 1904 Columbian*, the student yearbook of the junior class. Kent held this to be "the greatest—no, the only—honor [he] had received," a contention that the "records and grinds" section of the yearbook tends to confirm noting only his fraternity membership and participation on the class hockey team.[22] Squires, on the other hand, besides his own fraternity membership and participation in intramural hockey and baseball, had distinguished himself as member of the varsity track team. Among other accomplishments he set the university record in the pole-vault thus earning his yearbook accolade as "A man with a vaulting ambition," a sobriquet both witty and prescient.

FIGURE 2.14 *Editorial Board of* The Columbia Jester, *1902. Rockwell Kent and Frederick Squires appear on the back row center, left to right. Ely Jacques Kahn is seated on the floor, left. Rare Book & Manuscript Library, Columbia University in the City of New York.*

Likewise, Kent's classmates astutely distilled his deepest motivations when they wrote of him, "Ours is a high calling friend; Creative art demands the service of a mind and heart."[23] When they parted company at Columbia in 1904, Squires quickly entered practice forming a partnership within a year with another classmate, John Wynkoop. Kent on the other hand, who had been drifting ever more deliberately in the direction of painting and the visual arts while finishing his architecture degree, began using his talents as drafter and designer as a mainstay for his budding artist's career.

Squires & Wynkoop

Rockwell Kent recounted of his Columbia classmate that "Fred Squires was a post-grad, Williams man ... [and] had a number of talents: he was a fair hockey player, a good pole vaulter, probably a good architect, and certainly, when his subject was related to architecture, a gifted writer."[24] Born in Plainfield, New Jersey, Squires had graduated from Williams College in Massachusetts in 1900 with a bachelor of arts degree before embarking on the four-year BS program in architecture at Columbia.²⁵ Eight years of study were apparently deferral enough of Squires's vaulting ambition to build, for he immediately set himself the task of establishing a practice. While an architectural registration requirement had not yet been enacted in the State of New York, it is unusual that after his academic training he did not first seek some practical experience in another office before founding his own firm.²⁶ His professional partner John Wynkoop, for example, was continuing his training in the atelier of architect Donn Barber even as he and Squires began soliciting work.

Wynkoop was an Ohio native, a member of the Columbia class of 1903 a year ahead of Squires. *The Columbian* yearbook ascribed to him a lofty calling, "Art is the child of Nature"; and while not joining any extracurricular clubs or activities, he had gained recognition in his senior year when his student work was included in the T Square Club Annual Exhibition.²⁷ A perspective rendering of Squires & Wynkoop's first commission was included in the Eleventh Annual Architectural Exhibition of the T Square Club in 1905, and Wynkoop's watercolor esquisse for "A Market Cross" completed under the auspices of Atelier Donn Barber was displayed in the same show (Figure 2.15). Wynkoop gathered further recognition that same year when he was awarded

FIGURE 2.15 *John Wynkoop, Atelier Donn Barber, A Market Cross,* The T Square Club Eleventh Annual Exhibition 1904–1905 *(Philadelphia: McLaughlin Bros. Co., Ltd., 1905).*

first prize in the Paris Prize Competition providing him a scholarship to enter the Ecole des Beaux-Arts without examination where he studied from 1906–1908.[28] Wynkoop was thus abroad during the early years of his and Squires's ostensive partnership calling into some question the fullness of their collaboration since during those years they were an ocean apart.

Squires & Wynkoop's earliest successes in practice seem to have come primarily from Squires's Williams College connections where they garnered a commission for the design of The Gargoyle Gate, an entrance to the college's athletic ground, Weston Field (Figure 2.16). While the perspective exhibited in Philadelphia in 1905 was not included in the T Square Club

FIGURE 2.16 *Squires & Wynkoop, Architects; The Gargoyle Gate at Williams College*, The Hollow-Tile House *(New York: William T. Comstock Co., 1913).*

exhibition catalog, Squires later wrote about the origin and design of the project. Proposed by the Gargoyle Society, the school's student honor society, the little building was French Gothic in character in reference to its namesake, a compositional study in "symmetry without balance," and a form "in scale with Mount Greylock" whose prospect embraced its campus site. Squires waxed eloquent on the existential importance of the most modest of architectural compositions: "It can be seen that many considerations come into the designing of even this small structure, such as the character of the club, the handling of crowds, the layout of the college campus and even the consideration of the highest mountains in Massachusetts."[29]

In the years that soon followed, another commission came from Squires's alma mater for the design of the Phi Delta Fraternity House, his old chapter. First published in *Architectural Record* in 1908, the three-story project was a study in material expression in which "the characteristics and limitations of brick are ... recognized and respected, modeling and composition being subordinated to the textural effect" (Figure 2.17). The commentary concluded on a critically cautious note, however. "There are, in fact, so many features in brick and tile that the danger is a loss of dignity, but all this has been done with such delicacy that the result is interesting, revealing possibilities in a material which is destined to be a consequential element in the American architecture of the future."[30] The journal *International*

FIGURE 2.17 *Squires & Wynkoop, Architects; Phi Delta Theta Fraternity, Williams College,* Architectural Record *24 (1908).*

Studio took similar note of the project's decorative surface treatment in brick while also observing, "The steep pitched roof is fitting to the northern mountainous region and the twin-columned portico ... suggests the architectural traditions of a district settled at an early date."[31] In addition, the same essay gave special attention to Squires & Wynkoop's work in two other materials, hollow tile and concrete.

> The architects, Messrs. Squires and Wynkoop, have given considerable attention to work in this material. The use of hollow tile and other fireproof material they have carried to a point of facility with good results. Interesting dwellings have been built by them in New Jersey among the Oranges and in the neighborhood of Newark. The house built for Professor Lough at University Heights is said to have been the first terra-cotta tile house built in New York City. They have made an effective use of concrete beams, and hollow-tile walls.[32]

Based upon their record of publications and exhibitions, the years 1909 and 1910 were pivotal ones in the partnership of Squires & Wynkoop, indicative of an intense productivity in the brief years since founding their firm. During that two-year interval, Squires & Wynkoop published or exhibited almost twenty single family residences, two churches, two high schools, four fraternity houses, and one apartment house (Figures 2.18–2.19). A majority of the total of almost thirty projects were either already completed or then being brought to fruition. The exhibitions at the Architecture League of 1909 and T Square Club of 1910 included almost half of this oeuvre without

FIGURE 2.18 *Squires & Wynkoop, Architects;* "The First Terra Cotta House in New York," The Hollow-Tile House *(New York: William T. Comstock Co., 1913).*

FIGURE 2.19 *Squires & Wynkoop, Architects; Church of St. Luke the Evangelist; Roselle, NJ;* The Hollow-Tile House *(New York: William T. Comstock Co., 1913).*

overlap or repetition; and in December 1909, the journal *Architecture* published design proposals from the firm along with serious photographic portraits of the partners recognizing them in the captions as "Architects of To-day."[33]

The substantial body of Squires & Wynkoop's residential work was executed using terra cotta tile and concrete construction, an area of technical expertise that they sought to actively promote. Beginning in 1909, the partners, both separately and together, authored several essays in architecture and other trade journals that advocated the virtues and techniques of fireproof construction and that positioned their work at the cutting edge of efforts to integrate new building materials into residential construction. As Squires explained:

> The building departments of most of the towns where we have built have accepted fireproof construction after investigation, and in many cases have welcomed it in the hope that it would displace frame. Our clients have usually been men who could write the letters indicating an engineering degree after their names. Contractors, whenever they have been thorough workmen, have found no great difficulty in mastering the idea, and some of our best executed buildings have been the first attempt in this line of clever local masons.
>
> If, then, good contractors will give fireproof materials earnest thought, well-trained architects will give them careful study, and owners will pay

a higher price for a superior article, they will produce buildings of such a character that everybody will be glad that they can't be burned down. [34]

Squires and Wynkoop entered practice at a time when rising concerns about public safety and the hazards of shoddy construction were compromising architects' ongoing efforts to build up public trust and bolster their professional esteem. While progress in fire prevention and control had been made over the latter half of the nineteenth century, the rapid pace of commercial development was increasing the risk of urban conflagrations. A deadly fire at the end of 1903 consumed the Iroquois Theater in Chicago at the loss of over 600 lives.[35] Though avowedly "fireproof," the newly commissioned building lacked adequate fire separation between the stage and the house, and lacked adequate means of fire suppression, ventilation, exit lighting, or panic egress. As editorialized in *The Inland Architect and News Record*, "... the public has suddenly awakened and found that laxity and incompetence even to criminal carelessness has been the rule, and that of all the laws upon which the public relied for safety some have been dead letters for years and other evaded or ignored."[36]

A popular novel published early in the following year, Robert Herrick's *The Common Lot*, portrayed fictional circumstances of complicity among architects, developers, builders, and government officials that if not literally true nonetheless reinforced public suspicions about the inviolability of the architect's professional trust.[37] A devastating fire of the same year in Baltimore's downtown business district and another in San Francisco accompanying the great earthquake of 1906 severely tested the fire resistance of prevalent building practices and led architect and journalist F.W. Fitzpatrick to decry the nation's "annual ash-heap" and to assign to architects a significant blame (Figures 2.20–2.21).

> The folly of it all is pathetic, and certainly a reflection upon the intelligence of people. A million buildings are wiped out of existence inside of ten years. In New York they average 8,700 fires a year; in Chicago, 4,100. Our normal record is three theaters, three public halls, twelve churches, ten schools, two hospitals, two asylums, two colleges, six apartment-houses, three department stores, two jails, twenty-six hotels, one hundred and forty flats and sixteen hundred homes burned up every week in the year. Last year we indulged in 45,000 fires. The year before we burned up over 6,000 people. ...
>
> ... Architects are to blame, I say, because so many of them think only of the pretty exterior and dainty effects to be had inside with fine wood, etc. Everything is sacrificed to those considerations. The safety, the stability of the structure are minor considerations .... The average layman knows but little about fireproof construction. It is the architect's province, nay, his very duty, to educate his client in that respect. He has been derelict in that duty, and just to that extent do I charge him here with being an "accessory before the fact" to as near a crime as one can well come.[38]

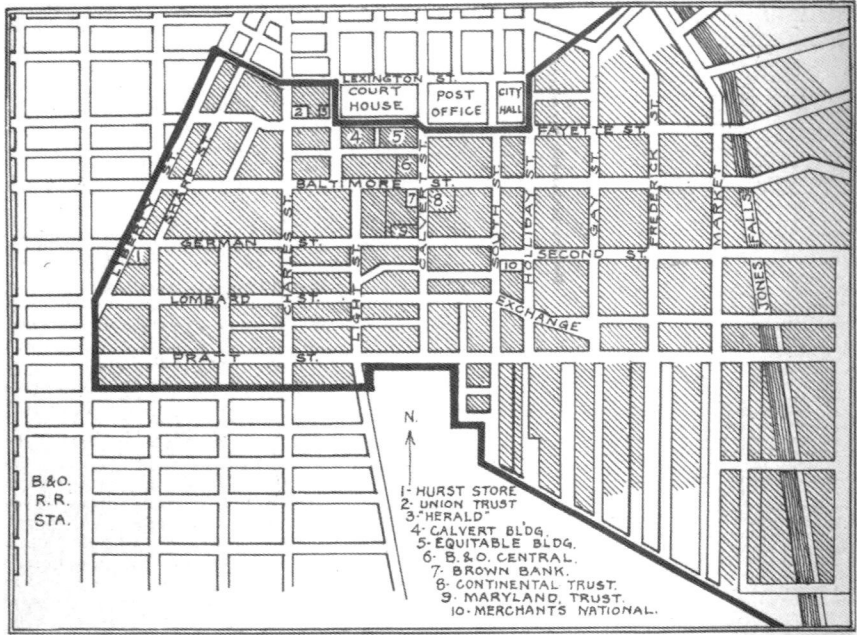

FIGURE 2.20 *Map of extents of Baltimore fire*, Inland Architect & News Record 43 (1904).

FIGURE 2.21 *Aftermath of Baltimore Fire*, The Brickbuilder 13 (1904).

The implications that architects were either unconcerned or uninformed on technical and financial considerations of fire protection, or that artistic intents were allowed to trump public safety, were serious charges that went to the heart of their ethical concern and professional competence. Such sober recognition of the interlinked, collective nature of professional status and repute increasingly mitigated in favor of state regulation of architects in the interest of safeguarding the life and property of the citizenry. Whatever internal or systemic logics may be offered as motive forces for professional formation—jurisdictional disputes, monopolistic tendencies, power-knowledge relationships—the field of architecture was feeling pressure at this time to submerge artistic intents within broader processes of technological innovation, statutory regulation, and progressive social reform.

It is within this milieu that Squires & Wynkoop became active proponents of the virtues of fireproof residential construction. Their argument for "the fireproof house as the American type" was very much in alignment with an editorial position taken by a Chicago architecture journal in the period following the Iroquois Theater fire: "It is time that the fire-proofing of all structures where loss of life by fire is possible be made part of every building ordinance and particularly in the line of residences and school buildings, for there the greatest danger lies. In other words, lives should be of more account than the property risk placed by an insurance company."[39] While the protection of life and property was an ethical imperative for architects, a favorable return on investment was a practical incentive for owners and builders alike. The architect's role was to educate those parties to the latent potential of hollow-tile and concrete house construction. Wrote Squires & Wynkoop, "Many a builder and owner today does not appreciate such hidden value and will not pay for it and these will have to be educated by the example of their wiser neighbors, who build for their children as well as for themselves."[40]

Owners and builders needed to be apprised of the value that would accrue from a combination of structural permanence, fire resistance, preservation of life, and reduced insurance rates. Indeed, architects themselves needed to be prodded beyond the technical conservatism of their practices to explore the benefits of new materials and approaches. There were practical impediments to experimentation, however. With office staff members typically lacking familiarity with new materials, firms were forced to rely upon the advice of engineers, manufacturers, or contractors, an abrogation of architects' own knowledge and expertise. The alternative was for architects to research new material systems on their own, an expense they were unlikely to recoup from project fees.[41]

Squires & Wynkoop helped fill this knowledge gap by sharing what they had learned in their own practice. No doubt, they had financial incentives as well. Several of their fireproof house designs had been specifically commissioned by journals aligned with or supported by advertising from the hollow-tile and concrete construction industries (Figure 2.22).[42] These too were some of the indigenous conditions that were shaping the fireproof American house, and as the architects maintained, "*inventiveness and commercialism* have led the way to the use of permanent and native materials."[43]

FIGURE 2.22 *Squires & Wynkoop, Architects; Demonstration house in stucco-covered hollow-tile commissioned by the journal* Building Progress; The Hollow-Tile House *(New York: William T. Comstock Co., 1913).*

Squires & Wynkoop as "architects of today" were clearly poised for success. Of the twelve projects the firm had included in the exhibitions of 1909 and 1910, six were houses of the fireproof American type. Their work in this vein was included along with that of more established firms in the Real Estate and Ideal Homes Show at Madison Square Garden. Former AIA President Frank Miles Day used an image of one of their projects as illustration for his introductory essay to *Inexpensive Homes of Individuality*, touted as a collection of some of "America's best country and suburban homes of moderate size."[44] In early 1910, the *New York Times* reported Squires & Wynkoop's most significant commissions to date, two twelve-story projects being developed by the Manhattan Office Building Company and part of an apparent "loft building boom" in the city.[45]

Despite the apparent success that the firm was enjoying, a rather cryptic public announcement appeared in mid-1911 stating, "The firm of Squires and Wynkoop, Architects, dissolved on May 1st, by mutual consent." According to that brief article, Wynkoop entered a partnership with a more senior architect, Percy Griffin.[46] Squires continued at his old office location, though he too soon formed a new partnership with Clifford Wendehack who was five years his junior.[47] What circumstances might have precipitated Squires & Wynkoop's sudden demise?

One hint of possible professional discord can be inferred from attributions given several published projects in the months and years following the dissolution of the firm. For example, while both partners are noted as architects of the loft project on East 16th Street, the firm's Mercantile Building on 7th Avenue is credited to Frederick Squires alone.[48] Perhaps the pressures of family life and the intense competitiveness of the business environment contributed to the split. The challenge of balancing the art, science, and business of architecture dynamically shaped any professional partnership. How partners divided and shared the various responsibilities of practice—job-getting, design, production, administration, supervision—largely determined the character and reputation of the firm and the quality and coherence of its output. Squires's and Wynkoop's respective class mottos from *The Columbian* may offer some insight into their professional predilections—one with his vaulting ambition and the other devoted to an ideal of art as the child of nature. If we trace the divergent paths they pursued after dissolving their practice, then it becomes quite evident in retrospect how prescient their yearbook profiles had been.

Wynkoop's early recognitions, atelier experiences, and fellowship in Paris at the Ecole des Beaux Arts cemented his reputation as a skilled designer, and many of the formal renderings published with attributions to Squires & Wynkoop bear a signature unique to his hand.[49] Wynkoop's new partner, Percy Griffin, had achieved some modest successes by the time of their professional union[50]; yet, their joint recognition as a firm, at least as measured in publications and exhibitions of their work, did not match the explosively productive period of Squires & Wynkoop's earlier success.[51] Percy Griffin's and John Wynkoop's professional trajectories were tragically truncated, however, with their premature, parallel deaths in 1921 and 1922 respectively, each one dying "after a week's illness with pneumonia."[52]

Frederick Squires, on the other hand, lived a long life and, as it unfolds, pursued several serial (and serializing) careers. Compared to John Wynkoop, Squires was likely the partner who was most active in cultivating a clientele from among his personal connections and also in advancing the firm's line of technical research into fireproof hollow-tile construction. While completing projects begun and in-progress at the time of Squires & Wynkoop's dissolution, he continued with his new partner Clifford Wendehack to champion the cause of the hollow-tile house. Beginning in 1911, he authored a series of ten monthly articles on the subject for the journal *Architecture and Building*, a step that would earn him the title of "contributing editor" and lead him into a variety of ventures as an architectural journalist.

Architecture and Building was a publication begun by long-established architectural publisher William T. Comstock, a first cousin of the infamous Anthony Comstock who gained notoriety as a crusader for morality and decency in his roles as Post Office Inspector and Secretary of the Society for the Suppression of Vice.[53] William T. Comstock began in the publishing business as a producer of maps and atlases and later acquired an architectural publishing house, A.J. Bicknell & Company, which he re-launched under his own name. He founded the magazine *Building* in 1882, characterized in its masthead as "an architectural monthly treating on all matters of interest to the building trades." The journal changed names, formats, and emphases several times through the years until it was finally re-christened *Architecture and Building* in 1911, "a magazine devoted to contemporary architectural construction."[54]

Squires's technical interests thus comported well with the journal's editorial emphasis upon new building materials, assemblies, and equipment and the perennial emphasis upon approaches to fire protection and suppression. Hollow-tile cladding of steel structure, reinforced concrete construction, fire egress standards, elevators, and sprinkler systems were among the journal's recurrent concerns. Squires's extensive research on hollow-tile construction led to the publication of a book on the topic in 1913, *The Hollow-Tile House*. The treatise significantly expanded upon the topics of his journal articles to include historical precedents of tile making and "Old World" stucco. Squires argued for the durability, safety, and economy of construction techniques he derived from his on-site building experiments with sand-casting and modular masonry units larger than brick, which he called "texture tiles" (Figures 2.23–2.25). The volume was illustrated with built residential works of his own design as well as those completed with partners Wynkoop and Wendehack. A number of the projects had been previously published and appeared in architectural exhibitions alongside the work of several New York colleagues also illustrated in the text.[55]

The culmination of Squires's hollow-tile thesis was the exposition of his "House of Three Inventions" for brother Lewis Squires at Netherwood, NJ. The epitome of his texture-tile techniques, the project demonstrated the technological innovations whose resulting architectural qualities of textured surface were, he claimed, "the result of millions of minute shadows." While obeying certain conventions of a scientific treatise, *The Hollow-Tile House* provided Squires with an apt format for a subtle form of self-promotion in an otherwise advertising-averse profession. After all, as his mouthpiece Tom Thumtack would later profess, "*It Is Professional to Educate.*"[56]

Certain rhetorical elements of *The Hollow-Tile House* foreshadowed the satirical literary project Squires would soon have in the works. For example, he offered several pointed criticisms aimed at owners, builders, and architects especially with regard to the architect's responsibility for guarding cost. He stated baldly, "The competitive bidding method by which the builder is usually selected is full of evils"[57]; and he implored owners not to saddle their architects with responsibility for domains over which they could exercise no control. He wrote:

> It is no disgrace to the architect that he is not a builder and has not the builder's knowledge, but the client usually thinks he ought to be as versatile as a janitor …. In the matter of costs, don't try to make him work the miracle of getting your fixed desires within your fixed price. The days of miracles are past.[58]

FIGURE 2.23 *Squires & Wynkoop, Architects; House for Mrs. J.J. Adams, construction of hollow-tile walls;* The Hollow-Tile House *(New York: William T. Comstock Co., 1913).*

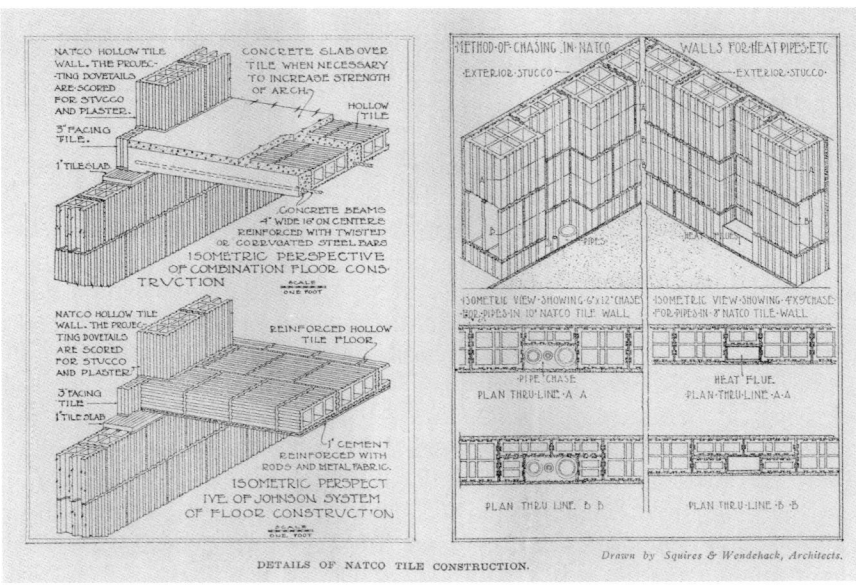

FIGURE 2.24 *Squires & Wendehack, Architects; details of tile construction,* The Hollow-Tile House *(New York: William T. Comstock Co., 1913).*

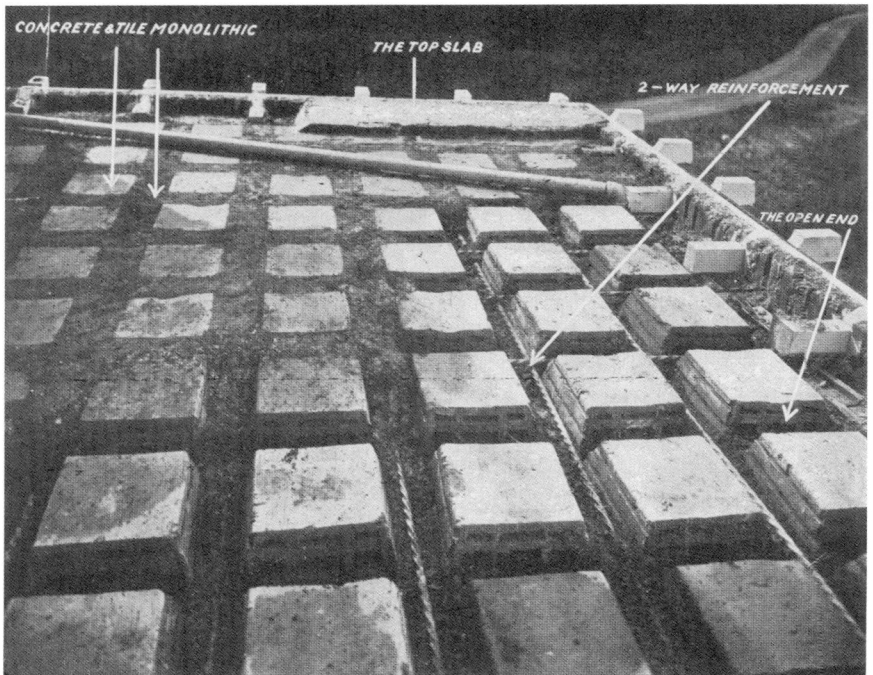

FIGURE 2.25 *Floor assembly construction using hollow-tile,* The Hollow-Tile House *(New York: William T. Comstock Co., 1913).*

Where Frederick Squires's biting critiques of the status quo cast *The Hollow-Tile House* as a vehicle for his unvarnished aspersions, when later conveyed in the wry manner of Tom Thumtack they were recast in the pages of *Architectonics* as the essence of keen wit. The title page of *The Hollow-Tile House* was likewise the harbinger of those coming attractions and collaborations, a flowing banner of a bookplate in the sky of a pristine arctic landscape, the unmistakable artistry of Squires's Columbia classmate Rockwell Kent.

By the time Squires conceived Tom Thumtack as his alter-ego, he had been busy at architectural practice for over a decade for the love of his art; but with a growing family, he also needed a steady income. The range of his residential and commercial projects, the enterprise of his technical research and construction innovations, and then his energetic pursuit of journalistic opportunities were all clear evidence of his striving in earnest. The understanding that he struck with his publisher, the William T. Comstock Company, for a series of humorous articles later to be compiled into books, must have held some promise of financial reward. To illustrate his tales and help bring them to life, he contacted his old friend from Columbia *Jester* days, Rockwell Kent, who reminisced years later in his autobiography about their collaboration:

The illustrating job that came to me at that period was quite good enough to yield me lots of fun in doing it. Fred Squires ... had turned his writing to good account in a series of amusing stories for an architectural periodical; and I had illustrated them. He now planned to publish these and additional stories in a book to be titled Architectonics, by Tom Thumtack, with illustrations by, anonymously, me. So with Fred standing over me, axe, as it were in hand, I made the drawings. "Come," he would say, "that's good enough. Let's have it." And, although most of them were not by any standards good enough, I would. It was a rush job, it had to be. Any money was as short as time. I think I got three hundred dollars for my work. Two hundred here, a hundred there, and twenty-five in bunches in between: all very well—but once again, how to get away?[59]

"How to get away" was a recurrent theme in Kent's life. Like Squires, he never lacked idealism or drive, though he often lacked material means and therefore found himself juggling a succession of short-term engagements sufficient to support his family, his wanderlust, and his painting. Interrupting his degree studies at Columbia, he strayed from architecture into art, later studying with noted artist Robert Henri and developing his own heroic, socially realistic style. Kent found early employment in the architectural offices of Ewing & Chappell, which he used as a home base and base of support for his artistic pursuits, freelance illustration jobs, and travels to distant horizons—Newfoundland, Alaska, the Southern Seas. He also became politically involved with Socialism, identified himself with the plight of Labor, and conceived his work as part of a larger human aspiration and struggle. By the time the illustration job came along from Fred Squires, Kent had already garnered recognition through exhibition of his art.[60] His anonymous association with Squires marked the effort as more a financial than a creative move. For Kent's efforts in making "194 drawings to illustrate the stories under the general title 'Architec-tonics'" along with a stipulation that he would "never sell, offer for sale or in any manner convey to any person the said drawings for publication purposes in any form in this or any other country," Frederick Squires promised the payment of $387.50.[61]

Not long after the publication of *Architec-tonics: The Tales of Tom Thumtack, Architect*, both Frederick Squires and Rockwell Kent, with different motivations, indeed found the means to get away. Kent had managed to move his growing family to Newfoundland where he could paint, though his sojourn was short-lived. Deported on suspicions of subversive activity, he found himself back in New York where, he remembered, "arriving penniless," and being met on his return by his old mentor and employer George Chappell with the promise of his old job.[62] Meanwhile, Squires abruptly relocated to Ohio and then on to Illinois where he joined his brother's petroleum drilling concern. His letter to Kent in September 1915 provided ample clue of the exigencies behind his parting and his abandonment of the field of architecture and a budding literary career:

Dear Rockwell,

I have your letter written from New York. You will notice that I have moved again which made me a little late in getting the letter after I arrived in McConnelsville.

Comstock reserved the right of not publishing the second volume [of Architec-tonics] if the first volume was a failure and this is what it proved to be. He took three stories out of the second set and gave me a three months note for fifty dollars for them and other notes for the royalty on "The Hollow Tile House" which I had assigned to Walter. This I explained to Mr. Chappell after he had been good enough to get back from the Buffalo party to whom he had disposed of the others, that "Temperamental" set.

Walter had such trouble with the first of Comstock's notes that he put the whole bunch into his lawyer's hands. Comstock has been able to pay one note and I think this is the one from which you are to get $35.00 and I have written Walter to send you a check for this. Comstock has gone back on the rest and simply paid the interest and got a sixty day extension.

There has been no royalty payment on the first volume Comstock claiming that only a dozen or so copies have been sold.

I have a contract for the production of a third book "Progressive Architecture" all the plates except one and all the text for which have been prepared and delivered. It is such a job getting money out of Comstock that I do not believe that I shall go any further with this book. It was my wish that I could get you to do all the decorations for it but I would not tackle it unless I was able to pay you cash direct in advance on my own responsibility which I am not yet able to do. Then I would let the royalty payments slide because it is easier making the money than getting it out of the publisher.

I'm sorry you could not continue your painting. It's a great pity that you are hindered by the need of earning money from filling your real place all the time.

Yours very truly,
Frederick Squires[63]

In his brief career as an architect, Squires demonstrated an affinity for engineering logic through his material research and its application to problems of progressive architectural construction. In his second career as a petroleum engineer and later employed with the Illinois State Geological survey, he invented innovative oil field processes and published two dozen technical papers on the subject, ultimately earning an honorary doctorate of science in recognition of his contributions.[64] On the face of it, it would appear that the wit with which Squires skewered the pretensions and preoccupations of the architecture profession through the mouthpiece of Tom Thumtack was in many ways his parting shot.

Ewing & Chappell

George Chappell and Charles Ewing, Rockwell Kent's erstwhile employers, had met around 1900 in Paris while studying abroad at the Ecole des Beaux-Arts. Ewing was from Washington, DC, and had studied at Georgetown University before taking courses as a special student in architecture at the Massachusetts Institute of Technology. Chappell, five years Ewing's junior, was from New London, Connecticut, and had graduated with a degree in architecture from Yale University. When the two returned to the United States from abroad, they separately sought employment as draughtsmen in two prominent New York architectural firms, each with strong Beaux-Arts orientations: Ewing in the office of Carrère & Hastings and Chappell at Lord & Hewlett.[65]

In those days, prior to widespread adoption of architectural registration laws, what separated a mere draughtsman from the accolade of "architect" was the possession of a client and a commission in-hand. When approached in 1904 to design a new home for a Westchester County widow and her family, Charles Ewing was joined by his friend George Chappell, each of them leaving their employers to establish their own firm. One of their first employees was the son of the client, a recently diplomaed architectural draughtsman from Columbia University named Rockwell Kent. Kent who was already set on a path that would straddle between architecture and art, reminisced in his autobiography about the early days at Ewing & Chappell.[66]

In the early booming years of their practice, Ewing & Chappell's social connections led to more residential commissions; to projects for members of the Vanderbilt family; and to university work for Vassar, Georgetown, and the newly established Connecticut College. Their work was regularly published in architectural journals and included in prominent architectural exhibitions of the day including those of the New York Architectural League in 1909 and the Philadelphia T Square Club in 1910. The 1909 exhibition included two institutional projects designed by the firm, the Cornelius Vanderbilt Memorial YMCA Building in Newport, Rhode Island, and the Sanders Chemical Laboratory at Vassar College in Poughkeepsie, New York.[67] The first of those commissions, a gift to the city from Alfred G. Vanderbilt as a memorial to his father, followed upon earlier work the architects had completed on the younger Vanderbilt's farm in nearby Pourtsmouth for a grand indoor riding academy (Figure 2.26). The eclectic designs integrated Colonial, Georgian, and French classicizing elements to yield results variously described as "Wrenian Baroque," "entertaining and attractive," or in the case of the science building at Vassar, "showing the Beaux-Arts tendency of those days to disregard surroundings in favor of individual expression."[68]

The T Square Club exhibition the following year in Philadelphia was devoted to domestic architecture, an arena in which Ewing & Chappell had been especially successful in preceding years beginning with Rockwell Kent's

FIGURE 2.26 *Ewing & Chappell, Architects; Interior, Riding Academy of Mr. Alfred G. Vanderbilt; Portsmouth, RI;* Architectural Record *21 (1907).*

mother's house. The house for Mrs. Kent, along with another for Rockwell's brother and several others in Tarrytown, New York, was published in 1909 along with the house included in the 1910 exhibition, a house for Richard E. Forrest, Esq., in Cedarhurst on Long Island—all compositions of rigorous local symmetries asymmetrically massed, interlinked commissions of the socially well-connected (Figure 2.27).[69]

Charles Ewing continued to solidify his professional standing through membership in the then very "clubby" American Institute of Architects; meanwhile Chappell's name appeared in New York newspaper society columns with rising frequency in association with the Society of Beaux-Arts Architects, especially in his role scripting entertainments for the group's increasingly elaborate charity balls.[70] For so many of these architects, their Paris school days had made lasting impressions, a spirit of hard work and frivolity that Chappell recounted and romanticized in a series of light-hearted essays for *Architectural Record* from 1910 and 1911 (Figure 2.28). Chappell wrote:

> Thus between master and students in their genial, free-and-easy, yet firmly constructed relation, the young American learns many lessons; what to do and what to avoid; what to say and what not to say, and as the weeks slip by and the day of the rendu draws near, he has grown to feel himself a part of the big machine, that astonishing machine, which, with the extraordinary looseness of its parts, runs so smoothly and with such power that it is an influence which is felt around the world.[71]

The "Paris School Days" articles appeared as one of the first of Chappell's journalistic forays as he strove to find his literary voice and define a critical

FIGURE 2.27 *Ewing & Chappell, Architects; House of Mrs. Rockwell Kent in Tarrytown, NY*; American Architect & Building News 96 (1909).

FIGURE 2.28 *George S. Chappell, "Charrette!" in "Paris School Days,"* Architectural Record 29 (1911).

persona. Chappell was writing at a time when the profession's lofty embrace of arts and letters was being nudged by concerns for business administration and rapidly changing building techniques. An early pair of essays on a seemingly innocuous topic, the architectural uses of lattice, for example, commenced with wry social commentary on the move from city to country which was propelling the rise of the American country house.

> We are returning to the country. The snug city-dweller no longer points the finger of scorn at Mr. Suburbanite, bundle-laden. The newspaper humorist and magazine wit less and less often shoots his darts at the painful joys of grass-cutting, snow-shoveling and other bucolic pastimes .... Back to the land! is the cry of the younger generations. Thus we have come to take an interest in gardens and their products. We pass beyond the simple axiomatic knowledge conveyed by that priceless volume and first aid to naturalists, "How to Tell the Birds from the Wild Flowers." We actually grow things, and boast about them and match cabbage-heads with our neighbors.[72]

In his citation of a book of humorous children's verse about birds and flowers that issued from the pen of an otherwise noted American physicist, Chappell offered a clue about the extreme range of vocations and avocations that then pre-occupied the educated elite. He also foreshadowed his own later literary pursuits.[73] During his Yale days, besides being active with the banjo and mandolin clubs, Chappell contributed to the *Yale Literary Magazine* and to the student humor publication, the *Yale Record*.[74] As noted in the introduction to an anthology of the first fifty years of the *Yale Record's* versifying wit, "Whatever undergraduate conversation may lack in weight of thought and height of theme, it abounds in humor—humor as harmless as it is genuine. And it is as natural for undergraduates to write verse as it is for them to sing in the shower-bath. All boys are poets at heart."[75] A notable number of Yale-educated architects, contemporaries and competitors in practice with Chappell, were also alumni of the *Yale Record*: Grosvenor Atterbury, Donn Barber, William Adams Delano of Delano & Aldrich, Chicago architect Howard Van Doren Shaw.[76] A weakness for satire and an appreciation of keen wit were defining attributes of these circles of social influence and arbiters of good taste.

At the same time when Chappell was helping to keep the Beaux-Arts spirit alive, he was also giving aid and support to Rockwell Kent's artistic aspirations. Chappell provided exhibition space free of charge to Kent and a self-organized group of independent artists seeking validation outside the bounds of the juried show system. While Kent was critical of the academic tradition, he was also derisive of the more avant-garde displays of modernist abstraction that he observed at the epochal Armory Show of 1913—works such as Marcel Duchamp's "Nude Descending a Staircase" or Georges Braque's "Violin." "The whole affair," he wrote, "was indicative of the current clash of ideologies of which the exhibits were abundant evidence – one of the two exhibits of the very gifted Raymond Duchamp-Villon being, as I recall it, a cheap electric bell, together with some lengths of wire, glued to a piece of common wall board, and entitled 'Architectural Sculpture.'"[77]

Whenever George Chappell was involved, it seems, worlds tended to collide and ironies multiplied. Such was the case in the same year as the Armory Show when Duchamp-Villon and Chappell—respective notaries for Cubism and Collegiate Gothic—found themselves paired in a short-lived collaboration for the design of new dormitories at the Connecticut College of Women. Ewing & Chappell had been awarded the commission based at least in part upon Chappell's family connections—his father had been an early donor and treasurer of the institution. Duchamp-Villon's vaguely Gothic "Façade Architecturale" in plaster displayed at the Armory Show had been an attempt to translate principles of cubism into a decorative, sculptural motive applied to architecture, his *Maison Cubiste*. As art historian Kevin D. Murphy has stitched together the story, artist and cultural impresario Walter Pach likely brought Duchamp-Villon to the attention of the Francophile architect Chappell who commissioned, and then later rejected, the union of these divergent stylistic strains of Gallic design intent.[78] Chappell's architectural conservatism should not, however, be interpreted as an aversion to modern existence but rather as a personal distaste for modernist displays. The duality of Chappell's business and creative lives, between his inner and outer offices, suggests an affinity for irony and uninhibited social intercourse disguised beneath the propriety of staid and familiar forms.

The Architects' Building

When D. Everett Waid published his first series of case studies of architects' offices in 1911 and 1912, the "broadening influences of pure architecture" was an underlying concern. In the second set of articles from 1913 to 1914, the emphasis shifted, as was evident in the series title, toward "The Business Side of an Architect's Office."[79] The dozen or so architects' offices newly profiled there were especially remarkable by virtue of being housed together in the same sixteen-story Park Avenue loft building. The co-operative enterprise had been developed and designed expressly for that purpose, for and by architects acting as their own clients. Looking more closely at Waid's cross-section through architecture culture of the Progressive Era, we can gain insights into not only changing operational methods structuring architects' drafting rooms and inner offices but also the web of social relationships extending from architects' reception rooms and outer offices into wider circles of business commerce and cultural display; architects in society interacting with their colleagues and competitors, contractors and clientele.

The Architects' Building, touted "as the home of a large group of T square and triangle men," had been anticipated with great interest from across the building trades and professions. According to Waid, "The building is interesting to the building world in general, because here the architects were their own clients and presumably handled the whole enterprise in an ideal way from the architects' point of view ...."[80] Located at the corner of Park Avenue and 41st Street in midtown Manhattan, it was completed on-schedule and on-budget, fully leased and occupied in mid-1913 by twenty-five architectural, engineering, and construction firms (Figure 2.29).[81] As reported by Waid:

> The fact that the building has accommodations for general and sub-contractors, decorators, material men, etc., would indicate a greater efficiency in handling the working forces of those who are fortunate enough to be numbered as tenants. One's office boy, with a tracing, can disappear into an elevator and in ten minutes bring back a blueprint hot and dry from an electrically lighted cylinder. Sets of drawings can be most conveniently delivered to contractors, and that contractor, called General, can quietly tap at the door and delicately insinuate that if F.S. details are not ready by such a date, the time of completion of the building will have to be extended. It seems quite ideal to be able to go next door for a criticism, or to borrow a draftsman, or to admire a set of competition drawings.[82]

FIGURE 2.29 *Ewing & Chappell with LaFarge & Morris Architects, The Architects Building in New York City. From* left to right: Architecture and Building 44 *(1912) and* Brickbuilder 22 *(1913).*

Designed in a collaboration between the firms Ewing & Chappell and La Farge & Morris, the project had been conceived seven years prior by architect Charles Ewing with the encouragement of his then-employer John M. Carrère.[83] The second and ultimately successful effort to launch the project came with the backing of other leading figures of the New York architectural scene. The speculative enterprise was described some years later by Ewing's by-then former partner George S. Chappell:

> A kingpin in the organizing group was the firm of McKim, Mead & White, and among others associated with them were Arnold Brunner, K. M. Murchison, Donn Barber and Charles A. Platt. With the addition of such well established construction folk as Post & McCord they formed a solid, powerful group. They had chosen an opportune time for their operation. It was just before the big jump in land values in this neighborhood and building costs were relatively low. They engineered a magnificent loan and put up a simple, practical building with an amount of capital that gave it the playful designation of the "Shoestring Building." It has been one-hundred-per-cent rented since its inception. Engineers, material men, fixture manufacturers and still more architects have flocked to the Architects' Building.[84]

In the first of his seven essays describing office arrangements of a dozen or so architectural firms, Waid gave a detailed account of the overall design of the Architects' Building. He made particular note of emergency egress and fire protection features in the steel frame structure, issues of perennial safety concern. He described the large window openings located close to the ceilings of the twelve-foot high spaces, a common sense consideration for flooding drafting rooms with natural light. He described material choices and budget trade-offs, offering that "the critical visitor should know that the owners fully and regretfully realized that, in economizing on plaster wainscot in corridors and omitting marble, they were incurring an increased maintenance cost."[85]

In addition to the overview of the building, Waid offered readers a peek inside the offices of the architects responsible for the building design. The previous office of LaFarge & Morris facing Madison Square had been profiled in Waid's first series of articles, so the reappearance of certain elements lends familiarity to the new mise-en-scène when we encounter again the outer reception room where an "attractive decorative effect is given by the books, a piece of tapestry, a large example of Japanese carving" and "a reversible table worth going a mile to see." Subtler shifts of inner office layout were mere responses to planning constraints, but others were suggestive of more significant organizational adjustments of the office's business paradigm. The partners now occupied private instead of shared offices, and additional rooms were provided for an office manager and superintendent.[86]

Likewise, the floor plan of George Chappell's and partner Charles Ewing's architectural office is as indicative of the firm's departmental organization as it is suggestive of the respective roles of the two partners. Ewing & Chappell's practice occupied the thirteenth floor of the sixteen-story building facing onto Park Avenue. According to the journal description:

> The plans show the possibilities of layout where the conditions are absolutely favorable. The architects in each case subdivided the space allotted them, always keeping in mind relative importance of space for drafting room, reception room, library, filing, etc., as to insure efficient administration. It will be noted that special attention has been given in both the offices shown to the matter of office entrances and the control of these. The operator of the telephone switchboard is in a position to direct all visitors to the proper department, quickly sending clients one way and contractors another and at the same time, can issue and receive drawings and is the better able to do all the useful things which are expected of that functionary.[87]

From the front office, clients could be quickly ushered into a formal reception room, "light gray and white in a simple and pleasing treatment"; meanwhile, contractors could proceed directly to the office of Mr. Allen, the firm's designated intermediary. Partner Ewing's office opened directly to the drafting room and was conveniently linked to Allen's while Chappell's office was closest to the clients' reception room and directly adjoined the firm's stenographers. Chappell occupied the corner office with triple windows, a suggestive pecking order when compared to Ewing's double and Allen's single. And more suggestive still, Chappell's office was equipped with an extra table from which we might infer an extra function, or an extra secretary, in addition to his partner's roll-top desk and drafting board (Figures 2.30–2.33). *Why did Chappell have an extra desk?*

Returning from Minnesota after a year away from New York, to serve as on-site construction superintendent for another firm, Rockwell Kent found himself back again "once more, New York; and in the draughting room of Ewing and Chappell, now moved to the Architects Building at 101 Park Avenue." Kent's memoires offer a particularly frank assessment of the inner workings of the firm and of his own role both inside the drafting room and out. He recalled the occasional arguments over his drafting board concerning matters of artistic intent between himself and his employers, sometimes caught in the middle between their own competing tastes.[88]

Kent credited himself with the renderings Ewing & Chappell used to "bait the hook" for the Connecticut College commission. He was therefore frustrated that despite his creative contributions to the project, he was typically kept out of site in the drafting room during visits from the College president in his role as client. So much for the nobility of labor; Kent was a "mere" draftsman. For Kent like his friend Frederick Squires

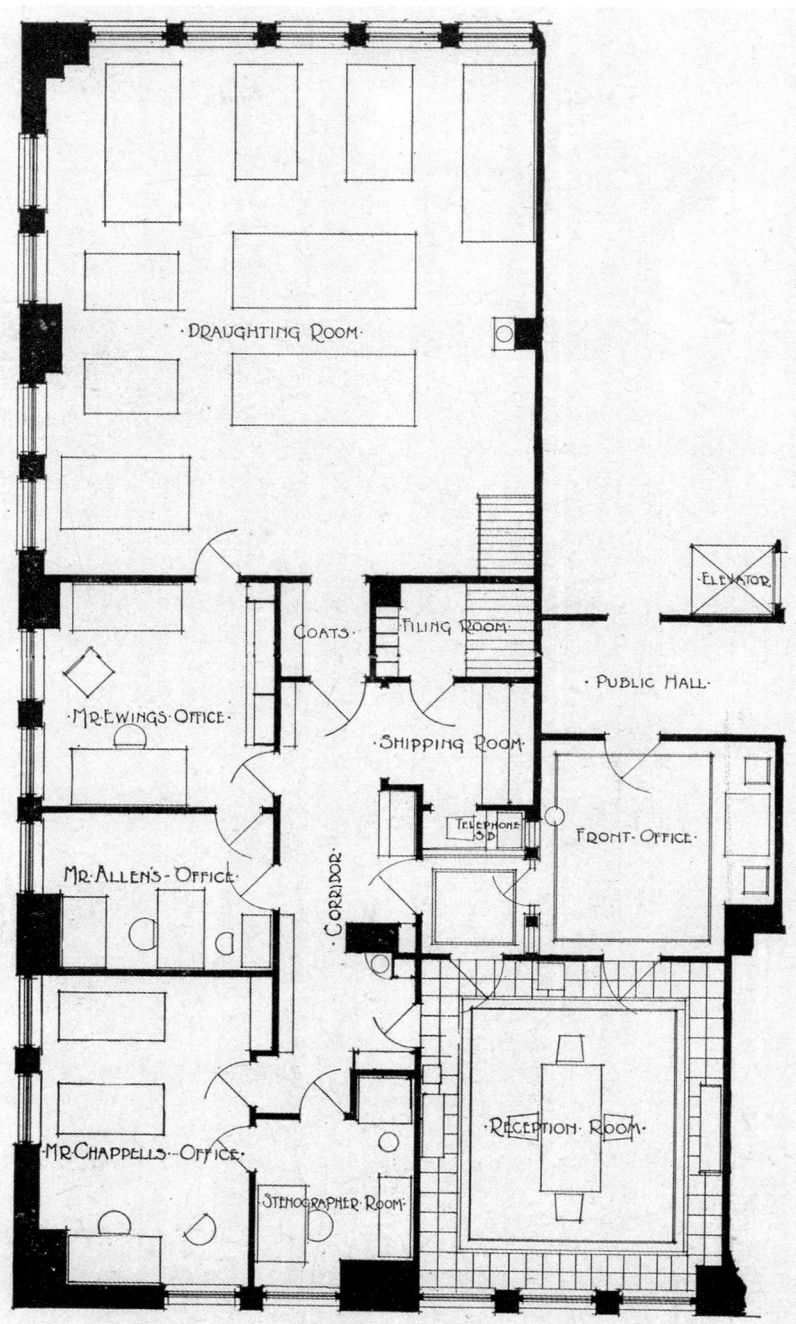

FIGURE 2.30 *Plan, Office of Ewing & Chappell in the Architects' Building,* Brickbuilder *22 (1913).*

FIGURE 2.31 *Reception Room, Office of Ewing & Chappell in the Architects' Building,* Brickbuilder *22 (1913).*

and apparently a number of others in the field, the daily grind of drafting room production and the frustrations of constant compromises demanded by the often adversarial interactions with the various players in the design and construction industry were made bearable nonetheless by an ethos of frivolity. As Kent reflected on the life of the inner office, "You just can't put a lot of fine fellows like young draughtsmen into a big room together, give them nothing in the world to do but rule a lot of lines on paper, and not expect to have things happen."[89]

Kent received recognition for his skill when a monograph on architectural renderers featured his work, and he worked in his capacity as a graphic renderer for several prominent New York firms to help bolster his income. But of his role at Ewing & Chappell it was remarked that "he is always welcome there because of his attractive personality as well as his artistic ability."[90] A 1915 collaboration published in the pages of *The Brickbuilder* brought together Chappell's increasingly parodical wit with his peripatetic and intermittent draughting room employee Rockwell Kent's illustrations. The two combined media to give irreverent interpretation to subjects of architectural history in a series of plates, "The Nomenclature of the Styles." The visual puns of

FIGURE 2.32 *Mr. Ewing's Private Office, Office of Ewing & Chappell in the Architects' Building,* Brickbuilder 22 *(1913).*

FIGURE 2.33 *Drafting Room, Office of Ewing & Chappell in the Architects' Building,* Brickbuilder 22 *(1913). Rockwell Kent is likely the drafter seated on the stool in the foreground. Note drafting tables configured on trestles.*

Kent's skillful woodcut prints combined with Chappell's tongue-in-cheek descriptions as in this genealogy of Grecian order (Figure 2.34):

> The well-known observation, that "architecture is frozen music," was doubtless made in reference to the early Greek article, [the Greek Freeze]. ... This type persists in cold storage form and shows amazing vitality considering the various uses to which it is put, as it serves equally well for temples, D.A.R. convention halls, court houses, railway stations, and bungalows. A rubber stamp of the Temple of Paestum is the *sine qua non* of the successful architect.[91]

Giving second thought to his own efforts, Chappell reflected in a letter to Kent, "It seems somewhat feeble to me on re-reading, but I suppose I look for too much to expect enduring charm in this light literature."[92] Despite any moments of self-doubt, the effort would mark just the first of many such collaborations joining Chappell's verses with Kent's images. At first intended for the insider entertainment of professional friends, the genre of work evolved to find an expanding audience for the duo's more broadly aimed caricatures of social mores and pretenses.

A transformative episode in this development came as an extension of Chappell's earlier-published reminiscences of atelier life and the ready appetite of his Society of Beaux Arts Architects friends to see the fellowship and ribaldry of their "Paris School Days" more broadly exposed to public display. In another of his collaborations, Chappell joined with fellow-architect and musical composer Kenneth Murchison in 1916 to write the libretto for a theatrical production about their Parisian life. Titled "Come to Bohemia," their operetta play was selected through competition to be presented on Broadway by the Stuyvesant Producing Company. According to reports published at the time: "[Chappell and Murchison] believed that the student atmosphere of the Latin Quarter in Paris had never been satisfactorily presented in the American stage, and together they have woven a romance around their own life there. The first scene is laid in the studio in which they lived, and the other scenes are quite as familiar to students who have entered the life of the Latin Quarter."[93]

Murchison was a Columbia graduate with whom Chappell had "lived and chummed" years before while studying in Paris. Besides being quite successful in his own architectural practice and noted for his designs for a series of impressive railway stations, Murchison had studied musical composition while in Paris with noted cellist and conductor Francis Touche and, according to one report, "spends his mornings in his studio and his afternoons at the piano and orchestra stand." Once back in New York, Chappell and Murchison had combined talents several times to stage and produce musical comedy entertainments for the Society's annual Beaux Arts Balls.[94] Murchison's office, too, was situated in the Architects' Building on Park Avenue.

FIGURE 2.34 Rockwell Kent and George S. Chappell, "The Nomenclature of the Styles: The Greek Freeze," Brickbuilder 24 (1915).

Back on the New York scene after his sojourns in Newfoundland as painter and artist, Rockwell Kent won a separate competition for the play's set design. His scenic paintings included what reviews described as "various exceptionally beautiful stage settings" including "the studio of some Latin Quarter artists ... striking in its details, with a perspective overlooking the housetops of bohemian Paris"; and "an exterior showing the boulevard tables and misty distances stretching away from the 'Café des Deux Magots,' in the [Place] St. Germain des Pres."[95] The play premiered in Atlantic City and traveled to Cleveland, Pittsburgh, Philadelphia, and New Haven before returning to the city for a rather abbreviated two-week Broadway run. The reviews were not kind, not even in Pittsburgh, where the critic declaimed, "It is a production intended to create an atmosphere and engage the eye. It does the latter but fails to do the former, for the authors have left that important ingredient out of both book and music."[96] But while "Come to Bohemia" had suffered an ignominious demise, George S. Chappell's literary career was just beginning.

Commencing in 1916, coincident with his forays into the theater, Chappell became a regular contributor to the popular American periodical *Vanity Fair*. Again, his witty verses were accompanied by the pen and ink or woodcut illustrations of Rockwell Kent who here first adopted his pseudonym of Hogarth, Jr.[97] These satirical pieces appeared like more entries for the duo's earlier "nomenclature of the styles," except here the styles were not historical or architectural but rather more broadly social and cultural, aimed at the evolving mores of contemporary metropolitan life. They comported well with the aims of the magazine as laid out by its editor, Frank Crowninshield:

> Now Vanity Fair means to be as cheerful as anybody. It will print much humor, it will look at the stage, at the arts, at the world of letters, at sport, and at the highly-vitalized, electric, and diversified life of our day from the frankly cheerful angle of the optimist, or, which is much the same thing, from the mock-cheerful angle of the satirist. This latter angle is sometimes a little foreign to our American artists and authors, and it will be one of Vanity Fair's most pleasant duties to wean them from their stiff, unyielding ways and make them, as the French periodicals have succeeded in making theirs, a little more free in their technique—a shade less academic and "tight"—a trifle more fluent, fantastic, or even absurd.[98]

Chappell's "poetic panoramas" of city life became more like armchair ethnographies. At first, his rhyming verses were inspired by fashions of "Th'Avenue," restaurant menus, and Greenwich Village flats (Figure 2.35). Over the next decade, his contributions expanded into essays in straight and punning prose on widely ranging, and sometimes wildly raging, topics: guests overstaying their welcome, marital infidelity, domestic harmony, men's social clubs, golf, manners, temperance, motor cars, weddings, and world war. He reveled, for example, in speculation about how he might have

FIGURE 2.35 *Hogarth, Jr. (Rockwell Kent) with George S. Chappell, "Th' Avenue," First published in* Vanity Fair *(January 1916).*

altered the national fate in its adoption of the 18th Amendment if he had only coined his rally slogan in time: "No Taxation Without Fermentation." *Vanity Fair* promoted Chappell and its stable of satirists by describing them as "humorists with a bite—witty with a dash of acid."[99] According to Brendan Gill:

> Chappell was a friend of Robert Benchley, …, Heywood Broun, Donald Ogden Stewart, …, and other well-known humorous writers of the period. A convivial group, they spent a lot of their time in speakeasies, as writers were expected to do in those days. It was said of Chappell that he was funnier even than Benchley, and Benchley appears to have agreed with this opinion.[100]

Chappell's name was also linked as co-author with that of humorist Dorothy Parker in the publication of *High Society*, a satirical guide to life in the upper circles, and he took over some of her duties as theater critic when she was famously fired from *Vanity Fair*.[101]

Parodies of then-familiar literary genres became a mainstay of Chappell's oeuvre, and he began to use his *Vanity Fair* platform, as well as his overlapping professional and social personas, to advance the cause of his mirth. In a series of magazine essays later compiled into book form, Chappell appropriated the nineteenth-century character of young Rollo from Rev. Jacob Abbott's twenty-eight volume series of books of the same name. While for Abbott, Rollo's curiosity about the world was aimed at the moral instruction of youth, Chappell's Rollo was far from innocent. Relocated from his simple country life, the modern Rollo gets his education from the city (Figure 2.36). According to a book review published in the *New York Times*, Chappell "describes Rollo's peregrinations among modern

FIGURE 2.36 *Hogarth, Jr. (Rockwell Kent) with George S. Chappell, Rollo and Uncle George,* Rollo in Society: A Guide for Youth *(New York: G.P. Putnam's Sons, 1922).*

flappers, weekend parties in the country, club dinners with his debonair Uncle George, explorations of Greenwich Village, and the eventual romance that changes Rollo from a boy to a man ...."[102] Warned an advertisement for the book, "If you fail to read *Rollo in Society* you are going to miss 47 laughs, 34 questionable quips and 19 of [Chappell's] sizzling slaps at modern customs."[103] As Chappell joshed in a newspaper interview, "All my writer friends say I am a brilliant architect, and all my architect friends say I am a corking writer, but my real profession is playing billiards. I used to claim I always built the houses to reflect the client, and almost all the houses I've built are low and rambling."[104]

Late in 1921, an essay published in *Vanity Fair* signaled the beginning of a whole new chapter in Chappell's literary career. With the title "My Amazing Discovery" and penned under the pseudonym of purported fellow of the Royal South Seas Explorers Union, Capt. Walter E. Traprock, the essay gave account of the discovery by this intrepid explorer of a new group of islands in the South Pacific, the Filberts—yes, full of nuts.[105] George Chappell lay behind the essay which served as a promotional teaser for his novel *Cruise of the Kawa*. The work was a burlesque fashioned after the genre of South Pacific travel adventures then in vogue.[106] A group of storm-tossed explorers find themselves thrust onto the beachhead of a new world and its genteel people whose flora, fauna, and native customs Traprock endeavored to record. Photographs in the book, staged in a studio, gathered Chappell's friends and colleagues from theater and publishing circles to give visual presence to his pretense—newspaperman Heywood Broun as the intrepid captain of the Kawa, Ezra Trippett; and dancer Margaret Severn as the Daughter of Pearl and Coral, Kippiputuona (pronounced "Kippi-put-you-on-a") (Figures 2.37–2.38).[107]

Chappell amused and amazed audiences as he extended the farce by offering public lectures about the Filbert Islands while appearing in full guise as Capt. Traprock. In a seemingly serious journal article, architect Egerton Swartwout conspired with Chappell to advance Traprock's "discovery" of the island's Fatu-Liva bird "with its unique gift of laying square eggs." Everyone in-the-know and especially those who knew George Chappell were all "in" on this elaborate joke.[108] In the next few years, Chappell continued this ruse with two new excursions to the edge, *My Northern Exposure* and *Sarah of the Sahara*, thus completing a veritable Traprock trilogy. In the former, Rockwell Kent, in a self-parody of his own serious and introspective travelogs to arctic climes, played the role of a savage Eskimo, "Makuik at mealtime" in the book's photographic illustrations (Figure 2.39).[109]

Once again in character as Traprock, Chappell headlined a group of publisher G.P. Putnam's stable of authors on a so-called Rough Writers rodeo and promotional tour of the West.[110] A New York newspaper declared Traprock to be the "Greatest American 'Kidder'" and quoted him at length on the virtues of kidding as "a splendid antidote for sentimentality." Chappell as Traprock elaborated upon the kidder's ethical code:

THE ARCHITECT'S OFFICE

FIGURE 2.37 *George S. Chappell in the guise of Walter E. Traprock, F.R.S.S.E.U.,* The Cruise of the Kawa *(New York: G.P. Putnam's Sons, 1921).*

FIGURE 2.38 *The W.E. Traprock Expedition,* The Cruise of the Kawa *(New York: G.P. Putnam's Sons, 1921). Publisher George Palmer Putnam appears standing at left in the guise of* Kawa *First Mate William Henry Thomas.*

FIGURE 2.39 *Rockwell Kent in Eskimo guise,* My Northern Exposure: The Kawa at the Pole *(New York: G.P. Putnam's Sons, 1922).*

"As I have said, effective kidding is done with profound seriousness," summed up the expert. "Furthermore, the champion kidder picks victims his own size, or bigger; he never kids weakness. He isn't afraid of his own extravagance. He is consistent; he never recants, weakly, at the end, with the remark, 'Oh, I was only kidding!' He may use a bludgeon, but never a poisoned dagger; he may be rough, but not vindictive. He 'sends 'em away with a smile—their smile!"[111]

The tenor of such mirth was not merely an echo of rebounding laughter in the salons and speakeasies of the otherwise bored metropolitan elite; it also redounded as a serious form of criticism in an age prone to censorship, prohibition, and sanctimonious moral reformers. Chappell was included in the roll-call of those authors, largely drawn from membership of the so-called Vicious Circle of the Algonquin Round Table, who pooled their talents in making what one reviewer called a "mass attack on the censor," a book of essays entitled *Nonsenseorship* (Figure 2.40). The continuing reach of the nineteenth-century Comstock Laws intended to suppress vice, the

FIGURE 2.40 Ralph Barton, "George S. Chappell Demonstrating His Outline of Censorship," Nonsenseorship *(New York: G.P. Putnam's Sons, 1922)*.

post-First World War paranoia about the infiltration of radical thought that fomented the Palmer Raids, and the passage of the Eighteenth Amendment to the US Constitution prohibiting alcohol were all assaults upon the very freedoms that the war was meant to secure. These writers turned their pens and their wit into swords and aimed them at "the oracle that always says 'no'."[112]

Chappell still maintained an active role in architectural practice even during the height of his literary phase though with projects not nearly so prominently featured on the pages of architectural journals as they had once been. Beginning in the mid-1920s, Chappell launched yet another vocation and assumed a new persona, that of architectural critic addressing a popular audience. Writing in *The New Republic* and under his own name, Chappell complained:

> Architecture is perhaps the most neglected, perhaps the most observed of all the arts. Newspapers and magazines do not fail to chronicle the latest achievements in the fields of drama, painting, sculpture and literature, and now moving pictures .... But of architecture we hear little except in the journals devoted exclusively to the interests of the profession. This apathy on the part of the average man is often only his fear of becoming involved in the technicalities of this most complicated calling.[113]

Thus, Chappell proceeded, through anecdote, analogy, and built examples to edify the public on the topic of architecture, to justify his belief "that no form of art enters so deeply, because so unconsciously, into the soul of our people." He endeavored to explain how modern needs and modern zoning had combined to make the skyscraper a distinctive expression of American culture.

A year later, a very similar though much-truncated argument appeared on the pages of a fledgling periodical, *The New Yorker*, once again pointing to Arthur Loomis Harmon's Shelton Hotel as exemplar of this emerging spirit.[114] In coming months, "The Sky Line" column became a regular feature of the magazine; yet, Chappell the critic had once again withdrawn behind the mask of a pseudonym, not "Traprock" this time but "T-Square," which in some ways may have just been Traprock-squared. Commencing the column regularly in 1926, Chappell laid the groundwork for Lewis Mumford and other successors to "The Sky Line" column for a genre of architectural journalism that oscillates even today between the edification of public taste on matters of "good design" and the evaluative standards that must be brought to bear in the mounting of serious social criticism. "The Sky Line" first presented a bantering and opinionated stroll down the avenues of the city and elicited via Chappell's very first column a contentious libel suit from an insulted architect, a controversy presaging contemporary brouhahas between hyperbolic critics and hypersensitive star-architects.[115]

Addressing his regular *Vanity Fair* column, with a typical tongue-in-cheek, to the taboo topic of men leading "Double Lives," Chappell reflected with candor nonetheless on the multitude of his own creative impulses.

> I have been thinking, more or less, about this double life business, for thirty years ..., and my conclusions, briefly, are, first, that most lives are double if not triple or quadruple, second, that this is all for the best, and third, that the most odious lives in the world are the purely single ones. ... [W]henever I hear it said of a man that he has spent his whole life doing only one thing, then I say that he has misspent it.[116]

Chappell's life had definitively transcended the bounds of a singularly focused professional practice, but there were costs for his fractured attention. Despite his antics and manic activity, he insisted to Kent in prior years that his life had "been along anything but a rose strewn path. With practically no income from my business and the cost of living what it is today, it has been a long time since I have had a night free from dire anxiety."[117] While remaining in the Architects Building on Park Avenue, perhaps in his same corner office, he withdrew from active partnership with Charles Ewing who had in turn joined with their former inner-office intermediary, Jerome Allen, to form Ewing & Allen.[118] Chappell set the scene in letter to his friend Rockwell Kent:

> Act II. The scene – my office, – back in my old annex to the present firm of Ewing + Allen, having moved in great dust, dirt and confusion last Saturday. Charles and Jerry are the same old plodders, they will probably be a great success. My room is in a mess, which I despair of ever getting completely cleaned up. There is my desk and three tables. Each day I clean one and by the time the round is made, no. 1 is in confusion again. It is like trying to carve for a large family.
>
> I expect within a few days to be plugging away on a competition for quite a large school to be built in Pelham Manor so I shall be burning the midnight Edison–juice and getting back to old habits. Building is still very quiet but not in absolute rigor mortis – its eyelids flutter a bit now and then, – a friend has asked me to go up to Mt. Kisco with him some day 'soon', – I am working on a house for a Mr. Barnes in New Haven, – several other things give me hope – and praise be to Allah! I still have my adorable little farm where I can take comparative refuge from the slings and arrows of outrageous fortune. Now if you will write me a 'love' letter I shall be very happy dear Rock –
> Yours as ever
> George[119]

The answer to the question posed earlier when examining the layout of Ewing & Chappell's office space must by now be quite apparent. *Why did Chappell have an extra desk?* Because as the years progressed he was leading a double and perhaps even a triple or quadruple professional life—as architect, playwright, journalist, author, lecturer, socialite, bon vivant. The outer offices of Ewing & Chappell's firm, like others in their Architects' Building on Park Avenue, were mirrors of an extended social tableau. Architects' offices incorporated overlapping circles of culture—elite, quotidian, commercial—rippling within a dichotomous modernity. Influences reverberated from outer to inner office and back again into the world, into spaces of public display, full of new moral sensibilities and artistic motives. By the time *The Handbook of Architectural Practice* was published in 1920, architects' offices had been transformed by technology, tempered by world war, and primed for profit. In many ways, the Architects' Building anticipated in built form the modern profession that *The Handbook* endeavored to chronicle.

> To return to the Architects' Offices for a moment. On the ground floor of the main building is one of our most fascinating architectural emporia, the Architects' Samples Company, where clients and architects may select practically every detail of material, be it brick, stone, marble, tile, shingle, trim, sash, stucco or what you will. Hundreds of firms show their "line" in this compact, useful assemblage. It is a sort of permanent exposition. One of the latest installations is a beautiful pipe-organ which plays solemn music, enveloping the minutiae of business in a deeply religious atmosphere, inspiring one cautious customer to whisper, "Let's sneak out before the collection."[120]

The career entanglements of George S. Chappell, Rockwell Kent, Frederick Squires, and Frank Miles Day can be traced to their overlapping social and professional circles, but they are also indicative of broader trends affecting American material life and cultural practices in the early-twentieth century. The historical terrain stretching between Civil War and world wars was a rollercoaster topography of Gilded Age excess, Progressive Era reform, Suffragists, Prohibitionists, speak easies and talkies, cables and wireless, all careening at an accelerating pace from the horse-drawn and steam-driven to the internal combustion engine. New modes of transportation, communication, artistic expression, and entertainment blurred boundaries of time and space. It was a period of ingrained prejudices, unmatched technological innovation, and exuberant economic growth.[121] After millennia of barely perceptible change, the building-related vocations were rapidly professionalizing and emerging as differentiated fields—architecture, engineering, and construction; building itself was being revolutionized by technological innovations in means of production, structural steel, indoor plumbing, electric lights, telephones, elevators, radiators, and machines of everyday life. The social practices of urban life were both stoking and devouring this change.

Chappell, Kent, Squires, and Day were caught in this whirlwind as well. While each entered their commonly chosen career along similarly privileged paths, all four were ultimately diverted as the centrifuge of architectural practice spun them in very different directions. Chappell, ever a gadfly, pursued an increasingly literary path while holding up a mirror to the vanities and preoccupations of his own social circles. Kent was drawn by wanderlust but drew in turn upon people and remote places to inspire the sublime landscapes and portraits of life and labor that were the subject of his increasingly political art. Squires dabbled in satire aimed at the foibles of his profession even while pursuing serious design research on fireproof construction, a fact making all the more ironic his early exit from the profession to pursue a career as a petroleum engineer. Finally Day, the eldest and perhaps steadiest of the group, was a recognized leader in the profession lauded as one who "combined to a rare degree the qualities of artist and executive."[122] As Chappell, Kent, and Squires were wavering in their commitments, Day embarked upon his final and what would arguably prove to be his most monumental contribution to the profession, "a treatise upon office administration."

CHAPTER THREE

Architect and Owner

At the turn of the century, architects were vying for their proper place, to be among the midwives of civil society. They were competing with each other and with adjacent fields—engineers, planners, builders—for credibility, legitimacy, and proximity to wealth and power. Just as architects were trying to shape themselves into a reliable profession, they were also dreaming of the ideal sponsors for their work. They imagined themselves educating owners to be the kinds of clients whose interests they could serve even while hoping for patrons who could serve and support them, in turn, in the cause of art. Frank Miles Day's and Frederick Squires's respective "handbooks" were part of this grander project. One aimed at regularizing and the other at ironizing architects' practices, but both were intended as primers for owners as well.[1]

The introductory argument of *The Handbook of Architectural Practice*, sandwiched between the tome's title page and its table of contents, was boldly proclaimed and succinctly stated. The "Purpose of the Handbook," Day proposed, was as "an aid to proper practice and efficient business administration ... in a field to which experience has heretofore been the only guide." Furthermore, it was expected "that the Handbook will give an insight into methods which might elsewhere be sought in vain and that it will aid in improving and standardizing common practice."[2] The emphasis upon methods of architectural practice and the business of administering a firm set this manual apart from Ancient and Renaissance treatises with which Frank Miles Day and his fellow acolytes of European architecture culture would have been so familiar. Vitruvius and Alberti discoursed primarily on design principles that underlay the art of building while giving only passing attention to the sorts of ethical concerns arising from day-to-day human interactions. *The Handbook* completely reversed this emphasis by making an explicit cause out of the manner and means of conducting the architect's quotidian business affairs while leaving principles of design and construction to the side.

The tacit knowledge of practice that is built up over time can be subtly transformed with each nuanced response to some variation in context or circumstance, as a feel for the game adapts to novel or unexpected conditions. The notion that such accrued experience could be translated into a set of explicit and readily applicable principles arose from a shared faith in standardization as a vehicle for the progressive improvement of professional practice. It was rightly anticipated that the new handbook could facilitate the transference of such experience across generations and to numbers far greater than the oral or apprenticeship traditions could ever achieve. There were inevitable consequences of this efficiency, however. Day's rationalization of his own office procedures tended to strip them of the very contingencies that made them effective in their parochial settings. Once vetted by an ensemble of professional peers and disseminated to a national audience, they took on the aura of universally applicable rules and thereby propelled the process of standardization. They also had the effect of narrowing the traditional range of acceptable modes by which architecture had been improvisationally practiced. Instead of a handshake and a nod, practice now turned upon ethical canons, contractual obligations, administrative procedures, and the bottom line.

A collection of practices

The Handbook of Architectural Practice was addressed first to architects, whether they be students, young practitioners just entering the field, or more experienced practicing professionals.[3] Besides its obvious orientation to architects, however, *The Handbook* was also addressed to owners with a suggestion that "it should be of value as enabling him the more intelligently to cooperate with his architect"—a rather audacious presumption, when considered from a consumerist perspective, about the direction in which deference was due. The motivation to instruct potential clients about the process of design and building, to shape expectations about architectural services as well as inform owners about their own responsibilities, was, once again, an aim tangentially shared with more venerable antecedents. In drafting *The Handbook*, however, Day confronted novel concerns that Vitruvius would never have encountered. New stresses were forming within the rapidly expanding design and construction industry as it took shape within a commercially oriented and increasingly litigious American business climate.[4]

The first draft of the preface to *The Handbook* that Day circulated to his invited reviewers was worded slightly differently from the version finally published. The text had originally asserted: "To the Owner, the Handbook should be of value *as indicating the orderly procedure which his work may be expected to take* and as enabling him the more intelligently to cooperate with his Architect."[5] Concerns arose, however, from among the solicited respondents, about whether the text went too far in suggesting to owners that the administrative procedures enumerated in the handbook were either necessary or prescribed. A committee of the Boston Society of Architects worried whether such specificity of procedure as presented in the main body of the text might not in fact open architects to accusations of malpractice should there be any variance from the suggested norm. The correspondents fretted that "an unscrupulous owner might use it against his architect as evidence, for instance, that the latter has not performed the services to the full of what would reasonably be expected of him, whereas the Hand Book does not and should not be construed as indicating that every architect should properly do all the things that are set down therein."[6]

Noted architect Ralph Adams Cram, then president of the Boston Society, expanded upon his committee's concerns and proceeded further:

> To raise the question as to how far this Hand Book will or may be accepted by owners or by the courts as an authoritative statement of the duties of an architect and whether, in case it is so accepted, it will not be possible for a litigious owner or a lawyer bent upon trouble, to claim that an owner has not received his full due because all the things set down therein have not been done. The Executive Committee has grave doubts as to the wisdom of publishing a document which may be so misconstrued.[7]

The Boston architects' concerns about "unscrupulous owners," or likewise "a litigious owner or a lawyer bent upon trouble," are particularly palpable indications of a profession that perceived itself under siege. Architects were grappling with the downside risks and potential rewards that accompanied the project of professionalization. Cementing good standing with owners was key to stemming the mounting challenge that they were receiving from builders.[8]

Status-minded practitioners were especially sensitive to the importance of elevating public perceptions about architects' professional scruples and competence. A full decade after establishment of the nation's first architectural licensing law in Illinois, the Chicago Architects' Business Association still recognized "that a structure is only as strong as its weakest parts" and therefore declared the importance of constantly ratcheting professional standards in order to extend "a hand backward to lift up and lend strength and encouragement to the weak, the timid and the faltering members of the profession."[9] In a period when architects still followed a range of vocational and academic paths into practice, Day's projection of an architects' handbook was responsive to this aim, to prod the profession into coalescing around some common standards of procedure and performance, thereby enhancing public trust.

Responding in his handbook revisions to the criticisms heard from Boston architects, Day dispensed with the controversial phrasing that had suggested

The Handbook could be treated as a definitive template for competent practice. Instead, he clarified the provisional nature of the handbook's contents and intents:

> The book is a collection of practices, each one of which may somewhere be found in use and many of which are everywhere in use. Yet it must be said at the outset that no architect, however highly his administrative methods may be developed, follows all the steps described in it, and that even though there may be many that he does not deem it necessary to follow, he may still conduct his practice with efficiency and with entire loyalty to the owner's interests.[10]

Notwithstanding Day's caveats, his "collection of practices," once published in handbook form, assumed the character of an authoritative rubric. Originating from Day's own office manual, the handbook could have never conveyed the full variety of regionally differentiated approaches to architectural practice then at play across the forty-eight contiguous states.[11] Once vetted, published, and promoted by the American Institute of Architects, however, the handbook became a virtual syllabus, a reference, and a guide. Formalizing this collection of practices had the effect of standardizing them, which in turn was to valorize them as a professional standard.[12]

Various forms of architectural service

In the very first of Squires's architect-tonic tales, Tom Thumtack turns the tables on his clients, not in his drafting room or the conference room but in a case raised in a court of law—"Client vs. Architect: A Plea" (Figure 3.1). Against plaintiffs' claims about architects' manifest impracticality, Thumtack mounts his humorous defense of the profession by demonstrating clients' complicity in shaping the unforeseen circumstances that bedeviled any project: the wife unable to sleep because her husband snores; the couple whose house is always crowded because of their own unchecked procreation; a smoke-filled living room and a client clueless about the flue. Thumtack argues that clients took credit for every design success while casting an accusing finger toward their architect for every imagined flaw. They fail to account, however, for their own mercurial desires, unrealistic budgets, and an ever-expanding project scope. Thumtack ladles the irony in his profession's defense:

> You have us dead to rights, oh clients! You have plausibly contended that the profession is probably neither useful nor ornamental and you have demonstrated that it is impractical. But how about yourselves? You and your friends around the festal board of your new home have hugely

FIGURE 3.1 Rockwell Kent, "Client vs. Architect: A Plea," Architec-tonics: The Tales of Tom Thumtack, Architect *(New York: Comstock, 1914)*.

joked about your architect. Don't you suppose he ever laughed at you? Are you so practical in your new role of client? Hasn't it occurred to you that he may have gone back to his office and caused a general ripple of amusement because you wanted to back the kitchen range against the ice box or because you and wifey fought like cat-and-dog over the wall paper before you'd even bought the lot?[13]

Tom Thumtack's witty courtroom ruses both index and satirize the increasingly litigious nature of architectural and building practice in turn-of-the-century United States.[14] Relationships between and among owners, architects, and builders were fraught with uncertainty, misperception, and mistrust. Indeed, the relationships were still finding their contractual form, being contested and refined under the sway of mercantilism applied now to services as well as to goods. Across millennia and diverse cultures, the functions and responsibilities that constituted design and building practice were being differentiated and variously defined, each responsive and attuned to local governing conditions, both material and social.

Past the preliminaries and prefatory notes, *The Handbook of Architectural Practice* introduced its first major topic, the Owner/Architect relationship.[15] That primary association comprised the essential link in all that followed, both in Day's manual and in the profession he was striving to encompass. Addressed to both parties, both to edify and advise, *The Handbook* detailed the mutual roles and responsibilities that constituted their bond: various forms of architectural service, the manner of selecting an architect, the architect's compensation, forms of contractual agreement, the role of consultants, the architect's status, the owner's duties. Each of these topics could be a source of friction or misunderstanding as might be readily gleaned from trade and professional journals of the era. Commentary on the topics elicited from Day's professional colleagues further confirms the tensions then at play—the recurrent conflicts and controversies issued from long habits of building culture, the increasing dominance of bottom-line oriented business logic, and the ongoing effort to both codify and challenge competing interests and advantages through legal and contractual means. In this sense, then, the drafting of *The Handbook of Architectural Practice* rendered a snapshot of the profession as an ongoing process of negotiation, as an active field of play.

Thus, in each of their respective handbooks, both Frank Miles Day and Frederick Squires tackled similar opening topics and addressed them to their essential and intended audiences—the nature of the Architect's relationship to the owner, or client.[16] The formality of directing or dedicating a work to a sponsor or potential patron comported with more ancient precedent and carried similar motives.[17] In such cases, there was a deliberate effort to shape the terms and expectations of patronage, to instruct architects' sponsors on their shared responsibilities, and thereby to construct a clientele appreciative of the role that the profession could best serve on its behalf. In each of Day's and Squires's efforts, one by sober discourse and the other by ironic wit, the authors were seeking to structurally and rhetorically position architects in close association with the commissioners of the work while differentiating themselves from the builder-executants. In the late-nineteenth and early-twentieth centuries, architects pressed to cement a professional advantage over builders in their functional relationship with owners on both legal and social bases, by shaping and standardizing their common contractual tools. Despite these attempts, architects' agency relationship with owners and their role as both judge and jury in disputes with builders remained perennial points of friction and dispute.

In *The Handbook*, Frank Miles Day succinctly instructed owners on the various kinds of architectural service that could be procured. "Architects," Day wrote, "are employed in sundry capacities," as executive, supervising, consulting, or associated architects, and in occasional miscellaneous employment. Architects might be employed for the full complement of services from design through development and detailing of the building project to contract administration and construction supervision. In complex, multi-building projects, they might be hired as master planner, to supervise the work of other architects on owner's behalf. They might be engaged as consultant to another architect based upon some area of recognized expertise. In special conditions, they might associate with another firm in a joint venture. Lastly, they might be called upon in rendering service as expert witnesses, providing independent assessments, as members of arbitration boards, organizing competitions, or adjudicating awards.[18] In turn-of-the-century America, the representative and representational roles of the architect were being clarified and defined within a new political economy of building, one still emerging from a tradition-bound building culture founded upon patronage and handicraft.

With the advent of the Uniform Contract of 1888, the inter-relationships between and among owners and builders, their capital and labor, were being formalized in contractual terms increasingly shaped by business motives—of profit, performance, and prestige.[19] By the beginning of the twentieth century, American architects were purposed as mediators in that relationship, the structural and functional paradoxes of which were at least partially of their own making. Despite ongoing assertions of architects' agency role—their authority to act on behalf of owners—it was nonetheless acknowledged that "Architects are not free agents …. They are subject to the conditions given by the owner …."[20] In addition to vague limitations on architects' agency function, we must also consider how contradictions in the respective parties' roles or responsibilities were exacerbated by shifting definitions of "the client" prompted at the turn of the century by the rise of commercial culture.

Just as the moniker "the architect" had become a short-hand for an increasingly bureaucratized organization supporting an amalgamation of creative and technical design expertise in a marketplace of products, services, and ideas, any singular notion of "the client" had become a figure of speech. "The client" was the personification of a branching decision tree composed of a complex bundle of interests, aims, ends, and means that could take the form of an individual, a business enterprise, a cultural institution, a public organ, or a corporate body. The available forms of architectural service described in *The Handbook* were indicative of that shifting reality, and Tom Thumtack's tales offer insights into the broad spectrum of architects' clientele.

Besides the sort of private, residential clients whose nouveau riche pretensions he caricatures as symptomatic of the age of conspicuous consumption,[21] Tom Thumtack characterizes the motivations of other kinds of public, institutional, and business-oriented clients. "Tom Thumtack, Detective" tackles the issue of small-town political corruption in the letting of public contracts. Our hero portrays the architect in the role of detective, necessarily alert to hidden signs of malfeasance through pay-offs and sweetheart deals, parochialism in favoring local architects and contractors, and the manipulation of bids (Figure 3.2). As Tom Thumtack observes, "Talk about the wickedness of great cities. Why, the per capita consumption of crookedness is greater in the country cities than anywhere else in the world."[22]

"The Pinch Hitter" peers inside the deliberations of a kind of collective client-by-committee, a hospital's board of directors sitting in review of designs submitted for an invited competition (Figure 3.3). When draftsman Thumtack delivers his firm's design proposal at the very last moment, his identity is confused with that of his tardy brother, a physician and member of the board who was running late. Finding himself empaneled with the other reviewers, Thumtack proceeds along a very tenuous line. He uses his

FIGURE 3.2 *Rockwell Kent, "Tom Thumtack Detective,"* Architec-tonics: The Tales of Tom Thumtack, Architect *(New York: Comstock, 1914).*

FIGURE 3.3 Rockwell Kent, another mistaken identity from "The Pinch Hitter," Architec-tonics: The Tales of Tom Thumtack, Architect *(New York: Comstock, 1914)*.

resemblance as a ruse to goad the board's competition advisor, "tyrranical old Professor Ward." Tom Thumtack savors the irony of the moment. "My blood was tingling anyhow with my love of theatrics, and like an adventurous youth of more romantic times, I wanted desperately to see the situation to its end. To sit in judgment of one's own drawings, wouldn't that appeal to any architect?"[23]

Another of Tom Thumtack's tales is especially germane to discourses and debates that were then swirling in architectural journals and in the real estate and trade press arising from the proliferation of a new and what some considered a particularly rapacious breed of profit-seeking developers. "The Speculative Builder" offers Thumtack's view of "a business as uncertain as fore-casting the weather and controlled by just as many subtle elements— the game of speculative building." Based presumably upon aspects of author Frederick Squires's own experiences in erecting the Mercantile Building on

Seventh Avenue in New York, the story lampoons the motives and appetite for risk of an investment-oriented builder named "Joy" (Figures 3.4–3.5). Tom Thumtack observes:

> The building game naturally appealed to this red-headed optimist because even when played within the rules, it has the other gambles faded to the ghost of a church raffle. Add to it the risks of real estate and the gamble assumes proportions. Now season the whole mess, as the cook book says, with the words 'New York City' and it is a wonder that the tracks and gambling houses afford a bit of competition.[24]

FIGURE 3.4 *Frederick Squires, Architect; The Mercantile Building, New York City;* Architecture and Building *44 (1912).*

FIGURE 3.5 Rockwell Kent, "The Speculative Builder," Architec-tonics: The Tales of Tom Thumtack, Architect *(New York: Comstock, 1914).*

What we recognize today as being akin to real estate development was in Tom Thumtack's tale a hybrid arrangement combining into one entity a building contractor and real estate speculator—in essence a builder and owner in one. That "red-headed optimist" was financially backed by private or corporate investors on the promise of healthy returns. In this tale, Thumtack had been engaged as an independent architect by Joy to provide him the requisite design services. Another manner of procuring design services that was operative at the time might involve a building company with its own internal staff of designers providing what today would be considered "turn-key" services to owners who contracted with them directly without an independent architect at all. A third alternative was possible and recognizable from pre-industrial precedents—a private owner or developer serving as their own architect, contracting directly with builders for the job.

These latter two arrangements were, however, increasingly proscribed by the professional canons of the American Institute of Architects for being rife with potential ethical conflicts wherever private interests might somehow compromise the public good.[25]

Each of these variations embodied vestiges of older practices, ones that had been commonplace prior to the rise of a model of practice privileging the architect's professional autonomy. Those gripping the mantle of "real architect," however, believed that the sheer scale of new building-development enterprises posed a growing threat to the institutional ideal of independent, professional, architectural practice. Early in the twentieth century, F.W. Fitzpatrick warned, "That spirit of commercialism that we have done so little to check, that we are powerless to check, and that so many of us have actually fostered, will be our undoing."[26] Especially at issue was the builder's challenge to the architect's direct relationship with the owner and the potential of this "new" arrangement to circumvent the architect's presumed agency and intermediary role. In 1907, alarms were sounded by architect Cass Gilbert at the annual convention of the American Institute of Architects (AIA).

> When a building corporation has grown great it assumes to control the situation. In New York and possibly in all our large cities, it may be truthfully said that not one in twenty of the important buildings (that such as cost half a million dollars and upward) are handled by private enterprise or are under the control of the architect as they formerly were. The building company employs the architect and assumes to control his design, and very largely does. And the man who opposes that system must find his opportunity in some other direction—certainly not in building important commercial buildings. The building company will be supported by the finance committee of the life insurance company that floats the loan and handles the stock and bonds. Ultimately the building company falls into the hands of a financial man or oftener of a financial committee, whose members may perhaps be a real estate man, a director of a bank or a broker, none of whom has any practical knowledge of building. These men care nothing so long as they can make a satisfactory report on the money invested.[27]

Besides their own growing sense of professional vulnerability, and as an argument in counterweight, architects expressed the view that owners had much to lose under terms of such arrangements, considering them to be "fundamentally prejudicial to the owner." As architect Henry S. Kissam suggested, "By such a relationship the builder is made the judge of his own work, and as every builder is a buyer of both labor and materials as well as a seller of them, he will judge his own work by the standard of its profitableness to himself."[28] Progressive Era reformers saw the profit motive in even more dire terms, adding urgency to the movement toward state regulation through licensing laws. A St. Louis architect voiced this warning:

Many of the structures erected throughout this country are not designed or erected by architects at all, but are constructed by speculators, mostly for financial gain. It is to be regretted that these parasites are permitted, under the authority of the law, to operate to the detriment of every decent consideration for the comfort, health, sanitation and art or the community. They are the outgrowth of the American's neurotic and revered effort to get rich quick, and reflect with wonderful fidelity the unmoral state of the country, whose greed for gold, if carried on to its logical conclusion, will undermine the foundations of our liberty.[29]

Despite such strident views, those "parasites" were now a significant portion of architects' clientele, hybrid combinations of owners, investors, and builders organized in pursuit of business profits. It was largely to those clients that architects had to make their appeals, and it was to their criticisms that architects were made to answer. Indeed, Mr. Day's handbook was intended as both a demonstration and a guide—to business-oriented clients of the architect's business savvy.

The selection of an architect

The *Handbook of Architectural Practice* succinctly described "two clearly defined methods of choosing an Architect ...: one, by direct selection; the other, by competition." The ostensible handbook aim, to inform Owners (or fledgling architects) about prescribed and accepted means of procuring architectural services, also served a more nuanced purpose. By the enumeration of various selection criteria and procedural etiquettes, *The Handbook* advanced a singular and narrowly focused definition of the professional Architect as it was then being advocated. "The architect of standing is primarily a gentleman ..., a man of intelligence and education, with all the breeding, tact, and virile honesty that this implies. If he is a member of the American Institute of Architects he has subscribed to a code of ethics that ensures the highest and most honorable type of service."[30] It was a definition congruent with the membership requirements of the AIA, and it was one that by its substance effectively promoted the exclusion from consideration of a wide range of design-and-building practitioners who in earlier days would have identified and solicited under the shared appellation of architect.[31] Contrary to discourses that prevailed in architectural journals about whether architecture was primarily an art or a business, *The Handbook* advice did not include design artistry among its comparative selection criteria at all. Instead, the recommended selection guidelines were aimed at preempting recurrent questions in circulation about architects' value and basic professional competence.

By direct selection

In outlining an approach to the direct selection of an architect, *The Handbook* advised:

> The Owner should give careful thought to the selection, since his interests depend so directly upon it. The Owner commits the expenditure of his money to the Architect, and though he may think he is in control of the situation, he is in a large measure helpless as to the way in which it is spent. In fact, he depends for a successful result almost as much on his Architect as does the patient on his surgeon.[32]

In order to gauge the Architect's reliability in the face of such vital financial risks, *The Handbook* encouraged comparison of professional candidates' respective levels of experience, their apparent technical knowledge and ability "to secure the best results without waste of space or money," their executive ability to authoritatively compel compliance with the construction contract, the congruence of their previous work with the Owner's current needs, and evidence of their "honesty and incorruptibility as are essential to the Owner's safety." "In brief," as *The Handbook* distilled the matter, "has the Architect established to the Owner's satisfaction his fitness, above others, to design the work and to control its execution?"[33]

While this question was proposed as an evaluative measure for owners to apply when selecting among individual architects, business-oriented clients aimed their barbed replies at the profession as a whole. In the years immediately preceding publication of *The Handbook*, a raucous back-and-forth argument erupted on the pages of trade and business journals concerning architects' overall competence. An article appearing in *Buildings and Building Management* journal offered "constructive criticism" and forensic analysis of "when the smaller city skyscraper fails to make an adequate return." A case study presented the "skyscraper proposition" of an owner, Mr. Mooney, acting as "a matter of civic and personal pride .... He wanted a good building, and he wanted it as a monument, but he saw no reason why it should not be a good investment as well." All seemed to go well with the process, up until Mr. Mooney "called in an architect."[34] According to the article, the combination of planning inefficiencies in the layout of the rentable office floors and a building cost almost double the owner's budget and the architect's own construction estimate yielded a balance sheet return "of a trifle over 5 percent on the total investment." The article implied that the architect's sheer incompetence delivered a building that did not pay.

A direct protest to the article was posted in the very next month's issue of the *Journal of the American Institute of Architects*. The editors did not dispute "the opinion that the failure of the building to pay might well be charged to bad planning"; rather, they took umbrage with the manner in which the term "an architect" had been tossed like some unsavory epithet as a means "of castigating a whole profession, or calling, for the mistakes of one of its members." While granting a gentlemanly benefit of the doubt whether the author had intended "to imply the wholesale incompetence of architects," the respondent nonetheless admitted with a surprising twist, "there are men practising architecture who are totally incompetent; but as this is a matter of almost common knowledge, the remedy lies in the choosing of the man—not in accepting incompetency and dishonesty as universal."[35] The flagship journal of the architects' professional organization thus implied that "the choosing of the man" was the inviolable patrician standard of professionalism, of honesty and incorruptibility, upon which the owner's selection of the architect should stand.

A follow-up article from the building managers' journal noted with some degree of understatement that their "series of articles on the small city skyscraper seems to have awakened rather a great amount of interest"—among both owners and architects. In those same pages, F.W. Fitzpatrick, architect and frequent critic of his own profession, joined the chorus in condemning architects' ways. Citing building statistics compiled in several cities by a financial institution, he claimed that "96 6/11 per cent exceeded the architects' estimates in their final cost", and that "78 per cent were ill-planned, in that the space was not made the most of, or the rooms were but poorly lighted, major sins that greatly reduced the income and made the buildings undesirable or hard to rent." Of that lot, Fitzpatrick suggested, "41 per cent were beyond remedy—abortions—buildings that no amount of revamping could ever whip into shape or profit." These inadequacies obtained, Fitzpatrick claimed, despite the fact that most of those buildings "were very attractive externally, highly ornate, some really artistic, showing evidences of infinite pains and some skill on the part of their architects in the way of 'design' ...." Fitzpatrick assigned fault for these sins not upon disreputable imposters, architects in name only; rather, he laid the blame "at the very foundation of the training an architect is supposed to get, in the mode of 'teaching' that is in vogue in our universities and schools of architecture 'in all its branches,' is injected into the long-haired youths who are taking their first steps towards the beaux-arts."[36]

The following year, *The Real Estate Magazine* presented a speculative builder's damning indictment—one deemed by the journal editors to be "forceful and logical"—of the high cost of architectural incompetence. The author, S. Kruse, cited two aspects of the owner–architect relationship—the architect's role as agent for the owner and the doctrine of a professional standard of care—that when so combined were avowedly unjust and counter to the owner's interests.

> [U]nder the doctrine of agency the mistake of the architects is the mistake of the owner and the consequent loss must be borne by the owner. ... The result under this system is that in a large building project, under the doctrine of agency, the owner places himself wholly in the hands of his architect and is wholly at his mercy.

We can readily imagine the predicament of the owner who falls into the hands of an unscrupulous or ignorant architect, and in this respect there is no practical difference between ignorance and dishonesty, as the results are the same. The reader will further realize the precarious situation of the owner, when we consider that practically eight out of ten so-called architects are wholly incompetent and unfit to undertake large building construction and determine the various problems incident thereto.[37]

Eight out of ten architects are incompetent? Digging further into Kruse's argument, it becomes clear that he is conflating all "classes" of architects into one disreputable lot. He thus reinforces with his accusations the very dilemma that the AIA had been confronting in its well-intentioned if paternalistic efforts to impose order upon an unruly mass of builders, speculators, dilettantes, and shysters all claiming to be architects in name, all the same.

Rather than lobbing the usual complaint about architects' frivolous fixation on their art, Kruse accused them instead of being overly focused on pecuniary gain, of deliberately not controlling building costs in order to maximize their percentage-based fees. Despite any protests to the contrary, architects of the most ethical sort could not be absolved of this accusation, he argued, for "In American communities, the commercial spirit will always rule. It is not a question of honor, or integrity, but solely a question of realizing as much money as possible on the smallest possible investment, either of time or money. ... This spirit pervades even the professions."[38] Kruse's complaints ran the gamut: that the average architect was incompetent, was impractical in design and construction, susceptible to kickbacks and bribes, charged an exorbitant AIA-dictated fee. Kruse rejected the assumption of an inviolable gentlemanly trust as the basis for a business transaction. He insisted instead upon the need to forge an ironclad contractual relation spelling out details of mutual obligations and expectations, mechanisms of penalty and reward, so that the owner was "at all times the absolute master of the situation." Indeed, he suggested as one remedy the "total elimination of the architect," proposing instead "to employ a competent and financially responsible construction firm which has in its employ qualified designers and engineers." He thus extoled the very same building corporations that the move toward professionalization of architects was meant to forestall.

Citing cases of owners' financial exigency precipitated by their architects' extravagant or incompetent plans, Kruse concluded with concrete proposals for the reform of the whole profession. He advocated for "either a change in the antiquated methods heretofore employed or stringent legislation, making the architectural profession a licensed profession, making the requirements for admission stringent and making him legally responsible for misleading estimates and opinions and fixing his compensation on the reasonable basis, say, 3% of the estimated cost."[39] The response to this critique and proposal was immediate, divided, and intense.

The next month's issue of *Real Estate Magazine* reported that Kruse's article had "aroused among the architects of the United States a difference of opinion, which promises to result in a controversy over the relations of owners and architects that should lead to some real reform in architectural methods. ... The property owner is certainly entitled to some protection at the hands of architects."[40] Likewise, and somewhat predictably, self-avowed "iconoclast" and "anarchist in architecture" F.W. Fitzpatrick endorsed the realtors' editorial premise though with doubts about the likelihood of architects in "their smug complacency and egotism" ever changing:

> In fine I can but repeat what I've claimed for a quarter of a century, that building has outgrown the practice of architecture, that the mode of procedure that we are trying to carry on as did our fathers and great grandsires is indeed antiquated, cumbersome, somewhat of a travesty and farcical and altogether unbusinesslike. ... I can't get rid of the notion that "architecture as she is practiced" is a back number, almost a closed incident.[41]

The AIA's official response to Kruse's diatribe, published right in the pages of *Real Estate Magazine*, came quickly from architect Frederick L. Ackerman, chairman of the organization's Committee on Public Information. Ackerman, too, was a critic of the status quo, one with a keen interest in the intertwining of social, economic, and political relations in the shaping of buildings and the urban realm.[42] For example, in a contemporary article in an architectural journal, Ackerman stated, "Do not lose sight of the fact that all the buildings erected within our cities are built not because of any desire on the part of the owner to make something beautiful, but rather from considerations purely commercial and economic ...."[43] Any sympathies Ackerman may have held for some of Kruse's criticisms of the profession were subsumed, however, within his rather supercilious rebuttal of the article which he characterized as "such a compound of ignorance, prejudice and failure to understand the simplest facts about a great and necessary profession ...."[44]

Despite Ackerman's elitist tone, his point-by-point engagement of Kruse's critique confirms the existence of architects' own anxieties about the current state of their profession. The AIA was a group of high-minded (and perhaps self-serving) individuals, an establishment not yet fully established, striving to elevate professional standards and thereby seize the title of architect from the grasp of those "eight out of ten" that Kruse had so accusingly condemned. Ackerman attempted to turn the tables, however, by questioning the motives of the "group of property owners, promoters and investors who go bargain hunting for professional services." Ackerman asserted that Kruse did "not possess the slightest inkling of what the professional men whom he so ruthlessly condemns are doing toward elevating the standards of the profession."

Ackerman addressed Kruse's suggestion that architects be subordinated to large building concerns by reminding that "the relationship between owner and architect recognized by custom as that of principal and agent is *not* a creation of the architect, but rather a *resultant* arising out of the relation between owner and contractor." The architect's essential role, he maintained, was that of arbitrator between owners and builders. It was not builders' role to insulate owners from architects; rather, architects should shield owners from builders! Likewise, in the matter of architects' agency for owners, Ackerman opined that the relationship must be based upon cooperation, and that architects could not and should not be held to account for conditions imposed or altered by owners beyond architects' control. While concurring with the rationale for the licensure of architects, Ackerman suggested that such laws if limited to the protection of health and welfare alone would be insufficient to ensure comprehensive competence in architectural practice. To the question of fees, Ackerman deflected his answer back toward the ever-increasing complexity of modern life that placed added demands on the discipline of design, that it accomplish a synthesis of diverse purposes beyond a mere assembly of parts.

Ackerman's ultimate argument was that the character of the architect was a reflection of the owner's own intentions. As the AIA's journal suggested in its editorial response, "Behind the incompetent in any profession will be found the incompetent man who is paying the bills."[45] Thus, while the cause of elevating the profession relied upon vocational reforms, it also required architects to edify public understanding; but in owners' direct selection of architects, the creation of a more virtuous and business-like profession was ultimately in owners' own hands. As Tom Thumtack advised on the matter of selecting an architect, "Remember, sir … you didn't hire him for a janitor."[46]

By competition

Of the second method of selecting an architect, *The Handbook* explained:

> Competitions are instituted to enable the Owner to choose an Architect through a comparison of solutions of the problem, submitted by sundry competitors. Of late, competitions have become less and less frequent. The method is now rarely employed, except for public work, for which it is sometimes required by law and in case of which it offers a safeguard against favoritism in the appointment. If a competition is necessary, it can be made successful only by conducting it upon such fair and equitable lines as conserve the interests of both Owner and competitors. [47]

The practice of conducting open or limited competitions as a means of soliciting architectural proposals and services, while dating from ancient times and utilized in the United States during the early Federal period, was romanticized and popularized by American architects returning from studies in Paris at the Ecole des Beaux Arts. The system of *concours d'architecture* was institutionalized in fledgling American schools of architecture and in the drafting clubs and ateliers in cities across the nation. Perhaps even more significantly, architectural competitions became the chief mechanism under the Tarsney Act of 1893 for selecting architects for the design of federal buildings, the culmination of a long-sought effort by the profession for private practitioners to gain access to publicly funded work (Figure 3.6).

Despite these mitigating circumstances, by the end of the nineteenth century many commentators held the opinion that architectural competitions were a means by which owners could extract "something for nothing" in the form of architects' uncompensated ideas and labor. An especially pernicious practice seems to have involved private owners soliciting "sketches" from several architects from among which might be

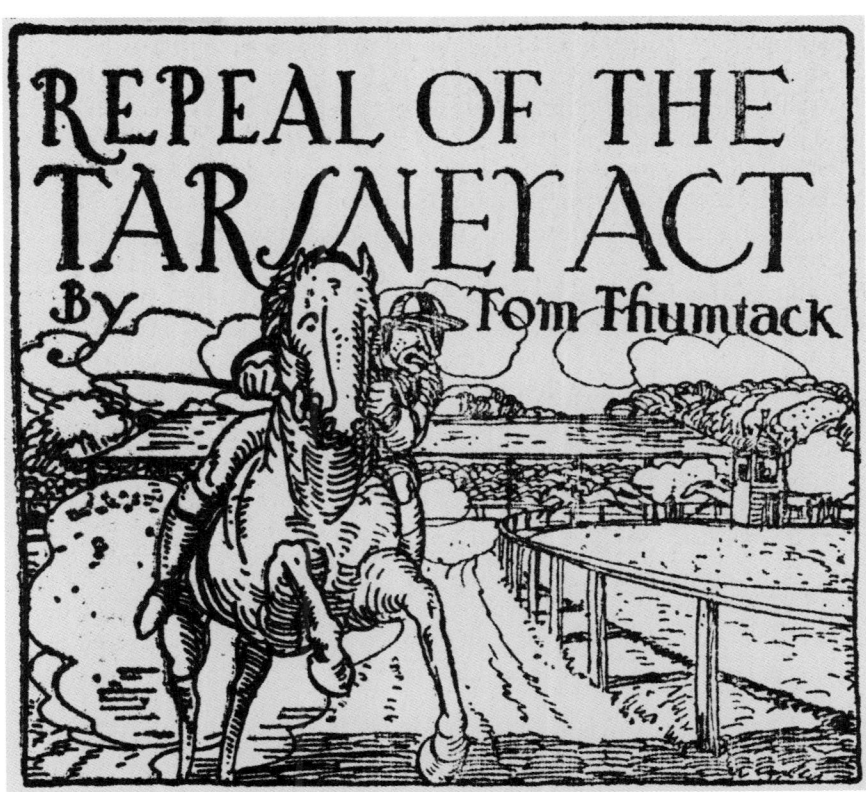

FIGURE 3.6 *Rockwell Kent, "Repeal of the Tarsney Act,"* Architecture and Building *47 (1915).*

chosen one for paid commission. Members of the AIA especially decried the demeaning manner in which colleagues were often willing to offer uncompensated services on the slightest chance of getting a job.[48] One journal editorialized that even when competitors were tempted to offer plans and specifications for a fee less than their worth, "It is probable that designs will be forthcoming in answer to their advertisement, just as iron, such as it is, may always be had for much less than the price of good material."[49]

Critics suggested that architectural competitions were at the root of a systemic undervaluation of architects' creative, intellectual capital that stymied progress toward a modern profession. The influential early architecture critic Maria Griswold Van Rensselaer was especially mindful of the deleterious effects of unpaid competitions upon broad efforts to bolster an American architectural profession still grasping for respect and legitimacy.

> That system of competitions which has been supposed the best aid to art and the best protection for the client is answerable for much that we deplore. Open, unpaid competitions are an abomination. It is folly, and something worse, to ask the members of a respectable profession to show us their ideas for nothing, and to expect to get their best ideas or the ideas of the best among them. Limited, paid competitions, where certain chosen artists are asked to submit schemes for comparison, and are promised a fair reward for their trouble, should stand on a different footing. But they are often managed with so total a lack of respect on the client's part, not only for art, but for mere labor, and so total a disregard for the precepts of business good-faith and common honesty, that they, too, have become a by-word and reproach. I cannot dwell upon this thorny subject here …. Let me only beg of my reader that, whether he be architect or client, he will never countenance in any way an unpaid competition; that, if as a client he shares in the management of a paid one, he … will not try to get something for nothing, or more than he asked for the price he agreed to pay ….[50]

Besides concerns about proper compensation, other issues of basic fairness plagued the conduct of competitions. The integrity of the adjudication process, the veracity of owners' intentions to build, lack of clarity and comprehensiveness of competition programs, variability of competitors' professional qualifications, and the potentially deceptive nature of architectural renderings were among the many criticisms aimed at competition conduct. In light of these concerns, it is ironic that the profession should have expressed as much enthusiasm as it did for the adoption of the Tarsney Act since it established formal architectural competitions as the means for the federal government to award public design commissions to private architects.

From the middle of the nineteenth century until the adoption of the Tarsney Act in 1893, primary responsibility for the design of federal buildings resided with the Office of the Supervising Architect of the US Department of the Treasury. This position and its staff contingent were typically appointed based upon political patronage rather than professional experience and expertise. The net result, architects charged, was artistically inferior to the best work being accomplished in private practice. Beginning as early as 1875, the AIA proposed and advocated legislation that would open the field of opportunity to private practices and thereby, they claimed, advance "the future standing of the nation in culture and art."[51] Once the act was adopted, its implementation was delayed until a change of presidential administrations brought the appointment of a more sympathetic Treasury Department regime willing to embrace the proposed reform.[52] With implementation of the law, the secretary of the treasury established protocols for the conduct of architectural competitions, based upon the AIA's advice, to address perceived abuses and long-standing concerns. These methods of conducting competitions included provisions for selecting competitors based upon merit rather than political patronage, appointment of an impartial jury, the stipulation of a professional fee for the winning competitor commensurate with the AIA's established schedule, and assurances of fairness and anonymity in the selection process.[53]

Given architects' established ambivalence toward competitions, it is unsurprising that not all of their concerns could be assuaged. Foremost among complaints was the financial burden that government competitions placed upon all but the winning competitors. In his presidential address to the 1908 AIA convention, Cass Gilbert indicted the "wasteful system" of competitions to which he attributed 90 percent of the profession's difficulties.

> The competition system has become so widespread that now it applies not only to government buildings but to all other classes of buildings. I think it would not be too much to say that the architects in this country annually expend over $1,000,000 in competitions from which they receive no return. How long can the profession stand this drain? And this is not all—to foot up the total you must add the profits that should have accrued from time and money expended, the wasted time and effort, the neglect of other duties, the depressing, the disheartening disappointments and the dissensions that ensue. If fault there be, it lies in ourselves. The correction is in our power.[54]

While recognizing the contributions of the Tarsney Act to the reform and standardization of procedures in the conduct of public competitions, the AIA's Committee on Competitions expressed regret "that this Act only applies to building controlled by on Department of the Federal Government." The committee outlined the various abuses of fairness and business ethics to which private competitions were prone:

The method of conducting competitions, except under the Tarsney Act in the United States, has been as varied as is the character of its people. They are instituted for many reasons: to give personal friends an opportunity to win a commission; to give the local architects a chance and through them secure business affiliations or advancement; to throw a sop to placate business elements, this giving an apparently fair opportunity to all competitors with the real intention of covering the appointment of a previously selected man; to secure the advantage of studying various schemes without expense; to secure the most artistic design and the most suitable arrangement of plan of the future building. It would seem hardly necessary to advise the professions to carefully avoid all competitions which have not clearly in view the selection the best scheme and the most skilled architect.[55]

The tendency of competitions to focus upon the artistic merits of design proposals was contrary, the committee maintained, to the full range of technical and administrative skills that were requisite qualifications for the successful fruition of any architectural project. All three attributes could be considered by an owner when following the direct selection method. The general position of the committee and the Institute, therefore, was to recommend "that an architect be employed upon the sole basis of professional fitness, without resort to competition."[56] Acknowledging nonetheless the likelihood that competitions would continue to be employed for private as well as public commissions, the committee sought to develop a competition code, fashioned in part upon the procedures established for the implementation of the Tarsney Act, that while being voluntary for owners would be compulsory for any AIA members wishing to participate. This effort culminated in 1909, under the committee chairmanship of Frank Miles Day, with the adoption of a position statement, "A Circular of Advice and Information Relative to the Conduct of Architectural Competitions," and a set of standardized program formats and contractual forms, all of which were ultimately included a decade later in *The Handbook of Architectural Practice*.[57]

The Tarsney Act, however, did not long endure. Subject to claims and counterclaims by supporters and detractors with regard to its cost-savings efficacy as public policy, as benefit to the profession, as boon to art and culture, the Act was unceremoniously rescinded in 1913.[58] The AIA, an early advocate of the Act though now a competition naysayer, was blindsided by the repeal and officially indignant. Some in the profession, however, applauded its demise. Curmudgeonly as ever, F.W. Fitzpatrick mocked the "wails" of the "inner circle" of architects, meaning members of the AIA, who were, he asserted, the chief beneficiaries of the law. "I think I am perfectly safe in saying," he continued, "that the legislation has done no good. The buildings carried on by private architects have been no better than the regular governmental product, have been the cause of endless rows and trouble, and have cost more to produce than those done in the usual way."⁵⁹

Tom Thumtack, for his part, was unsentimental about the Tarsney Act repeal which he considered no more than a "well-conducted game of chance." From Thumtack's point of view, in government-run competitions, "There is no other gamble where the chances are half so long or the purses half so short. Uncle Sam's dealer, Tarsney, has stacked the deck on us." So in the dark cloud of the Act's repeal, Tom Thumtack could find a silver lining, "the chance to get a minimum fee for hard work and full value given." But in singing his lament, Tom Thumtack acknowledged the precariousness of the architect's fee and the profession's self-defeating willingness, to tender its services for free: "The Tarsney Act is dead. Dead but not forgotten. Hope springs eternal in the gambler's breast and some day will rise up one greater than Tarsney who will enact a law whereby our Uncle Sam again will get, from the architectural profession, with its hearty consent, something for nothing."⁶⁰

Fees, contracts, and consultants

The value of architects' services, the scope of those services, and—as seen in the case of competitions—even the right of architects to be paid at all were matters of perennial friction as the owner–architect relation evolved. As one architect bemoaned, "It seems to be the general impression in many uninformed places ... that an architect makes a few sketches taking a few days of his time and for this work receives an enormous fee."⁶¹ Meanwhile, architects held the view that they were woefully underpaid. Even as the overhead costs of their practices rose—more drafting staff for more detailed drawings, more engineering consultants, more supervisory responsibility—their fees were subject to constant downward pressures—from cut-rate competitors, from bargain-hunting clients, from full-service construction firms.

Over the course of the nineteenth century, a fee structure based upon a percentage of construction cost was derived from arcane precedent, institutionalized as a schedule of charges, and tested in the courts. The services connected to those fees were suggested by custom but were variable in practice and only vaguely described in the AIA's standard schedule of fees.⁶² Despite such elusiveness of purpose, architects were never free agents; rather, their actions were conditioned by local circumstance and adjusted to the divergent motivations, proclivities, and proficiencies of the other players in the game.⁶³ Architects' dual if potentially conflicting roles—as owner's agent on the one hand and as unbiased arbitrator of disputes with builders on the other hand—had been tangentially codified in 1888 in the terms of the Uniform Contract between owners and contractors. The AIA, however, did not turn its full attention to the formalization of architects' and owners' contractual relationship until almost thirty years later. In that endeavor as in others, Frank Miles Day played a leading role.

Over the intervening years, architects' services and offices were expanding to accommodate the changing scale and complexity of construction projects. Rather than a single practitioner with a few drafters, "the architect" in a burgeoning metropolis might be a firm of some size, its personnel stratified by function and rank. Architects had to coordinate the retinue of technical consultants whose participation the increasing technological complexity of buildings had spawned. Firms were organizationally challenged to provide adequate administrative oversight and construction supervision in the face of changing project delivery methods that the rise of general contracting entailed. Architects' mastery of the science and technology of building and their authority over the construction site were being incrementally ceded to others. Likewise, architects' livelihoods were being threatened by competition from well-financed speculative design and construction firms and by other actors unencumbered by the professional strictures of the clubby AIA.

The AIA's adoption of ethical canons requiring its members to disavow pursuit of any financial self-interest in building was a necessary and timely measure to bolster public trust as well as safety. It was part of an effort to differentiate those architects subscribing to the tenets of an ethical professionalism from the rabble of a construction industry otherwise rife with disrepute—a perception supported by facts but also reinforced by class-based biases and stereotypes. While contractual rationalization of owner–architect relations arguably enhanced mutual understanding among the parties and thereby averted potential disputes, it also institutionalized a more operationally restrictive definition of proper architectural practice where more fluid ethical boundaries had once pertained. The unintended consequence of imposing a static and paternalistic paradigm of propriety upon one segment of a dynamic and rapidly diversifying industry, however, was to limit the profession's own agility in the face of accelerating social, technological, and economic change. The AIA's assertion of principles of an avowedly more ethical professionalism left its members only the narrowest of claims to a moral high ground and to the art of architecture as their exclusive expertise domain.

"Fees—A Reductio Ad Absurdum"

Tom Thumtack was especially attuned to the ironies of architects' financial plight and to the structural paradoxes of fees based on a percentage of construction cost (Figure 3.7). In giving voice to architects' frustrations through his fictional mouthpiece, author Frederick Squires no doubt drew upon his own experiences in architectural practice during the boom years of New York City loft building in the early-1900s.[64]

FIGURE 3.7 Rockwell Kent, "Fees: A Reductio Ad Absurdum," Architecture and Building 46 (1914).

The shopkeeper who offered his wares below cost and claimed to make his profit by selling them in big quantities, had nothing on the architectural profession for business acumen, for our schedule of minimum charges is founded on just such logic. For example: We're paid on a percentage of the cost, but the capable architect is the one who keeps down the cost. Therefore, by doing his best he reduces his compensation. ... The client wants to keep the cost down, and his architect must help him in this, but the less the cost of a particular job, the less is the compensation and the less is likely to be the beauty of its execution from which the architect obtains his reputation.[65]

Given the structural paradoxes of risk and reward inherent in this system, Tom Thumtack is left to surmise, "The only reason that I have been able to find for the present illogical scheme is that you have got to have a scheme."

The *Handbook of Architectural Practice* described three "methods of paying the architect": by a percentage of final construction cost, by a set fee plus the cost of the architect's expenses, or by salary in cases of employment by a governmental or corporate body.[66] Of these three, the first was most widely in use and received the lengthiest explanation. Over the years leading up to publication of *The Handbook,* the relative benefits of this customary method were under increasing scrutiny as architects realized the competitive disadvantages of a system in which the harder you worked the less you were paid. Owners, of course, were skeptical from the other direction, assuming architects' self-serving motives to run-up the costs.

The suggestion of a percentage-based fee for architectural services calculated upon final construction cost had become conventionalized decades before the AIA first published the 5 percent stipulation in its schedule of charges in 1866.[67] The standardized fee structure itself became one defining trait of an AIA-anointed architect that separated its members from the ranks of wage-based mechanics. Neither the universal applicability of the fee structure nor its ultimate collectability was guaranteed, however, among even the small coterie of AIA members.[68] The percentage-based fee could become a bone of contention with more commercially minded clients seeking to purchase a material product in the form of drawings and specifications rather than the more nebulous and difficult-to-understand services of design and construction supervision. The fee structure was thus an easy target for rate-cutting competitors, those perhaps un-pedigreed and less devoted to advancing the fraternal project of professionalization or those seeking the collection of "illegitimate fees" through kickbacks and bribes. As one architect complained, "… the illegitimate fees exacted … in some cases far exceed the legitimate. So true is this that to gain the illegitimate some men cut almost to nothing the legitimate fees and as inducement for preference over honest and conscientious competitors."[69]

Where did the 5 percent fee originate? Even as architects struggled to hold the line with clients that a minimum fee of 5 percent was usual and proper, they themselves were not at all convinced that the minimum fee was even adequate to cover the basic overhead expenses their practices incurred. Turn-of-the-century wisdom held that the standard charge by percentage fee of construction had originated in Europe. One writer, for example, contended:

> Our present system, if it deserves that name, is in reality nothing but an obsolete rule of the 18th century established for the public buildings of France as a fair average for a rather uniform class of work which, therefore, takes no account whatever of the infinite variety of modern types of buildings, conditions of employment, individual requirements, standing of practitioner, etc., and the application of which to modern work is indeed, as [English architect] George Edmund Street is said to have remarked even fifty years ago, "a great absurdity." … This custom

was enacted into law during the French Revolution, was adopted by most architectural bodies as the only precedent available and gradually spread to other countries.[70]

The first self-declared professional architect in America, Benjamin Latrobe, had explained this practice a century earlier in justifying to a client his proposal for compensation:

> It is in France, Germany & England the established custom of Architects, (in England confirmed by many decisions of the Courts) to charge for their works, 1., a commission of 5 prCent on the whole amount of the expence incurred in executing their design, –2., a certain sum for fair drawings, if furnished, according to their difficulty, number, or beauty; –3., if the work be at a distance from the usual residence of the Architect,– all travelling expences, & a certain sum pr day for loss of time.[71]

Latter-day critics attempting to trace the lineage of the customary fee structure would likely have agreed with Latrobe's sentiment, though with a rationale from quite a different historical perspective. They suggested that when "the American Institute [of Architects], without particular consideration of the different customs of England and America, adopted unmodified the official schedule of the Royal Institute of British Architects naming 5 per cent as a 'minimum charge'," it had misconstrued the relevant application of the fee, to a full rather than to a partial slate of services.[72] It was therefore suggested that as a result of this disjunction, "in the United States the architect renders more service for less compensation than is the rule abroad."[73] Architect Arne Dehli explained:

> European and American conditions in the architectural profession are not at all identical, and neither are those of the building trades. The conditions of architects' employment vary considerably in the different European countries and are everywhere different from those prevailing the United States; in England, for instance, the five per cent. rule really means seven and one-half per cent. in addition to the wages of the superintendent, two and one-half per cent. on the cost being added for quantity surveying.[74]

In more direct terms, that would equate to 5 percent for design, 2.5 percent for quantity surveying or estimating, and an additional negotiated fee allocated to construction supervision. Glen Brown, then AIA Secretary, lent further credence to this argument with his careful assessment and comparative analysis of prevailing practices and charges in France, England, Russia, Germany, Italy, and Switzerland. In no example did the 5 percent fee pertain for the full complement of services during all phases of both design and construction.[75] Instead, variable conventions applied, as in the English case, by the owner's provision of extra compensation beyond the architect's basic fee for the preparation of material estimates and full-time on-site job supervision by a clerk of the works.

In the United States, by contrast, the 5 percent fee stipulated in the AIA's schedule of charges was ostensibly a minimum charge but was nonetheless described as covering full architectural services inclusive of construction supervision. At the turn of the century, American architects were still regularly hiring, directing, and coordinating multiple trade contractors on owners' behalfs in lieu of general contractors, tasks entailing significant outlays of time and labor expense. Architects tried to minimize the extent of their supervisory obligation, but this came with a concomitant loss of quality control. They might also try, in the manner of their European colleagues, to compel owners to independently employ a clerk of the works acceptable to and reporting directly to the architect's firm. Architects' increasing difficulty in adequately fulfilling their supervisory obligations was arguably one among several factors precipitating the rise of the system of general contracting and speculative construction firms. The result was to further constrict architects' potential revenue stream by allowing, for example, general contractors to collect the supervisory fee that architects had earned but never successfully claimed or collected.

At the AIA's annual convention of 1908, Frank Miles Day introduced a motion on behalf of the Board of Directors for a new schedule of charges raising the customary minimum fee from 5 to 6 percent. As AIA President Cass Gilbert noted in his opening address, "That the demands upon the architects both in professional service and in the cost thereof have enormously increased is a well known fact. The schedule when adopted some forty years ago represented fair remuneration for that time, but it does not represent fair remuneration now."[76] The motion, which passed unanimously, obviously hit a nerve as architects felt the financial squeeze between rising practice costs and the rising standard of living. One editorialist observed, however, that while "high-priced architects" may feel little effect of the increase, "architects who have found it difficult to convince their clients that their services were worth five per cent will find it even more difficult to convince their clients that their services are worth six per cent." "Standard-rate architects" would likely be at even greater risk from "cut-rate architects" and from the "speculative builders, whose owners believe that they cannot pay the Institute's fees."[77]

For his part, Tom Thumtack rued such bitter ironies that architects' shortsighted insistence upon the minimum fee perpetuated. "Who," he asked, "will be the prophet to lead architects to better profits?"[78] His own suggestion, echoing a growing number of practitioners in the 1910s, was to implement a fee structure on a "business-like basis," one that would recoup "the cost to the architect of getting out the work plus a reasonable profit."[79] The "fee plus cost" method, it was hoped, would appeal to the sensibilities of even a hard-nosed business client, one who could sympathize with the architect's unique pecuniary equation. Architects and their critics alike acknowledged, however, how generally unaware the public was about the architect's high production costs: the investment in drafters, superintendents, and stenographers, along with the expense of maintaining a large office space to house a diversified workforce.

A banker sympathetic to architects' cause advised them on how best to make their case in terms that a business-oriented client could understand. As antidote to the client's "lack of knowledge of the cost of drawing," he advised architects to keep meticulous accounts to "explain to the client in details of dollars and cents and hours and minutes" the real expense of drafting. To the complaint that there was a "lack of explicit determination of what the client is paying for," the banker begged architects for more precision in describing their services; to be explicit about "what is meant by *supervision*," because the typical client, he claimed, is "confident that he is not getting the supervision to which he is entitled." On his final points, uncertainty about the actual functions of the architect and the "lack of evidence of commercial return on good design," the banker urged architects to educate the public and to educate themselves, in the first instance about the high standards that the profession endeavors to uphold in both the public and private interest; and second, to better appreciate the role that good planning plays in profits, in the pro forma performance of commercial real estate. Deriding the AIA's schedule of charges, the banker encouraged architects to "educate [the client] to a belief in your capabilities, and not present him with a printed slip of what [fees] the Institute decrees."[80]

In 1915, the concept of a fee plus cost system for the calculation of architects' charges was raised at the annual AIA convention. While reaffirming its confidence in the percentage of the cost of building system, the Board of Directors admitted a caveat: "But the questions are being asked with increasing frequency: Is a percentage system a logical one? Is it fair either to architect or client?"[81] Holding close to precedent, the Board issued its response:

> The percentage method has been in use since the foundation of the Institute and is the method with which the public is familiar. Whether he likes it or not, the client understands it and can estimate the cost. It would therefore be most unwise to sweep away that which has become an established custom, a custom recognized by the courts, and set up a substitute which even though more equitable to both parties to the agreement, is as yet generally unknown and untried.[82]

Despite any hesitations or deference to tradition, the convention approved in principle the acceptability of the fee plus cost system as an alternative to the percentage-based system as a means of calculating architects' charges. The very next year it issued a detailed circular of information about the system and confidently proclaimed, "This system of charging places the Architect in a position where he can advise the Owner on the investment of his money without having his professional remuneration in any way affected by the final amount actually expended."[83] The accounting for time and labor costs yielded a transparency that any banker or business-client might appreciate, though quantifying the added value of architects' design services like the intangibles of artistic virtue remained a challenge in a bustling construction economy where willingness to assume risk was quickly becoming a prime index of due reward.[84]

Agreement between owner and architect

It was with a wisdom grown of the profession's accrued collective experience that *The Handbook* soberly advised: "A clear understanding between Owner and Architect as to their relations and obligations is of utmost importance. So many unforeseen situations may arise during the designing and erection of a building that neither a verbal agreement … nor a mere exchange of letters, is an adequate guarantee against misunderstandings."[85] Despite this sage advice, and irrespective of ongoing efforts since the 1880s to standardize the contractual relationship between owners and builders, the relationship between owner and architect was often left deliberately vague. Indeed, the AIA did not turn its attention to standardizing terms of the owner and architect agreement until 1916. When it did, it was under the meticulous committee leadership of Frank Miles Day.

In a lecture to architecture students around the turn of the century, one architect offered this advice on client relations: "Talk not too much about what you will do. Promise little, promises are easy to make, and hard usually to keep. Besides, if the owner is an experienced businessman, as he usually is, he knows this well already, and he will rely on you more, the less you promise."[86] A treatise on the legal aspects of construction in circulation at the same time suggested that some architects' penchant for contractual vagueness and their procrastination in coming-to-terms might be attributed to certain inherent traits:

> Some persons are afflicted with an excessive timidity or politeness, which leads to an habitual fogginess of expression in their business dealings, as if they feared to wound the feelings of others by a brusque directness of demand or reply, and many more, under the influence of a craftiness which is not incompatible with timidity, habitually conceal their real intentions, and make their bargains in vague terms, to which they hope to be able later, after they have been accepted, to ascribe a meaning very different from that which the party who accepted them had in mind, and much more advantageous to themselves.[87]

Rather than merely explaining the motivations of "some persons," this proto-psychoanalysis could have been applied to the profession as a whole.

Over the course of the formative nineteenth century, architects had conjured a role for themselves out of the existential gap between owners and builders. The architect's role on the American continent was only loosely constrained by European precedent; rather, it continually shifted with respect to the needs and opportunities of the situation at hand. Within certain limits and understandings, the architect's function could be adjusted to provide whatever ratio of vision and know-how was necessary to compensate for insufficiencies in the other two. Free of institutional fixity, architects were able to exercise "a craftiness not incompatible with timidity or politeness" in order to insinuate themselves into such representative and representational roles as circumstances might allow.

The Uniform Contract of 1888 had formalized the roles and mutual obligations binding owners and contractors to each other, but in its designation of architects as owners' agents, it left the full nature and meaning of that relationship essentially undefined. Architects acting on behalf of owners were to: make drawings and specifications that remained their authors' property, supply contractors with additional details to provide further instructions, answer questions or doubts with just and impartial decisions that were final and conclusive, make fair and reasonable valuations of work added or omitted, condemn all noncompliant work as unsound or improper, be allowed to visit and inspect the work at all times and places, and certify any changes in contract time. The manner by which architects were to consult or advise the owners while acting on their behalfs in these matters was neither specified nor implied.[88]

The AIA's "Schedule of Charges and Professional Practice of Architects, As Usual and Proper," in use at the time of the adoption of the Uniform Contract, was similarly vague. Some procedural sequence of services over the first half of the project was suggested by a list of incremental fees due and collectable after the completion of each phase of work. These were described as "preliminary studies, general drawings, specifications and details." The nature of the architect's interaction with the owner during the course of this work was never described, however. Fully one-half of the total fee was assigned to "supervision of works," that portion of contractual engagement between owner and contractor addressed in the Uniform Contract, though again the mode of consultation between owner and architect was not addressed. Indeed, the fee schedule description of supervision, while reiterating terms of the Uniform Contract, also provided caveats of what it was not. The schedule distinguished supervision from "the continuous personal superintendence which may be secured by the employment of a Clerk of the works" as an extra service chargeable to the owner. It should also be noted that despite big differentials of architects' own time and labor associated with alternative modes of project delivery, the architect's role in advancing a project from design into construction by the hiring of builders, whether through multiple or single contracts, whether with bid or negotiated prices, was neither listed as an explicit service nor associated with a specific fee. Architects may not have been free agents, but under the loosely drawn legal obligations some of their services seem to have been free, or at least not fully accounted.

Burdened with its onerous tasks and its attention "so engrossed by the revision of the [other] documents," the Committee on Contracts and Specifications had been unable to turn its attention to formalizing the owner and architect relationship through a parallel standardized contractual form.[89] That effort came to fruition in 1916 with publication of the first edition of the Standard Form of Agreement Between Owner and Architect. Prior to that adoption, architects had typically followed their own habits of practice or the owner's preferences in the drafting of some letter of agreement. While not explicitly a contractual form with space for codicils and signatures, the AIA's "Schedule of Charges" regularly served that substitute role either in lieu of a separate letter or by embedded references to it therein.[90]

The Schedule of Charges and associated services combined with the architect's responsibilities as enumerated in the Uniform Contract (governing the period of construction) thus served in tandem to suggest the full scope of the owner–architect relationship. The architect's commission to act as an agent on owner's behalf was never explicitly assigned to the architect by the owner; rather, it was merely assumed as a fait accompli. Indeed, the Uniform Contract's designation of the architect as "Agent of said Owner" was an understanding arrived at by architects and builders in owners' absence, with architects negotiating on owners' behalfs. Architects themselves had asserted their agency for owners, and builders had cagily agreed. The fuller implications of this compact would only gradually emerge.

Ironically, the newly minted contract form of 1916 was little more than a refined version of the AIA's old schedule of charges that had been periodically updated since 1866. That form, like the new contract, focused more upon the determination of fees based upon a percentage of construction cost than upon the description of services. An additional, alternative form was authorized in the following year to allow for the fee-plus-cost approach. The new contract did not broach in any manner whatsoever the highly charged issue of the architect's standing as the owner's agent during the course of construction, nor did it make reference to the much-contested general conditions of the contract for construction.

One consideration did migrate, however, between the two contractual forms: the issue of arbitration. Where builders had succeeded in binding architects' decisions to review by independent arbitration in cases of challenge or dispute, architects here adopted the same mechanism in their relationship with owners. This was presumably an attempt to forestall litigation that might arise from architects' actions taken on owners' behalfs. The continuing vagueness of the architect's relationship to either of the other parties merely echoed observations still operative from the previous century. "How far an architect can go in carrying out his undoubted duty, that of endeavoring to see that the contractors comply with their agreements, is, unfortunately, not determined. There is no question that here the architect is agent for the owner, but the owner's rights are as undefined as his own."[91]

Employment of engineers and other consulting specialists

The Handbook was prefaced by a familiar formulation, essentially Vitruvian in character, of architecture as an amalgam of art, science, and business. And while the interdependence of these three cognitive domains may seem self-evident and even universal, by the turn of the twentieth century their interrelationships, like those among architects, builders, and owners, were often quite antagonistic. The art and science of architecture and building, once empirically reconcilable through the shared logics of geometry and construction, became fractured by the dual instrumentalities of technology and commercialism. Engineering, as the apotheosis of physics and economy, became a rival to art as the raison d'être of architecture, proudly proclaimed by architects as their exclusive professional domain. Tom Thumtack, too, acknowledges in one of his missives the architect's existential paradox, embedded linguistically in the name itself: "It is the Absolute Divorce of the Practical and the Artistic" (Figure 3.8).

> Our profession's name consists of two words referring respectively to art and science, and we who practice Architecture should practice Art and Science. But through our mispronunciation of the word, Art has gained undue emphasis. Mr. Practicalissimus doesn't care for Art, so give him Science. He admires and respects Science in the inverse ratio to the way he admires and respects Art …. This being true, and wanting to sell what Mr. Practicalissimus is in the market to buy, let's change the accent and put the emphasis on the Tect. Or, better still, reverse the word. Offer him the service of a Tectarch.[92]

Besides changing their name, how could architects reconcile and integrate their compositional art with mathematical analysis of multiple technical systems—steel skeleton structure, mechanical, electrical, plumbing, and conveyance? How were architects supposed to coordinate their design efforts with all those consulting engineers? Could engineers turn the tables on architects and engage them instead to superficially ornament their structures; or once so emboldened, displace architects altogether as the arbiters of design? Perhaps of most urgency in consideration of architects' already inadequate fee structure, who was going to pay? From the owner's perspective, negotiating reimbursement of the architect's engineering expenses only foreshadowed the builder's battle for "extras" during the construction phase yet to come.

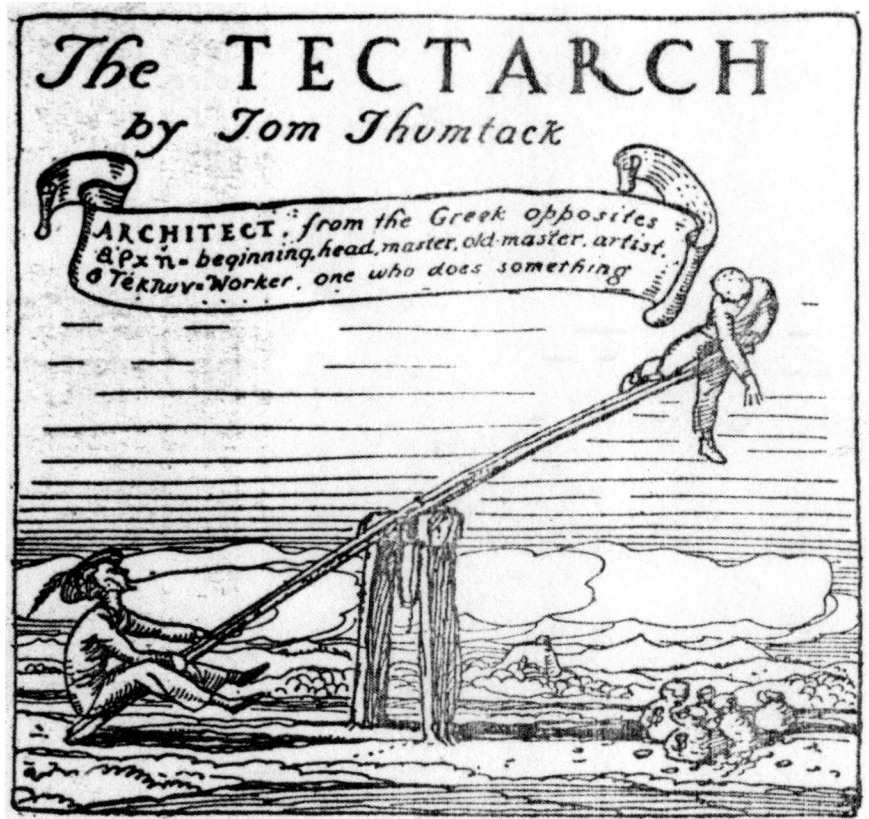

FIGURE 3.8 Rockwell Kent, "The Tectarch," Architecture and Building 47 (1915).

These dilemmas were already becoming apparent in the last quarter of the nineteenth century, to architects and engineers alike. In 1878, one architecture journal editorialized:

> The separation of architects and engineers into two professions is quite a modern device. The engineer's profession is in fact a young and strong-minded daughter of the architect's begotten of the modern tendency to the mechanical development of science and to the division of labor. Needlessly divided sympathies separate those whom the family relation and common interests ought to keep in close union.[93]

The historical emergence of the engineer as intermediary between architect and builder on the technical–analytical plane mirrors the differentiation of roles that called forth the architect as social and functional mediator between builder and owner. In pre-industrial times, all the essential branches of architectural knowledge—the arts of planning and designing, the application of empirical science to problems of construction, techniques of material craft and assembly—could be jointly claimed and were fluidly shared among a spectrum of building actors, from dilettantes to drafters to mechanics. While architects could cite ancient precedents to justify their claims to a superordinate, guiding position among the other agents of construction, engineers could assert with increasing confidence the critical importance of their own realms of technical expertise.

Compared to the architect's generalist knowledge, engineers offered the kind of specialized experience with emerging technologies, modern building practices, and approaches to organization and cost control that were redefining the construction industry. The engineer's application of science to everyday problems—to the utilitarian purposes of civil and military infrastructure; to the mechanical innovations propelling manufacturing and commerce—had inevitable impacts upon more intimate, built, and inhabited realms typically within the purview of architectural design.[94] "The gap between the professions has widened," it was observed, "till in our day we have seen architects who are either innocently ignorant or superciliously disdainful of the whole theory of construction, and engineers who attempt the most imposing monument without any concerns of architectural teaching."[95] Owners, navigating the archipelago of expanding building types and competing knowledge domains, needed the sort of captain of construction whose judgment they could trust to fill that gap, but it was not at all clear at the turn of the century whether either the architect or the engineer was the obvious or exclusive choice.

Having become accustomed to subordinating construction—and builders—to their guiding artistic vision, some architects were loath to cede any control to consulting engineers, "to be simply the master mind which gives assent to things of which he is often profoundly ignorant." Rather, they clung to the idea of an "all-around architect," one who "may be less scientifically exact than the specialist, while really knowing and appreciating far more, in an architectural sense," about the practical and technical needs of building.[96] The resistance to external expertise might be understood as merely a romantic reaction against the onslaught of a technological fait accompli, but it also manifested the profession's growing sense of economic vulnerability as the architect's reliance upon a growing retinue of technical specialists further eroded their fees.[97] For their parts, engineers struggled to secure their own livelihoods by demonstrating the essential value of their professional service, though they too questioned the proper hierarchy of building design expertise.

Civil engineer Corydon T. Purdy offered his thoughts on the matter in a paper presented at the 38th Annual Convention of the AIA held in 1905. Purdy characterized "the advent of the rolled beam" and mechanical equipment as harbingers of "a new age in building construction" in which "the engineer has suddenly, as it were, become a distinct factor in the building problem." As compared to the profession of architecture, he admitted that the engineering profession was still in its infancy, and while gaining in public esteem was mostly expected to perform work on a salary basis rather than for the consideration of a fair and commensurate fee. He argued, "If a relation is ever established between the engineer and the architect, which will be conceded to be the proper one by both professions and by the public, we may fairly expect that relation to be one which will work for the advantage of all concerned—the architect, the engineer, and the owner."[98]

While engineering exactitude was now requisite for matching material capacities with architectural aspirations and owners' cost constraints, Purdy noted a continuing reticence of turn-of-the-century architects to employ professional engineers as consultants. Those architects or firms unable to perform their own structural designs typically relied instead on the calculations provided by steel manufacturers' in-house technicians. This latter arrangement presented architects with both professional and ethical dilemmas, for consultants' fees did not really disappear; rather, they were shifted into material costs. This lack of price transparency could be corrosive of the bonds of mutual trust so essential to maintaining harmony among contractual partners. Likewise, such arrangements could compromise architects' ability to maintain full creative control. For his audience of generalist architects, Purdy enumerated a full spectrum of specialist interactions—from the architect's dream of ultimate autonomy to the nightmare of subordination that they most feared. All of these alternatives, Purdy contended, were currently "in vogue":

1. The architect may do the work himself, without assistance.
2. The architect may have the work done by some manufacturer.
3. The architect may have the work done by the builder, or the owner, with his consent, may have it done in that way.
4. The architect may employ the engineer as a part of his own force.
5. The architect may associate the engineer with himself as a partner.
6. The architect may employ a consulting engineer, who has his own independent office and practice.
7. The architect may be associated with such an engineer, employed directly by the owner, without any personal arrangement with him in relation to the matter, or
8. The engineer may have control of all the work, with the architect more or less subordinated to him.[99]

Purdy methodically considered each option in turn, pointing out potential conflicts or objections that were insurmountable in all cases but one, the employment of the consulting engineer in independent practice. Purdy's proposal was as diplomatic as it was prescient, balancing the architect's need for creative control with due respect for the engineer's professional contributions.

> The architect in full control of the planning and execution of every great architectural undertaking, retaining structural and mechanical engineers who have their own independent practice, and sharing with them the emoluments and the honors of their achievements, the engineer laboring independently within his own province, without limitations, except by the financial and architectural conditions of his problems, receiving adequate compensation while he maintains the position of the architect; such is the ideal relationship of architect and engineer; and particularly so if both individuals are broad-minded and reasonable, and over all, there be mutual sympathy.[100]

Still, the "question of compensation" constituted a primary difficulty in architect and engineer relations. As Purdy well-recognized, "It always seems a hard thing to spend so large a part of the architect's commission in one sum." First and foremost, and in contrast to the architect's efforts to extract additional compensation from the owner sufficient to cover necessary consultant expenses, Purdy proposed: "The engineer's compensation should be paid by the architect, because that is most in keeping with the subordinate relation of the engineer." To recoup that outlay of expense, Purdy proposed raising the architect's fee chargeable to the owner from 5 to 7.5 percent of construction cost. From past experience, architects already knew this well-intentioned notion was easier said than done. As builders had done almost two decades earlier, Purdy called upon architects through the AIA to confer with engineers in an effort to put their relationship "upon a better basis."[101] Despite this invitation, consultant's fees, as well as their regular services, would remain unsecured for the foreseeable future, classified as a reimbursable expense contingent upon the architect's own success in the course of contract negotiations.

Another account of "The Relations of Specialists to Architects" given at the same convention immediately following Purdy's presentation made clear that structural and mechanical engineers were not the only consultants competing for a portion of the architect's fee. And despite Purdy's entreaties for comity, this architect cast consultants' role with an air of disdain. The speaker contended, "The landscape architect, the interior decorator, the glass designer, being [consultants] in whom the artistic sense is indispensable, are perhaps the most difficult of all to control." Landscape architecture was not yet solidly established as a profession, its practice considered "an anomaly" and its purpose not well-understood. Glass and mosaic designers could not be "trusted undirected with a work of importance"; and "regarding the interior decorator," it was avowed, "there is no possible slaughter worse than that he can accomplish ... with an otherwise harmless if not entirely wholesome architectural interior." Engineers by comparison received a modicum of praise, since "the really capable engineer has no sentiment of hurt pride in admitting that he knows little of art." [102]

Ingrained cultural and intellectual antagonisms, as well as economic competition, plagued architects' and engineers' relationships from both sides. One editorialist observed:

> The [engineer] has regarded the architect's ideas as chimerical or impracticable, as based on imperfect knowledge and experience of iron and steel; while the architect has looked upon engineer's work as crude and inartistic, based on mathematical theories and formulas which leave much unsatisfied and which seldom give any sense of pleasure. These antagonistic opinions have, of course, prevented any *entente cordiale* between the professions, and have rather widened the gulf which separates them. While regarding each other from such opposite standpoints, we cannot wonder that differences have been magnified, and that any agreement between them has been rendered more difficult of accomplishment.[103]

A decade later, these frictions were still apparent, even exacerbated by academic rivalries and intellectual inversions, where Beaux-Arts-based architecture curricula were embedded within colleges of engineering. Architect William J. Steele reminisced, "How well we remember the lordly air with which our engineering fellow students discussed the mysteries of calculus in our presences. How much they enjoyed the imputation that we of the architectural bar-sinister had elected our course because it was easier than theirs. How well we remember the way the 'Fine Arts' were tagged and set aside and feminized!" It was, thus, from a very different position compared to nineteenth century experience that this same architect admitted the profession's dependence upon external expertise:

> Let [the architect] gladly, in the bigness of admitting that he can't know everything, make use of any and every kind of a specialist that walks; but, in God's name, let him pay for it. ... Only so can we hold our ground against the 'specialists' who now, grown tired of playing their little second fiddles, are invading the architect's territory and entire commissions ....[104]

Between the first and final drafts of *The Handbook of Architectural Practice*, various justifications for the extra costs of consultants' services were rehearsed and revised as architects and handbook authors struggled to explain to owners and themselves how the technical requirements of contemporary building had outpaced their professional mastery and control. The unpublished draft of the first handbook edition, largely written by Frank Miles Day himself, didactically summarized the argument for architects' expanded fee.[105] In this extended excerpt, Day conveys the visceral stresses architects had been bearing in the face of rapid technological change:

> The Owner, not accustomed to the practice of the profession, is surprised to find in Article 5 of the Schedule of Charges that he is expected not merely to pay the Architect a commission on the entire cost of the work but that he is also to reimburse the Architect the charges of engineers for heating, ventilation, mechanical plant, and electrical work, and he would like to know why this is so. ...
>
> For centuries the list of trades, the work of which went to form a completed building, changed but little, when of a sudden, and within a single fifty years, were added steam-heating, mechanical ventilation, electric light and power, hydraulic and electric elevators, and other equally technical developments of the applied sciences. The Architect staggered along under his added burden for years, trying to keep himself abreast of subjects, each one of which, developing as rapidly as it did, was sufficient to fill the mind of a specialist. Many expedients were tried, but at last it became clear that, if these branches were to be competently handled, it must be by skillful disinterested experts acting in harmony with and under the general direction of the architect.
>
> Formerly a single set of by no means complicated drawings sufficed for all the work of a building, however important. After the change, three or four sets were needed: one, as before, for the trades in general; another for the steel or reinforced concrete structure; a third for boilers, heating, ventilation, elevators, etc.; a fourth for electric equipment with its generators, panel boards, ducts, wires, outlets, etc. With the increased number and elaboration of the drawings came an equal or greater increase in the complexity and length of the specifications.
>
> By whom were specialists in these new branches to be paid? Architects attempted to assume the burden, only to find that in addition to it there fell on them the duty and expense of adjusting in great detail and at much cost, the design of the building to the needs of the intricate apparatus that it had to house. The result was what might have been expected. The Architect ceased to make a living, and he said to the Owner: "If you instruct me to employ experts, as you certainly ought, you must pay for their services yourself; as for me, the fact that I have to arrange your building in most intricate ways to suit these emanations of modern science and to make their outward manifestations tolerable has thrown on me an expense for which you scarcely repay me by the part of my commission arising from their cost."
>
> The experienced and intelligent Owner, to secure the best results in branches of the work so charged with potential trouble, is willing to reimburse the Architect the fees paid by him to such specialists because such an Owner understands that engineers of larger and more varied practice than it is possible for anyone in the regular employ of an architect

to possess, are needed successfully to solve the complicated problems of modern domestic engineering.[106]

Reactions to Day's discourse were generally positive and supportive, though consensus apparently formed that it might be wiser, in addressing owners on the topic of consultants, to say less.[107] An alternative text, much simplified and condensed, retained only a brief passage of Day's original.[108] In lieu of Day's complex explanation, it offered as analogy and aspiration the practices of a sister profession. "As a logical sequence, the Architect finds himself in much the same position as a general practitioner in medicine. While he is responsible for the success of his work as a whole, he must know when to consult with a specialist if he would have every detail reflect the best practice in each special field."[109]

Architects had long recognized the importance of educating clients about the overhead costs entailed in the conduct of architectural practice. To the expense of maintaining a skilled and effective drafting force for production of drawings and other technical documents, to the cost of on-site construction supervision that often exceeded their fee, architects now added the engineer's, their sometimes competitor's, commission for providing the technical expertise so essential to the execution of their basic tasks. *The Handbook* appealed not to Mr. Finedesign, but to the sort of client that Tom Thumtack called Mr. Practicalissimus, about whom there was much to admire. As old Thumtack observed:

> It is indisputable that he is in the best position to encourage architecture provided he can be made to want it, for he has demonstrated that he gets what he wants. Our mistake has been that we have tried to do business with him by offering him the ornamental when he was in the market for the useful. It may emphasize this mistake the more when we recall that modern markets have advanced faster selling brains than feelings.[110]

The architect–owner relationship

The relationship that obtained at the turn of the century between owners and their architects, between architects and their clients, was defined in a big part, but not in sum, by their pecuniary ties. Fees were an ongoing preoccupation of American architects due to the AIA's adoption of an inadequate fee structure based upon a misconstrual of European practices. Even if flawed in their favor, owners still had every reason to question the arrangement, since it serendipitously rewarded architects for their failures to constrain construction costs. Yet, *The Handbook* insisted that the owner "owes duties to the Architect other than the payment of bills" and that the architect's fundamental posture in relation to the other actors was an ethical one "of trust and confidence."¹¹¹ In order to cement their professional status and ostensibly to bolster public trust and confidence, the AIA promulgated a set of principles of professional practice and adopted a canon of ethics. Meant both to compel members' compliance and to mold clients' expectations, these documents institutionalized norms of behavior more akin to an age of chivalry than a teaming age of business enterprise. At the same time, *The Handbook* and other sources sought to remind profit mavens of their civic duty as patrons of the architect's art.

The architect's status

In an effort to position architecture as an ethically based service profession, *The Handbook* sought to shape public perceptions by appeal to the better-known fields of medicine and law:

> [The Architect's] relation to the Owner bears some likeness to that of the physician to his patient or of the attorney-at-law to his client; each is chosen because he is assumed to possess skill and ability in his calling .... Just as the physician should refuse, even at the patient's solicitation, to treat his case in a manner medically unsound, or as the lawyer should refuse to bring or defend an action under conditions repellent to the moral sense, so the Architect should refuse to lend himself to the erection of an unsafe, unsanitary, inconvenient, or unsightly structure. Such an obligation may, under certain conditions, require him to give up his employment.[112]

By both design and default, architects were ethically entangled with their clients at multiple junctures of intersecting and competing interest in an arena increasingly shaped by conflicts over the bottom line. As *The Handbook* explained, the architect's representative function shifted over the course of any project from that of owner's adviser to owner's agent to arbitrator and judge in owner-and-builder disputes. In each instance, architects rendered services and verdicts based upon representational instruments of their own device. Thus, while architects' drawings and specifications ostensibly served as objective intermediaries in negotiating owner-and-builder agreements, architects' interpretations of them when rendered in their mediator role were subject to suspicions from both sides. Whose interests were truly being served?[113] Architects' assertions that their unique expertise and professional ethos were elastic enough to ensure performance of all these roles without any taint of self-interest stretched thin owners' and builders' credulity and only eroded architects' project authority.

Architects may have owed their livelihoods to owners, but *The Handbook* declared that their loftiest ethical obligation was to the art and science of architecture, to each other and to themselves: "As a master of his own art and of the arts and sciences allied to it, the Architect owes to them and to himself an obligation not to violate their canons."[114] Since its founding in 1857, the AIA's implicit code of conduct had been the moral code of a gentleman as applied to art, science, and business, a high ideal that separated the organization's members from all disreputable pretenders to the name. Subsequently, a shared Schedule of Charges had established a common fee discipline among architects as "usual and proper" on the principle that commissions should be granted by an owner solely on consideration of professional merits for the job rather than on the basis of competitive cost. In 1894, the AIA's annual convention adopted a resolution meant to reinforce architects' fee solidarity, "That the practice of soliciting patronage, by furnishing sketches for work under terms other than as provided for in the adopted Schedule of Charges, is considered as unprofessional."[115] The following year, the Board of Directors reported:

> At no time in the history of the Institute has the question of the ethics of the profession been as frequently and so constantly under consideration and discussion, as during the last year. Your Board does not therefore feel that the standard of professional practice has been deteriorating and that unprofessional conduct is more in evidence than formerly, but rather that higher ideals have obtained, and lapses from professional conduct excite more notice and more opposition. Still they feel that unless checked the competition for business among the vast and increasing number of architects will lead to a constant adoption of those ... unprofessional methods, which would be condemned if they were practiced by lawyers, physicians or clergymen.[116]

The manner by which architects solicited commissions, provided gratuitous services by participation in competitions, advertised, or accepted favors from contractors or suppliers was among the topics of perennial concern for those anxious to elevate the principles and thereby the public standing of the profession. The Boston Society of Architects gave early attention to the adoption of a locally applicable code of ethics for its membership, and other AIA chapters gradually followed suit.[117] Partially in an effort to bring uniformity to the locally variable ethical codes, the AIA adopted its first nationally applicable Canon of Ethics in 1909 during the presidency of architect Cass Gilbert. In his charge and challenge to the convention on the topic, Gilbert called for "an ethical code so broad that it will cover all right conduct." He warned against "the hasty adoption of a narrow code which would place the technical stigma of 'unprofessional conduct' upon honorable practitioners .... Let us sternly rebuke those forms of practice which infringe on moral right, which place selfish interest above the general good, or tend to lessen the dignity or lower the tone of the profession." Gilbert reasserted the gentleman's creed in reminding his colleague architects that "it is character, not codes" that should govern an individual's most important personal and professional relationships.[118]

The code adopted in 1909 included twelve ethical canons, three of which limited the manner in which architects could engage with builders and building trades. After centuries of productive ambiguity that had fostered overlapping operational boundaries, the AIA code of ethics was definitive in its functional separation of architecture and building, declaring that it was unprofessional for an architect "to engage directly or indirectly in any of the building trades."[119] While this prohibition was meant on one level to reassure owners that their architects shared no financial interests with builders that could compromise either quality or cost, it also asserted a professional, territorial jurisdiction over design.

In earlier days before widespread professional licensure, use of the title of "architect" was unregulated by law. A full spectrum of mechanics, builders, and engineers could assert their operative right to the title as easily as could those claiming special privilege by virtue of prior education, training, or practice—or membership in the AIA. The incremental process, initiated by Illinois in 1897, of enacting uniform registration laws for architects grew as an extension of states' constitutionally granted authority for safeguarding public safety. While the AIA had been officially ambivalent about registration laws over intervening years, following the First World War and aligning with other reformist attitudes, it moved in 1919 to encourage advocacy among its state components for the adoption of such laws.[120] To aid in this effort, an AIA committee drafted a model code intended to promote uniformity of interstate standards.[121] As an exclusive professional organization, AIA members had laid a special *moral* claim upon the title "architect" based upon gentlemanly accords on matters such as fees and ethical competition. The enactment of state registration laws defined a process for validating an exclusive *legal* claim based upon the satisfaction of certain minimum standards of competence. Establishing legal claim to the title of architect was not the same, however, as a prohibiting practice of architecture under another name.[122] The AIA could only condemn as "unprofessional" the practices of those competing commercial interests such as building companies and designing builders that performed their same functions but with salaried architect-designers employed in-house. At the same time, as a matter of professional ethics, AIA architects prohibited themselves from building.

The balance of the dozen ethical canons, nine in number, essentially dealt with the manner by which architects interacted with each other in their competition for clients and commissions.[123] Four of these dealt specifically with the mechanism of the formal architectural competition where used by owners as a means of selecting an architect. Aspects of the AIA's "circular of advice" on the conduct of competitions, previously discussed, were deemed to be of such significant import in upholding professional integrity that they were elevated to the level of ethical canon. This included prohibitions against participation in non-sanctioned competitions and any efforts to influence competition outcomes. Four additional canons set "golden rules" for the profession by specifying the manner in which architects competed among themselves. They should neither speak ill of another architect, undercut another's efforts in seeking work, nor compete for a commission solely on the basis of professional charges.

Most vexing among all the dozen canons was the one prohibiting AIA members from paying for advertising. The accompanying "Principles of Professional Practice" offered only the sparest of explanations, suggesting the principle was assumed to be self-evident: "Advertising tends to lower the dignity of the profession."[124] In an age in which the profession was being challenged by commercial competition from large building companies, architects clung to an increasingly anachronistic standard adopted from Roman antiquity. Regarding the solicitation of work, Vitruvius wrote:

> Other architects go about and ask for opportunities to practice their profession; but I have been taught by my instructors that it is the proper thing to undertake a charge only after being asked, and not to ask for it; since a gentleman will blush with shame at petitioning for a thing that arouses suspicion. It is in fact those who can grant favours that are courted not those that receive them. What are we to think must be the suspicions of a man who is asked to allow his private means to be expended in order to please a petitioner? Must he not believe that the thing is to be done for profit and advantage of that individual?[125]

In considering some of architects' more subtle forms of self-promotion, Tom Thumtack, for one, was of the humorous opinion that the AIA's "cannon" was "on too fine a trigger" (Figure 3.9). A well-placed article in the real estate section of the newspaper or the practice of importuning contractors to purchase illustrated advertisements in trade publications were common stratagems for circumventing the spirit if not the letter of the ethical rule. Among other insidious practices, Tom Thumtack pointed to architects' incessant and unseemly social climbing, wondering why "cultivating people for ends ulterior to friendship is not condemned like advertising." He asked:

> Is it not possible that the sin of their advertising is condonable …? Is it not true that the days when advertising was taboo were the days before the star appeared in moving-pictures, before the lawyer learned his law in terms of business and before the doctor used the motor? Is it not true that the faster pace of modern business requires a readier channel between [the buyer and the seller], between the client and the architect?[126]

In the face of broad public misunderstanding about the purpose and practice of architects, Tom Thumtack proposed, in answer the AIA's advertising

FIGURE 3.9 Rockwell Kent, "*Advertising: Reports from the Canon of Ethics,*" Architec-tonics: The Tales of Tom Thumtack, Architect *(New York: Comstock, 1914).*

prohibition, to "provide … for the canon this new ammunition. 'It is professional to *educate*.'"

When Frank Miles Day invoked Vitruvian authority on the solicitation of services in an early draft of *The Handbook*, he unleashed a torrent of reviewers' objections.[127] The views about the sway of hidebound tradition echoed Tom Thumtack's ironic critiques and presaged an imminent if nuanced adjustment in the AIA's posture toward advertising. The need to educate the public about the value of an architect's services and the need to compete with other groups not similarly constrained by ethical rules were common arguments that could not, one correspondent offered, be "dismissed with a quotation from even so high an authority as Vitruvius."[128] This view was best articulated by Chicago architect John L. Hamilton:

As for the theory that an architect should undertake a charge only after being asked, and should not engage in solicitation or promotional work, I believe that this accounts for the ingrown timidity so frequently found among architects, and their lack of touch and understanding with the business world. I believe that the Institute should advocate and encourage what I would call, for want of a better name, "Scientific Salesmanship"— first, for the purpose of educating the public on the value of architects' services; second, for widening the horizon and acquaintance himself, and third—for the purpose of leaving him free to compete, in the most effective manner available, with the large and growing groups under various titles other than architects, who are performing the same or similar services.[129]

In his update to other committee members, Day reported, "I find a good many of our correspondents are strongly opposed to giving such prominence to the part about the solicitation of work."[130] The Vitruvian reference was accordingly eliminated from the text and matters pertaining to proper and improper solicitation were relegated to the "Circular of Ethics" in the appendices of *The Handbook*. Developments the following year led to the elimination of the canon pertaining to advertising altogether, and the AIA's Board of Directors admitted the degree to which the issue had become a bone of contention for the organization.

It is an easy step from the subject of Public Information to that of Advertising, but in such a change of subject just now it is somewhat like stepping off a wharf into a stormy sea. The waves have been beating higher and higher in recent months and the Institute has been bombarded with private and public admonitions to wake up and take cognizance of the rising storm ....
In order to survey this vexing question once again a committee was appointed which presented a report to the Board at its September meeting, and this report in substantially its original form is presented to the Convention for consideration.
The substance of this report is that advertising to excess is a question of bad taste, that it is practically impossible to define and control matters of taste by legislation and that it is better therefore to remove advertising from the list of punishable offenses and revise the Canons of Ethics accordingly.[131]

In eliminating the advertising stricture from its ethics code, the organization revised its advice to members on standards of professionalism in order to emphasize the distinction between good and bad taste in advertising practices: "Advertising of the individual, meaning self-laudatory publicity procured by the person advertised or with his consent, tends to defeat its own ends as to the individual as well as to lower the dignity of the profession, and is to be deplored."[132]

In the more than sixty years since its founding the AIA had endeavored to insulate architects from the business and labor of construction and thus to define the field as exclusively a gentlemanly profession. Toward that end, the ethical principles it confirmed in 1918 were still being observed another sixty years later when a newspaper headline announced in 1978, as if out of another era, "Architects Will End Ban on Advertising: Code of Ethics Is Revised to Allow 'Dignified' Presentation in Print, but Not on Television."[133] On this like so many other issues that embroiled the profession, architects' status-seeking efforts blinded them to their own protectionist, and often self-defeating, motives. Their aims to distinguish themselves from their intermural rivals and to elevate themselves above their erstwhile collaborators lurked behind a self-righteous if hidebound morality. *The Handbook* could thus state without any irony the sincerity of its ethical aspirations: "The Architect's position is one of trust and confidence, and it is fundamental that he should act in absolute and entire good faith throughout."[134]

The owner's duties

To garner the professional status to which *The Handbook* aspired, architects needed a species of client fully commensurate with that ideal. The difficulty, of course, was that the AIA could not very well regulate the character and motivations of owners just as it could not so easily impose its principles of practice upon the eclectic field of non-AIA members, unregistered architects, or various building agents and intermediaries. Indeed, different kinds of clients with different kinds of needs and motivations might well be served by different kinds of "architects" rather than one authoritative, theoretical type. Tom Thumtack suggested that clients could have different opinions about whether the best architect for them should be a "draft horse" or a "race horse" (Figures 3.10–3.11); but, as he further confessed, evoking the terms of the Owner–Architect Agreement:

> I'll tell you the truth, I went into architecture because I was an artist, and now I'm an architect in the sense that I'm a specially trained artist in building. I'm not a good superintendent. I superintend because I have to and that's the truth of it. If your fee would allow it I'd hire a practical Johnnie to do superintendence, and leave construction to him. But your pay wouldn't stand it.[135]

The Handbook of Architectural Practice was intended as much to indoctrinate potential clients as it was to coach inexperienced practitioners about the defining terms of owner–architect relations. *The Handbook* instructed, "Not every Owner realizes that he owes duties to the Architect other than the payment of bills. Perhaps the highest of these duties is the unwritten one of sympathetic cooperation, without which it is hardly to be

FIGURE 3.10 *Rockwell Kent, a work horse from "Temperament,"* Architecture and Building *47 (1915).*

FIGURE 3.11 *Rockwell Kent, a race horse from "Temperament,"* Architecture and Building *47 (1915).*

expected that the Architect will produce his best work or feel a sustained devotion to his client's interest."[136] That "unwritten" owner's duty was one that architects nonetheless idealized. Their relationship with owners was a form of reciprocal exchange, both material and symbolic, a *quid pro quo* of sympathy and devotion. As one architect advised, "After a choice has been made, the architect and client should have a heart-to-heart conference. A successful solution of a problem ... is only possible when the client allows his architect to see the 'inner man'."[137] Or, as another suggested, "It is through this intimate relationship of architect and client that great results have been achieved, and the client himself, in a certain way, becomes part architect in the transaction."[138]

In the late nineteenth century, popular magazines recognized the need to educate the American public about the architect's role, noting that "the common popular feeling towards the architectural profession is a feeling of distrust." This level of distrust was attributed in part to a lack of refinement in public judgment, an inability to recognize the value of art in an otherwise practical pursuit. Posing the question, "are we just to our architects," *Century Magazine* bemoaned the public's conflicting expectations of that ostensibly vital profession:

> So we ask [the architect] now to satisfy impossible desires, now to be infallible, and now to suppress himself and follow our lead. And we are so uncertain as to his right pecuniary rewards that sometimes we expect him to do without any and again believe in the likelihood of his dishonesty because he works for a commission regulated upon the cost of the building he erects.[139]

Noted architectural critic Mariana Griswold Van Rensselaer voiced similar sentiments in laying down her first and second commandments to the public: "an artist is needed for an 'unimportant' as well as for an 'important' building," and "when we set an artist to work we should let him work as freely as possible." She continued with admonitions to the American public: "You do not see that it is just as foolish to refuse professional help in building as in law or medicine, and a great deal more selfish; nor, when you ask an architect's help, do you follow and help him with half enough docility and trust." Favoring sacred values over business returns, she asked, "Is this not, in truth, the heart of the matter—loyal trust on the client's part, loyal service on the architect's?"[140] In Van Rensselaer's formulation, the price of the architect's loyal service was the client's docility and trust.

Besides these "unwritten" duties, the owner was of course obligated to fulfill the more prosaic terms enumerated in the "Standard Form of Agreement between Owner and Architect," terms *The Handbook* endeavored to explain. These included, for example, the need to clearly and frankly outline the program of requirements and the project budget, for "concealment in such a matter naturally sets up distrust of him in the Architect's mind." Providing accurate and legally valid descriptions of the project site, giving close attention to all project documentation submitted by the architect, and rendering prompt decisions on matters requiring approval were key considerations enabling the architect to act and allowing the project to progress. In addition to these proactive contractual duties, *The Handbook* warned of one important area where the owner was *never* to act: "The Owner, whether at the work or elsewhere, owes it to the Architect and the Contractor, not to give orders to the Contractor or any of his people. All orders should be given through the Architect, otherwise misunderstandings and confusion result."[141]

This principle of separation constituted the essence of the architect's agency during construction, to be an active mediator, no mere intermediary, between the owner and the builder. The drawings and specifications that comprised the contract were manifestations of both requirement and intention, but they were subject to interpretations for which the architect reserved final say—to safeguard the owner's interests against builders' claims for "extras"; to safeguard the architect's own prerogatives of artistic intent. Both assertions of the architect's authority were nonetheless contested, still subject in builders' minds to arbitration and review.

Owners and architects each could legitimately lay claim to rights of authorial origination, but their collaborative roles became increasingly competitive when circumscribed by contractual agreements, legal precedents, profit motives, and an ever-more exacting division of labor. *The Handbook of Architectural Practice,* an embodiment—in Chicago architect Charles E. Fox's apt phrase—of "the thought of the profession as crystallized into form after many discussions," conveyed the fragility of this relation. According to *The Handbook*:

> The Owner does not generally realize how difficult it will be for him and his Architect to remain on a good footing from the making of the first studies to the completion of the building and how much reasonableness, restraint, and tact both must continually exercise, if the building is to be an entire success and if they are to find themselves on terms of cordiality at its finish.[142]

Such difficulties were no doubt at the source of Tom Thumtack's less tactful if tongue-in-cheek declaration, that "Architecture would be a fine profession if it were not for the clients."[143]

The introductory section of *The Handbook* devoted to "The Architect and the Owner" was only seven pages in length, but its brevity belied the historically conditioned complexities that their relationship entailed. The social and functional disambiguation of architects from owners, of architects from builders, was impossible to ever fully realize because creative ambiguity was embedded at the core of their relations. Tensions between art and science, art and business, art and society, were motive forces propelling the art of building. While the architect's art was indeed subject to the laws of supply and demand, it still oscillated between practical problem-solving and an edifying cultural pursuit. By their design services, architects aspired to provide the kind of "constructive reasoning," by which entirely new demands might be created.[144]

CHAPTER FOUR

Architects and Builders

In the three decades spanning between the adoption of the Uniform Contract of 1888 and the drafting of the first *Handbook of Architectural Practice*, the relationship between architects and builders underwent substantial transformation. In the early contractual codification of owner and builder relations, the architect embraced the role of owner's agent and wielded substantial authority over contractors without compunction. The architect occupied a privileged position in the whole contracting process with the ability to influence owners in their invitations to bidders and then selection, and sometimes shopping, among the bids. The drawings and specifications that formed the basis of those bids were left vague for the time to be elaborated later during construction with supplementary details that served, in the architect's sole discretion, as reasonably inferable developments of the original designs. The architect could interpret the drawings and specs, accept or reject the work of the trades, direct changes and approve charges, and still assume the role of impartial umpire and judge in owner and builder disputes. Thirty years later, this status quo no longer adhered. What had changed?

Early membership in the architecture profession in this nation was drawn from ranks of both owners and builders, not from some pre-formed vocation; but beginning in the latter half of the nineteenth century, the aims and practical impacts of academizing and professionalizing efforts in the United States were to differentiate the architect from the builder class by ever closer alignment with owner-elites. Visionary, socially well-positioned, self-anointed architect-leaders strove to raise the stature and influence of the profession so that it might be counted among the essential arbiters of an increasingly nationalized building culture. These early efforts to shape a unified and exclusive public identity for "the architect" were laden, however, with unintended consequences. In pursuit of social position and influence, architects ceded ever more authority for the technical, managerial, and economic aspects of building to a new class of construction intermediary, the general contractor. The ironic effect was a gradual abdication of the very authority that the profession so painstakingly sought.

A formative chapter in this history unfolded at the turn of the twentieth century as the shifting relationship between architects and contractors became increasingly palpable. Internal debates and sounds of alarm about the rising influence of the general contracting system marked a moment in time when architects fretted about the changing shape of their profession even while acquiescing to a new order of project responsibility and control. The American Institute of Architects' (AIA) unilateral effort to modify the terms and assumptions of the uniform contract governing relations among owners, builders, and architects became a flashpoint for controversy as architects sought to ameliorate the effects of their diminished standing through the re-assertion of tradition-bound prerogatives. Contractors, on the other hand, emboldened by organizational solidarity and empowered by alignment with business-oriented clients' economic interests responded by directly challenging architects' presumptive authority as impartial and final arbiters of all contractual disputes. When it was published in 1920, *The Handbook of Architectural Practice* incorporated this history; it distilled a century of conflict and collective experience into standardized contractual instruments, best practices of professional procedure, and a compendium of administrative forms.

Card games and boxing matches

One of Tom Thumtack's earliest essays laid out a satirical but telling account of the dynamics joining architects and builders. Focusing upon a central player in the drama of any architectural project, the story entitled "Contractors" brought to the fore the architect's chief antagonist in their competition for the favor of the client (Figure 4.1). While each rival entered separately into a direct contract with the client, the two were indirectly bound to each other in a triangular relationship meant to achieve the owner's goal. Tom Thumtack, wizened by experience, likened the architect's and contractor's early relationship during the bidding process to a card game (Figure 4.2). The contractor was a gambler in a sea of uncertainty and risk, armed with a little bit of skill and a whole lot of bluff; yet, in this phase of the relationship, the architect held cards close to chest while waiting for the contractor to reveal a bid.

> [The contractor's] mind is the melting-pot for weather, human nature, estimating, strikes, prices, panics, tariffs, floods, wrecks, owners, architects, banks, delays, materials, subs, plans and past performances. From this melting-pot he pours his final figures and each melting-pot

FIGURE 4.1 *Rockwell Kent, the client at ringside from "Contractors,"* Architec-tonics: The Tales of Tom Thumtack, Architect *(New York: Comstock, 1914).*

FIGURE 4.2 *Rockwell Kent, the card game from "Contractors,"* Architec-tonics: The Tales of Tom Thumtack, Architect *(New York: Comstock, 1914).*

pours different figures, while Tom Thumtack sits back and hides his cards behind his fingers and only bets after his opponent has spread his cards, face-up, upon the table. No melting-pot for Tom. To him figures talk and he knows every bidder's figures. Tom knows them all and each contractor knows only his own and isn't very sure of those. It is a melting-pot against a stacked deck and who do you think should win?[1]

The architect's seeming advantage over the contractor in the poker game of the bidding process shifted to the competitive arena of the boxing match during construction when the builder held the distinct advantage (Figure 4.3). The real competition was the battle for "extras"—the contentious terrain that lay between the contractor's guesswork of a bid and the architect's vagueness of design specificity. As Tom Thumtack explained, "Some [contractors] are fighters and some are cajolers and some are only crooks. Their strength lies in the fact that neither of their adversaries, architect or owner knows a thing about the 'costs'." When it comes to cost, Thumtack maintained, contractors never contract, they only expand.[2]

The matrix of social transactions governing design and building practice has historically been portrayed in terms of the distinct motivations of a cast

FIGURE 4.3 *Rockwell Kent, "Contractors,"* Architec-tonics: The Tales of Tom Thumtack, Architect *(New York: Comstock, 1914).*

of three emblematic actors: owner, architect, and builder. Yet, as has been previously suggested—first, in consideration of the relationship between owners and builders and then that between architects and owners—the architect's distinct mediating role and intermediary functions only gradually emerged. Over the course of the nineteenth century, the architect's close association with and affinity for the builder were as likely to apply as their position as the owner's advisor or agent. Indeed, a spectrum of hybrid arrangements pertained, and the architect's orientations continually shifted in response to the pressing demands of the day.

Besides working with clients to develop design proposals, architects typically engaged and hired the various trades directly and supervised them on their clients' behalfs. Within each trade, the individual workers were employed by an organizing chief who assembled their labor in order to enter into contracts with clients, through the intercession of the architect, for services on a job-by-job basis. Within this scenario, the architect was able to maintain contact and familiarity with the trade laborers actually performing the work, whether engaging them directly or through an intermediary—the employing contractor, a designated foreman, or a recognized master of the trade.[3] Projects were initiated with scant detailed description beyond basic plans and elevations, while further detailed elaborations were supplied by the architect to the builders as needed for more precise guidance.

This orderly narrative is not meant to suggest, however, that such close proximity always bred harmony or that construction sites were idyllic and conflict free. One trade journal account from the late nineteenth century illustrated in dramatic fashion some of the tensions that underlay the architect–builder relationship. As reported from Keokuk, Iowa with the headline "An Architect's Death by Violence," we learn of "a criminal case of a great deal of interest to superintending architects":

> The State charged C. A. Calhoun, a building contractor, with manslaughter of an architect, A. Lourie, in causing his death by pushing him off the first story of a building, which he was superintending, into the cellar, whereby his neck was dislocated, producing incomplete paralysis, resulting in death in five months after the injury. The contractor had threatened to throw the architect off the building if he persisted in asserting that certain of the window-frames were not plumb.[4]

The system of direct engagement with the trades ostensibly afforded the architect and the client thereby served greater construction oversight, material selectivity, and creative control. It also cast the architect in a potentially conflictive position in the hiring role, subject to contractors' perceptions and accusations of unfairness in making selections among competitive bidders. With privileged knowledge of each trade contractor's respective bid, an unscrupulous architect could shop for lower bids among familiar or favorite contractors, could exact kickbacks for the favor of a contractual award, and could surreptitiously manipulate assumptions about material specifications. How commonly such abuse of authority was exercised is difficult to surmise. It certainly comprises a significant theme of discourse in trade and architectural journals of the late-nineteenth and early-twentieth centuries.[5] The professional ill-repute and untrustworthiness of architects vied with that of builders as a prominent public concern. Indeed, some opinions held that the very function of the architect was dictated by the client's need for a detective at the construction site, a spy to keep constant watch over the builder's ploys to circumvent quality whether through shoddy construction or the supply of inferior material. Likewise, it was recognized that the client's spy, the architect, could be susceptible to corruption as well.[6]

Over intervening decades, such concerns provided stimulus for the establishment of both self-policing professional standards and advocacy for state-legislated qualifying exams. While an elite faction of the profession might uphold a code of honor as defined by its gentlemanly status, or another an aspiration to the ideal of architecture as art, the motivation for profit-making within a booming post-Civil War business climate was an undeniable factor within the spectrum of vocational orientations comprising the field. As acknowledged by the Chicago Architects' Business Association in the early twentieth century, "unless the entire tone and character of the architectural profession can be advanced, it is useless for the individual to attempt to stem the tide of the general public disregard, in some cases almost contempt for the integrity and real worth of the profession."[7]

It was the builders, however, who first advocated regularizing the terms of their contractual engagement with owners when they called upon architects to parley with them as interlocutors on owners' behalfs. As one architect recounted:

> Several years ago the question of contract relationship came up between contractors and architects; darkened clouds appeared, only to be brushed away when this Institute appointed a committee on uniform contract to meet with a like committee of the National Association of Builders. It was not without misgivings on our part, that we feared little would come of it. The result was they met us half way, and after a few years of work and revisions, etc., it proved very successful.[8]

It was especially successful from architects' point of view since they were able to formalize for themselves a role and set of functions that had previously been ad hoc and variable. In the first four clauses of the relatively compact sixteen-clause contract, architects positioned themselves as essential agents of the owner's contractual interests even while asserting the absolute authority of their own avowedly impartial judgment. As stated in the second clause of that contract:

Should it appear that the work hereby intended to be done, or any of the matters relative there to, are not sufficiently detailed or explained on the said drawings, or in the said specifications, the Contractor shall apply to the Architect for such further drawings or explanations as may be necessary, and shall conform to the same as part of this contract, so far as they may be consistent with original drawings, and in the event of any doubt or question arising respecting the true meaning of the drawings or specifications, reference shall be made to the Architect, whose decision thereon, being just and impartial, shall be final and conclusive. It is mutually understood and agreed that all drawings, plans and specifications are to remain the property of the Architect.[9]

Architects at once absolved themselves of errors or omissions, uncertainty and risk. They contractually positioned themselves as the ultimate arbiters of quality irrespective of any potential ambiguities in their instruments of service, the drawings and specs. The fact that builders freely or at least grudgingly entered into such contracts meant that when challenged in court these high-handed terms tended to carry the force of law to the general advantage of owners against the builders. Builders had succeeded, nonetheless, in drawing architects as owners' agents into negotiations with them as an organized body on a coequal basis. Just by contractually formalizing certain practices of received custom, builders were able to mark those conventions in time and in light of prevailing conditions. While architects may have seen the Uniform Contract as affirmation and fulfillment of an elevated professional status, builders understood it instead as the framework of an ongoing process, subject to renegotiation as changing conditions and emerging opportunities might require.

General contractors

As the scope and complexity of building projects intensified in the period of economic and commercial expansion following the conclusion of the Civil War, the practical ability of architects to manage their intermediary role as hiring agent and superintendent of the various trades was under increasing stress. To adequately fulfill this traditional role would require the architect to increase the number of construction-oriented staff to meet the growing demand of day-to-day inquiries and inspections; yet, the commonly accepted fee structure for architectural services based upon percentage of construction cost was deemed inadequate to cover costs of this increasingly time-intensive service. Into this widening managerial gap entered a new kind of construction intermediary, functionally serving the roles previously played by the architect as gatherer and organizer of the trades—the general contractor.[10]

The general contractor might be an experienced builder, for example, a carpentry or masonry contractor already accustomed to a primary role as coordinator of subsidiary trades within the scope of the larger work; on the other hand, the general contractor might be more of a business agent lacking deep construction knowledge or experience but instead possessed of keen instincts for brokering the deal. Where the architect had customarily negotiated multiple contractual arrangements with individual trade contractors on behalf of the client, the emergent system placed the general contractor in that pivotal role with the trades, with all its opportunities for increased organizational efficiencies as well as more determined exploitation of labor.

While this new arrangement relieved the architect of the burden of some of those ever-expanding responsibilities, the net effect was a far more profound shift in the structure of the architect's professional service. On the one hand, the architect was distanced from the newly denominated "sub-contractors" through intervention of the general contractor. On the other hand, the architect's exclusive relationship with the client was, in relative terms, demoted as well by the effective elevation of the general contractor to the level of the client's prime contracting agent, a much more powerful role than any prior sub-contracting trade had enjoyed. As architects came to realize, the overhead and profit that constituted the general contracting fee were an income stream they had now denied themselves. At the same time, the new contracting system required ever more work on their parts to produce sets of increasingly detailed drawings and specifications in advance of the construction phase as the basis for more exacting competitive bids.

By the turn of the century, architects' doubts about the larger impact of the system of general contracting began to fester. Journal essays appeared with titles such as "The Necessity for Abolishing General Contracting," "General Contracting a Menace to Architects," or "The Place of the General Contractor." As one essayist observed, "The architect appreciates that in some ways the intervention of a general contractor will save some work in looking after details, but a reasonable examination should convince even the most prejudiced that there are many evils in the system affecting owner, producer and architect." Among the enumerated evils were the direct and indirect costs that the general contractor passed along to the owner as well as the general contractor's increased power to squeeze the bid prices of sub-contractors and to force onto their shoulders the bulk of accumulated risk.[11] As one journal editorialist fretted:

> Should the system of general contracting prevail, there seems to be nothing to hinder it going one step farther. ... [Just] as the tradesmen are under the system simply workmen for the general contractor, when the general contract system is fully matured the general contractor will be employing the architects practically as draftsmen, or doing their portion of the work without them altogether. The general contractor would

hardly be blamable, as he would simply be following out and perfecting a system encouraged and facilitated by the architect, and which without interference will run its natural course.[12]

Noted Chicago architect Dankmar Adler recognized the value of competent and highly organized general contractors but bemoaned as "nuisances" those other sorts he deemed "adventurers who, being themselves without any of the essential facilities for the erection buildings, are compelled to employ subcontractors for the execution of every part of the work which they have undertaken to perform." At the same time, he outlined the nagging problems of the construction enterprise that led business-oriented clients to embrace the general contractor as a means to control price, schedule, and the innumerable conflicts to which uncoordinated trades were prone. Adler admitted, "There are many great undertakings which must be carried to completion under great difficulties and in very quick time, and under conditions which demand ... a strictness of accountability and a degree of personal responsibility which ... are difficult to attain by any other means than the intervention of a general contractor."[13] Adler challenged his own profession to imagine a compelling alternative nonetheless, where architects might again be in charge.

> Suppose an architect were to arise with courage enough to say to his client, "... I am ready to extend my guarantee from that of quality to one of total cost and time of completion of building, provided that I am sufficiently remunerated for the assumption of this risk, and I will take suitable measures for satisfying you as to the value of this my guarantee." The same policy which leads the owner of a building to concentrate the responsibilities of the many minor contractors upon one general contractor would lead him also to eliminate the general contractor, and to concentrate all the responsibilities in the person of a properly remunerated architect. But before this can be done, architects must become good organizers and good executive officers, and must learn to exercise a command over the details of construction of buildings, and acquire a mastery of problems of finance, which at the present day are not considered among the prominent characteristics of the average architect.[14]

Ironically, it was a trade contractor—one familiar with the abuses that general contractors could exact upon the laboring classes in extracting the lowest bid—who appealed to architects as allies of labor. Echoing architect Adler's challenge, this contractor pleaded his case, "That the architect increase his functions to include those exercised by the general contractor, and adjust his scale of commissions to include this extra service, adding to his establishment a department of superintendence, supervision and control in the hands of a man or men properly qualified for this work."[15]

Over the intervening decade, the profession swung back-and-forth like a pendulum between attitudes of victimhood and resolve in the face of the challenges of general contracting and competitive bidding. There was recognition, for example, that the old system of multiple contracts by which the architect separately engaged and coordinated the trades was most appropriate for smaller buildings like residences where architects could remain in direct contact with craftspeople and closely monitor the progress of the work. Larger projects, however, called for a level of staffing, oversight, and organizational acuity greater than architects could typically provide.

> When an office building, or a large factory or warehouse, or a great flat building, is to be erected, … it is then that the general contractor appears on the scene as a mediator between architect and workman whose value is recognized. He takes the entire contract and is responsible for every detail of it. He gives ample bonds for the whole work, and shoulders the responsibility which otherwise would be divided up among two dozen or more smaller and perhaps less responsible contractors. If he is an enterprising and up-to-date contractor he employs a superintendent who is a practical engineer and who takes upon himself almost all the load of providing the proper material whenever needed; guarding against delays by keeping the several contractors moving in their regular order, one moving out of the way of another; inspecting and regulating the work from the standpoint of an engineer quite as much as of a superintendent. Such a man is valuable in smoothing over rough places in the busy architect's life and in reflecting credit on his employer, the general contractor.[16]

A special committee of the AIA was commissioned during the presidency of Frank Miles Day, 1906–07, to report to the convention on what were widely perceived to be the negative impacts upon the profession of the general contracting system. The committee, chaired by architect Cass Gilbert, summarized the conditions that had led to the rise of the general contractor and the current state of affairs: architects' retreat from responsibility—in the face of growing project complexity and in favor of their own short-sighted convenience. "At any rate," Gilbert reported, "we were willing to accept what seemed an easy way, by attempting to load the whole responsibility on one [contracting] firm. But by this the general contractor has become the arbiter of the building trades." Large building companies had been bolstered by the full confidence of their financial backers. Operating on a large scale, they were capable of squeezing material costs, dictating terms to labor, and even hiring architects as their employees. The report concluded:

> In our present judgment, there may be times when we should advocate the employment of a general contractor, but as a rule it should be the sentiment of the architects of the country *to deal with the men that do the work* (applause) and that so far as possible, we should induce our clients

to revert to the old system of letting special contracts for each important branch of their work and particularly advise them that contingencies may arise which we cannot foresee, but ask them to charge the contingent fund against the five to fifteen per cent profit that will be charged by a general contractor or broker and let them pay a portion of the balance to the architect for his additional services.[17]

A resolution was unanimously passed by the convention and distributed in print along with a copy of the full committee report to the entire AIA membership. It put the organization on record that the general contracting system "is one which menaces the entire architectural profession and, if carried to its logical conclusion, would make impossible 'the honorable practice of architecture.'"[18] Not all architects were quite so certain of the threat, however. One responded directly to the committee's printed report by suggesting that architects were being unprogressive in not recognizing and meeting the new corporate realities of owners and contractors alike.[19] Another architect also demurred from the broadening consensus and urged consideration from the standpoint of the general contractor, warning colleagues that the contractual authority vested in the architect was subject to abuse, and that:

> Quite too often, in his zeal to protect the owner under all contingencies, [the architect] forgets that contractors also have rights which are no less important, and draws up specifications and contracts so one-sided that responsible bidders either refuse to figure at all, or add such a margin, to protect themselves, as brings the cost far above the owner's expectation or the architect's estimate …. The disposition to over-reach the contractor [can be] so manifest as to create a feeling of mistrust not only as to the plans themselves, but the architect who made them.[20]

Despite such diverse and reflective attitudes among individual architects, the official organs of the profession set out to reclaim the very mastery of the construction site it had inadvertently conceded to general contractors. To return to Tom Thumtack's mixed gambling tropes, of the card game and the squared circle, a new match was to be wagered, this time in the contractual arena. Architects tried to stack the decks with unilateral revisions to the Uniform Contract. General contractors replied with loaded gloves and some counter-punches of their own.

Architect as owner's agent

As judged by its widespread use in the construction industry, the Uniform Contract had maintained its popularity as the standard form of agreement between owners and contractors since its adoption in 1888.[21] Over years of use, the terms of the Uniform Contract remained largely intact, though minor refinements in the text were occasionally implemented upon agreement of architects' and builders' respective organizations. In 1901, a joint committee was convened with the National Association of Builders to make a more thorough review, and in the following year the AIA's Committee on Contracts and Liens reported several proposed changes and simplifications, the most notable of which was elimination of the clause designating the architect as the owner's agent.[22] While the committee offered no explanation of what had precipitated this change, we can gather from contemporary sources the sort of conflicts that architects' unchecked exercise of their agency authority had caused.

In his treatise on construction law published in the preceding decade, architect and legal scholar T.M. Clark had observed:

> The questions of how far the architect is an agent for the owner, and is empowered to bind him by his actions or decisions, is one of extreme importance to the profession. The ordinary contract between owners and builders leaves this point somewhat indefinite, and architects, particularly the young and zealous ones, frequently get into trouble through not knowing how far they are entitled to help their employer without his consent.[23]

The mere deletion of the agency designation from the language of the Uniform Contract did not put the issue to rest. Where architects were most apt to encounter difficulties was in ordering on-site alterations without the contractor's full agreement about whether the changes would constitute contract "extras," or extra charges; and in case they did, without first obtaining the owner's authorization for the increase in price—which by the way might also accrue to the architect's advantage through an increased fee.

Again under the presidency of Frank Miles Day, the AIA initiated a concerted effort in 1906—on its own this time, without participation from builders—to revise the owner and contractor agreement, ostensibly to update the general conditions of the contract and to integrate and standardize the AIA's suite of bid-related forms. While the Uniform Contract was still widely used, it was also being regularly amended to suit local customs and architects' preferences about administering their project authority. Finding a "wide divergence of practice" across the nation with regard to the contract's general conditions, the committee's high-minded aim was to establish "a code of Practice covering the letting and administration of contracts which will, in marked distinction from the chaotic illogical system of the past, tend to place the relations of Architect, of Owner and of Contractor on a sounder as well as a higher basis and at least in that sense be 'standard.'"[24]

The committee developed editorial methods that foreshadowed Day's approach a decade later when he would tackle the much larger task of organizing the *Handbook of Architectural Practice*.

> After obtaining from some twenty-five of the leading architects throughout the country, copies of their General Clauses and contract forms, the Committee held a meeting in New York and adopted a tentative arrangement or index covering all the subject matter contained in the various specifications submitted, and Mr. Pond of Chicago very generously undertook the laborious task of collating, copying and arranging this material in accordance therewith. This resulted in a volume containing some hundreds of clauses, and at a subsequent session of the Committee also held in New York early last Summer, a plan of elimination and a general constructive principle was adopted.[25]

Where the Uniform Contract of 1888 had contained only sixteen clauses, the committee's four-year effort yielded, after continual sifting and multiple revisions, a new set of general conditions that numbered sixty-three.

In circulating its drafts of the standardized documents seeking members' feedback, the committee broached some unresolved issues that had for years stoked uncertainty and doubt. One issue in which all participants had a stake was determination of both the nature and limits of the architect's role as the owner's agent. The committee solicited members' opinions about what the AIA's official position should be on "this matter of Agency" as well any information about how local customs might apply:

> From the outset of the Committee's work it has been confronted with the question as to whether the Architect was or was not to be construed as the Agent of the Owner. Of course his status would be clearly determined in any form of contract, were such a contract made between the Owner and the Architect, but at present a very large majority of work is done simply on the basis of the Institute Schedule of Practice and Charges or private schedules in which no definition occurs of the Architect's legal status in this respect. It appears that in ordinary practice he becomes the agent at special times and occasions by special authorization from the Owner, and at other times acts simply as counselor, but it is probable that he is regarded by the generality of contractors as the Owner's agent and his orders are carried out on that understanding.[26]

Correspondence between then committee member Frank Miles Day and prominent Boston architect Robert D. Andrews (1857–1928) sheds light on the controversy surrounding the architect's role as owner's agent.[27] Among the unreconciled structural paradoxes of architectural practice of the era, architects were presumed to act on the one hand as agent in the interest of the owner and on the other hand as impartial judge of the owner's contract disputes with the contractor. This duality constituted a conflict of interest in which architects might act as judges of their own actions, whether taken on their own or their owners' behalfs Despite decades of precedent in which this paradox had ruled, Andrews declared his "very definite conviction that it is in the highest degree impolitic for the profession to allow itself to be forced into a position where the impartiality of an architect's decisions may be questioned." He summarized his own firm's alternative approach to serving the client, in the first instance, not as agent but as professional advisor; and then, in administering the contract, not as agent but as impartial judge.

> I assume that the architect's position after the signing of a [construction] contract is essentially different from his position before the contract is signed. In the latter case the architect is a professional advisor, working confessedly in the interest of the owner who employs him, simply because there is no one else whose interest is involved, unless it be his own. The architect is not then the owner's agent, but his advisor, and he renders his advice through the medium of drawings and written descriptions. A scheme having been approved, and the drawings and specifications completed, the architect conducts the business of receiving figures as preliminary to a contract. When the contract is signed, and the architect named therein as the judicial interpreter of its conditions, he becomes bound by the terms of the contract to act as a neutral without inclining to the interest of either party. The fact that his payment for this service comes through the hands of the owner in no way invalidates this conclusion, inasmuch as the monetary arrangement between the owner and contractor is one which serves to adjust and distribute upon both parties the compensation the architect receives.[28]

Andrews's analysis is insightful even if his suggested remedy, the elimination of the concept of agency from the rubric of contractual relationships, did not fully relieve architects of ethical dilemmas, for example, when confronting the potential remediating costs of their own oversights or omissions. He himself admitted:

> It does sometimes happen that in non-essential matters of construction we arrange with the contractor to balance an increased expense here by a lessened expense there, but this is only done without the owner's knowledge and approval when the modifications are of such minor character that they fall under the head of interpretations of the contract rather than of changes in it.[29]

Such undocumented changes, hinging upon architects' interpretations of what was "minor" or "non-essential," were exactly the kinds of contractual judgments that a builder might dispute.[30]

It was thus very much in contractors' interest that architects *should* be identified as agents of owners, so that owners could be held to account financially for the actions of their architect-agents. Andrews reached this same conclusion when conferring with William H. Sayward of the Boston

Master Builders Association. Sayward, who had been present at the drafting of the original Uniform Contract in 1888, conveyed builders' strong support for including the agency clause in the construction contract:

> The builder's reason for wanting that clause in the contract was that it makes his position much safer. The architect having supervision of the work, and therefore knowing what goes on, by his failure to interrupt any work or to condemn it, is virtually giving the owner's sanction to it, if the architect is the recognized and credited agent of the owner. This applies equally well to work done outside the contract terms as to that within those terms. The builder, therefore, simply has to say that the architect tacitly sanctioned what he was doing, in order to establish his claim to payment. It is then up to the architect to show that the owner instructed him to incur the extra work in question. In other words, if the clause "acting as agent for the owner" stays in the contract all the risk and hazard of the situation is thrown by the builder upon the architect and owner conjointly, and they must wrangle the matter out.[31]

Lacking either consistent methods or administrative tools for ordering project changes and documenting owners' approvals, architects could quickly find themselves with roles reversed, no longer in the position of deciding judges but as defendants among the ranks of the accused. Builders recognized the agency clause less as an emblem of architects' authority than as a chink in owners' contractual armor. As Andrews intimated in his letter to Day, "I think the builders have shown more shrewdness than the architects in this matter, and I think it is high time that we free ourselves from the noose which they have thrown around our necks."[32]

Besides Andrews's opinions on the matter, the Committee on Contracts and Specifications reported receiving responses to its queries on the status of the architect as owner's agent from a majority of AIA's component chapters. From these, the committee reached a rather equivocal conclusion:

> It appears that the custom is widespread of regarding the architect as the owner's agent; on the other hand, a strong minority holds that he should not be regarded as the agent, and advances good reasons for that opinion. The Committee, inclining to this latter opinion, has drafted an Article ... expressing it, but believes that the whole question is one on which further legal opinions may be valuable, the decisions of the Courts being various and the practice in the past by no means uniform.[33]

Article 40 of the first standard edition of the General Conditions of the Contract published in 1911 thus advanced a much circumscribed concept of limited agency while reaffirming the architect's key interpretive role. It stated: "The parties to the Contract recognize the Architect as the interpreter of the Contract Documents, and in that capacity he is to define their true intent and meaning. He is not the agent of the Owner except in structural emergencies ... and except when in special instances he is authorized by the Owner to act."[34] This stipulation in the newly standardized form was just one example of how the revised set of general conditions reflected the proprietary views of the architecture profession filtered through the lens of the AIA.

Neither builders nor any of their representative organizations had been invited by architects to collaborate in drafting the new contractual forms, an inversion of the situation in the 1880s when builders initiated the contract-drafting effort that culminated in publication of the Uniform Contract. This perceived slight along with justifiable claims of embedded biases evoked a hue and cry from builders and a very public rejection of the new contractual forms. Builders' complaints about architects' high-handed tactics had been mounting over the years since the first adoption of the Uniform Contract. The criticisms, shared privately among like-minds at local builders' exchanges, became increasingly public when expressed on the pages of construction industry journals and at the annual meetings of their national trade employers' associations. The bill of particulars highlighted several clusters of concerns revolving around conduct of the bidding process, the administration of the contract for construction, and the relationship between general contractors and subcontractors. These three realms of concern all converged at the boundary of the architect's responsibilities under the terms of the contract for construction. Foremost among these was the architect's role as both creator and interpreter of the instruments of service, the working drawings and specifications. To be sure, architects shared many of the same concerns but from a very different perspective.

When William Sayward had argued previously for the explicit designation of the architect as the owner's agent, his aim was to tag the owner with responsibility for the architect's instructions as given on the owner's behalf. What Sayward recognized then, he reiterated two decades later as he summarized the structural paradox of the architect's dual authority as both owner's agent and contract interpreter:

> It is true that in carrying on building work under the conditions described it has constantly been insisted that the architect may also assume the function of a judge, and act as an unprejudiced referee upon disputed points; but, as a matter of fact, this purpose, however sincere, defeats itself, for under such a rule the architect is called upon for a service which only a superman could fully render. The differences which arrive at the stage of dispute are almost invariably based upon interpretations of the instruments which the architect himself is responsible for, and, as in the practice of law a judge is not considered acceptable in a case where he is personally interested or to which he is intimately related, so in disputes arising out of building work it is equally inappropriate that the architect be placed in the position of absolute arbiter on all points arising

in the carrying out of work based upon his own design. But the practice has been in vogue for many a year, and out of it has grown this wholly undesirable and in most cases unjustifiable feeling that the architect in his decisions leans perceptibly in favor of the employer, that is, the owner.[35]

Sayward's view, as one long engaged in the organization of contractors, was that "the only way in which general reforms can be secured or reasonably fair conditions can be maintained is through united action."[36]

Builders organize

Grasping the role of collective organization within the building industry of the early-twentieth century is complicated by shifting frames of reference that blur definitions and perceptions—of exactly who should be considered an employer and who an employee. The simplest formulation might involve a single owner who engaged hired-hands directly, to work on that owner's behalf. This straightforward relationship was complicated, however, by continual elaborations within the hierarchy of design and construction that inserted a retinue of intermediaries between owners' capital and laborers' hands. Master crafters who assembled laboring crews became trade contractors. The chief among these might be designated a primary contractor, or perhaps self-declared an architect, one who engaged other contractors on owners' behalfs With the emergence of the general contracting system, the so-called contractors were effectively demoted to the role of subcontractors, now answerable to the general contractor rather than being accountable to the owner directly or else indirectly through the architect as owner's agent.

Architects and general contractors, both, were de facto employees of their clients, whether as individuals or organizations. Some owners were also speculative builders who employed architects as staff. Meanwhile, architects' own offices were departmentalized with personnel of specialized function. Was a junior drafter in an architect's office an extension of management or a laboring stiff? While trade laborers organized into unions for the purpose of collective bargaining, trade unionism was considered antithetical to the professional ideal.[37] Labor unionized; management formed associations—to deal with labor. Such overlaps and ambiguities in the status of architectural work complicate relations among principals and staff, designers and technicians to the present day.

When the AIA (along with the Western Association of Architects) negotiated the terms of a uniform contract with the National Association of Builders in the 1880s, architects ostensibly represented the concerns of owners even while advancing their own profession-building intents. The National Association of Builders, on the other hand, as an association of master builders-cum-contractors, represented their own economic interests as employers against the demands of both the labor force and the owners by whom they were in turn employed. Construction laborers had to fend for themselves through unionizing, collective bargaining, and—as was frequently necessary—strikes.[38]

Indeed, concerted action by laborers in the building trades to assert their rights and oppose abuses was one important factor spurring the establishment of trade employers' associations in urban centers such as Chicago, New York, and Boston in the last decades of the nineteenth century.[39] Having risen from the same ranks as the laborers, master builders were not altogether lacking in empathy for the worker's plight. The effort to organize master builders on a national scale, as in the case of the National Association of Builders, was recognition of the need to reconcile the requisites of fair and decent work conditions common to each trade—issues of wages and hours, the training of new workers through apprenticeship, the right to organize, conditions of dismissal—with the variable methods and customs that pertained across different localities. According to William Sayward, "The various communities of builders in the principal cities of the country were all working in ignorance of the principles and actions of each other, and this ignorance caused frequent and disastrous discord."[40] Within an increasingly nationalized construction economy, it was felt that common standards should apply.

One approach to averting strikes that gained purchase over the course of the industrializing nineteenth century was the establishment of a contractually mandated arbitration process to hear and reconcile disputes between employers and employees. In the face of a series of debilitating bricklayer strikes in New York and Chicago in the late 1880s, the ad hoc establishment of arbitration committees, composed of equal numbers of trade employees and their contractor-employers along with an additional neutral party or umpire, had provided the means for overcoming negotiation impasses. A turn-of-the-century treatise on the topic extolled the period as "the Arbitration Age" and predicted that its application to the building industry would be as beneficial to the relations of architects, contractors, and engineers as it had proven in labor disputes.

> The bringing about of arbitration is a voluntary act on the part of disputants, who by its means select their own judges, and it becomes, when properly conducted, a speedy and inexpensive, and should be a friendly way of finally adjusting and determining almost any dispute which may arise in connection with construction work .... Arbitration must appeal to honest men, and to men who think right. It is not for the unprincipled, and men whose sole desire is to get the best of each other. It is an honest and manly way to settle an honest difference between man and man.[41]

The National Association of Builders, with Sayward as secretary, took the lead in advocating a standardized regime of construction arbitration to be adopted by the construction industry and applied nationwide. Sayward's National Association was careful to support the rights of labor to organize and to recognize the positive contributions of labor. Their aim, nonetheless, was to isolate contentious issues that applied within particular trades in an effort to avert the conflagration of sympathetic strikes by other trade unions.[42] Sayward insisted, however, that the inception of trade employers' associations was not merely a response to labor strikes but was also a means for builders to win sufficient recognition and respect from owners and architects in order to negotiate with them from a position of collective strength. As Sayward described the circumstances that then applied:

> The true relation of the builder toward the owner and architect was found to be almost invariably poorly understood, and the practices and methods prevailing were almost as many and as diverse as the number of architects and owners. The practice of one office would perhaps be entirely distinct from the practice of the nearest neighbor, while the practices of the whole as a class had become abnormally developed upon the side of the owner, the interests of the builder and contractor being as a whole substantially ignored.[43]

The early fruit of contractors' efforts to bring order out of this chaos was of course the participation of the National Association of Builders in drafting the Uniform Contract of 1888. That document gave added impetus to the standardization of the owner–builder relationship where so many parochial attitudes had applied, thus lending contractors some security against arbitrary contractual conditions. Where the architect was specifically implicated in the owner–contractor relationship, as an adjudicator of disputes between those parties by means both "just and impartial" and "final and conclusive," builders accepted the status quo but did not bend to it. They succeeded instead in gaining adoption of one contractual clause subjecting an aspect of the architect's customary administrative authority to external arbitration in cases of dispute. In the event of a contractor's disagreement with the architect's "fair and reasonable valuation of work" added to or deleted from the contract, owners were now committed to the same process that builders' associations were employing with labor union disputes. This achievement undermined the architect's traditional authority and set a precedent for future contractual challenges.

William Sayward

William Sayward's long career as an advocate for the interests of builders commenced in Boston. A builder and a contractor like his father, he was described as "a very popular public reader, possessing rare powers of imitation, combined with a good physique, strong facial expression and great dramatic force."[44] Born in 1845, he had seen the rise of the general contracting system in the post-bellum era from the perspective of a "contracting builder," a sub-contractor within the newer denomination of constructor roles. He understood firsthand the potential abuses in the "manipulation of sub-bids" by general contractors that robbed the subs of "a single dollar of profit" even while the general contractor was able to impose an overarching percentage as a coordinator's fee. "The practice," Sayward posited, "places too much temptation in the way of unprincipled men."[45]

Sayward understood the attractions that the general contracting system might hold for architects, "the greater simplicity obtained by combining the various departments of labor under one or two contractors, thus relieving [the architect] of much care and responsibility." Sayward held the view, however, "that in reality the task of the architect would be much simpler if he did not delegate any portion of his responsibility," for architects and their staff could thereby remain in much closer proximity to the craft laborers rather than working through an intermediary unknowledgeable about the particular trades. "To my mind," Sayward wrote, "there is but one method of reform for this evil, and that is to 'reform it altogether.' Each contractor for separate portions of the work should make his contract direct with the owner or supervising architect, and then there can be no question in regard to the perfect fairness of the system."[46] Sayward understood, even earlier than architects did themselves that the intercession of general contractors between labor and owner displaced architects' authority over construction as well as their proximity to and empathy for the trades.

Sayward was a relentless advocate for the establishment of local builders' exchanges, and his organizing efforts focused first in Boston and then more widely afield as secretary of the National Association of Builders. Sayward promoted the construction of centrally located meeting venues where contractors of the various trades, general contractors, and material suppliers could convene on a daily basis to compare notes and conduct business, to interact socially and build rapport. Sayward described the benefits of builders' closer association: systematization of construction practices across the nation, the establishment of uniform wages by trade, solidarity in negotiations with labor, improvement of working methods, consideration of the apprenticeship system, and establishing—with architects—some uniformity of contractual relations with owners. Builders' exchanges in cities such as Philadelphia and New York even included exhibition spaces for the display of building materials and assemblies for the benefit of the public, counterpoints and complements to the ubiquitous architectural exhibitions of the day underwritten by builders and builders' exchanges as sponsors (Figures 4.4–4.6).[47]

Sayward was an enthusiastic champion of local efforts in Boston to institutionalize arbitration as a means of reconciling disagreements and avoiding recourse to disruptive strikes and lockouts, and in his role as an

FIGURE 4.4 *Exchange Room, Master Builders Exchange, Philadelphia,* Carpentry and Building *12 (1890).*

officer of the National Association of Builders, he was a leading proponent of binding arbitration nationwide. Toward that end, he offered testimony in Washington and traveled to New York City to propose the establishment of a national arbitration network, "to substitute for old antagonisms and crude methods of attack and repulse [with] a system of arbitration through a permanent central court of settlement and appeal."[48] Further efforts to establish a truly unified national organization of trade employers and contractors were hampered, however, by the split within employers' own ranks reflective of local customs that favored either an "open shop" or "closed shop" approach to labor practices and material supply. Sayward was a strong proponent of Boston's "open shop" tradition as a model for others and argued:

> If employers abandon their distrust of unions and enter into friendly business relations with them, unions must abandon their distrust of non-union men and concede the right of their fellow workmen to join, or refrain from joining, their bodies .... By the abandonment of its attempt to coerce people into joining it opens the surest road for accession to its ranks of those who may come of their own accord, but won't be driven.[49]

New York City trade employers, on the other hand, upheld the opposite view in support of the "closed shop," a means of protecting that city's construction market from the incursion of outside and non-unionized

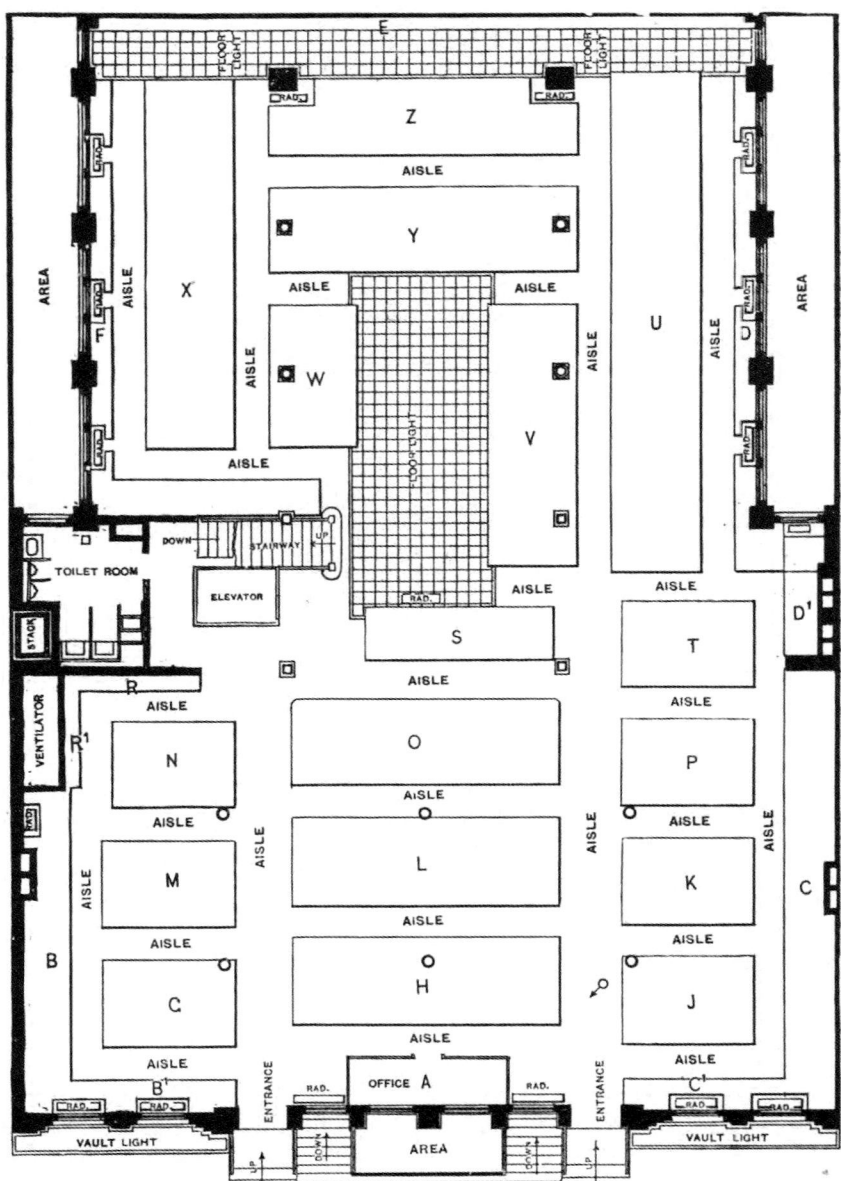

FIGURE 4.5 *Floor plan of Permanent Exhibitions Department, Master Builders Exchange, Philadelphia,* Carpentry and Building *12 (1890).*

FIGURE 4.6 *Diagrams of masonry assemblies erected to illustrate materials and workmanship, Master Builders Exchange, Philadelphia,* Carpentry and Building 12 *(1890).*

competitors. Sayward's influence, and that of the National Association of Builders, began to wane on just this point as his organization's conciliatory approach to "the establishment of more harmonious relations between employers and workmen"[50] was supplanted by a new organization's more antagonistic approach to making "a solid stand and united front against organized labor's unjust exactions and insufferable petty tyrannies."[51] The Building Trades Association of New York, formed as a builders' exchange and local offshoot of Sayward's National Association of Builders, soon repositioned itself as an employers' union, the Building Trades Employers' Association, in an effort to marshal greater collective force in its dealings with the plethora of trade-specific labor unions. Subsequent efforts to geographically broaden the movement through creation of a National Building Trades Employers' Association were splintered, however, again due to disagreements over whether the organization was to favor an open or a closed shop orientation.[52] Still, another organization emerged a few years later founded on closed shop principles, the National Association of Builders' Exchanges.⁵³ With the tide apparently turning in a more confrontational direction, Sayward's old organization—having championed cooperation with labor for twenty years—greeted the new association with apparent disdain:

> In view of the fact that a movement is on foot to create a National Association of Builders' Exchanges, which aims to control employers in the building trades by copying the methods of trades unions, this National Association [of Builders] condemns such propositions and declares that any and all attempts to establish mandatory bodies either among employers or among workmen are fundamentally wrong, and lead inevitably to oppression. Employers are urged to avoid such complications.⁵⁴

Out of this convoluted genealogy of associations, and despite any naysayers' barbs, the newest of these organizations thrived, though it too sparked confusion when it was re-christened as the (all too familiar-sounding) National Building Trades & Employers Association in 1912.⁵⁵ It was this very association which soon came to the urgent attention of the AIA and especially to those responsible for the still-fresh revisions just issued in the previous year of the AIA's suite of standardized contractual forms, the Committee on Contracts and Specifications and architect Frank Miles Day.

A "Critical Analysis"

On the surface, relations between architects and builders fostered at the local builders' exchanges remained convivial. Banquets with speeches and good cheer provided venues for the sharing of views, even on difficult topics addressing builders' concerns. At a joint meeting of the Boston Society of Architects and the local Master Builders' Association, it was reported that "the delightful freedom of the occasion was further increased as the dinner proceeded by the accompaniment of piano and cornet, and a song written for the occasion by W.H. Sayward, Jr., entitled 'Architect and Builder,' expressive of the unity of the two professions in their work and spirit." Thereafter, Sayward in the role of toastmaster introduced a speech outlining builders' dependence upon the accuracy and detail of architects' drawings, the difficulties engendered by "blanket clauses" in architects' specifications, and the need to protect the rights of sub-contractors in the general conditions of the contract. An architect delivering a response on behalf of the profession "said that he had expected something rather more 'red hot' than the remarks which had been made, but suggested that possibly builders are little too afraid of the architects. He agreed with the speakers, but would go them one better in their own cause."⁵⁶

Despite any good feelings that flowed from these social encounters, rumblings of builders' discontent began to echo in a much more public way. Frank Miles Day signaled his alarm at these new developments in a letter to Chicago architect Allen B. Pond:

> I believe Mr. Atterbury has written to you about the numerous articles antagonistic to the Institute documents which have emanated from the National Building Trades and Employers' Association and that some arrangements would have to be made for a conference with that Association. Mr. Sturgis, however, wishes our Committee to make very sure that that Association has really a national status and is composed of men with whom we ought to treat ….
>
> Judging by the articles which this Association has published, it is their desire that most of the binding force be taken out of the Institute documents and that everything, even the architect's decisions as to the quality of workmanship and materials be referred to arbitration. If we go into conferences with these gentlemen and that may after all be the best way of stopping their campaign, we will have to exercise a good deal of patience and firmness.[57]

Day wrote to other acquaintances and AIA members in various cites trying to ascertain whether the National Building Trades and Employers Association was a legitimate and truly representative organization; and "whether they are the kind of men seriously to consider their affair with us or whether they intend to use us as an aid to self-exploitation."[58] Day expressed his worries in another letter to a committee member:

> The National Building Trades and Employers' Association has vigorously attacked the standard documents of the American Institute of Architects. It has carried on a newspaper campaign with great spirit and has rallied to its support some two hundred associations of diverse character, credit men, improvements associations, builders' organizations etc. These have been caused to pass resolutions condemning the fairness of the Institute documents. So unfounded and biased were these attacks and so wide spread were they that it was thought well some time ago to consider agreeing to a conference with the Association to determine what their desires really were and to see whether without sacrificing the spirit of the documents, some changes could be made in them which would make them acceptable to the Association. It, however, appears very important to ascertain what we can about the status of the Association and report the facts thus ascertained to the Board of Directors of the Institute at its January meeting.[59]

Day's and his colleagues' concerns were not exaggerations. As reported from the builders' annual convention held in Washington, DC in 1913,

"One of the principal topics of discussion ... had to do with the 'Uniform Contract' ... and the adoption of resolutions recommending that every effort be made to have laws passed in the various states, similar to the one now in force in Pennsylvania, providing for an equitable interpretation of plans and specifications." Presumably, such provisions would nullify standard contractual assertions that the architect's interpretations of the drawings and specifications were in any way final and conclusive.[60]

Activist officers of the national builders' organization from Baltimore and Louisville mounted a publicity campaign to air their grievances in order to seize the public's support—as well as architects' attention. The deployment of a localized strategy to gain news exposure was coordinated nationally through trade journals and addressed to the builders' exchanges. For example, it was reported:

> The Builders' Exchange of Louisville made an arrangement for a page more or less in the Saturday afternoon edition of one of the local daily papers to be devoted to building subjects. This not only makes the paper in question of particular interest to all builders but it also makes it worth more as an advertising medium to the contractors and it places the building industry of the city before the public in better shape ... which helps the cause considerably.[61]

The third annual convention of the national association was held in Louisville, Kentucky, in January 1914. Another change to the group's name only added to architects' and others' confusion, however, as the National Building Trades and Employers' Association reverted to its pre-1912 appellation, the National Association of Builders' Exchanges. As was reported in the trade press, "A whirlwind business session, an enthusiastic spirit of organization and a determination to wage a persistent campaign for the betterment of conditions of contracting in the United States marked the proceedings."[62] The target of builders' unanimous contempt was the AIA-issued general conditions of the contract for construction, published in 1911, which architects had unilaterally revised and expanded.

Rabble-rousing speeches at the convention impugning the AIA's general conditions, and architectural practice in general, elicited multiple cheers from among the delegates. The newly elected president of the association, Harry L. Lewman of Louisville, excoriated the architecture profession, its feudal modus operandi and allegedly harmful practices.

> The present system employed in the preparation of contracts and specifications ... is a relic of antiquity and is an outgrowth of the practice years ago when the builder was merely a mechanic. It brings about a subserviency upon the part of the contractors, which is highly detrimental to the interests of the building business, but more important still, it greatly restricts and stifles competition. The consequences of a

system of such uncertain provisions are bound to be harmful both to the owner, the contractor and to the allied interests. Under this system, or rather lack of system, employed in construction, a specification lacking in definite description, filled at every crook and turn with arbitrary and incomprehensive clauses, is prepared and upon this the contractor is asked to make a bid. He is immediately faced with the proposition that his interests will be wholly dependent upon the manner in which the authority is exercised, and what ought to be a close, careful and accurate estimate based upon known facts, becomes a question of his estimate of the personal character and disposition of the supervising officer. In this age which has produced such effective business machines, working with marvelous precision, is it not to be regretted that we are still struggling along with such primitive methods, which are wholly inadequate for present day practice?[63]

Lewman summed up contractors' complaints by declaring, "As the lines are now drawn ... it appears that the real issue in this controversy is whether the architect shall be the final interpreter and judge without appeal of the plans and specifications which he creates for the use of commercial interests."[64]

The convention answered Lewman's charges with decisive action in resolutions passed without dissent. First, the builders approved "an analysis of the sixty-three articles of contract documents proposed by the American Institute of Architects" in 1911. Second, they issued a threat, that if representatives of the AIA did not meet with them and "agree with standard and equitable conditions," then they would proceed with publication of their analysis "with a view of giving publicity to the existing conditions in building construction and make an educational campaign against the present extremely hazardous and expensive conditions." Finally, in order to further press the urgency of their concerns and to apply additional pressure, the builders approved an alternative uniform contract for temporary use in lieu of the architect-drafted forms.[65] The new contract form, containing twenty-one articles and an additional thirty-one general conditions, replaced the architect's presumed interpretative authority over the drawings and specifications with the contractor's broadened rights of appeal to arbitration with the owner as a means of seeking redress.[66]

The architects were swift to respond. Indeed, it was reported even while the convention was still in progress that Frank Miles Day as chairman of the Committee on Contracts had sent word that the AIA's Board of Directors would meet in coming days to act upon builders' concerns.[67] Day soon had in his hands a copy of the builders' "yellow pamphlet entitled 'Critical Analysis'" laying out their complaints against the 1911 version of the AIA's general conditions of the contract. In sharing that document with other committee members, Day insisted that they "must take fully and frankly all the criticisms contained in this pamphlet, however offensive their presentation may be."[68] The Board of Directors, feeling "very indignant about the attacks of the Trades' Association," and being wary about their motives, was at first reticent to confer with the upstart builders' association. Instead, Day and other committee members reached out to William Sayward who had been familiar to them since the early days of the National Association of Builders with whom the AIA had negotiated in 1888.

Sayward and Day corresponded on the topic of the new builders' association, and Sayward, it appears, was working behind the scenes to circumvent the aggressive tactics of the (now-called) National Association of Builders' Exchanges with his own proposals—under the aegis of his old National Association of Builders—for revisions to the uniform contract. Day suggested in his reply that the two might find a meeting of minds regarding "how a stable and worthy association of builders could be brought about."[69] Besides contemplating how to thwart the influence of the more strident builders' association, Day's committee was also hearing criticisms from architects themselves about the length of the AIA's new standardized forms, albeit with continued support for underlying principles affirming the architect's authority.

Perhaps still not fully comprehending the seriousness of the builders' substantive critiques, Day suggested to his committee that "we might shorten the forms by throwing into the appendix some of the subjects of slight importance and I think we could considerably shorten them in appearance by more compact typography."[70] Despite those initial ruses and reactions to the builders' grievances, Day and members of the AIA's Standing Committee on Contracts and Specifications soon found themselves conferring in earnest with a representative group of the National Association of Builders' Exchanges.

Arbitration versus arbitrariness

Meeting in Philadelphia in the fall of 1914, Frank Miles Day presided as chair over the joint conference with builders. Day reviewed the history of the development of the standardized documents and outlined a process for their ongoing revision. Builders were not offered the imprimatur of co-authorship, however, as had been the case with the Uniform Contract of 1888. The AIA's Board of Directors had already decided:

> The Institute should seek the advice of builders and architects generally, but that it ought to be in a position to adopt such forms as seemed best to it, without having to compromise on questions of principle; in other words, that it should not enter into any further agreement with any association of builders jointly to publish documents, but that the Institute should publish its own documents.[71]

The architects took the position that they were willing "to confer with all national associations of builders, steam-fitters, electricians, and others connected to the work of building," but those trades whose respective organizations responded to the architects' invitations deferred instead to the National Association of Builders' Exchanges as their sole representative effectively rendering the negotiations a bilateral affair.

In spite of any trepidation the parties may have harbored upon entering the meeting, comity prevailed; and as was reported at the time, "it soon became apparent that a spirit of moderation and a sincere desire for the betterment of the document animated all present."[72] As Day later reported, "What had seemed so formidable in print became the subject of calm discussion. The documents were gone over article by article, and we cleared each others' minds."[73] The discussions over the two days of this preliminary meeting focused upon two broad areas of concern: the extent to which contractors might seek recourse through arbitration for architects' summary decisions and contract interpretations; and the manner in which sub-contractors should contractually relate to general contractors, architects, and owners. Contractors' specific concerns, numbering "no less than two hundred faults,"[74] were sprinkled throughout the sixty-three provisions of the general conditions. Given the brevity of the scheduled meeting as compared to the range of issues to be considered, the Philadelphia conferees focused first on forging a set of shared principles. The fine grain of agreement was left to be ironed out in subsequent meetings, then to be later affirmed by the membership of the respective organizations.[75]

Regarding the matter of subcontracting, the rise of the general contracting system had fundamentally altered the relationship between and among owners, their architects, and the trade laborers who had once been effectively in owners' direct employ. In former days, the architect had acted as the owner's agent in directly engaging the trade contractors, supervising the progress of their labor, and certifying their requests for payment. Under the newer system, conflicts could arise in the ambiguous zone between the architect's and the general contractor's authority over the day-to-day supervision of the work. Trade contractors and their employees might be uncertain about, first, whether they were bound to the owner or to the general contractor for receipt of their contracted pay; and second, whether the architect's job-site instructions were green lights for extra work for which they could legitimately claim extra charges. Indeed, this ambiguity could prove especially unfair to subordinate contractors vulnerable as they were to malfeasance by nefarious actors, whether they be owners, architects, or general contractors. In consideration of the revised general conditions, architects and builders agreed that relations had to be clarified "that sub-contractors should so far as practicable be bound to the terms of the contract between the owner and the general contractor"; and "that the owner shall not be involved in the relations between the [general] contractor and the sub-contractor."[76] Trade laborers were employed by subcontractors, subcontractors by general contractors, and general contractors by owners. Architects, the erstwhile master builders, were definitively distanced from craft laborers by the more exacting hierarchy of contractual relations. The architect's role as owner's agent in relations with physical laborers, long-sought and then fraught with difficulty, was now subjugated to the general contractor's intermediate authority.

The second major issue embroiling architects and contractors concerned the finality of architects' decisions rendered in their role as interpreter of the contract for construction. Builders had long doubted the possibility that architects could credibly perform as impartial judges when they were being paid by owners and when the drawings and specifications comprising the substance of the contract in need of interpretation were instruments of their own device. Since 1888, recourse to arbitration of disputes had been contractually sanctioned in only limited cases such as whenever the fair value of changes or extra work could not be agreed. The new set of general conditions issued by the AIA in 1911 "made arbitrable all matters that related to extras, extension of time, damages between various contractors, damages as between the owner and the contractor." In all matters of dispute not strictly defined as subject to arbitration, architects reserved to themselves ultimate say. Still, contractors took the view that "every decision that the architect might give, under the contract, should be subject to arbitration."[77] According to Frank Miles Day, architects posted a question in reply:

> "Do you insist that the color of a wall, or the excellence of a piece of carving, shall go to arbitration, if the builder does not like our decision?" They said, "We do not take such an extreme position." We were, however, unable to draw such a line. At our four days' meeting it was arranged that the architect should make primary decisions on all claims of the owner or contractor, and on all matters relating to the work, or interpretation of the contract drawings, leaving any architect using this document free to fix such limits of arbitration as he chooses.[78]

Authority over the selection of a paint color may seem a trivial point with more weighty issues at stake, but architects' concerns were clearly conflicted. Where contractors were focused upon fairness and the profitability of construction as a business, architects were fixated upon ultimate outcomes and aesthetic effects. Architects also recognized, however, the economic disadvantages of long-coveted prerogatives of professional practice that the general contracting system had brought to the fore. As builders entered negotiations with architects, they were clear about their own priorities as had been hotly debated at their convention: "the regulation of the drastic and autocratic power of the architect."[79] They could no longer countenance existing forms of contract in which it seemed "more to [their] advantage to submit to injustice than to risk antagonizing the architect by complaint." After years of perceived abuse, contractors and builders had come to feel "that their property rights ought not to be subjected to the ultimate decision of a single person—architect, engineer, superintendent, or inspector—who is closely connected with the original controversy."[80]

Architects were as surprised by the passion of builders' assault as they were lacking in sound rebuttals to its reason. In reports to the respective organizations about the negotiations, both architects and builders extolled the cooperative spirit of give-and-take and compromise that had prevailed in talks where they had convened as equals. The contractual accommodations granted and received by the two sides, however, were quite asymmetric. Where the 1911 version of the general conditions had granted to the contractor only a handful of matters that were subject to arbitration, in so doing it had exclusively granted to the architect "final decision of all [other] questions arising" under the contract. After negotiation of new contractual terms, however, the balance of power had been effectively reversed. Except in a few cases where the architect's deciding authority was preserved, all other matters were made subject to arbitration. According to Article 10 of the new general conditions of the contract, "The Architect's decisions, in matters relating to artistic effect, shall be final, if within the terms of the Contract Documents. Except as above or as otherwise expressly provided in these General Conditions or in the specifications, all the Architect's decisions are subject to arbitration."[81] The primary concession that architects won from builders was reflective of their professional imperative, but it was a meager return compared to what they had given away.

The provisional resolution of contractors' complaints about the general contract conditions whittled sixty-three articles down to a more manageable forty-five. Contractors' public campaign against architects' power concluded in an atmosphere of apparent comity. The negotiated terms, however, bolstered the standing and responsibility of the general contractor and brought to a close an era in which the architect's professional authority was presumed to be either symbolically or contractually inviolable. Boston architect William Stanley Parker, an advocate of broadened arbitration protocols who had participated in negotiations with builders, prepared a point-by-point comparison of the first and the revised editions of the standard forms. As he suggested, even the smallest turns of phrase were loaded with historical assumptions, and minor revisions in terminology were evidence of architects' growing recognition of the problems that flowed from their old autocratic ways.[82]

> There are only minor changes in the form of the Agreement from that of the First Edition, yet some indicate a fundamental change in attitude toward building operations. At the bottom of the first page the words "to the satisfaction of the architect" are omitted. This is a relic of a past day when the contractors all knew the whims of each architect for whom they worked, and the architect seldom attempted to define what he wanted to such an extent that he who merely read could estimate. Today it is more and more common for contractors to

figure on plans and specifications drawn by an architect for whom they have never before done work, and who, very likely, has his office in a more or less distant city. Estimates must be based on words and symbols that can be interpreted in light of common practice, and the personal element eliminated so far as it cannot be expressed in black and white or blue and white. The architect will surely be called upon to pass on the work, but the criterion is not the architect's personal satisfaction but the satisfaction of the terms of the contract. It is not what the architect meant to say that constitutes the contract, but what he actually said and indicated on the drawings. Contractors must be considered not mind readers but businessmen. The performance of the contractor must, therefore, satisfy the requirements of the plans and specifications, not merely the whim of the architect, and the present wording of Article I of the Agreement makes this clear.[83]

FIGURE 4.7 *Rockwell Kent, the squared circle from "Contractors,"* Architec-tonics: The Tales of Tom Thumtack, Architect *(New York: Comstock, 1914)*.

Builders had argued that architects, in their assumed role as fair and impartial arbiters, were guilty of egregious arbitrariness. In applying their interpretive judgment to the terms of a contract that they themselves had drafted and drawn, architects were able to wield undue agency and control. The knockdown blow in this boxing match, to return to Tom Thumtack's apt analogy, was the builders' insistence on owners' contractual acceptance of broadened dispute resolution through external arbitration as a guard against architects' demonstrable bias. Architects' acquiescence to this provision, as well as to the principle that communication with subcontracting trades must always be mediated by the general contractor, effectively severed architects' direct exchange with laboring trades while diminishing the authority of architects' judgment in the eyes of their own clients. Tom Thumtack conveyed a sense of architects' cruel awakening to their weakened position in the competitive conflict of construction: "Comes a struggle for breath! A wakening to pain! A desperate nausea! I've come back to consciousness only to find myself sagged back on my corner-ropes, weak from a terrible drubbing. I look though puffed eyes cross the squared circle and see my grinning antagonist waving the check for his extra" (Figure 4.7).[84]

A new standard of care

In presenting the outcome of his committee's arduous efforts to AIA colleagues at their annual convention, Frank Miles Day strove to place the newly revised standard forms into a context and to forestall misapprehensions.

> There seems to be a notion that because the Institute has prepared a form of contract it has some desire to impose this form upon its members and architects generally. Nothing is further from the mind of the Institute. Practitioners of standing know their own minds, as to their contracts. They may find something good in the forms, however, and if so they will use it, and there is not the slightest thought in the minds of the Institute or its committees that it can, or even wishes to impose such a document upon anybody. There are, to be sure, members and others who have not had facilities for forming their own minds, who may think the document a good one, and wish to use it. There are certainly many younger practitioners who would be aided by the existence of such a document. They could use it or draw from it. But our friends the builders, I fear, have some idea that such a document will come into universal use. That is an idea which no one ought to hold. If the Institute can assist in formulating good practice, can prepare a document in which things are reasonably stated as between the owner and his contractor, that is all it can do. It must leave the question of its use absolutely to those who wish to use it. (Applause.)[85]

What Day could not then admit, *The Handbook of Architectural Practice* would necessarily reflect. Many of the challenges that builders launched toward the status quo of architectural practice became the basis of a new standard of care. As attorney William B. King who led negotiations with architects on builders' behalf had predicted: "A broader measure of arbitration will lead to greater care in the drafting of specifications .... [I]t will help the present movement toward the standardization of specifications and the exact expression of ideas in regard to material and workmanship. It will also make an architect careful before he makes a decision."[86] Day's handbook advice a few years later indeed confirmed King's predictions and demonstrated the extent to which contractors' criticisms had clarified architects' priorities. On the topic of "Working Drawings," *The Handbook* advised:

> The Institute's "Circular of Advice Relative to the Principles of Professional Practice" (Appendix B) says: "As the Architect decides whether or not the intent of his plans and specifications is properly carried out, he should take special care to see that the drawings and specifications are complete and accurate, and he should never call upon the contractor to make good the oversights or errors in them nor attempt to shirk responsibility by indefinite clauses."[87]

Notwithstanding architects' capitulations to contractors' righteous demands, the first edition of *The Handbook* still conveyed a level of suspicion toward general contractors and disdain for the impact of competitive bidding upon the integrity of the whole construction enterprise—shopping for the lowest bids instead of ensuring the highest quality and squeezing subcontractors at every step:

> It needs little imagination to picture the result of such a course on the quality of the work; and the course is not an unusual one. Such contractors are mere brokers of other men's services. Their interest is not in the integrity of the work. They do not long keep up even an appearance of directing it, for as soon as trouble comes they throw onto the Architect the burden of the fight with incompetent subcontractors. Such results of competitive bidding are as repugnant to honest and capable builders as to architects.[88]

The rise of the general contractor had been a response to changing economies of scale—of building technology, business finance, and the division and unionizing of labor. Architects of an earlier era had been general contractors *avant la lettre*—assembling the trades for the owner's purpose, devising details on the spot just as needed and in close conversation with the artisanal crafts. General contractors, on the other hand, assumed many of the architect's intermediary duties but without titular rights to the nobler name. The result of the institutionalization of architecture as a profession was to progressively abdicate managerial control and to become increasingly remote from a direct engagement with labor.

It is uncanny but not inexplicable how what once seemed so essential to the profession could have been systematically undone—all in the course of forty years. The tactical advantage that architects first won in aligning their own and owners' interests was later felled by contractors' greater organizational savvy. In advancing strategic business goals, contractors were able to appeal directly to owners' commercial interests in ways that architects had generally been unprepared to match.

It is ironic, therefore, that *The Handbook of Architectural Practice* rather than fully embracing the very business sense it first promoted sought instead to turn back the clock. As had been emotionally proposed back in 1913 before the brouhaha with the National Association of Builders' Exchanges erupted, Day's *Handbook* again advocated a partial return to the "separate contract system" in hopes that architects might reclaim for themselves the general contractor's role they had once so enthusiastically relinquished.[89] Thus, architects were forced to confront the unintended consequences of their earlier actions. The way forward appeared to them as if reflected in a rearview mirror, visions of an idealized past (Figure 4.8).

FIGURE 4.8 *Rockwell Kent, the rearview mirror from "Contractors,"* Architectonics: The Tales of Tom Thumtack, Architect *(New York: Comstock, 1914).*

CHAPTER FIVE

Tools, Technology, Practice

The fifteen editions of *The Handbook of Architectural Practice* published to date chronicle a century of changing contexts and constructs of US architectural practice. They have distilled aspects of the collective experience of American architects into a concrete form. Over that time, *The Handbook* was never aimed to revolutionize architectural practice; rather, its function has been to reproduce the profession in an evolutionary way. Because ongoing handbook revisions have inevitably lagged behind the breaking waves of business enterprise and technological innovation, they always seem vaguely anachronistic no matter how up-to-date. The constant race to chronicle the normative practices of a mutable profession became tangibly evident in 1963 when *The Handbook* adopted a loose-leaf, three-ring binder format. Individual sections could be independently modified, new procedures supplanting old in a process of unceasing revision, "testimony to the turbulent, swiftly changing conditions surrounding practice."[1]

The Handbook was the grand vision of a single individual with access to a national network of broad-based, locally inflected professional expertise. When published in 1920, it was dedicated "to the memory of Frank Miles Day of Philadelphia under whose constructive and able leadership this Handbook was undertaken and written and whose untimely death alone prevented him from carrying it to completion." Day's premature death in 1918 never put the project at risk, however. The clarity of Day's purpose and the monumental effort that he had already expended were motivations enough for his committee members to see the project to its proper completion.[2] Today, it is a complex document with multiple authors of wide-ranging expertise and subject to ongoing revision.

It is not possible within the scope of the present study to trace all of the formative conflicts and controversies molding architectural practice over the intervening decades since *The Handbook* was first published. The aim of this final chapter is much more focused—to reflect upon, to theorize, ongoing tool-driven transformations of architecture practice in a historical light; to illuminate them by comparison to the changes wrought by the organizational and procedural tools first introduced into practice over a century ago. As should by now be quite evident, the process of drafting and publishing the very first *Handbook of Architectural Practice* was itself a technological innovation. That act and the effort leading to it both codified previously inchoate relationships and promulgated new instruments of design and building production. The stricter division of actors' roles and the setting of definitive standards helped to regularize outcomes and expectations and, presumably, to elevate architects' public esteem. In so doing, the professionally sanctioned boundaries of "proper" architectural practice were considerably narrowed as compared to preceding eras, a limiting effect that was a correlate of the process of professionalization itself.

Tools of architectural practice

Every tool is a bundle of social relations. This premise may be applied to the whole complement of architects' tools—to the legal contracts, working drawings, specifications, software, administrative forms, and to architects' own offices and employees—even to architects themselves. The challenge is to parse those tools; to trace their networks of force and relation in the transactional purposes to which each is put. *The Handbook of Architectural Practice* was itself such a tool; or perhaps more aptly, it was a kit of tools. It charted a programmatic "Agenda for Architects" by describing project procedures and then collating the necessary administrative forms for authorizing and directing their execution.[3] It situated the practice of architecture, as both science and art, within the bounds of American political economy, of business and law. Over successive editions and generations of architects, it has served as "a barometer of practice as it developed to accommodate shifting political and economic realities, construction booms and busts, a relatively recent liability crisis, and the information age."[4] Each edition has provided a synchronic slice through the dominant modes of architectural practice then in-play. By looking across the historical grain of the handbooks, it is possible to identify where continuities of practice have reigned and disruptions occur.

From the perspectives of social and cultural theorists of the nineteenth and early-twentieth centuries, the formation and ongoing transformation of professions as operative social categories were implicitly tied in both cause and effect to the alienation, anomie, and disenchantment symptomatic of capitalist modernity: class conflicts among competing economic interests (Karl Marx), the emergence of functionally differentiated laboring roles bound together in organic solidarity (Émile Durkheim), or the process of bureaucratic rationalization flowing from the spirit of capitalism itself (Max Weber).[5] Subsequent sociologists of professions, in deriving alternative explanatory models, extended those theories in typological, functionalist, and other ideological directions. Deterministic structures and social processes were attributed as underlying, latent causes of the characteristic traits and motives of professions—jurisdictional competition over disciplinary boundaries for purposes of social closure and market control.[6] More recent efforts to account for the production and reproduction of complex associational forms like professions point in varying degrees away from structuralist causality toward the situated actions of individual agents joined together in constructive practices. In such an approach, "the social" can neither be objectified as a thing nor should it be rendered an underlying explanatory cause; rather, the very possibility of "the social has to be explained instead"—through a methodical mapping of specific associations in which tools and things, too, have agency.[7]

The history of *The Handbook* reviewed thus far demonstrates that the formation of architects' tools and indeed the gradual emergence of architects as mediating actors were as much a result of the concerted agency of individuals—both alone and through committees and organizations—as they were the manifestation of any invisible causal force. As has already been suggested:

> In the United States, ... historians have often had a difficult time identifying individuals responsible for buildings of colonial vintage. It was not that the individuals responsible for design were not given credit in the historical record, but that the functions of design had not been constituted as operations associated with a discrete author. The beginnings of the professionalization of architecture lie in the formation of such an author or creative agent. This was not simply a matter of importing architects or ideas from Europe, but of constructing design as a social practice situated both culturally and structurally in the American context.[8]

To be sure, the American milieu that shaped the architecture profession was far from homogeneous. Distinct modes of practice developed in relation to local customs. The construction community in Boston championed the virtues of arbitration; New York City's laboring trades were strident in upholding their closed-shop protections; Philadelphia's master mechanics long held sway over piecework prices; and in Chicago, architects first emerged in the role of builders' drafters and only later as owners' go-betweens. Until general contractors began appearing on the scene here and there, architects played the essential hiring and supervisory roles themselves. From such a rich diversity of approaches to architectural practice, how do we explain the march toward standardization that *The Handbook* both chronicled and abetted?

The architect's role had at first been fluid and amorphous, not necessarily named, adaptable to local situations, to the needs and capabilities of the other stakeholders. Indeed, the architect might in fact have *been* one of the other actors playing a dual role, an owner-designer or designing builder. Thus, "the architect" that emerged was a contingent character rather than an absolute functional type. The architect was a mediating agent and translating mechanism linking the ends and means of construction that locally prevailed. The essential variability in the constitution of the architect both reflected and propelled shifting relations between owners and builders, still the primary actors. When the Uniform Contract of 1888 formalized the architect's role as owner's agent, however, that representational agency became *the* structuring principle of architectural practice.[9]

The formalization and rationalization of locally disparate practices into increasingly standardized and homogeneous organizational routines reflected a broader national trend of political, economic, and technological incorporation,[10] but the rise of the respective local associations of architects and trade employers could carry this process only so far. Communication and commerce across the geographic expanse fostered awareness of shared vocational interests, the comparison of local best practices, and the integration of status-building efforts. In the course of drafting *The Handbook*, common problems of practice were identified by Frank Miles Day and his far-flung correspondents and addressed by various committees of the American Institute of Architects (AIA), but their proposals for new tools and new tool configurations were only tangentially ever aimed at cutting operational costs. Rather, they were intended to elevate the standards of practice, to assert professional authority, and to cement professional prestige.[11]

The proliferation of contractual tools over the course of the late-nineteenth and early-twentieth centuries—for the configuration, description, procurement, and administration of construction—was an ongoing development of the architect's agency relation. New tools were forged to accommodate the expanding scope and scale of projects—and the intensifying demands of business and law. In *The Handbook* examples that follow, some instruments of architectural practice are examined for the ways in which they extended, masked, or displaced different dimensions of the architect's projective agency as it had been coalescing over time.[12] Once architects were empowered to represent and provisionally act for owners, the intermediation of drawings and various bureaucratic forms enforced their intentions at the construction site even as they themselves physically withdrew.[13]

Drawings and specs

As Tom Thumtack ironically suggested in likening construction rivalries to first a poker game and then a boxing match, the architect's power pivoted on the fulcrum of the bid process. From a position of apparent strength and holding all the cards—as project author and interpreter; as owner's advisor, privy to competitive bids—the architect was soon exposed, once construction had commenced, to the contractor's relentless pummeling—attempts to exploit every error or omission; to recoup every loss through an extra charge. In translating clients' spatial, programmatic needs into buildable form, architects were challenged to balance precise descriptions with as yet unknown contingencies, to predict ultimate ends without fully controlling construction means or cost.

It is instructive to note the ways in which owners' intents were displaced into and then projected, via architects' agency, into enabling representational media, the architect's instruments of service. This transference was evident from the architect's very first interpretive projections of the owner's problem—surveys of budget, needs, and site—into preliminary sketches and schematic proposals. Indeed, *The Handbook* advised, "The Owner should clearly state the requirements of his problem and should frankly name the amount that he is willing to spend. Concealment in such a matter naturally sets up distrust of him in the Architect's mind."[14] Architects endeavored to strike a proper balance among competing demands through iterative visions and revisions. Their designs were manifest in scaled graphic representations conveying the full scope of the building project along with textual supplements prescribing exact material attributes and qualities of finish. Those working drawings and specifications provided a common reference for contractors' estimates of material and labor, cost and time. But once a contract was struck, the architect's role shifted again, still the owner's advisor but now the agent and interpreter of the "properly inferable" true intents of the contract documents, tools of their own device.[15]

We have seen the ways in which drawings and specifications steadily increased in importance over the years. Yet, contractors complained, many architects persisted in the old ways as prescribed in the conditions of the contract in the hope of eliciting the lowest possible bids whether or not based upon thorough and accurate documentation. In earlier days, the drawings and specs could remain relatively vague, providing general outlines of project scope to be developed through constant on-site consultation throughout construction. With the intercession of the general contractor, however, the architect's drawings and specs needed to be fully elaborated before construction commenced, to provide an authoritative basis for sub-contractors to calculate more exacting bids to be assembled into the general contractor's concrete price proposals. For this higher standard of performance to succeed, however, required that architects be omniscient, that their representations be clear and complete, that sub-contractors be able to accurately estimate from the information at-hand, and that general contractors be mind-readers of architects' intents and motivated by altruism rather than profit. None of these, of course, was ever the case.

Contractors further complained that once bids were awarded and construction commenced, architects were able to exercise autocratic and arbitrary power in the administration of the contract and in the interpretation of their own contract documents. If construction details were left vague for purposes of bidding, then their elaboration during the process of construction could lead to intractable disputes and feelings of ill will. While any supplementary details issued during the course of construction were supposed to be reasonably inferable developments of the drawings and specs, the general conditions granted to architects final judgment of their very own intents as well as discretion regarding whether or not contractors were entitled to extra compensation under the terms of the contract. Wherever documents may have been inaccurate or contradictory, architects could find refuge in the contractually granted interpretive authority that stipulated: "in event of any doubt or question arising respecting the true meaning of the drawings or specifications, reference shall be made to the Architect, whose decisions thereon, being just and impartial, shall be final and conclusive."[16] Contractors and architects were thus locked in ongoing debates over what was included in the contract and what constituted an "extra." Under the old Uniform Contract, appeal to arbitration to settle intractable disputes was allowed only under limited circumstances, and even those provisions could be circumvented by an obstreperous owner's refusal to participate in naming an arbitrator.

Besides consternation over the level of detail included in the working drawings, another arena of recurrent tension was the architect's specifications. In the 1910s, "specifications" referred both to the contractual terms and stipulations included in the owner–contractor agreement and to the textual supplements to the working drawings. Where the drawings ostensibly provided objective information with regard to geometrical, positional, and dimensional attributes of building designs, the specifications provided qualitative standards of acceptable material, craft, and performance. These too were rendered subject to the architect's interpretation. According to Tom Thumtack, "The perfect specification would be the essence of three lectures to a visitor from Mars on 'How to Properly Construct a House,' by an earnest artist, a careful builder, and a shrewd attorney …. A perfect specification writer should have graduated from Columbia Law School and Drummond's Detective Agency and then taken a course in palmistry to cover the unforeseen contingencies" (Figure 5.1). Despite his ironic idealizations, Thumtack admitted nonetheless that the state-of-the-art of specification writing was far from perfect.

> At present the object is to get it all your own way, so that taken in connection with the "uniform contract" by no possible contingency can the "party of the second part" have any chance at all. So the specification tries hard to be legal and just as hard to be inclusive, and when it is the result of real legal advice and real building experience, I have no doubt that it is as efficient as its sound is formidable. But, as it is usually done, it is merely verbose and contradictory. Like the time and forfeit clauses in

FIGURE 5.1 Rockwell Kent, "*Specifications*," Architec-tonics: The Tales of Tom Thumtack, Architect *(New York: Comstock, 1914).*

the contract much of the specifications cannot be enforced. A great deal of it is in the nature of a blanket, and horse and man know how hard it is to keep a blanket on especially when it is needed. Moreover the architect writes his specifications and sometimes lets the contractor tell him just what they really mean. On the other hand, I've known strong men to let enormous contracts on next to no specifications at all, and through the force of their own personalities require an excellent observance of the principles of good construction.[17]

Builders derided the legalistic jargon of architects' specifications as nothing more than self-absolving efforts at obfuscation. Blanket clauses protected architects from their own errors and omissions and shifted risk and responsibility onto the backs of builders. "Or equal" clauses could provide architects with wide latitude for ratcheting standards of quality beyond what the contract reasonably required. Builders shared tales of the most egregious abuses, as in the case of "the architect who added to his specifications, 'Any other work or material necessary to complete this structure shall be done and furnished by the contractor without additional charge,' or requiring the contractor to supply anything that the city building ordinances call for that are left out of the plans."[18] In advancing the interests of the owner, or in covering their very own hides, an architect could quickly forfeit any pretense of being a fair and impartial judge.

As we have seen, contractors' associations successfully pressured architects to yield important concessions to their valid complaints when the general conditions were revised in 1914. Abandoning any insistence that their interpretive adjudications of contract disputes were "final and conclusive," architects agreed to revised contractual terms that stipulated, "Except as above or as otherwise expressly provided in these General Conditions or in the specifications, all the Architect's decisions are subject to arbitration." As one commentary on the revised documents noted, "There has been a growing tendency … for Architects to recede from this position of dictator as being a logically untenable one, and one that does more harm psychologically than it does good practically."[19]

In the halcyon days of integrated effort between masters of craft and the laboring trades, the application of templates and squares, plumb bobs and levels had provided sufficient guidance to the workers to make their work true. In some genealogies, the architect first emerges as drafter, as just another tool of the builder; but in other lineages, the architect is a signifying master, not for the builder but as owner's agent, one now estranged from the laboring crew. The drawings and specifications bound owner and contractor together contractually through the architect's representational agency. At the same time, they inserted a new mediating distance between the architect and the site, its material and labor. *The Handbook* of 1920 acknowledged how far professionalizing efforts had come in displacing the architect's old improvisational methods:

> The Architect owes to the Owner, and to all who may be connected with the work, the duty of making the working drawings and specifications as complete, clear, and thorough as it is possible to make them. They are, in a certain sense, the most important of the documents constituting the contract. It is in them, quite as much as in supervision and administration, that the Architect must exhibit the "due diligence and reasonable skill" that the law requires of him. Their careful preparation is the best form of insurance against trouble during the execution of the work. On their quality depends exactness in estimating and effectiveness in competitive bidding.[20]

The give-and-take with builders on the site was replaced by increasingly exacting standards of practice. The presumption that drawings and specifications could constitute a transparent and totalizing system of description, free of errors or omissions and with no room for misinterpretation, demanded a level of omniscience, however, that was impossible to meet. It exposed architects in their hubris to new levels of responsibility increasingly beyond their technical competence and liability for conditions beyond their control.

Supervision and superintendence

Among the precipitating causes for the emergence of the general contractor and the letting of work under a single contract was recognition that architects had exceeded their capacity to maintain a robust and continuous presence at the building site. This was not in itself a retreat from the visceral reality of construction but rather an admission of the existence of a more pressing, economic reality now driving the professionalization of architectural practice. Architects held tightly to their tradition-bound fee schedule of 5 percent of construction cost as one emblem of their elevated standing with respect to the laboring trades. As was previously noted, however, that schedule was based upon erroneous assumptions and misconstrued precedents. Where the AIA's schedule of charges stipulated 5 percent of construction cost for full professional services including (at first) superintendence, European antecedents applied the 5 percent fee only to the design portion of the project with additional fees assessed during the estimating and construction phases.

Under the old American paradigm, architects may have initially provided less detail in their working drawings and specifications, but they were directly engaged in hiring and directing the separate trade contractors on owners' behalfs. The architect's on-site role included the provision of additional details on an as-needed basis, working through the problems at-hand with the craftspeople who would execute the solutions. As the size and complexity of projects grew, and as an architect's scope of practice expanded, then the staffing obligation to provide a regular site presence became an increasingly onerous financial burden under the limitation of the stipulated fee. As *The Handbook* noted in its efforts to recalibrate owners' expectations, "It must be perfectly evident to the reasonable Owner that the Architect cannot, consistently with his other duties, be personally present at the work any large proportion of his time, and that he cannot be expected to pay for continuous superintendence."[21]

By 1888, architects had already begun to distance themselves from any expressed or implied commitment for a continuous presence at the construction site. For the edification of owners, they differentiated between architects' contractual responsibility for periodic supervision and a more constant on-site representation through superintendence—for which an extra fee applied.[22] In an effort to distance themselves from architects' previously assumed obligation, *The Handbook* confirmed:

> The custom of the profession is that when mere supervision will suffice, the Architect furnishes it, but that when continuous superintendence is needed the Owner pays the salary of the clerk of the works. Even in the latter case the Architect gives supervision, and usually quite as much of it as in the former ....
>
> Supervision is no very certain guarantee against bad work; superintendence is so to a much higher degree, but neither will turn a bad mechanic into a good one. The inexperienced or ignorant Owner is perfectly willing to award his work to the lowest bidder, saying, "Let the Architect see to it that the Contractor gives me a good job." He defeats his own ends by pretending to believe that the Architect has some occult power unknown to other men.[23]

With evident awareness of the historical contingencies that had theretofore governed use of the term "superintendent"—as either the architect's or the contractor's respective roving, on-site representatives—*The Handbook* invoked the more ancient term "which for hundreds of years has been used as the title of a person skilled in building superintendence, acceptable to the Architect, acting in the Owner's interest, paid by him and continuously or almost continuously present at a structure in process of erection." In the game of shifting agency, the clerk of the works mediated between the architect and multiple trade contractors, the trade contractors mediated between architects and mechanics, and the architect effectively mediated between mechanics' labor and owners' capital. In each case, specific aspects of the architect's representative agency had been displaced into a new instrument of functional control.

The qualities and capabilities of clerks of the work were clearly derivative attributes of the architect's own idealized persona. In instinct if not in training, *The Handbook* suggested, the clerk of the works should be like an architect: able to interpret the drawings and specs; have the foresight of an artist in anticipating ultimate effects and the reason of an engineer to avert any risk for "the work to proceed to disaster." And perhaps most poignantly, in light of and acknowledgment of the architect's gradual resignation from day-to-day participation at the building site, the clerk of the works had a special role in bolstering the esprit de corps of the workforce. *The Handbook* advocated that the clerk of the works should exhibit a level of "diplomacy and tact" befitting a deep affinity with the cause of the laboring trades:

> While the clerk of the works must see that work is done properly, he should not let the mechanics feel that they are under espionage. He must make them feel a pride in doing things well. He must lead them to understand that he is there to aid them in the proper execution of their work, and that he does not intend to make captious use of his authority or to find petty fault.[24]

Shop drawings

Just as an architect might spring forth whenever a builder's drafter, seizing an opportunity, skirted their employer to claim a client of their own, then we can infer a parallel process in which a clerk of the works might emerge from behind the architect's shadow to assume a new, independent role—the general contractor. To an owner already primed to consider project superintendence as an "extra service" not included in the architect's basic fee, elevating the clerk of the works to the role of general contractor could, plausibly, simplify everyone's lives, both owner's and architect's alike. Rather than the architect acting on behalf of the owner to hire and direct multiple trade contractors each with their own contracts and prices, the general contractor could streamline the administrative effort—consolidating multiple contracts into one, assuming responsibility for hiring and coordinating the trades, solving problems on-the-site, managing quality and performance, charting progress and payments. Every one of these discrete functions had devolved in some fashion from the architect's comprehensive role.

One consequence that followed from the new mode of project delivery, however, was a greater separation of architects (and their supervisory designees) from the building trades. In earlier times, tangible and intangible benefits accrued for all parties in that critical knowledge exchange. Foremost among these was the architect's direct experience with material processes and problems of construction—not to mention a possible by-product of mutual respect. In negotiating new general conditions of the contract in 1914, however, architects acquiesced, for the sake of clarity in the lines of command at the construction site, that their communications with the trades, the newly christened "subcontractors," could only flow through the intermediation of the general contractors. To facilitate the necessary accommodation between the architect's design propositions—manifest in drawings and specs—and the specific means and methods employed uniquely by each trade, shop drawings attained a heightened importance as a medium of interpretive elaboration. As *The Handbook* sought to explain:

> No matter how carefully the Architect's drawings may be made, they do not completely cover the constructive details of all the trades employed upon the work, nor would the masters of those trades wish the Architect to enter more fully than he does into such details. The drawings made by the several trades, the so-called shop drawings, are a necessary step between the Architect's drawings and actual construction. Even if it were proper for him to do it, the Architect could not make the shop drawings acceptably to the mechanics because in most cases, such drawings speak not merely the language of the trade but the language of the very shop in which the work is to be made.[25]

The greater reliance upon shop drawings as a medium of exchange between architects and mechanics was a role reversal from earlier times when architects, as master mechanics, made large-scale profiles and details as needed during the course of construction to guide the work of the trades.[26] In the emergent relation, the "shops" produced fabrication and setting details to inform and prompt decisions from designers at a distance from the building site. Review and approval of shop drawings, the abstracted formalizations of means and ends, could not ensure, however, that the information transferred between fabricators' shops and architects' offices would be either transparent or error-free.

The heightened technical opacity of shop drawings—reflecting the proprietary knowledge specific to each trade—required ever greater specialization and division of effort within architects' own offices.[27] The increasing departmentalization of architects' firms between design and execution became a regular topic of architectural journals.[28] Operating remotely from the site, architects could find themselves in the risky position of giving approval for fabrications the systemic implications of which they might not be able to fully fathom or coordinate at the time. Architects insisted, therefore, that contractors share responsibility with them for the unintended consequences that shop drawing approval might command. Under conditions of increasingly fragmented project knowledge, the general conditions of the contract thus stipulated: "The Architect's approval of such drawings or schedules shall not relieve the Contractor from responsibility for deviations from drawings or specifications, unless he has in writing called the Architect's attention to such deviations at the time of submission, nor shall it relieve him from responsibility for errors of any sort in shop drawings or schedules."[29]

Change orders

While Day was drafting *The Handbook* in 1917, no transaction in the entire building enterprise was more fraught for dispute than in the day-to-day handling of "Changes in the Amount of the Contract." Each of the contractual constituents—owners, architects, and builders—had their own tactical interest in the outcome of change order requests even while contractually and financially bound to each other for a larger pursuit. Despite the terms of the architect's professional standard of care, *The Handbook* avoided undue promises about the technical adequacy of architects' representations in projecting ultimate building costs; instead it expressed a significant caveat: "So intricate is the process of drawing and specifying a modern building that it is scarcely possible even for the most expert to foresee and exactly describe every item that will be needed in its construction."[30] How could anyone not sympathize with the unpredictability of the building process? Yet ironically, architects found themselves exposed on either side to accusations of incompetence, poor faith, or both, for the proliferation of "extras," irrespective of the fact that escalating costs were just as likely spawned by owners' changeable minds or the over-optimism of contractors' original bids.

In drafting *The Handbook*, the manner by which various firms managed the process of tracking and accounting for changes in construction cost was a topic of some consideration. In Day's back-and-forth with his correspondents, there is evidence, however, that neither the terminology nor the procedural instruments for executing project changes had yet been fully standardized. For example, D. Everett Waid commented on Day's first handbook draft:

> Change order to my mind should mean a change in the contract or in the work done under the terms, but not necessarily a change in cost. The most important function of change orders frequently is to show that the contractor has proper authority for varying or departing from specifications, and at the same time protecting both parties' interest by showing that no change in price is involved. If there is any change of price involved, then a credit order or an extra order should follow the change order as soon as possible. The change order form herewith has been found a fine safeguard against surprise extras. Note its provisions, particularly the stringent rule that none shall be issued by a Clerk of the Works without emergency reasons and also that, no matter whomsoever issued, it shall be immediately confirmed or countermanded by the architect.[31]

The distinction between minor changes or tweaks made on-site—"field orders" in quasi-military parlance—and more significant changes requiring adjustment in contract cost was evidently not yet fully formalized in all quarters.[32] What is clear, however, is a growing recognition of the limits to architects' agency authority, the need to secure proper authorizations, and to keep owners thoroughly informed. *The Handbook* noted:

> Article 24 of the General Conditions of the Contract makes it plain that the Architect has no right, except in emergencies, to alter the contract sum, either by ordering extras or by accepting deductions, unless so authorized by the Owner. Such an authorization may be general, the Architect being constituted the Agent of the Owner for such purposes, but the Owner, under ordinary conditions, will be loath to grant to another so great a power over his purse, and the Architect, if well advised, will be unwilling to accept so heavy and unnecessary a responsibility.[33]

The early establishment of the architect as owner's agent had been an important precedent for the formalization of US architectural practice. In application, however, agency was an ambiguous authority that carried unwelcome liabilities that architects would ultimately come to rue. Foremost among its jeopardies was architects' exposure to accusations of high-handedness or double-dealing in approving—or disapproving—extra charges due to contractors for the performance extra work. On the other hand, contractors could try to take advantage of architects' supposed authority for contract interpretation by claiming from the owner extra charges for the architect's every on-site instruction or request. In an era when drawings and specs were left intentionally vague, architects claimed wide latitude to make interpretive judgments about their true intents. During construction, architects were supposed to favor neither owners' nor builders' interests; rather, they avowed themselves independent agents neutrally administering the contract terms. With architects' fee based upon a percentage of construction price, however, owners could well wonder in cases of rising project costs whether their architect and general contractor might somehow be in cahoots. To such suspicions, *The Handbook* replied, "It is a mistake to assume that such changes are as a rule welcome either to the Architect or to the Contractor. Except in rare cases, they are to both a source of delay, annoyance and loss."[34]

The quantity system

Where so many construction industry frictions converged—those sources of "delay, annoyance, and loss"—was in the competitive bid system for establishing construction cost. Each of the architect's representational tools and executive mechanisms described in the foregoing sections—the drawings and specs, the clerk of the works, shop drawings, and change orders—addressed specific transactional needs within larger project processes. Over the years, the crucial juncture between design and construction, the bidding phase, had been tackled as well. Under Frank Miles Day's leadership, the AIA began as early as 1911 to standardize bidding procedures and instructions to bidders to ensure greater transparency and a semblance of fairness. These procedural adjustments could not overcome, however, what many considered to be fundamental fallacies of the competitive bid system:

> One, that a modern building can be described by drawings and specifications with sufficient completeness to provide for an accurate computation of costs, and, hence, for bids on its construction that are fairly competitive; and the other, that the contractors' business is that of selling finished work, and that he is essentially a merchant, who should, but by no means always does, possess a specialized knowledge of the suitable and economical use of the things he buys and sells.
>
> The first of these false assumptions leads us direct to a consideration of the sufficiency of the architect's service, while the latter involves a study of the contractor's status under this form of contract.[35]

Even before the solicitation of bids, architects struggled then as now to provide owners with meaningful preliminary estimates of construction cost. As *The Handbook* advised:

> Preliminary estimates are a test of intellectual honesty. The temptation to name too low a price in fear of displeasing the Owner or in the hope of luring him on is too strong for some minds. Such a course leads to bitter disappointment on opening the proposals and to the heartbreaking work of cutting all that is best out of a design to get a lower bid.[36]

The Handbook cautioned owners that the bid process was volatile and could yield significant differences between high and low bids and thus pleaded that "the Owner must in justice forbear hasty judgment if the Architect fail to display the gift of divination."[37] The more distant architects were from the day-to-day economics of construction, the less capable they were to provide detailed estimates of material and labor costs. Good record-keeping of past projects could assist the architect in making ballpark estimates based upon "cubage," or averages of cost-per-cubic-foot of similar work. Or the architect could appeal for courtesy estimating assistance from eager contractors hungry for work with implied promises of preferential consideration for future jobs.[38]

Subject to criticism first and foremost in precedence were the accuracy and dependability of that most important of project representations, architects' drawings and specs. We have heard these complaints before; perhaps we still do. One ardent critic of the profession, himself an architect, stated the indictment bluntly: "The drawings emanating from the average architect's office are unintelligible and lacking in pertinent information and detail, and it is not an exaggeration to state that the specifications are rubbish." The critique continued:

> The explicit purpose of the drawings and specifications is to define and limit the amount of work to be performed under the contract. This they should do with such clearness and precision that there can be no doubt in the bidder's mind as to the amount and character of the work called for, and that all of the bidders may compute their estimates upon precisely the same basis. It is in the failure of the drawings and specifications to perform this essential function that we find the roots of all of the evil, corrupt and ethically dishonest practices in the building business, and the compelling need for reform.[39]

In fairness to architects, any quest for perfection in the construction documents was severely compromised by other mitigating factors. Based upon old expectations and precedents, the requirement for more detailed and complete drawings was in direct conflict with mounting pressures of time and production cost. Architects had to produce more drawings for increasingly complex buildings in a shorter time in order to optimize budgeting of an already inadequate fee, one contractually stipulated by misguided professional schedules and clung to as an emblem of status. The consequences of such haste could be errors and incompleteness in the drawings and specs. Meanwhile, where the general conditions of the contract, laden with "blanket clauses," had allowed the architect great latitude in making clarifications and interpretations during the course of construction, the threat of appeal to arbitration increasingly limited the possibility of design improvisations and problem-solving on-site.

The consequence of these factors was to summon the worst of behavior from among competitive bidders. Understanding the improbability of making an accurate valuation of construction based upon architects' inevitably imperfect drawings, bidders focused instead on making their wagers in the horse race of estimating.[40] In order to maximize chances of winning the bidding competition, it was held that the general contractor:

> ... according to his judgment in the circumstances, shaves off the figured profit and even cuts the figured cost [of the sub-contractors], if he thinks it necessary, considering carefully the character of his competitors, his chances for recouping the probable losses showing on the bidding sheet through substitutions of cheaper materials for those specified, through securing profitable extras, and through taking advantage of ambiguities and omissions in the drawings and specifications and the discrepancies between them. He does these things not by preference but by necessity. He must first secure the work and then exert himself to the utmost to make a profit.[41]

The systemic flaws of competitive bidding and their correlation with the rise of general contracting were well-recognized on all sides—by both architects and builders as chief actors and adversaries; by owners as chief beneficiaries of the "mercenary spirit of modern industrialism" in their quest to maximize profits by extracting the lowest bid.[42]

As early as the 1890s, arguments were launched by G. Alexander Wright (1852–1918) for an instrumental intervention into the flawed competitive bidding process, a conversation that was to stretch for over thirty years, ultimately to no avail. Wright was an English-trained architect and quantity surveyor who emigrated from London to San Francisco in 1890. He brought with him an advocacy for the quantity surveying system as a possible remedy for dysfunctions he observed in American construction practice.[43] In England and other European countries, the quantity surveyor was an intermediary between the architect's preparation of drawings and the contractor's preparation of a bid. The quantity surveyor's very specific task was to devise a bill of material quantities that could be provided to all competitive bidders as the common, objective basis for their prices. In Wright's opinion, this approach would simplify the redundant practice whereby individual bidders made their separate estimates based upon the architect's potentially ambiguous construction documents. Instead, the quantity surveyor was charged with scrutinizing the drawings and specs for clarity and completeness and then alerting the architect whenever inconsistencies or gaps were found and thereby allowing for appropriate clarifications or corrections. Thus, as Wright described the advantages of the system, "all interpretations should be made before the contract is awarded and not afterwards, at least as far as the human mind can determine."[44]

Besides establishing objectifiable quantities as a common basis for competitors' bids, the quantity system tackled the sensitive issue of how the very real costs of estimating were to be borne. Wright's and others' arguments highlighted the inefficiency of the prevailing system in which the full estimating expense was borne by each separate bidder. Accepting on the law of averages that a competitor was only successful, for example, on one out of ten bid attempts, then the combined expense of preparing all ten bids had to be embedded as part of the general contractor's overhead costs and effectively "hidden" in the single successful bid. Under the quantity system, however, the quantities were only estimated once and shared with all competitive bidders. By common agreement, the surveyor's fee could be added as a line item to the winning bidder's bid form or else appended to the architect's fee. As has been noted, early American architects, still emerging from the ranks of mechanics, had apparently misconstrued and deviated from European precedent when they established their own standard fee structure. Extra assessments were variously charged for preparation of bills of quantities and the services of fulltime construction superintendence. To an American client focused on the bottom line, it might have been expected that the full array of services should already be included in a single fee. From the early days of US architectural practice, there had clearly been a problem in translation on a very essential point.

Congruent with the vocalization of trade employers' complaints that arose with the AIA's peremptory revisions to the general conditions of the contract, discussions about the merits of the quantity system were significantly amplified beginning in 1913. Back-and-forth debates ensued on the pages of both architectural and construction-oriented trade journals.[45] One journalistic provocateur, architect Sullivan W. Jones, took strident views in favor of the quantity system and chaired a newly established AIA committee devoted to study of the issue. In their first annual report, the committee recapitulated Jones' general arguments about the corrosive effects of prevailing practices and the failure of architects' drawings and specifications to function effectively for the purpose of estimation:

> Competitive bidding is fast degenerating into a disgraceful scramble, from which the contractor who will take the longest chances generally emerges as the successful bidder. These conditions are undermining the contractor's moral stamina and are fostering and encouraging business brigandage in the field of building instead of honesty and efficiency. We are all more or less familiar with the manifestations of this form of

decadence; and, indeed, we are all finding it increasingly more difficult to secure thoroughly honest work under the lump-sum contract awarded through competitive bidding.[46]

Frank Miles Day included a chapter on "The Quantity System" in *The Handbook,* laying out the critiques of the prevailing system and the advantages that the quantity surveyor system was assumed to achieve. Respondents to his draft expressed contrasting views on a scale between skepticism and certainty about the prospects for widespread adoption of the system. Day himself remained ambivalent on the topic. He wrote: "The Quantity System is used at present in the United States only to a very limited extent, though interest in it is growing and its advocates and users are increasing in number. It is difficult to prophesy through which channels the system will finally develop and become established as the rule of practice."[47] An early advocate of the quantity system, G. Alexander Wright responded at length to Day's tepid endorsement. Wright voiced frustration that his twenty years of advocacy had yielded so few results and openly questioned the seriousness and commitment of the AIA to deal with such an essential challenge to the profession: "That so much indifference is exhibited in such an important matter is equally strange, because if once properly understood and endorsed by the Institute, would be of so much benefit to the profession, their clients, and to the Building Industries of the entire country."[48]

The AIA's intermittent attention to the matter did finally yield an encouraging outcome, however, when in 1921 the respective organs of architects, engineers, and general contractors concurred on a scheme for implementing the quantity survey system. Their concerted initiative grew out of a study of industrial inefficiency commissioned by the American Engineering Council of the Federated American Engineering Societies, *Waste in Industry.* The building industry was among six cases comprising the study, and "duplication in figuring quantity by all bidders" was identified among the sources of construction industry waste that came under scrutiny.[49] There seems to have been broad consensus about the intertwined nature of the problem, and even rare agreement among factions of architects, engineers, and builders about the potential for the quantity surveying system to provide a basis for a solution. But as is well-known, this proposed innovation in US architectural practice did not take hold. As a later edition of *The Handbook* summarized:

> Prior to 1920 the quantity system was used in America only to a very limited extent. Interest in it had, however, developed and in 1926 a group of Quantity Surveyors established a national organization to standardize procedures and form a basis of recognition of persons qualified to perform this technical service. Whether as a principal result of the depression of the nineteen thirties or otherwise this national organization apparently ceased to function after a very few years, and by 1940 little active interest in the Quantity System was apparent except so far as the services of those

trained in quantity surveying were employed by individual Contractors to take off the quantities on which their estimates of cost would be based.[50]

Progressive Era optimism about the potential for reform and post-war planning for a modern world initially sparked optimism in all quarters of American society. In the construction sector, forward-thinking architects, engineers, and constructors sought new mechanisms for transforming entrenched habits of a hidebound industry. Thence ensued in short order the boom of the Roaring Twenties, the gloom of the Great Depression, and the urgent efforts of the Second World War. Among the many tolls of those events, however, were the requisite energy and appetite to implement such a significant retooling of practice as the adoption of the quantity system would have likely entailed.[51] With the rise of socialism, some may have considered the quantity system as a foreign device unsuited to the American competitive spirit. Others may have simply seen it as an evolutionary dead-end in an ongoing process of innovation and change. What is clear from this and the foregoing examples, however, is that the bundles of social relations by which "the architect" was assembled were being incrementally restructured; they were being re-wired in order to mediate old conflicts and to channel new sources of systemic stress. Over the intervening decades, as the tools of practice had expanded, architects' agency had been steadily displaced.[52]

New tools of practice

In one of his most arresting tableaus, architect Tom Thumtack finding himself pitted against the contractor in a boxing match sets the stage: "On their hands are the four-ounce gloves of misunderstanding and the rules are the Queensbury rules of the uniform contract and they fight in the squared circle of the scope of the specifications. Mr. Owner sits at the ring-side to cheer the victor or berate the vanquished." Then the architect, finally on the ropes and reeling from his head-on collision with the pugilist contractor's iron fist, beholds an apparition as he wavers on the edge of consciousness (Figure 5.2). It is a vision of cooperative spirit, unity of purpose, good will:

> Then I seemed translated to a happy land, full of crisp airs and pleasant sunshine. Before me was going up a splendid building and by my side was the strong figure of a man who was my brother-worker, and near us both stood a master who with kindly interest encouraged us to work together. He had two purses and on one I saw my name and on the other saw my brother's name and from them was paid to each his wages for duties done in furthering the building. In my hand was a compass and in his a trowel. When I saw his square paper cap, a great light broke upon me. This brother-helper was the builder. He and I were working side by side

FIGURE 5.2 *Rockwell Kent, architect on the ropes from "Contractors,"* Architectonics: The Tales of Tom Thumtack, Architect *(New York: Comstock, 1914).*

with one great purpose; to perfect for our employer, his great bee-hive of a building. ... Between us both and toward our venerable employer, flowed mutual helpfulness. Each was his agent.[53]

Thumtack's vision may have been a flashback to a simpler time, a déjà vu. Was it also a premonition of a possible future? Architects at the turn of the twentieth century already romanticized an earlier era of omniscient "master builder," and that shibboleth of the construction industry persists even to this day. Emergent moderns anticipated a new Middle Ages where skilled though docile workers, industrially integrated in their efforts but in need of managerial direction, might fabricate architects' rationally construed designs.[54]

Over the decades stretching between the Civil War and the First World War, the respective agents of ownership, design, and construction were bound by the same legal principles, economic interests, and technology-driven procedures that were paradoxically forcing them apart. The once-blurred and shifting identities among owner, architect, and builder begat three distinct operative roles, but unresolved tensions simmered among them, nonetheless. Conflicts barely concealed beneath the surface of project practices could arise wherever any actor was motivated to exploit another's weakness or to promote a tactical strength.

Arguably, all the great challenges that the construction industry confronts today were already present when *The Handbook of Architectural Practice* was first published in 1920. Like then, the building profession still grapples with prediction and control of performance outcomes but for projects of ever-increasing scale, cost, technological complexity, environmental impact, and social consequence. Then as now, the competitive viability of the architecture profession was under serious pressure. In reaction and response, mediating tools and alternative methods of delivery were fashioned to enhance the communicative accuracy of building information; the estimation of labor and material, overhead and profit; the interaction between design and fabrication; the management of schedule and cost; the distribution of risk and reward.

The standardization of practice a century ago was primarily in service to the project of professionalization, still in its early stages. Standards-setting was a means for both elevating trust and excluding competition. A "grand bargain" struck among nascent professions, society, and the state established self-regulating and entitled franchises of expertise to serve the public interest. Professions were thus able to claim the mantle of altruism in order to legitimize their own self-interest.[55] As social assumptions shifted from a paternalist to a more consumerist orientation, however, professions were slow to adapt. Technologically driven changes in the marketplace of ideas and services further exacerbated those disjunctions even as professional capabilities were continually streamlined or enhanced.

In quest of heightened efficiencies, the impacts of new tools and applications may be quickly felt in the unsettling of established systems and practices. More difficult to gauge may be the longer-term collateral consequences of such success. The general aims of becoming more integrated and collaborative in any field may serve shared goals like increasing social equity or promoting environmental sustainability. They can also become vehicles advancing narrow economic interests—where fungible sources of capital and expendable pools of labor are subject at ever-accelerating rates to outsourcing, automation, and obsolescence; where "everything is productive but nothing is labored."[56] Whether all these goals are mutually achievable, and to what extent professions must change in order to serve those competing ends, are fundamental questions that hang in the balance in this era of inexorable social and technological upheaval.

Clarion calls from a century ago for the return of a collaborative spirit, entreaties to infuse the building enterprise with common purpose born of shared risks and incentives were already, even then, tinged with nostalgia. Are they any less so today, now reincarnated as "building information modeling" (BIM) and "integrated project delivery" (IPD)? Or, do our new tools instead open up untapped capacities, the chance for more diverse agents and constituents to participate in the process, to help set the terms of a new compact that will govern relations among development, design, and construction in the new millennium? Rather than being mesmerized by new tools of practice, architects and their cohorts need to understand emerging technologies critically, in a historical light.

BIM and IPD

The formalization of craft-based traditions under the sway of industrialization was a necessary stage in the technological conversion of US architectural practice. It was a process that *The Handbook* both codified and propelled. Differentiating themselves from among the mixed interests of capital and labor, of owners and builders, architects enacted standards of ethical practice through auspices of the AIA. They enforced among themselves a uniform fee structure, eschewed unseemly self-promotion and competition, divested themselves of financial interests in building, and stood aloof from the material processes of construction. The intermediary tools that architects devised—more exacting drawings and specifications, general contractors and clerks of the works, shop drawings and change orders—facilitated their remote project control but gradually displaced their mediating agency.

Almost as soon as new relationships began to congeal, architects had second thoughts about the strict divisions of labor that their professionalizing efforts demanded and that standardization entailed. Architects were particularly concerned, for example, about the cascade of unintended consequences flowing from the intercession of the general contractor and the rise of the single stipulated-sum contract. By yielding to general contractors' responsibility for gathering bids from the separate trades and by insisting upon site superintendence as an extra fee-for-service, architects ceded their most direct means of exerting project control—through unfiltered intercourse with labor and cost. As Frank Miles Day outlined in his 1908 speech to the Philadelphia Builders' Exchange, "the growing dislike and distrust of the general contracting system" could be traced to a litany of complaints. Among these were the dubiousness of claims that general contractors could provide certainty of cost and the inflated promise that their intercession would "relieve the owner of responsibility." Day bemoaned "the folly of competitive bidding" in which the award of work to the "lowest and worst bidder," a "mere broker" of the trades, led to "frequent inefficiency" and "work lags" owing to the general contractor's "non-supervision of quality."[57]

Despite its rise in importance, the reach of the so-called single contract or general contracting system was never absolute. Its adoption paralleled, for example, the ascent of the "vast construction company" in which the primary actors were not always so categorically distinct. Large design-build firms such as the George A. Fuller Company might have a business-savvy architect at the helm or some enterprising master builder; real estate interests might support their business finance model. They might contract directly with owners for a completed building on a cost-plus-fee basis, employ their own architects and engineers in-house, broker contracts with trade labor, and manage the material supply chain along with the construction process.[58] The

Hoggson Brothers Building Method assured clients that their combination of design, engineering, and construction services into one business entity would streamline workflows and relieve them of immeasurable stress and concern (Figure 5.3):

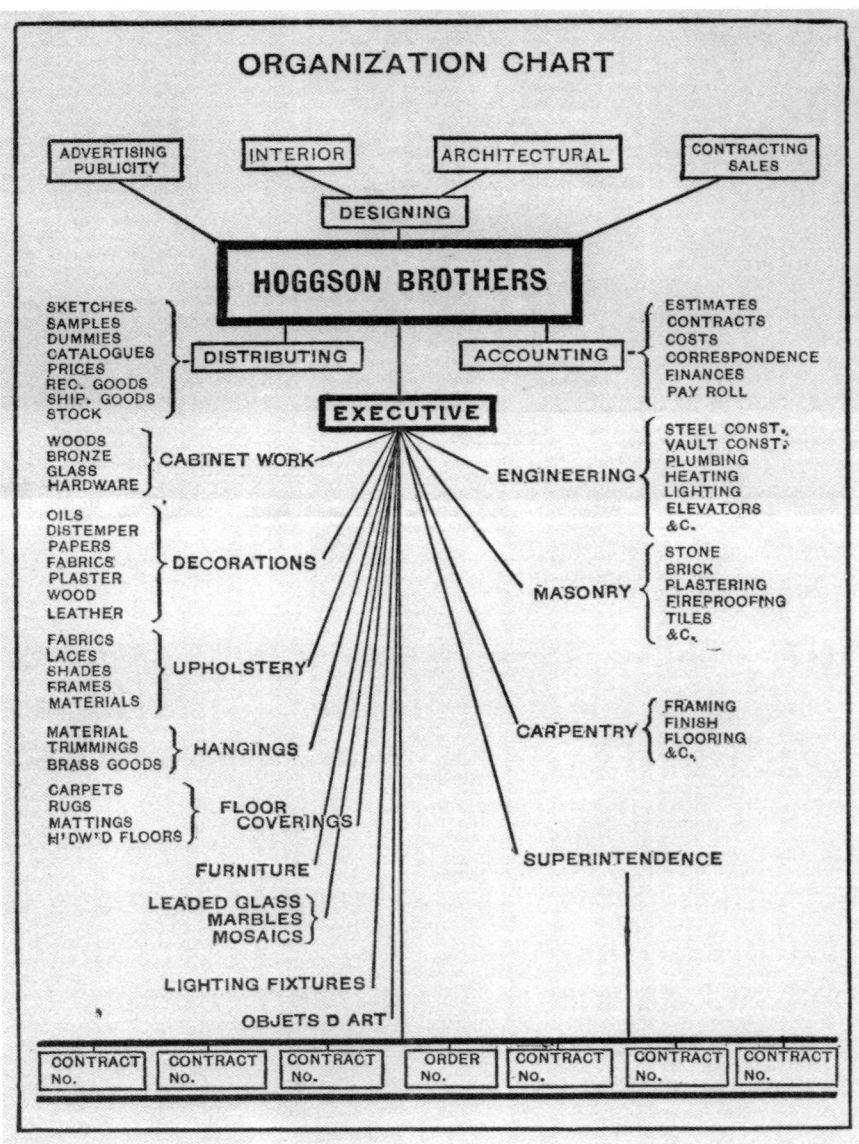

FIGURE 5.3 *Organization Chart*, The Hoggson Building Method *(New York: Hoggson Brothers, 1910)*.

From this time on you are free from the cares of the undertaking. The greatest hindrance to successful building has been removed—namely, divided responsibility. The architect will have no cause to blame the contractors, nor the owner to blame the architect. We become responsible to you for the whole task from first to last. Your only responsibility is the voluntary and pleasing one of expressing your wishes regarding the sketches, plans and selection of materials as they are laid before you. By a provision of the contract you reserve the privilege, however, of withdrawing at any time prior to actual building operations.[59]

Architects fretted, however, that large construction firms could pose a threat to their status, recasting them from autonomous professional practitioners back into the role of builders' employees—a matter of significant concern again today as venture capitalists and big data firms set their sights on disrupting the construction industry.[60] Independent general contractors represented a nuisance to architects as well. They could actually complicate rather than simplify architects' administrative duties while drawing a more lucrative fee. With such realizations, architects were soon reconsidering the benefits of the old multiple contract system that had been so readily abandoned, but they were constrained at the same time by the protective standards that they had adopted in order to set themselves apart. The restrictive terms of the AIA's Standards of Professional Practice—against advertising, building contracting, unsanctioned competition, or overlapping financial interests—had been essential in their time for establishing public trust in a field rife with malfeasance and incompetence. By mid-twentieth century, however, with the world transformed by war, those gentlemanly strictures were increasingly anachronistic and had become material impediments to progress.

Changes in the landscape of US architectural practice emanated both from the bottom-up and from the top-down. As we have seen, local customs governing building enterprise had historically held sway in cities across the nation; and despite the homogenizing effects of technologically driven trends, parochial practices could still spur broader innovation and change. In the Atlanta of the 1960s, for example, two architects schooled at Georgia Tech following the Second World War pressed at established bounds of AIA sanctions to experiment with novel approaches that we now understand to have been fully precedented in the past. In practice with his father, a young George Heery was experiencing firsthand the increasing pressures of time and cost exerted by the growing complexity of building and the bitter wages of economic inflation. He saw competition coming from "not so much other architects as they were the design-build contractors who claimed faster delivery and lower costs to the owner."[61] In response he pioneered early approaches to the nascent field of construction management in an effort to recapture some of the professional responsibility earlier abdicated by architects to general contractors and clerks-of-the-work.[62] John Portman made waves in Atlanta and far afield by creative engagement in the financing of projects self-initiated and self-designed. While provoking ethical questions at the time, he thus reasserted the once familiar model of owners being their own architects and prompted interest in the revived prospect of architects as developers.[63]

Before the advent of contractual uniformity in the late-nineteenth century—and even after—there have been as many manifestations of "the architect" as there were types and varieties of clients and species of builders and trades. Together they formed a dynamic system of intertwined exchange shaped by local and regional building cultures. Professionalizing efforts to restrict the title of architect, to contractually segregate roles and responsibilities among architects, owners, and builders, had the paradoxical effect of both defining disciplinary boundaries and delimiting professional reach. In pursuit of elevated ethical standards, architects foreswore their financial interests in building—the very benefits which owners and builders continued to reap. All the organs of professionalization and state registration, education and accreditation, were coordinated to serve an increasingly narrow and restrictive model of practice even as the marketplace demanded greater flexibility and responsiveness to ever-changing conditions and demands.

Over the final quarter of the twentieth century, sociologically oriented researchers turned their eyes to the profession and practice of architecture in a manner that challenged much of the received wisdom about the efficacy of status building efforts of the preceding century. Successive economic downturns and shocks to the energy supply called into question the stability and sustainability of overly romanticized views of professional autonomy and the exposure of dominant practice models to an increasingly imbalanced system of risks and rewards.[64] Dana Cuff, extending the analysis of Robert Gutman, was especially prescient in identifying ways in which the fragmentation and specialization of professional roles on the cusp of the digital turn were necessitating new orders of flexibility in the formation of alternative models of practice, ones that were increasingly elastic, mosaic, and nomadic in response to economic uncertainties and project complexities.[65] Architects' retinue of possible services was expanding, but it was a menu still organized as prix fixe rather than à la carte—based upon the old basis of professional fee as a percentage of construction cost.

In the 1970s, and again in the 1990s, architects faced governmental challenges to their professional autonomy when the AIA was compelled to enter into a consent decree with the US Department of Justice after allegations of illegal constraint of interstate commerce under the terms of the Sherman Act of 1890. The AIA's code of ethics was specifically cited for prohibiting architect members from competing against each other for commissions on the basis of professional charges.[66] Thus, one of the foundational tenets of US architectural practice, the upholding of a common fee-basis for services, fell by the wayside. Other long-held ethical standards such as restrictions on advertisement or self-promotion and injunctions against architects serving as contractors in "design-build" modes of delivery were likewise overturned in the following decade.[67]

The "design-bid-build" approach to construction procurement is tagged today as the "traditional" method of project delivery; yet, at the turn of the nineteenth and twentieth centuries, the single contracting method (their "design-bid-build" equivalent) epitomized a world reversed from pre-industrial norms. In current parlance, it would be considered a "disruptive innovation." It is ironic, therefore, that digital-era tools and today's integrative project methods are misconstrued as the precipitating causes rather than the unanticipated effects of ongoing processes of professional transformation. The leap into the future is resuscitating the hybrid disciplinary agencies of the past—the designer-builders, the builder-developers, the developer-designers, and unique fusions of all three as para-professional, multi-disciplinary consultants, and design assistants. Is this the "happy land" of practice that Tom Thumtack foresaw in his punch-drunk hallucination?

Some descriptions of IPD as method and BIM as enabling tool echo in their idealistic rhetoric Thumtack's panacea of mutual helpfulness flowing among co-equal agents. According to the AIA's guide, "This is the world of Integrated Project Delivery":

> Technological evolution coupled with owners' on-going demand for more effective processes that result in better, faster, less costly and less adversarial construction projects are driving significant and rapid change in the construction industry. ... IPD leverages early contributions of knowledge and expertise through utilization of new technologies, allowing all team members to better realize their highest potentials while expanding the value they provide throughout the project lifecycle. At the core of an integrated project are collaborative, integrated and productive teams composed of key project participants. Building upon early contributions of individual expertise, these teams are guided by principles of trust, transparent processes, effective collaboration, open information sharing, team success tied to project success, shared risk and reward, value-based decision making, and utilization of full technological capabilities and support. The outcome is the opportunity to design, build, and operate as efficiently as possible.[68]

Based upon such aspirations, IPD might be construed in its essence as an idealized structure of social relationships implicitly critical of the adversarial, market-based system that has long prevailed. In its avowed reversal of familiar historical developments by which material, ideas, and labor were divided, it suggests a return to a prelapsarian unity among the trifecta of building agents.[69] Its expressed goal of enhanced efficiency, however, aligns architecture ever more closely to the visions of Henry Ford, Frederick Taylor, and Adam Smith.

Not unlike the protagonists in Tom Thumtack's dream, "working side by side with one great purpose," it has been suggested that "IPD process methods work hand in hand with BIM and leverage the tool's capabilities."[70] BIM is extolled as "a tool, not a project delivery method," a key instrument for realizing the integrative practice agenda; but if as suggested earlier, every tool is a bundle of social relations, then what are the social relations that are being bundled inside of BIM? BIM organizes inputs and outputs in an effort to manage the human tangles of disfunction and dispute that have been the hallmark of design and building practice for over a century: the imprecision of drawings, the ambiguity of specifications, the unpredictability of cost, the inevitability of change, the separation of design intelligence from construction know-how, and the estrangement of architects from the building site. By "shifting the focus from individual processes to project workflows and seamless interactions," it is anticipated that the "ultimate solution" of optimization and efficiency could be at-hand.[71]

It can also be argued, however, that digitally augmented designers modeling ever more complex building forms, surfaces, systems, and assemblies merely disguises the essence of managerial efficiency with the cloak of autonomous creative control. Behind the computer screen, that opaque picture plane, a new boxing match takes place in the intricate web of national and international standards organizations. Those standards-setting bodies are also proxies for proprietary interests, large software producers competing for market advantage over the means of design and building production. By defining the technical parameters enabling cross-platform interoperability of digital modeling, simulation, fabrication, and management tools, the virtual terms of a new uniform contract are being set.

Within one integrated platform, all the old tools joining drawings and specifications, quantities and costs, scheduling and coordination, shop drawings and change orders may be linked. Thus, in its own way, BIM has the potential to seamlessly integrate the kinds of procedural logics—interactions among designers, builders, owners, and users before, during, and after project construction—that *The Handbook of Architectural Practice* first sought to codify in 1920 and that the profession has been elaborating ever since. Achieving this vision would be the culmination of a century of effort to align architectural practice and education with the political economy of construction in a global marketplace of goods and services. BIM is thus as much a metaphor as it is a medium for a virtual collaborative future in which, it is imagined, the master builder may be reborn—the ultimate rationalization of the building industry through optimization, prediction, and control—of production, performance, and cost.

Would this mark a new beginning, a clear break with the past where, finally absolved of pesky old rivalries, co-equal collaborators might consider anew what important social purposes a reunified construction industry might serve? Or could we find instead that human nature still prevails and that, in spite of industry optimism and best intentions, BIM- and IPD-driven projects remain just as susceptible to suspicions of greed—of kickbacks and corruption among public officials, software providers, and favored designer-builders—as were the ethical fears of olden times—of rigged competitions, architects and builders in cahoots, "of lies for bricks and knavery for mortar"?[72] Automated "clash detection" may be a boon for avoiding costly construction errors by coordinating the efforts of design disciplines and the trades; but still, as this history of practice has shown, the profession itself has been constituted by those same structuring tensions. A century of effort to detect clashes of interest and to ameliorate contractual conflict has yielded only provisional managerial remedies. Emergent and re-emergent models of architectural practice are as indicative of those unresolved tensions as they are prognostic of new technological capabilities.

Before committing themselves too quickly to another totalizing vision of architectural practice, past experience suggests that architects would be wise to remember the unintended consequences that an earlier quest for contractual uniformity entailed. Rather than adopting particular practice platforms as techno-contractual *faits acomplis*, architects should reassert their own agency—and their rights as software consumers—to tailor their own tools, each to their own purposes: to program their own agendas; to script their own routines; to specify their own constructions. Instead of clinging to hard-won claims to an ever-shrinking title, architects are once again free to assume the gamut of speculative and constructive roles historically ceded to owners and builders. The proliferation of alternative, hybrid models of professional practice might be a desirable outcome of the reversal of architects' diminished agency. Like the one suggested in Tom Thumtack's dream, more regionally diverse and locally inflected approaches to practice could emerge—"a happy land, full of crisp airs and pleasant sunshine."

Architectural practice, artificial intelligence

Historical reflection on the birth of the first *Handbook of Architectural Practice* from a century ago has served as a convenient lens for considering the creative transformations of the architecture profession on either side of that arbitrary divide. The foregoing theoretical speculations on historical processes of profession-formation have been pursued for the potential insights they may offer about present patterns and unfolding conditions. As consideration of BIM and IPD just showed, one hazard of cumulative historical amnesia is that, over the course of a century or even a generation, forgotten structures and their inherent contradictions can too easily be obscured by novel tools and their effects. The mirror of history is inadequate as an optic for seeing the future, however. As American journalist and utopian thinker Edward Bellamy observed, "One can look back a thousand years easier than forward fifty."[73] (Today, it can be just as difficult to look forward five!) Rather than offering feeble predictions of a contingent future, the final aim here is to suggest some performance specifications for whatever forms of architectural practice may, in the course of time, emerge.

In reviewing the formation and transformation of the US architecture profession since 1870, one can identify several developmental stages that correspond to general tendencies in other professions as they emerge from their respective vocational roots.[74] In the first stage, craft-based and locally variable bundles of inter-related services are provided by variously skilled and trained practitioners to their respective publics and clientele. As this historical account of architectural practice has shown, such a state of affairs prevailed in the United States through much of the nineteenth century and even into the twentieth century. The claim to the title of architect could be and was asserted by individuals across a range of skill-based crafts and avocations. The chief disadvantage of such titular fluidity was that ill-repute associated with even a single practitioner could adhere to all the other architects so-named.

In a second stage of development overlapping with the first, we can see efforts being made to bring uniformity to the variable local practices in order to elevate the quality and consistency of the work, to bolster expectations and professional identity, and thereby to garner public trust. From the founding of the AIA in 1857 to the adoption of a Uniform Contract in 1888 to the publication of *The Handbook of Architectural Practice* in 1920 and even *Architectural Graphic Standards* in 1932, we can see reflected the underlying motives of this process. Architectural practice was being standardized through adoption of ethical codes and the development of contractual tools and administrative instruments by which the accrued experience of the profession, so propagated, could become the operational norm. Over the ensuing century until today, the early process of standardization only intensified as it inexorably propelled a third stage of development enabling the systematization of architects' knowledge base and the automation of its productive tools.

Paralleling the transition from agriculture to industrial manufacturing to an information-oriented economy, professional work has continually been analyzed and reorganized to answer adjacent expectations and demands. Beginning in the 1920s with the promulgation of "A Standard State Zoning Enabling Act" by Herbert Hoover's US Department of Commerce as well as advocacy in favor of uniform and standardized building codes, the US construction industry has been substantially integrated nationwide based upon intertwined economic, juridical, and technological ties. Public officials in their respective roles and locales manage zoning, permitting, and inspection processes as an extension of the policing power granted to them by the states. Despite occasional lapses in design adequacy and construction safety or news of malfeasance in biddings or other nefarious acts, the industry—understood in its broadest sense—has accrued over a century-and-a-half a level of respectability commensurate with the proportion of the gross national product annually at its command.

National studies of architectural education and practice contributed further momentum to the process of modernizing the profession. The influential "Princeton Report" of 1967 commissioned by the AIA called for sweeping reforms in design education to encompass broader environmental concerns to meet the challenges of the time: exploding information and the specialization of tasks within an increasingly complex design and building enterprise.[75] A study of architectural education and practice commissioned in the 1990s, the so-called "Boyer Report," further advanced the idea of "standards without standardization" as one of seven goals for the reform of the architecture profession.[76] The reciprocal relation between architectural practice and educational curricula, along with interlinked organs of registration and accreditation, became increasingly important motive forces ratcheting professional standards, performance expectations, and public accountability.

The rise of computation in architecture also ensued in the post-Second World War era. Computational tools were being crafted to aid and assist increasingly complex planning, design, and construction processes. A variety of new tools emerged from innovations in engineering, communication, and manufacturing that then entered architects' offices and unsettled old routines—among them: computer-aided drafting and design and a host of automated means for sorting, editing, and processing words, numbers, and images. These new tools then redounded upon their sources initiating new cycles of innovation and experimentation projected through computer-numerically controlled fabrication machines. Over the course of this iterative process, many roles have been redefined, new ones created, and some, like the vocationally trained drafters of old, have mostly disappeared from view.[77]

While the internal logics and logistics of design interacting with construction were being incrementally and systemically refined, architects' extrinsic relation with their publics has remained largely unchanged. The media spotlight that shines upon a small subset of high-profile, brand-name designers only serves to obscure the essential, public-serving role of the profession. Some question, however, whether the old paradigm of self-protecting and proprietary professional expertise in whatever fields, accessible to the relatively few, can remain a viable delivery model for a media-saturated, networked society in the era of ubiquitous computing. Indeed, the proliferation of various software and scripting applications already enables many firms to aggregate and customize those tools to their own and their constituents' specific productive ends. Like other sectors and services, will professions be swept along or simply be swept aside by technological advances in manufacturing and e-commerce, big data, and machine learning?

In the next stage of this story, we must anticipate exploitation of the full capacities of our digitally networked world in the technological transformation of professions and their practices.[78] When extended to the field of architecture, however, this application of technology does not automatically arrive at the same promised land that acolytes of integrated practice might hope or expect. The aim of democratizing practical expertise, making it more readily accessible and affordable to the public at large, would presumably allow greater access to "professional services" by people who need them most but can afford them least.[79] High-level controls reflecting public priorities in zoning, fire safety, sturdiness, and energy efficiency could be encoded as operational defaults. Debates over the fraught working relationships among architects and engineers from a century ago could be definitively recast as mere matters of algorithmic detail. The continued modularization of professional functions into automated routines might then challenge the very model of professional work and the subdivision of knowledge domains as has developed since the nineteenth century. Architects and other professionals would thus be gradually displaced as the exclusive agents of their own expertise.

Do the rise of automation and expert systems necessarily portend an absolute end of professions? Not necessarily, but some believe they could significantly alter the kinds of work and numbers of jobs in the workforce reserved for the bespoke, craft-based applications of judgment, knowledge, and skill that we came to exclusively associate with professions in the nineteenth and twentieth centuries.[80] When many aspects of professional work have been decomposed into a series of routine tasks enabled by responsive devices programmed to learn, will every worker really need to be a fully educated and trained professional in the manner presumed in the past? Already, fields of law and medicine have seen a proliferation of para-professional intermediaries who with focused and specialized training are able to competently discharge key responsibilities once considered to be the exclusive purview of fully educated and licensed professionals. Granted, there is likely to be a continuing demand for architects as "independent" agents to serve the edifying interests of private, public, and institutional clienteles. The numbers of creatives commensurate with ongoing expansion of the knowledge base, however, would likely be proportionately fewer than the legions of intermediary agents needed to translate new principles and processes into accessible standards, systems, and income-earning or open source applications.[81]

For the architecture profession, existential questions and disbelief must surely follow such stark prognostications. Will artificial intelligence render "the architect" a mere expert system, an autonomous vehicle of design?[82] It does appear that the entire construction sector is poised for an industry makeover. The full integration of digital design and fabrication processes with supply chain logistics and industrial-scale automation would be the logical realization of calls from over a century ago for the elimination of waste through systemic innovation and reform of hidebound practices. The acceleration of change is already experientially evident, a background of everyday life.

The decomposition of architects' broad responsibilities into so many discrete tasks had already commenced in the late-nineteenth century, as we have seen, with the legal and ethical separation of ownership, construction, and design. Each of these realms is constituted by its own internal logics and decision-making structures further complicated by intertwining connections between and among the three, all set within locally variable socio-economic contexts. At each juncture in this matrix of relations, opportunities are rife for the further decomposition of sub-routines and tasks and then the articulation of intermediary applications and translating agents to perform discrete but interactive functionalities all fed by a polyglot of data points and sources. Building simulation models promise to become co-extensive and interactive with their built environments and the inhabitants that they support.[83]

The licensure of architects first arose in a climate in which civic-minded and self-interested elites petitioned the states and were granted a franchise and competitive advantage over avowedly less qualified practitioners to protect the health, safety, and property of the people. The upholding of standards and the assumption of risk became distinguishing characteristics of twentieth-century professionalism. In the intervening decades, many of those same purposes once staked to individuals have been embedded within the institutional frameworks governing practice—through education, accreditation, registration, building codes, zoning ordinances, construction standards, representational conventions, corporate structures, and a multitude of consultancies and pro formas. Just as the agency functions of the architect have been decomposed and distributed among a retinue of frameworks and actors, so too should it follow that risk and reward be collectively shared among all those who stand to profit or fall. In an era of distributed expertise within the organs of vast corporate bodies, should the licensing of individual practitioners still be the exclusive means of safeguarding the public interest?

The automated edifice of practice will require a complex architecture indeed, one with an equally diverse retinue of visionaries, artists, communicators, experts, craftspeople, technicians, programmers, processors, editors, database managers, gamblers, custodians, and crew. The Architects Building from 1913 already foreshadowed that co-working future—a speculative, cooperative enterprise and communal work space where architects—both as owners and owners' agents—along with engineers, general and sub-contractors, material suppliers, and blueprint makers co-located to facilitate collaboration, conviviality, and common enterprise. From its perch on Park Avenue, the Architects Building was just one node in a vast social network facilitating design and construction—its flows of ideas, information, material, labor, and capital.

Rather than wallowing in despair or vainly resisting de-professionalization, architects need to re-examine the edifice of practice and prepare for a grand conversion.[84] Architects like other professionals will need to re-educate themselves, or reconceive altogether how to educate themselves and others, not for the singular profession as they have known it, but for the multifarious roles that the new "mangle of practice" will demand.[85] Where professionalizing efforts of a century ago withdrew the architect from both the site of construction and its field of financial interest, new tools have the potential to thrust architects by whatever names back more organically into the heart of the action, into a multitude of pluralist practices. The challenge will be to avoid the same sort of totalizing uniformity that nineteenth- and twentieth-century professionalization incurred.[86]

Following a century and a half in which architectural education became increasingly homogenized as it was severed from architectural practice, greater responsibility for educating architects must again reside within the building industry itself. Social, economic, and technological pressures increasingly challenge the university monopoly in liberal and professional education. Ever-escalating educational costs further privilege a class of architectural workers best oriented by their social backgrounds to facilitating the interests of economic elites. To counter this trend, any truly integrated construction industry must strive to make the design and building field more upwardly mobile and accessible to those whose community environments are most in need of transformation. It must be more inclusive of those whose full participation has been historically hindered, whether by socio-economic circumstance or by race or gender-based discrimination.

Within a reformed model, variably disciplined design, development, and construction firms, large and small, could help bear the educational and training costs for those least able to pay. They could support students' general education through liaisons with local universities for access to remote and resident instruction while restructuring the work itself as part of a built-environment curriculum. Indeed, internet-based resources could enable factories, fabricators, and firms to offer as part of their expanded services, and in collaboration with far-flung networks of university, industry, and cultural partners, a full spectrum of vocational, para-professional, and professional training and certification opportunities congruent with local and regional needs. Rather than merely reproducing a hidebound profession or exacting claims upon a title, the aim of such efforts would be an ongoing expansion of opportunity, laying foundations of social justice by sowing seeds of hope in the very communities they serve.[87]

Such progressive vision as the present demands was already palpable a century ago when Frederick Squires concluded his monograph on contemporary construction methods with a challenge to the field of architecture born out of optimism for modern means:

> We live in days of progress. Make of them days of building progress! Two million women vote! The moving picture talks! We telegraph through boundless space! Then shall we use Egyptian bricks? Shall we make Roman concrete, without steel? Shall we exhume our house plans from

Pompeii? The day and generation cry advance! They crown initiative! And if architecture and building are to reflect the spirit of these stirring times, let their dead past bury its dead and their pulsing present build monuments to progress."[88]

Rather than a romanticized return to the age of the medieval master builder, architects might entertain some alternative tropes. Daedalus, the cunning worker, was the mythical inventor (and thief) of the very tools that launched an avocation. Like Daedalus, contemporary architects as agents of their own self-invention are governed by a structure of risk in a "process [that] develops inexorably in terms of its own logic."[89] A century and a half ago or more, architects' assertion of agency for others established the core of a social identity; it is what set them apart from builders and formed the basis of the US architectural profession. As the architect's agency was dissipated into more and more tools and instruments, the architect ceased to be a solitary individual or even an independent firm. Like Daedalus, the embodiment of cunning and inventiveness, "the architect" that we are now assembling is recast as a pervasive social mechanism, an embedded principle of systemic craft and problem-solving ingenuity everywhere apparent but increasingly difficult to see.

A conversion

Tom Thumtack (or is it Frederick Squires this time?) teases us with the promise of a final story. It could be another tale about doppelgangers, mistaken identities, the sacred and the profane, building inspectors, or history detectives. Alas, only Rockwell Kent's unsigned illustration survives; Thumtack's yarn, unfortunately, is not attached. The image is cataloged in the archives of Squires's and Kent's alma mater where they had sketched and lampooned their time away as architecture students in the Columbia School of Mines (Figure 5.4). The title of this untold tale is "'A Conversion' by Tom Thumtack."

Four builders stand around a fire at night, illuminated by its warming glow, enveloped by billowing smoke. It is a convening of the trades. The air is crisp and the sky is clear, filled with stars or else agitated with a blizzard. The object of their animated discussion and product of their labor, a textured hollow-tile wall stands tall but incomplete. Bemoaning the difficulty of integrating structure with the technical demands of electrical, plumbing, and heating subs, Squires had once observed, "Nothing is so heartbreaking as to see a carefully erected tile wall cut all to pieces by these three trades."[90]

We might recognize the scene from before; for, it resembles a photograph from Squires's architectural treatise on the hollow-tile house (Figure 2.23).

FIGURE 5.4 *"A Conversion by Tom Thumtack." Artist's proof, 1914. Rockwell Kent Papers; Box 21; Squires, Frederick; Rare Book and Manuscript Library, Columbia University Library. By permission of Plattsburgh State Art Museum.*

The wall is unfinished just like his story, both stopped mid-course. Frederick Squires's sudden exit from the profession of architecture, decamping first to Ohio and then to Illinois to join his brother in an oil drilling business, was apparently a career conversion already waiting in the wings. With a growing family to feed, a hardscrabble profession, and a publisher not paying promised royalties, it does not appear that Squires hesitated long before leaping at the new opportunity. After such an intense sprint toward the high bar of architectural practice, his pole vaulter's vaulting ambition seems to have launched him right out of the box.

Leaving the architecture profession behind, Squires does not seem to have ever looked back, but it does appear that he carried his architect's curiosity, inventive spirit, and sense of adventure with him into new domains. A technical paper that he published in 1949 provides a few biographical details about the author to round out this unfinished picture.

> Frederick Squires, petroleum engineer for the Illinois State Geological Survey, is credited with the first successful applications of repressuring and intentional water flooding in the Illinois oil fields. He holds degrees from Williams College and the School of Mines of Columbia University. He formerly was partner and field manager of Squires Brothers, Remlik Oil Company and Dinsmor Oil Company, which were organized at the inception of secondary recovery. He has invented several oil field processes and has contributed a number of technical papers on petroleum engineering.[91]

Nowhere is there even a hint of Squires's previous professional occupation! Instead, out of his earlier incarnation as an architect, distinct but related personas had emerged: engineer, bricoleur, inventor.

We know of one last conversion that Frederick Squires undertook. For his own home in Champaign, Illinois, he found two almost identical vernacular frame houses, both L-shaped in plan. Leaving one intact, he had the main section of the other hauled by horses to the other site, marrying the twin houses on new hollow-tile foundations to form an integral H-shaped abode. With unifying additions and shingles cladding the exterior, he carved a warm and homey interior rich with arts and crafts-inspired detail.[92] It does not seem at all accidental that the home he wrought for himself bears a mirror's resemblance to the Best House exhibited by Squires & Wynkoop at the Architecture League in 1909 (Figure 5.5). Like Tom Thumtack playing the double role, architect Squires had become his own client; and as has perhaps already been suspected, satire and autobiography were never very far apart in his allegorical architec-tonic tales. When read in that light, Squires's comments about design conversions convey an implicit philosophy of architectural practice relevant for present times as well.

> But it is in the rejuvenating of old buildings that one finds the best place to try the whole bag of tricks. The fact that the house of thirty years ago was seldom designed by an architect, but was well and soundly built by carpenter or mason, gives the redesigner a chance to be the wonder worker who gives new lamps for old. The carpenter's house, for very lack of attempt at any architectural design, was of simple form and outline, and this simplicity lends itself gracefully to modern adornment by skilled hands.

The variety of professional trajectories pursued by Frederick Squires and indeed by his contemporaries and collaborators Rockwell Kent, George

FIGURE 5.5 *Squires & Wynkoop, Architects; Country House for Mrs. E.L. Best; Bronxville, NY;* The Hollow-Tile House *(New York: William T. Comstock Co., 1913).*

S. Chappell, and Frank Miles Day reveals the heterogeneity of interests that underlay architectural practice undergoing its own Progressive Era conversion. While architects maneuvered for social position as a requisite of professional advancement and prestige, shared notions about professional boundaries—the technical and ethical functions of the architect—were tending to fracture and diverge. As in any process of cultural ferment, we can find both residual and emergent tendencies simultaneously at play during those times and ours, each brushing against the grain of a dominant order of practice. Then as today, we can find new relationships forming, and new architects being assembled, wherever the interests and abilities of otherwise independent agents cross or align in novel and often ephemeral ways. Recognizing the complex set of interactions that constitute any field, we may better understand how architecture, far from being a static formation, has perennially developed new operational standards, ones that respond to shifting situations and aspirations; to the motivations of actors, their functions and tools (Figure 5.6).

A century now after the first publication of *The Handbook of Architectural Practice*, old questions still arise. They are ethical questions; they are questions of the architect's constructive role in society; and they are symptoms, all, of the perennial play of practice and technology, of capital and labor. Contemporary debates about constructability and sustainability, social responsibility and cultural appropriateness, digitally enabled routines,

FIGURE 5.6 *"Finis." Artist's proof, 1914. Rockwell Kent Papers; Box 21; Squires, Frederick; Rare Book and Manuscript Library, Columbia University Library. By permission of Plattsburgh State Art Museum.*

and performance-oriented practices all beg for an extra measure of historical awareness to temper hubris with humility. As this narrative suggests, the interplay of competing interests as well as choices among alternative paths has historically ordered the field of professional practice in ways we have hardly begun to fathom.

NOTES

Introduction

1. For overviews of the early history of architectural publication in the United States, see Dell Upton, "Pattern Books and Professionalism: Aspects of the Transformation of Domestic Architecture in America, 1800–1860," *Winterthur Portfolio* 19, no. 2–3 (1984): 107–59; Mary Woods, "The First American Architectural Journals: The Profession's Voice," *Society of Architectural Historians. Journal* 48, no. 2 (1989): 117–38.

2. The specific reference here is to Burton J. Bledstein, *The Culture of Professionalism: The Middle Class and the Development of Higher Education in America*, 1st ed. (New York: Norton, 1976).

3. Regarding variable notions of disciplinarity in the field of architecture, specifically in relation to architectural education and the general process of professionalization, see Mark Linder's essay "Disciplinarity: Redefining Architecture's Limits and Identity," in *Architecture School: Three Centuries of Educating Architects in North America*, ed. Joan Ockman and Rebecca Williamson (Cambridge, MA; Washington, DC: MIT Press; Association of Collegiate Schools of Architecture, 2012), 291–98.

4. This study aligns with those strains of social thought that bring the issue of practice into focus and to the foreground of attention. Rather than treating practice as the mere enactment of underlying principles, theories, or structuring relationships, current approaches to practice in fields of sociology and anthropology tend to emphasize contributions of individual agency and action in the constitution of larger systems of order and the construction of structures of power and meaning. The structure/agency duality is especially evident in the field of architecture where the play between "systems of professionalism" and locally conditioned forms of practice suggests a dynamic, responsive, and reciprocating process of exchange, where residual, dominant, and emergent approaches to action continuously interact. For an overview, see Jane Fajans, "Practice: An Anthropological Approach," in *International Encyclopedia of the Social & Behavioral Sciences*, ed. James D. Wright (Amsterdam; Boston: Elsevier, 2015), 782–87; Sherry B. Ortner, "Theory in Anthropology since the Sixties," *Comparative Studies in Society and History* 26, no. 1 (1984): 126–66. Key influences in the formulation of the present study include: Pierre Bourdieu, *The Logic of Practice*, trans. Richard Nice (Stanford, CA: Stanford University Press, 1990); Michel De Certeau, *The Practice of Everyday Life*, trans. Steven F. Rendall (Berkeley: University of California Press, 1984); Michel Foucault, *Discipline & Punish: The Birth of*

the Prison, trans. Alan Sheridan, 2nd ed. (New York: Vintage Books, 1995); Clifford Geertz, "Thick Description: Toward an Interpretive Theory of Culture," in *The Interpretation of Cultures: Selected Essays* (New York: Basic Books, Inc., 2000, 1973); Anthony Giddens, *The Constitution of Society: Outline of the Theory of Structuration* (Berkeley: University of California Press, 1984); Bruno Latour, *Reassembling the Social: An Introduction to Actor-Network-Theory*, Clarendon Lectures in Management Studies (Oxford; New York: Oxford University Press, 2005); Sherry Ortner, *Anthropology and Social Theory: Culture, Power, and the Acting Subject* (Durham, NC; London: Duke University Press, 2006); Raymond Williams, *Marxism and Literature* (Oxford, UK: Oxford University Press, 1977).

Chapter 1

1. In consideration of how Edward Said's concept of "traveling theory" may be applied to the portability of standards of architectural practice across cultures, see George B. Johnston, "Traveling Professions: How Local Contingencies Complicate Globalizing Tendencies in the Standardization of Architectural Practice" (paper presented at the Seeking the City: Proceedings of the 96th ACSA Annual Meeting, Houston, TX, 2008), 15–22; Edward Said, "Traveling Theory," in *The World, the Text, and the Critic* (Cambridge, MA: Harvard University Press, 1983), 226–47. In a similar vein, Bernard Bailyn's "deeply contextualist approach to history" is invoked here as a methodological aim: "I ... had been surprised to see the dominant cluster of ideas, beliefs, and attitudes that came to light when the Enlightenment platitudes were put aside and one concentrated on what the leaders of the Revolutionary movement were actually saying, where their ideas had actually come from, how those ideas had cohered, and how, though derived from a different world, they had articulated circumstances unique to North America." See Bernard Bailyn, *The Ideological Origins of the American Revolution* (Cambridge, MA: Harvard University Press, 1992), v.

2. T. M. Clark, *Architect, Owner and Builder before the Law: A Summary of American and English Decisions on the Principal Questions Relating to Building, and the Employment of Architects, with about Eight Hundred References, Including Also Practical Suggestions in Regard to the Drawing of Building Contracts, and Forms of Contract Suited to Various Circumstances* (New York: Macmillan Company, 1894), 180.

3. Dell Upton has sketched the pre-1860 terrain of architectural training and practice in Joan Ockman and Rebecca Williamson, *Architecture School: Three Centuries of Educating Architects in North America* (Cambridge, MA; Washington, DC: MIT Press; Association of Collegiate Schools of Architecture, 2012), 36–65.

4. Such might be the case of Drayton Hall along the Ashley River near Charleston, SC. See Arnold Berke, "Searching for Palladio: How Did One Italian Architect Shape Some of America's Greatest Houses?" *Preservation* 61, no. 4 (2009): 40–43; George W. McDaniel and Carter C. Hudgins, "Mystery

at Drayton Hall: The Surprise Appearance of a 1765 Watercolor Sheds New Light on a Palladian Past," *Magazine Antiques* 177, no. 4 (2010): 148–51.

5   Such narratives comport with the east-west dialectic of cultural distinction and dissemination that inform so much of the American imaginary. See, for example, Frederick H. Baumann, "Relation of Architect to Contractor and Journeymen," *Inland Architect & News Record* 6 (1885): 60–61.

6   W. W. Boyington, "Differences between the Methods of Architectural Practice Prevalent Now and Those of Fifty Years Ago," *Proceedings of the 21st Annual Convention of the American Institute of Architects* 21 (1887): 102–06.

7   Notions of cultural dispersion as charted by researchers in the field of material cultural studies are of particular interest in this regard. See Henry H. Glassie, *Pattern in the Material Folk Culture of the Eastern United States* (Philadelphia: University of Pennsylvania Press, 1969). More recent attempts to account for the "red state/blue state" divisions in the US political map have pointed to the diverse cultural orientations of North American colonists that became geographically and socially ingrained. See Colin Woodard, *American Nations: A History of the Eleven Rival Regional Cultures of North America* (New York: New York: Viking, 2011).

8   "The Need of Unity," editorial, *American Architect and Building News* 1 (1876): 2–3. William Rotch Ware was the nephew of noted architectural educator William Robert Ware (1832–1915). Henry F. Withey and Elsie Rathburn Withey, *Biographical Dictionary of American Architects (Deceased)* (Los Angeles: New Age Publishing Co., 1956), 632–33. *American Architect and Building News*, first published in 1876, was "the first American periodical with a future," having a sustained run until 1938 when it was absorbed by *Architectural Record*. Mary Woods, "The First American Architectural Journals: The Profession's Voice," *Society of Architectural Historians. Journal* 48, no. 2 (1989): 118.

9   "The Need of Unity," 2–3.

10 Boyington was born in Springfield, MA, and received some training in architecture in New York under a Professor Stone. He arrived in Chicago, according to his own account, at about the age of 14. Withey and Withey, *Biographical Dictionary of American Architects (Deceased)*, 71.

11 Boyington, "Differences between the Methods of Architectural Practice Prevalent Now and Those of Fifty Years Ago," 102–06.

12 Ibid., 104. Boyington fails to account for the esteemed tradition of very highly skilled master builders that had been long-established in Philadelphia and that exercised a notable influence through its guild organization, the Carpenters' Company of the City and County of Philadelphia.

13 Frank Eugene Kidder, "The Architect as a Builder and as an Engineer," *Inland Architect & News Record* 29 (1897): 22.

14 C. H. Blackall, "Fifty Years Ago," *American Architect* 129, no. 5 (1926): 7–9.

15 William P. Bannister, "The Practice of Architecture," *American Architect* 129, no. 5 (1926): 41–42.

16 Kidder reports on a contemporaneous address by an English architect on the topic "An Ideal Architect," that "sets forth an ideal standard, which should

be approached by all architects. In this address he says: '[The architect] must, in every sense of the word, be an artist. He must be a constructor. He must be an engineer.'" Notwithstanding his sympathies with his English colleagues, Kidder admits that disintegrative trends in education and practice increasingly frustrated realization of that ideal. Kidder, "The Architect as a Builder and as an Engineer," 22.

17 Magali Sarfatti Larson, *The Rise of Professionalism: A Sociological Analysis* (Berkeley: University of California Press, 1977), xv–xvii. The American Institute of Architects was established in 1857, architectural studies were established at Massachusetts Institute of Technology in 1867, and Illinois was the first state to implement the licensure of architects in 1897.

18 E. H. Kendall, "Report of Special Committee on Uniform Building Contract," *Proceedings of the 21st Annual Convention of the American Institute of Architects* 21 (1887): 69. The short-lived Western Association of Architects was founded in 1884 and merged with the AIA in 1889. Comprised primarily of mid-western practitioners with a majority of its membership from Chicago, the WAA's more inclusive membership requirements were a significant contrast with the more elitist orientation of the AIA. See Cecil D. Elliott, *The American Architect from the Colonial Era to the Present* (Jefferson, NC: McFarland & Co., 2003), 78–81; Mary N. Woods, *From Craft to Profession: The Practice of Architecture in Nineteenth Century America* (Berkeley: University of California Press, 1999), 38–42.

19 A cogent and informative account of the history of the development of the AIA's standard contracts can be found in American Institute of Architects, *The American Institute of Architects Official Guide to the 2007 AIA Contract Documents* (Hoboken, NJ: John Wiley & Sons, 2009), 12–37. Besides the establishment of a standard schedule of charges for architectural services in the years following the Civil War, calls had been issued as early as the 1870s from leaders of the profession such as Richard Morris Hunt and Thomas U. Walter for the establishment of some standard form of construction contract, though none of these efforts were brought to fruition until the late 1880s.

20 P. B. Wight, "Building Contracts," *Inland Architect and News Record* 9, no. 4 (1887): 33.

21 Ibid., 33–34. As it is noted in the speech transcript, Wight was at that time the general manager of the Wight Fireproofing Company of Chicago, an innovator in fireproof doors, and in that capacity apparently ranked himself among the mechanics, master builders, and contractors in attendance at the convention. He was, however, also an architect and had been active within the American Institute of Architects since 1866 while still in practice in New York and served as that organization's national secretary 1869–1871. Withey and Withey, *Biographical Dictionary of American Architects (Deceased)*, 657; American Institute of Architects, *The American Institute of Architects Official Guide to the 2007 AIA Contract Documents*, 13, 20–21.

22 Wight, "Building Contracts," 33.

23 Ibid.

24 "Talking to the Builders," *New York Times*, 27 November 1889, 4. The words and sentiment are those of William H. Sayward speaking two years

later to the Building Trades Club of New York City about the purpose of organizing builders.

25 See O. P. Hatfield, Alfred Stone, and J. H. Windrim, "Report of Special Committee on Uniform Building Contract," *Proceedings of the 22nd Annual Convention of the American Institute of Architects* 22 (1888): 62–63. Oliver Perry Hatfield (1819–91) practiced architecture in New York, was an early member of the American Institute of Architects, serving for a time as the Treasurer of that organization. Withey and Withey, *Biographical Dictionary of American Architects (Deceased)*, 271. William Sayward (1845–1934) served as Secretary of the National Association of Builders for over fifty years. He was instrumental in negotiating the terms of the 1888 Uniform Contract and remained a force for recognition of builders, and an irritant to architects, throughout his career. Charles A. Sayward, *The Sayward Family: Being the History and Genealogy of Henry Sayward of York, Maine and His Descendants: With a Brief Account of Other Saywards Who Settled in America*, Variation: Genealogy & Local History (Ipswich, MA: Independent Press, 1890), 154–55.

26 "The Contractor shall and will well and sufficiently perform and finish, under the direction, and to the satisfaction of [insert name] Architect (acting as Agent of said Owner), all the work included in the [insert project description] agreeably to the drawings and specifications made by the said Architect, ..." "Form of Contract Adopted by the Joint Committee of the American Institute of Architects, the Western Association of Architects, and the National Association of Builders," (Washington, DC: American Institute of Architects Archives, 1888), Article 1.

27 "Should it appear that the work hereby intended to be done, or any of the matters relative thereto, are not sufficiently detailed or explained on the said drawings, or in the said specifications, the Contractor shall apply to the Architect for such further drawings or explanations as may be necessary, ... and in event of any doubt or question arising respecting the true meaning of the drawings or specifications, reference shall be made to the Architect, whose decision thereon, being just and impartial, shall be final and conclusive." Ibid., Article 2.

28 "Should any alterations be required in the work shown or described by the drawings or specifications, a fair and reasonable valuation of the work added or omitted, shall be made by the Architect, and the sum herein agreed to be paid for he work according to the original specification, shall be increased or diminished as the case may be."

29 "Should the Contractor at any time refuse or neglect to supply a sufficiency of properly skilled workmen, or of materials of the proper quality, or fail in any respect to prosecute the work with promptness and diligence, or fail in performance of any of the agreements on [] part herein contained, such refusal, neglect or failure being certified by the Architect, the Owner shall be at liberty, after three days written notice to the Contractor, ..." "Uniform Contract of 1888," Article 12.

30 Wight, "Building Contracts," 33.

31 National Association of Builders of the United States of America, "Official Report of the Third Annual Convention" (Boston: National Association of Builders of the United States of America., 1889), 6.

32 Ibid., 25–26.
33 Ibid., 36–43.
34 John S. Stevens, "Report of the Committee on Uniform Contract," *Official Report of the Ninth Annual Convention of the National Association of Builders of the United States of America* 9 (1895): 38–40.
35 Louis D. Brandeis, "Suggestive Form of Contract Printed for the Boston Society of Architects," *American Architect & Building News* 37 (1892): 7.
36 American Institute of Architects, "Proceedings of the Thirty-Fifth Annual Convention of the American Institute of Architects" (Washington, DC, 1901), 42.
37 "Important Revision of the Uniform Contract," *Inland Architect & News Record* 40 (1902): 36.
38 American Institute of Architects, "Proceedings of the Thirty-Fifth Annual Convention of the American Institute of Architects," 42.
39 Clark, *Architect, Owner and Builder before the Law*, 180.
40 As Emile Durkheim would suggest a continent away but close in time, "… when men unite in a contract, it is because, through the division of labor, either simple or complex, they need each other. But in order for them to co-operate harmoniously, it is not enough that they enter into a relationship, nor even that they feel the state of mutual dependence in which they find themselves. It is still necessary that the conditions of this co-operation be fixed for the duration of their relations. The rights and duties of each must be defined, not only in view of the situation such as it presents itself at the moment when the contract is made, but with foresight for the circumstances which may arise to modify it. Otherwise, at every instant, there would be conflicts and endless difficulties. We must not forget that, if the division of labor makes interests solidary, it does not confound them; it keeps them distinct and opposite …. [E]ach of the contractants, while needing the other, seeks to obtain what he needs at the least expense; that is to say, to acquire as many rights as possible in exchange for the smallest possible obligations." Émile Durkheim, "Progressive Preponderance of Organic Solidarity," in *Émile Durkheim on Morality and Society, Selected Writings*, ed. Robert Neelly Bellah (Chicago: University of Chicago Press, 1973), 97–98.
41 German sociologist Georg Simmel observed, "Exchange is not merely the addition of the two processes of giving and receiving. It is, rather, something new. Exchange constitutes a third process, something that emerges when each of those processes is simultaneously the cause and effect of the other." Georg Simmel, "Exchange," in *On Individuality and Social Forms; Selected Writings*, ed. Donald N. Levine (Chicago: University of Chicago Press, 1971), 57.
42 As a leading and very active member of the architecture profession, Day's correspondence and papers provide significant insights into the pressures shaping US architectural practice in the period between the Civil War and the First World War. Notable repositories of Day's materials are the manuscript collections of the Architecture Archives of the University of Pennsylvania in Philadelphia and the American Institute of Architects Archives in Washington, DC. A PhD dissertation focuses primarily upon the work issuing from Day's

architectural practice. While not delving deeply into the matters treated here with regard to Day's authorship of the *Handbook of Architectural Practice*, that work provides useful insights nonetheless into turn-of-the-century architectural practice. See Patricia Lawson Heintzelman Keebler, "The Life and Work of Frank Miles Day" (PhD, University of Delaware, 1980).

43 Frank Miles Day, "Letter to J. Lawrence Mauran, Et Al. Dated 6 January 1917," in *AIA Office Files Autograph: Waid, Dan Everett (1864–1939)* (Washington, DC: American Institute of Architects Archives, 1917).

44 Ibid.

45 Day served a two-year term as president of the AIA from 1906 to 1907.

46 The records of correspondence related to the drafting of *The Handbook of Architectural Practice* reveal Day's assiduous process of sifting through the letters, striking through every read passage with a vertically oriented pencil line and then compiling all the salient comments in master lists, each point to be addressed in turn.

47 American Institute of Architects, *The Handbook of Architectural Practice* (Washington, DC: Press of the American Institute of Architects, Inc., 1920), 11.

48 John L. Hamilton, "Letter to Frank Miles Day Dated 7 February 1918," in *AIA, Office Files, Documents: Handbook, Evolution of, 1915–1917* (Washington, DC: The American Institute of Architects Archives, 1918), Box 1 Handbook, Evolution of, 1915–17.

49 William B. King, "Letter to Frank Miles Day Dated 14 September 1917," ibid.

50 H. G. Heddinger, "Response Dated 15 September 1917 to Frank Miles Day Letter of 8 August 1917,"ibid.

51 Warren Powers Laird, "Letter to Frank Miles Day Dated 8 October 1917," ibid. At the time of Day's premature death, Laird observed, "Mr. Day combined to a rare degree the qualities of artist and executive, and his influence was potent in the advancement of both the quality of American architecture and the standards of professional practice under which it is wrought into being. To few men is it given thus to aid in moulding both the methods and ideals of a great profession." "Frank Miles Day: An Appreciation," *American Architect* 114, no. 2219 (1918): 15–16.

52 At the turn of the century, Frank E. Kidder sensed the expanding scope of architects' responsibility and the dilemmas thus entailed: "Of course one can hardly expect to master all of the problems of architectural styles and proportions, building construction, the strength of materials and structures and the details of plumbing and electricity by the time he is twenty-two or twenty-three years old, and it is questionable if a person should be allowed to assume the responsibility of directing operations that require this knowledge at such an age." Kidder, "The Architect as a Builder and as an Engineer," 22.

53 *The Handbook of Architectural Practice*, 11.

54 Representative examples of such turn-of-the-century literary portrayals are reviewed in Herbert Croly, "The Architect in Recent Fiction," *Architectural Record* 17, no. 2 (1905): 137–39. Harvard-educated Croly (1869–1930) served in his early career as editor of *Architectural Record* from 1900 to 1906. In later

years, his authorship of *The Promise of American Life* (1909) and role as founding editor of *The New Republic* (1914) place him among the founders of American liberalism and as an intellectual force of the Progressive Movement. "Herbert Croly Dies at Santa Barbara," *New York Times*, May 18, 1930, 31.

55 Frederick Squires, *Architec-tonics: The Adventures of Tom Thumtack, Architect* (New York: Comstock, 1914). The journal *Architecture and Building*, published in New York by William T. Comstock from 1911 to 1932, was a continuation of several other journals including *Architects' and Builders' Magazine* (1899–1911) "devoted to the interests of architects, engineers, builders, woodworkers and persons contemplating building." The publication in book form of previously published serial essays was a typical practice of this and other architectural journals of the era. The *Tom Thumtack* essays were published serially for most of 1914 and 1915. The book version was originally intended to comprise two volumes, but only one volume was ever published. A total of twenty-one separate essays were published in either journal or book form. "Volume One" of the book included fifteen chapters plus an introduction and conclusion. Of that number, only nine of the stories had been previously published in the journal. An additional six installments previously published in the journal did not appear in the book and were likely intended for inclusion in the anticipated second volume. There is suggestion of the existence of at least one additional, unpublished story, "A Conversion," the text of which has not been located. The completed illustrations for the story have been identified among archival materials. See Rockwell Kent, "A Conversion," in *Rockwell Kent Papers, c. 1885–1970* (Columbia University Rare Book & Manuscript Library, 1914), Box 13, Book Illustrations, Squires, Architec-tonics.

56 Squires, *Architec-tonics*, 13.

57 "Architects of To-Day," *Architecture* 20 (1909): 177–84; *The Nineteen Hundred & Four Columbian: The Year Book of the Junior Class*, vol. 14 (New York: Columbia University, 1902), 319.

58 Frederick Squires, *The Hollow-Tile House* (New York: The William T. Comstock Co., 1913). As in the case of the Tom Thumtack stories, the essays comprising *The Hollow-Tile House* had previously been serialized in the pages of *Architecture and Building*.

59 Squires, *Architec-tonics*, 29.

60 Ibid., 25–33.

61 Ibid., 55–63.

62 Ibid., 15–24.

Chapter 2

1 While positioning himself as something of an owner's advising angel, Thumtack suggests a mode of project delivery we might recognize today in which program and construction managers guide owners through the complex process of engaging design professionals and managing the design and construction process on the owner's behalf.

NOTES

2 Frederick Squires, "Tom Thumtack, Client," *Architecture and Building* 46, no. 12 (1914): 457–59.

3 H. S. Kissam, "The Principles of the Business Management of Office Practice of Architects," *American Architect & Building News* 94, no. 1702 (1908): 45. Descriptions of late-nineteenth-century firms such as Burnham and Root included plans showing spatial organization along with detailed descriptions of office organization and methods. See "The Organization of an Architects Office: Parts I–IV," *Engineering and Building Record* 21, no. 6, 11–13 (1890): 81, 83–84, 95, 165.

4 Frederick Squires, *Architec-tonics: The Adventures of Tom Thumtack, Architect* (New York: Comstock, 1914), 132–33.

5 *The Handbook of Architectural Practice* (Washington, DC: Press of the American Institute of Architects, Inc., 1920), 20. D. Everett Waid (1864–1939) was a prominent New York architect, having practiced previously in Chicago after studying at the Art Institute and the Columbia University School of Architecture. Henry F. Withey and Elsie Rathburn Withey, *Biographical Dictionary of American Architects (Deceased)* (Los Angeles: New Age Publishing Co., 1956), 622–23. During the period of the development of *The Handbook of Architectural Practice*, Waid served as Treasurer of the American Institute of Architects and was a frequent correspondent with Frank Miles Day on matters of its contents. Day had specifically solicited Waid's input with a handwritten note: "The subject of the Handbook is so near akin to matters that have greatly interested you and on which you have written that I shall value anything that you may send me looking to its improvement." Frank Miles Day, "Letter to D. Everett Waid (Undated August 1917)," in *AIA Office Files Autograph: Waid, Dan Everett (1864–1939)* (Washington, DC: American Institute of Architects Archives 1917), AIA Committees F-Hi, Box 16L. Indeed, the concise title of the handbook was Waid's recommendation in lieu of Day's more cumbersome original title, "An Architect's Handbook of Professional Practice and Business Administration Issued by the American Institute of Architects." D. Everett Waid, "Letter to Frank Miles Day Dated 8 November 1917," in *AIA, Office Files, Documents: Handbook, Evolution of, 1915–1917* (Washington, DC: The American Institute of Architects Archives, 1917), RG 801 SR 8 Box 1.

6 "How Architects Work I: Offices of Noted Architects," *Brickbuilder* 20, no. 12 (1911): 249.

7 The first set of essays were published between 1911 and 1912, inclusive. Ibid.; "How Architects Work II: Offices of Noted Architects," *Brickbuilder* 21, no. 1 (1912); "How Architects Work III: Offices of Noted Architects," *Brickbuilder* 21, no. 2 (1912). An earlier series of essays from the late-nineteenth century published in an engineering-oriented journal had profiled several architects' offices, among them two in Chicago that were of particular interest for being inserted into larger buildings of their architects' own design—Burnham & Root in the Rookery Building and Adler & Sullivan in the Auditorium Building. "The Organization of an Architects Office: Parts I–IV," 83–84; "New Offices of Adler & Sullivan Architects, Chicago," *Engineering and Building Record* 22, no. 1 (1890): 5.

8   "How Architects Work II: Offices of Noted Architects," 10.
9   "How Architects Work III: Offices of Noted Architects," 38.
10 Neil Harris, *Cultural Excursions: Marketing Appetites and Cultural Tastes in Modern America* (Chicago: University of Chicago Press, 1990), 111–31; Tony Bennett, *The Birth of the Museum: History, Theory, Politics* (New York: Routledge, 1995), 59–88.
11 Paul Cret, "The Utility of Exhibitions," in *T Square Club Catalogue of the Eleventh Annual Architectural Exhibition 1904–1905*, ed. William S. Vaux and Richard Erskine (Philadelphia: T Square Club, 1905), 9–10.
12 Ibid., 10–11.
13 Ibid., 9–12.
14 Indeed, builders in both Philadelphia and New York maintained their own "permanent exhibitions of building materials … where the architect and client may see a most complete and instructive display of all branches of the building industry." See W. H. Sayward, "The National Association of Master Builders," *Carpentry and Building* 12 (1890): 135–51. Harvey Wiley Corbett, "Year Book of the Architectural League of New York and Catalogue of the Twenty-Fourth Annual Exhibition," ed. Architectural League of New York (New York: Kalkhoff Company, 1909), 165; "The Sixteenth Annual Architectural Exhibition" (Philadelphia: Philadelphia Chapter American Institute of Architects; The T-Square Club, 1910), 206–07.
15 "The Architect, the Contractor, the Publisher: Not a Fable," *Inland Architect & News Record* 26 (1896): 55. As reported in 1918, the AIA proscribed such practices, citing the ethical impropriety of compelling such advertisements. "Resolved, That the Board of Directors condemns the issuance of catalogues of architectural exhibitions which are supported by advertising, as injurious to the profession because the support so given is in the nature of a contribution which the advertiser dislikes to refuse to make, rather than a payment made for value received, and believes that those holding such exhibitions should give consideration to other unobjectionable means for financing them." "Wrong Methods of Advertising the Architect," *Architecture* 37, no. 4 (1918): 104.
16 "Sixteenth Annual Exhibition of the T-Square Club," *American Architect* 97, pt. 2, no. 1791 (1910): 162.
17 Kent's renown as an architectural renderer is confirmed in his autobiography as well as by his being featured in a monograph of his work. Besides his work for Ewing & Chappell, Kent completed freelance work for the firms of Aymar Embury II, Henry Hornbostel, Delano & Aldrich, and John Russell Pope among likely others. "Monographs on Architectural Renderers. The Work of Rockwell Kent," *Brickbuilder* 23, no. 7 (1914): 167–69; Rockwell Kent, *It's Me O Lord: The Autobiography of Rockwell Kent* (New York: Dodd, Mead & Company, 1955), 250–51, 73–74.
18 Kent, *It's Me O Lord*, 65.
19 Ibid., 47–50. For a discussion of the role of the manual training movement in setting US educational agendas in the late-nineteenth and early-twentieth centuries, see George Barnett Johnston, *Drafting Culture: A Social History of Architectural Graphic Standards* (Cambridge, MA: MIT Press, 2008), 9–52.

NOTES

20 Kent, *It's Me O Lord*, 68–69.
21 "Six Publications Run by Columbia Graduates," *New York Times*, January 4, 1903, Magazine Section, 1.
22 Kent, *It's Me O Lord*, 70; *The Nineteen Hundred & Four Columbian: The Year Book of the Junior Class*, vol. 14 (New York: Columbia University, 1902). Since *The Columbian* was a chronicle of the junior class, Kent at the date of this publication had not yet begun his contributions to *The Jester*.
23 *The Nineteen Hundred & Four Columbian: The Year Book of the Junior Class*, 14, 314, 19.
24 Kent, *It's Me O Lord*, 69, 277.
25 "Obituary: Frederick Squires," *Williams Alumni Review* 48, no. 11 (1956): 33; Beverly Seyler, "Frederick J. Squires, 1879–1956, Petroleum Engineering," *ISGS History Heritage Memorial* (2006), http://isgs.illinois.edu/frederick-j-squires; Karen Lang Kummer, "National Register of Historic Places Registration Form: Frederick Squires House" (United States Department of the Interior, National Park Service, 2011).
26 New York initiated architectural registration in 1915. "The History of NCARB," (Washington, DC: National Council of Architectural Registration Boards, 1994), 1, Table 1.
27 *The Nineteen Hundred & Three Columbian: The Year Book of the Junior Class*, vol. 13 (New York: Columbia University, 1901), 301. See "Elevation of a Town Church" in *Catalogue of the Annual Architectural Exhibition for 1902–1903*, ed. William C. Hays (Philadelphia: T Square Club, 1903), 77.
28 "John Wynkoop, Architect," *New York Times*, December 14, 1922, 21; James Philip Noffsinger, *The Influence of the École Des Beaux-Arts on the Architects of the United States* (Washington, DC: Catholic University of America Press, 1955), 102.
29 Frederick Squires, "The Gargoyle Gate," *Arts and Decoration* 1, no. 1 (1911): 130; *The Hollow-Tile House* (New York: The William T. Comstock Co., 1913), 180; "Gargoyle Gate at Weston Field," MIT Libraries DOME, http://hdl.handle.net/1721.3/144989.
30 "Phi Delta Theta Fraternity House, Williams College," *Architectural Record* 24, no. 3 (1908): 242–43.
31 "Recent Work by Squires and Wynkoop," *International Studio* 37, no. 148 (1909): cviii–cix.
32 Ibid.
33 "Architects of To-Day," *Architecture* 20 (1909): 177–84.
34 "Fireproof Houses," *American Architect & Building News* 96, no. 1755 (1909): 53–55. Other publications in the arena of hollow-tile construction include: "Fireproof Houses," *Carpentry and Building* 31, no. 10 (1909): 329–31; John Wynkoop, "The Design and Construction of a Concrete House: Part 1," *Cement Age* 8, no. 5 (1909): 314–20; "The Design and Construction of a Concrete House: Part 2," *Cement Age* 8, no. 6 (1909): 426–41; "The Design and Construction of a Concrete House: Part 3," *Cement Age* 9, no. 1 (1909): 10–19; Architects Squires and Wynkoop, "The

Fire Proof House as the American Type," *Western Architect* 16 (1910): 107–08; Frederick Squires and John Wynkoop, "A Concrete House: A Description of the Constructive Features, Including Reinforcing, Heating, Ventilating and Electric Wiring of a Concrete House," *Cement Age* 11, no. 4 (1910): 188, 200–08.

35 Sara E. Wermiel, *The Fireproof Building: Technology and Public Safety in the Nineteenth-Century American City* (Baltimore: Johns Hopkins University Press, 2000), 203–05. Anthony P. Hatch, *Tinder Box: The Iroquois Theatre Disaster, 1903* (Chicago: Academy Chicago Publishers, 2003). The Iroquois disaster is still considered one of the deadliest single-building fires in the history of the United States.

36 "Attention Called to Theater Construction (Editorial)," *Inland Architect and News Record* 42, no. 6 (1904): 41.

37 Robert Herrick, *The Common Lot* (New York, London: The Macmillan company, 1904).

38 F. W. Fitzpatrick, "Our Annual Ash-Heap," *American Architect & Building News* 89 (1906): 151–52. See also: "Lessons of the Baltimore Fire," *Inland Architect & News Record* 43 (1904): 10–14; "San Francisco: Notes after a Thorough Investigation of the Results of the San Francisco Disaster," *Inland Architect & News Record* 47 (1906): 79–81.

39 "Necessity for Fireproofing Schools and Residences (Editorial)," ibid. 45, no. 1 (1905): 1.

40 Squires and Wynkoop, "The Fire Proof House as the American Type," 107–08.

41 Wynkoop, "The Design and Construction of a Concrete House: Part 1," 314–20.

42 These include houses commissioned by the journals *Cement Age* and *Building Progress*.

43 Squires and Wynkoop, "The Fire Proof House as the American Type," 107–08. Emphasis added.

44 "Real Estate Show. To Open at Madison Square Garden This Week—Unique Show," *New York Times*, May 15, 1910, 14; *Inexpensive Homes of Individuality* (New York: McBride, Winston, 1911), 3–16. Day described one of Squires & Wynkoop's fireproof houses from Mountain Station, NJ, as "based on modern English work but not to the sacrifice of a straightforward development of plan in simple materials."

45 One project was for a "high-grade office and loft building" at 114–116 East Sixteenth Street, and the other was a "loft building on the northeast corner of Seventh Avenue and Twenty-fourth Street," a project that was predicted to contribute to the "long expectant development [of Seventh Avenue] into a high-class commercial thoroughfare." "In the Real Estate Field: Loft Building Boom Stimulates Realty Market," *New York Times*, February 16, 1910, 15; "New Era Dawning for Seventh Avenue," *New York Times*, May 22, 1910, 67. It is unclear whether a third loft building located on 25th Street was ever realized. See "Perspectives of Three New York Loft Buildings Designed by Squires & Wynkoop Architects," *Architecture and Building* 42, no. 12 (1910): 506.

46 "Art and Architecture: Squires & Wynkoop Dissolve Partnership," *Architecture and Building* 43, no. 9 (1911): 22. Griffin was approximately fifteen years Wynkoop's senior. He had studied architecture at MIT in the 1880s and trained in the office of H. H. Richardson before founding his own practice. "News from the Classes: 1885," *The Technology Review* 23, no. 4 (1921): 631–32; "Percy Griffin [Obituary]," *New York Times*, March 16, 1921, 9.

47 According to his 1921 application for AIA membership, Wendehack did not attend a university but rather accrued some twenty years experience in Atelier Donn Barber (where no doubt he was familiar with Wynkoop) as well as experience in the offices of W. W. Bosworth, Pell & Corbett, and for short periods in other offices. He received some Beaux-Arts training in Paris (though he does not appear in the list of officially inscribed students), and he conducted independent studies in Rome. He lists the duration of the Squires & Wendehack partnership as four years, from 1911 to 1914. By the end of his career, Wendehack had established a substantial reputation for his expertise in the area of country club design. Clifford Wendehack, "Application for Membership," in *AIA Historical Directory of American Architects*, ed. American Institute of Architects (Washington, DC: AIA Archives, 1921); "Clifford Wendehack, Architect, 62 Is Dead," *New York Times*, May 16, 1948, 68; Henry F. Withey and Elsie Rathburn Withey, "Wendehack, Clifford C. (1885–5/15/1948)," in *Biographical Dictionary of American Architects (Deceased)* (Los Angeles: New Age Publishing Co., 1956), 643; Clifford C. Wendehack, *Golf & Country Clubs* (New York: W. Helburn, Ind., 1929).

48 Also, renderings of Griffin & Wynkoop's loft building on 32nd Street bears uncanny similarity, along with Wynkoop's distinctive graphic technique, to Squires & Wynkoop's 16th Street project designed at almost the very same time. Architect Frederick Squires, "Mercantile Building at N.E. Cor. 24th St. and 7th Ave., New York," *Architecture and Building* 44, no. 5 (1912): 222–24; Squires and Wynkoop, "Loft Building at 114–116 E. 16th Street, New York City," ibid., no. 7: 305–07; "Mcadoo Building in 32d Street," *New York Times*, September 17, 1911, 103.

49 John Wynkoop's distinctive diagonally oriented signature appears on his work included in the catalog of the 1904–05 T Square Club Exhibition. Thereafter, the characteristically refined renderings of Squires & Wynkoop's practice bear a similar mark.

50 Besides several private and institutional projects, a residential block of townhouses on W. 74th Street in Manhattan, New York City, received special critical attention. "A Residence Block, West 74th Street, New York: The Clark Estate Houses," *Architectural Record* 20, no. 5 (1906): 404–10.

51 Among projects receiving some notice in published accounts were the firm's project for a loft building (similar in aspect to the two loft buildings attributed to Squires & Wynkoop), a women's jail, and a sanctuary for the congregation of the Seventh Church of Christ the Scientist, all in Manhattan. "Mcadoo Building in 32d Street," 103; "Better Care for Women Prisoners in New Jail Which City Will Erect," *The Sun*, March 22, 1914, 2; "Will Build for [Christian] Scientists," *The Sun*, December 31, 1918, 9.

A factory for Pierce-Arrow and a perspective rendering a New Detention Center for Women were exhibited at the thirteenth annual exhibition of the Architecture League in 1915.

52 "Percy Griffin [Obituary]," 9; "John Wynkoop, Architect," 21.

53 For the genealogical connection between the publisher and the morality crusader, the sons of two brothers, see Cyrus B. Comstock, *A Comstock Genealogy: Descendants of William Comstock of New London, Conn. Who Died after 1662—Ten Generations* (New York: The Knickerbocker Press, 1907), 65; "William Tompkins Comstock: July 14, 1842—January 16, 1910," *Architecture and Building* 42, no. 12 (1910): 18; Heywood Broun and Margaret Leech, *Anthony Comstock, Roundsman of the Lord* (New York: Albert & Charles Boni, 1927), 36. The *New York Times* reported that Anthony Comstock "had been the centre of controversy during most of the forty-three years of his career as a crusader because of the differences of opinion over what constituted the dividing line between indecency and art." As the newspaper recounted, "One of the most discussed of Mr. Comstock's raids was upon the Art Students League Building at 15 West Fifty-Seventh Street. On August. 2, 1906, he caused a police patrol wagon to be backed up in front of the league's doors, where it was loaded with about 1,000 copies of 'The American Art Student,' a catalogue published for students. The alleged offence of the catalogue was the showing of five nude figures which had been selected by the Board of Control of the league as examples of the work done by its students. Miss Ann Robinson, book-keeper of the league, was arrested." "Anthony Comstock Dies in His Crusade," *New York Times*, September 22, 1915, 1, 6. William T. Comstock's architectural publications tended to deal with the construction side of architecture as opposed to the artistic emphasis of other journals and exhibition catalogs of the day.

54 The evolving names and masthead emphases of the journal provide a cross-section through changing attitudes about the organization of professional expertise and trade labor in the architecture field: (1) *Building*, 1882—"an architectural monthly treating on all matters of interest to the building trades"; (2) *Architecture and Building*, 1890—"published every Saturday devoted to art, architecture, archaeology, engineering, and decoration"; (3) *Builders Magazine*, 1899—"devoted to the interests of builders, carpenters, woodworkers, and persons contemplating building"; (4) *Architects' and Builders' Magazine*, 1899—"devoted to the interests of architects, engineers, builders, woodworkers and persons contemplating building" and later "devoted to the interests of architecture, building and engineering"; and (5) *Architecture and Building*, 1911—"a magazine devoted to contemporary architectural construction."

55 This included projects from Aymar Embury II, Grosvenor Atterbury, and McKim, Mead & White.

56 Frederick Squires, "Advertising: Reports from the Canon of Ethics," *Architecture and Building* 46, no. 8 (1914): 163.

57 *The Hollow-Tile House*, 43–44.

58 Ibid., 61.

59 Kent, *It's Me O Lord*, 277.

60 Ibid., 225–78. Rockwell Kent's life is far more interesting and relevant to topics surrounding the present study than can be fully accounted here. Kent's autobiographies and correspondence at the Smithsonian have been mostly scoured for references to his experiences as an architecture student, employee of Ewing & Chappell, and associations with Frederick Squires. Besides these sources and Kent's autobiographical/philosophical travel logs, see David Traxel, *An American Saga: The Life and Times of Rockwell Kent*, 1st ed. (New York: Harper & Row, 1980).

61 Frederick Squires, "Correspondence to Rockwell Kent Dated 3 February 1914," in *Rockwell Kent Papers, [circa 1840]–1993, bulk 1935–1961* (Washington, DC: Smithsonian Institution Archives of American Art, 1914).

62 Kent, *It's Me O Lord*, 303.

63 Frederick Squires, "Correspondence to Rockwell Kent Dated 15 September 1915," in *Rockwell Kent Papers, [circa 1840]–1993, bulk 1935–1961* (Washington, DC: Smithsonian Institution Archives of American Art, 1915).

64 "Obituary: Frederick Squires," 33.

65 Geoffrey E. Melhuish, "National Register of Historic Places Registration Form: Timber Point House in Biddeford, Maine" (United States Department of the Interior, National Park Service, 2013), 16–20; "George Shepard Chappell [Obituary]," in *Obituary Record of Graduates of Yale University Deceased During the Year 1946–1947* (1948), 47–48.

66 Kent, *It's Me O Lord*, 89.

67 Corbett, "Year Book of the Architectural League of New York and Catalogue of the Twenty-Fourth Annual Exhibition."

68 "Two Riding Academies," *Architectural Record* 21 (1907): 229–35; "Vanderbilt Gives $100,000: Will Erect Y.M.C.A. Building as Memorial to His Father," *New York Times*, November 7, 1907, 9; James L. Yarnall, *Newport through Its Architecture: A History of Styles from Postmedieval to Postmodern* (Newport, RI: Salve Regina University Press, 2005), 170–71; "Sanders Chemical Laboratory, Vassar College," *American Architect* 123, no. 17 (1923): 54. Alfred G. Vanderbilt, at age 37, was aboard the Lusitania when it was sunk in 1915.

69 "A Cottage on Oak Road, Tarrytown, N.Y.," *American Architect & Building News* 96, no. 1754 (1909): 52; "A House on Cobb Lane, Tarrytown, N.Y.," *American Architect* 96, no. 1754 (1909): 52; "House of Douglas Kent, Esq., Tarrytown, N.Y.," *American Architect & Building News* 96, no. 1754 (1909): 52; "House of Richard E. Forrest, Esq., Cedarhurst, L.I., N.Y.," *American Architect & Building News* 95, no. 13 (1909): 15; "Houses of Mrs. James Mcnaught and Mr. E.E. Ling, Tarrytown, N.Y.," *American Architect & Building News* 96, no. 1773 (1909): 259; "House of Mrs. Rockwell Kent, Tarrytown, N.Y.," *American Architect & Building News* 96, no. 1773 (1909): 259; "Portfolio of Country Residences. Residence of S.B. Lord, Cedarhurst, L.I," *Architectural Record* 28 (1910): 306.

70 "Architects in Costume: Beaux Arts Society Dines and Enjoys a 'Hysterical' Melodrama," *New York Times*, February 8, 1913, 24; "Ball of the Fine Arts: Beaux Arts Architects to Give First Dance at the Astor," *New York*

Times, December 22, 1913, 9; "The Ball of the Fine Arts," *New York Times*, February 15, 1914, 59. The Society of Beaux-Arts Architects was founded in 1894 by American alumni of the Ecole des Beaux-Arts for the purpose of promoting academic design culture in the United States through its atelier-based educational programs. See "To Found an Academy of Architecture," *New York Times*, January 23, 1894, 4. Founding members of the board of trustees included Charles F. McKim, Ernest Flagg, Richard H. Hunt, Walter B. Chambers, William A. Boring, and John M. Carrère.

71 George S. Chappell, "Paris School Days: How the Student Lives and Works at the Ecole Des Beaux Arts (Part 1)," *Architectural Record* 28 (1910): 37–41; "Paris School Days: How the Student Lives and Works at the Ecole Des Beaux Arts (Part 2)," *Architectural Record* 28 (1910): 350–55; "Paris School Days: How the Student Lives and Works at the Ecole Des Beaux Arts (Part 3)," *Architectural Record* 29 (1911): 139–43.

72 "Lattice—Its Use as an Architectural Embellishment—Part I," *Brickbuilder* 22, no. 5 (1913): 105–08; "Lattice—Its Use as an Architectural Embellishment—Part II," *Brickbuilder* 22, no. 9 (1913): 201–04.

73 Robert Williams Wood, *How to Tell the Birds from the Flowers: A Manual of Flornithology for Beginners* (San Francisco; New York: Paul Elder and Company, 1907). Wood (1868–1955) is noted for his contributions in the field of optics through advances in ultraviolet and infrared photography. The Editors of Encyclopedia Brittanica, "Robert Williams Wood," Encyclopedia Brittanica, Inc., https://www.britannica.com/biography/Robert-Williams-Wood.

74 "George Shepard Chappell [Obituary]," 47–48.

75 Cyril Hume, Thomas Caldecot Chubb, and Francis Woolsey Bronson, eds., *The Yale Record Book of Verse, 1872–1922* (New Haven: Yale University Press, 1922), 7. See also Henry S. Ely, Brian Hooker, and Wells Southworth Hastings, *Yale Fun: A Book of College Humor in Poetry, Pictures and Prose, Chosen with Loving Care from the Yale Record of the Past Eight Years; Conceived in the Sanctum, Founded on Foam, and Dedicated to the Humorous Faculty* (Hartford, CT: R. S. Peck, 1901).

76 "The Yale Record" article available through Wikipedia, while not consistently documented or attributed, provides a historical list of notable alumni associated with the publication. "The Yale Record," Wikipedia.org, https://en.wikipedia.org/w/index.php?title=The_Yale_Record&oldid=803048197.

77 Kent, *It's Me O Lord*, 316. Despite such ideological frictions, Kent later found himself in the company of Marcel Duchamp and Man Ray as part of the organizing committee of the First Annual Exhibition of the Society of Independent Artists. See Society of Independent Artists, "Catalog of the Frist Annual Exhibition of the Society of Independent Artists" (New York: William Edwin Rudge, 1917).

78 "Woman's College Buildings Will Be of the Tudor Type: Architects Ewing and Chappell of New York Selected to Design Structures–Bids to Be Asked Soon and the Work Will Be Rushed to Completion," *The Day [New London, CT]*, July 15, 1913, 3; Kevin D. Murphy, "Cubism and Collegiate Gothic: Raymond Duchamp-Villon at Connecticut College," *Archives of American Art Journal* 32, no. 1 (1992): 16–21.

79 This second set of essays notably included accounts of new offices for several firms whose old offices were described in the earlier series, "How Architects Work." D. Everett Waid, "The Business Side of an Architect's Office with a Description of the Architects' Building, New York," *Brickbuilder* 22, no. 8 (1913); "The Business Side of an Architect's Office: The Office of Mr. Donn Barber," *Brickbuilder* 22, no. 9 (1913); "The Business Side of an Architect's Office: Description of the Offices of Messrs. Henry Bacon; Ford, Butler & Oliver; Ludlow & Peabody; H. Van Buren Magonigle and Kenneth Murchison," *Brickbuilder* 22, no. 11 (1913); "The Business Side of an Architect's Office: The Office of Messrs. McKim, Mead & White," *Brickbuilder* 22, no. 12 (1913); "The Business Side of an Architect's Office: The Office of George B. Post and Sons," *Brickbuilder* 23, no. 2 (1914); D. E. Waid, "The Business Side of an Architect's Office: The Office of Messrs. Mann and Mcneille, New York," ibid., no. 5; D. Everett Waid, "The Business Side of an Architect's Office: The Offices of Mr. Howard Greenley and Messrs. Taylor and Levi," ibid., no. 3.

80 In addition to Ewing & Chappell, LaFarge & Morris are listed as associated architects for the project. "The Business Side of an Architect's Office with a Description of the Architects' Building, New York," 179–81; T-Square [Pseudonym of George S. Chappell], "The Sky Line," *The New Yorker* (1927): 64–66.

81 See for example "An Office Building for Architects," *The Building Age* 34, no. 8 (1912): 428–29; "Midtown Building: Remarkable Contrasts Shown on Various Side Streets," *New York Times*, September 1, 1912, x11.

82 Waid, "The Business Side of an Architect's Office with a Description of the Architects' Building, New York," 179. "F.S." refers to "full-scale" details, and the "General" is the general contractor whose rise is chronicled in the following chapter.

83 Ibid., 179 Ewing had been employed for about four years at Carrère & Hastings prior to forming his own firm with George S. Chappell. Charles Ewing, "Form of Application to Qualify by an Exhibition of Executed Work for Candidature as Associate Member in the American Institute of Architects," in *AIA Historical Directory of American Architects*, ed. American Institute of Architects (Washington, DC: AIA Archives, 1907).

84 It is worth noting that Chappell was writing anonymously at the time, as an architectural critic, about the virtues of a project that his own firm had designed. T-Square [Pseudonym of George S. Chappell], "The Sky Line," 64. The success of the project merited a twenty-story addition in 1927, though both buildings were demolished in 1979 to make way for construction of a 49-story office tower.

85 Waid, "The Business Side of an Architect's Office with a Description of the Architects' Building, New York," 180.

86 "How Architects Work I: Offices of Noted Architects," 251. Compare to "The Business Side of an Architect's Office with a Description of the Architects' Building, New York," 181.

87 "The Business Side of an Architect's Office with a Description of the Architects' Building, New York," 181.

88 Kent, *It's Me O Lord*, 273–74.
89 Ibid., 274–75.
90 "Monographs on Architectural Renderers. The Work of Rockwell Kent," 167.
91 George S. Chappell and Rockwell Kent, "The Nomenclature of the Styles, Adam Style—Greek Freeze: A Humorous Theory Illustrating in Caricature Familiar Schools and Phases of Architecture," ibid. 24, no. 1 (1915): 23–24; "The Nomenclature of the Styles, Early Christian—Rococo: A Humorous Theory Illustrating in Caricature Familiar Schools and Phases of Architecture," *Brickbuilder* 24, no. 2 (1915): 71–72.
92 George S. Chappell, "Correspondence to Rockwell Kent Dated 10 April 1915," in *Rockwell Kent Papers, [circa 1840]–1993, bulk 1935–1961* (Washington, DC: Smithsonian Institution Archives of American Art, 1915).
93 "Architects as Composers," *The American Contractor* 37 (1916): 76B; "About Alumni: Kenneth M. Murchison," *Columbia Alumni News* 7, no. 23 (1916): 707; "Unique Organization Launches Production," *Washington Herald*, April 30, 1916, 2.
94 "Unique Organization Launches Production," 2; Catherine W. Bishir, "Murchison, Kenneth M., Jr. (1872–1938)," in *North Carolina Architects & Builders: A Biographical Dictionary* (Raleigh, NC: Copyright & Digital Scholarship Center, North Carolina State University Libraries, 2015); Withey and Withey, *Biographical Dictionary of American Architects (Deceased)*, 435. Besides other talents, Murchison was apparently noted for his impressions of George Washington! For an account of the work of Francis Touche, see Jann Pasler, *Writing through Music: Essays on Music, Culture, and Politics* (Oxford; New York: Oxford University Press, 2008), 372–74.
95 "'Come to Bohemia's' New Haven Tryout Attracts Most of Forty-Second Street Far from Home," *The Sun*, April 27, 1916, 7; "Kent Wins," *The Evening World*, February 26, 1916, 12; Charles M. Bregg, "In the Theaters Last Night: 'Come to Bohemia'," *Pittsburgh Gazette Times*, March 28, 1916, 11.
96 "In the Theaters Last Night: 'Come to Bohemia'," 11.
97 Kent recounts the selection of his pseudonym in conversation with *Vanity Fair* editor Frank Crowninshield. Hogarth, Jr. was chosen in homage to William Hogarth, the eighteenth-century cartoonist and social critic. Kent, *It's Me O Lord*, 306–08.
98 Frank Crowninshield, "In Vanity Fair," *Vanity Fair* 2, no. 1 (1914): 15.
99 "'Now Listen Quietly' [Advertisement for Vanity Fair]," *House Beautiful* 46–47 (1920): 160.
100 Brendan Gill, "The Sky Line: Prospectus," *The New Yorker* (1987): 106–09.
101 Fish, Anne Harriet, Dorothy Parker, George S. Chappell, and Frank Crowninshield. *High Society: Advice as to Social Campaigning, and Hints on the Management of Dowagers, Dinners, Debutantes, Dances, and the Thousand and One Diversions of Persons of Quality* (New York: Putnam, 1920).

NOTES

102 "Rollo in Society. By George S. Chappell [Book Review]," *New York Times*, September 10, 1922, 33.

103 "Rollo in Society [Advertisement]," *The New York Herald*, September 8, 1922, 3.

104 Young Boswell [pseudonym of Harold Stark], "Young Boswell Interviews George S. Chappell," *New York Tribune*, November 25, 1922, 11.

105 Walter E. Traprock [Pseudonym of George S. Chappell], "My Amazing Discovery: Introducing the Filberts, a New Group of Islands in the South Seas," *Vanity Fair* (1921): 57, 92.

106 These include Frederick O'Brien's *White Shadows in the South Seas* (1919) of which George Chappell wrote, "Perhaps nothing will ever equal the furore caused by the 'White Shadows,' but it must be remembered that that was our first real taste of O'Brien and we liked it a lot. I am by way of becoming an O'Brien addict. Most travel books, I must confess, bore me almost to tears. The traveler so seldom knows how to write. But in Frederick O'Brien we have that amazing combination of a world wanderer who is at once vagabond, poet and accomplished literary gentleman." George S. Chappell, "The South Sea Man Again [Book Review of *Atolls of the Sun* by Frederick O'Brien]," *The New York Herald*, November 5, 1922, 7.

107 *The Cruise of the Kawa Wanderings in the South Seas* (New York and London: G.P. Putnam's Sons, 1921); "Off with the Mask," *The New York Herald*, January 1, 1922, 7.

108 Swartwout used the fictional square eggs as evidence to satirically refute artist Jay Hambidge's serious theory of dynamic symmetry in classical design, a hypothesis whose accuracy Swartwout otherwise disputed. Egerton Swartwout, "Greek Proportions, Theoretically and Otherwise," *American Architect [and] the Architectural Review* 120, no. 2381 (1921): 379–83. Swartwout's veiled satire was likely in response to an article in the previous month's issue: James A. Kane, "The Hambidge Theory of Symmetry and Proportion in Greek Architecture as Relating to Architectural Design," ibid., no. 2378: 261–65.

109 George S. Chappell, *My Northern Exposure: The Kawa at the Pole* (New York: G.P. Putnam's Sons, 1922), 146–47.

110 "Rough Writers Start West for Annual Oregon Round-Up: Weaponless, Except for Typewriters, They Follow the Advice of Horace Greeley and Hope to Penetrate as Far as the Pacific Coast," *The New York Herald*, September 10, 1922, 2; Walter Trumbull, "Pendleton's Great Roundup Has Savor of Old West: Annual Spectacle, Attended This Year by Rough Writers from the East, a Joyous and Colorful Occasion," ibid., 15 October.

111 Marguerite Mooers Marshall, "America's Champion 'Kidders' Make United States a Great Nation; Happy National Trait Saves People in Nerve-Trying Situations," *The Evening World*, June 21, 1922, 3.

112 Herbert S. Gorman, "Mass Attack on the Censor [Book Review of Nonsenseorship by Heywood Broun, Et Al.]," *New York Times*, September 10, 1922, 35, 39; *Nonsenseorship: Sundry Observations*

Concerning Prohibitions, Inhibitions, and Illegalities, ed. George P. Putnam (New York and London: G.P. Putnam's Sons, 1922); Broun and Leech, *Anthony Comstock, Roundsman of the Lord*.

113   George S. Chappell, "The Shelton," *New Republic* 38 (1924): 43–45. Chappell describes at length The Shelton, a thirty-story bachelor hotel designed by architect Arthur Loomis Harmon. See "Thirty-Story Bachelor Hotel," *New York Times*, June 11, 1922, 106.

114   The article was discretely attributed to "R.W.S." Based upon the similarity to Chappell's piece in *The New Republic*, one may infer that Chappell was behind *The New Yorker* piece as well. In any case, subsequent "Sky Line" columns were signed with the pseudonym "T-Square" which are widely credited as being Chappell's work.

115   The lawsuit that resulted from Chappell's biting comments about the design of The Delmonico Building, designed by H. Craig Severance, forced *The New Yorker* to apply new standards in its editorial definitions between matters of opinion and matters of fact. Kathy Roberts Forde, *Literary Journalism on Trial: Masson V. New Yorker and the First Amendment* (Amherst: University of Massachusetts Press, 2008), 90–91.

116   George S. Chappell, "Double Lives: Their Interest, Their Advisability and Their Beauty," *Vanity Fair* (1922): 49.

117   "Correspondence to Rockwell Kent Dated 29 January 1919," in *Rockwell Kent Papers, [circa 1840]–1993, bulk 1935–1961* (Washington, DC: Smithsonian Institution Archives of American Art, 1919).

118   See the entry for Allen, Jerome Ripley (1871–12/20/1928) in Withey and Withey, *Biographical Dictionary of American Architects (Deceased)*, 17. Chappell maintained office space in the Architects Building well into the 1930s and appears to have continued sharing space with Ewing & Allen until about 1924. James Ward, *Architects in Practice, New York City, 1900–1940* (J & D Associates: Union, N.J., 1989), 14, 23.

119   Chappell, "Correspondence to Rockwell Kent Dated 29 January 1919."

120   Chappell is here describing the ground floor of the annex addition to the Architects' Building completed in 1927. T-Square [Pseudonym of George S. Chappell], "The Sky Line," 65. See also "Architect's Building New North Wing, New York," *Architecture & Building* 59 (1927): 182.

121   Socially sanctioned attitudes of racism, sexism, and anti-Semitism among the metropolitan elites of the period are evident in Frederick Squires's ventriloquism of Tom Thumtack as well as in George Chappell's missives about Paris and New York. The presence in architectural offices of the day of such nonchalant slights of class and standing may be gauged by an examination of Egerton Swartwout, *An Architectural Decade: Ten Years with McKim, Mead & White*. Ed. Jesse Smedley (Seattle, WA: Amazon Digital Services LLC 2014). Regarding US technological innovation and economic growth in the period 1870–1940, see Robert J. Gordon, *The Rise and Fall of American Growth: The U.S. Standard of Living since the Civil War*

(Princeton Economic History of the Western World) (Princeton: Princeton University Press, 2016).

122 Warren Powers Laird, "Frank Miles Day: An Appreciation," *American Architect* 114, no. 2219 (1918): 15–16.

Chapter 3

1 Working from distinct points of view, sociologists Robert Gutman and Magali Sarfatti Larson have each tried to describe some of the historical complexities of the architect–owner relationship in order to theorize and explain the dynamics of late-twentieth-century architectural practice. See Robert Gutman, "Patrons or Clients?" *Harvard Architecture Review* 6 (1987): 148–59; Magali Sarfatti Larson, "Emblem and Exception: The Historical Definition of the Architect's Professional Role," in *Professionals and Urban Form*, ed. Judith R. Blau, Mark La Gory, and John Pipkin (Albany: State University of New York Press, 1983), 49–86; George B. Johnston, "Traveling Professions: How Local Contingencies Complicate Globalizing Tendencies in the Standardization of Architectural Practice" (paper presented at the 96th ACSA Annual Meeting, Houston, TX, 2008), 15–22.

2 American Institute of Architects, *The Handbook of Architectural Practice* (Washington, DC: Press of the American Institute of Architects, Inc., 1920), 7. The text describing the "Purpose of the Handbook" did not appear, however, in subsequent editions.

3 Approximately fifty schools of architecture had been established in the United States by 1920, but paths into the profession by means other than academic degree still predominated. For a compilation of North American schools of architecture in order of their establishment, see Joan Ockman and Rebecca Williamson, *Architecture School: Three Centuries of Educating Architects in North America* (Cambridge, MA: Washington, DC: MIT Press; Association of Collegiate Schools of Architecture, 2012), 415–21.

4 According to US government analysts, economic growth in the 1920s was reflected in a surge of construction in both residential and non-residential sectors linked to technological innovation in areas of electrification, internal combustion engines, chemistry and petrochemicals, and telecommunications. See Robert Shackleton, "Total Factor Productivity Growth in Historical Perspective," Working Paper Series (Washington, DC: Congressional Budget Office, 2013), 7–8. An informative account of the impact of these innovations on daily life can be found in Robert J. Gordon, *The Rise and Fall of American Growth: The U.S. Standard of Living since the Civil War* (Princeton Economic History of the Western World) (Princeton: Princeton University Press, 2016), 25–318.

5 Emphasis added. "An Architect's Handbook of Professional Practice and Business Administration," in *Handbook of Architectural Practice - 1st Ed. Not Published File* (Washington, DC: The American Institute of Architects Archives, 1917), 1.

6   Henry H. Kendall, George B. Will, and Chester N. Godfrey, "Report [Dated 25 October] of Committee Appointed to Examine and Report on the Draft for an 'Architects' Hand Book of Professional Practice and Business Administration …'," in *AIA, Office Files, Documents: Handbook, Evolution of, 1915–1917* (Washington, DC: The American Institute of Architects Archives, 1917), Box 1 Handbook, Evolution of, 1915–17.
7   Ralph Adams Cram, "Transmittal Letter Dated 26 October 1917 from Boston Society of Architects to Frank Miles Day," ibid., Box 1 Handbook, Evolution of, 1915–17.
8   This topic is the focus of Chapter 4.
9   "Chicago Architects' Business Association," in *Handbook for Architects and Builders*, ed. Emery Stanford Hall (Chicago: Chicago Architects' Business Association; Wm. Johnston Printing Co., 1908), 17.
10 *The Handbook of Architectural Practice*, 7.
11 Based upon established conventions of local building culture, the conduct of architectural practices could vary subtly or significantly from city to city. Building regulations were still largely a local affair, and markets for material and labor were highly localized as well. As we will see, there were also divergent attitudes between midwestern and northeastern cities with regard to issues such as arbitration and the relationship between architect and builder.
12 The AIA's Committee on Contracts and Specifications, of which Frank Miles Day was a member, was especially active in the period 1909–1911 in the standardization of the contract documents governing the relations among architects, contractors, and owners. In the explanatory notes published along with draft editions of the documents, it was stated: "While the Committee realizes that any standard documents may be subject to more or less modification in different sections of the country, it has been its aim, while attempting to make a specific document which could be used in actual practice for standard classes of work, at the same time to produce one which might be regarded as a species of a code of reference as representing the judgment of the Institute as to what constitutes the best practice of the profession. Even those Chapters which have reported that *under their local customs* [emphasis added] they do not think the documents as issued could be actually used, have been almost unanimous in stating that they considered them valuable for reference purposes and as a basis upon which modified forms could be constructed suited to local conditions." "Report of the Standing Committee on Contracts and Specifications of the American Institute of Architects on the Standardization of Documents," in *Frank Miles Day Collection (1861–1918)* (Philadelphia, PA: The Architectural Archives, University of Pennsylvania 1911), FMD 059.241 Box 6.
13 Frederick Squires, *Architec-tonics: The Adventures of Tom Thumtack, Architect* (New York: Comstock, 1914), 19–20.
14 Architecture journals regularly published reports on court cases and decisions related, among other things, to architects' attempts to collect fees from clients. The case of *Hunt vs. Parmly* is one well-known example described in Cecil D. Elliott, *The American Architect from the Colonial Era to the Present*

(Jefferson, NC: McFarland & Co., 2003), 46–47. See also H. Edwards-Ficken, "The Case of H. Edwards-Ficken, Architect: Against the New York Athletic Club," *American Architect & Building News* 19, no. 528 (1886): 69–70; "A Suit for Architects' Fees," *Inland Architect & News Record* 13, no. 7 (1889): 99; "Supreme Court Decision on Architect's Fees," *Inland Architect & News Record* 31 (1898): 31.

15 This was a significant change from the order of the early draft of the handbook widely circulated for commentary and critique. In that edition, Day devoted the first section to "Memoranda of Procedure and Practice." This entailed a rather detailed checklist, step-by-step, of the administrative actions typically followed in any project including suggested formats for financial bookkeeping, timekeeping, logging correspondence, transmittals, approvals, and changes. A consensus of respondents questioned both the placement and the wisdom of this checklist, some faulting its over-prescriptiveness and any implication that its contents were requirements of good practice rather than mere suggestions or examples. Ultimately, these criticisms prevailed, and while the "memoranda of procedure" were included in the first published edition of the handbook, they were relegated to the appendix. At the same time, the relationship of owner and architect was brought forward in the ordering of the handbook contents. This reflected a particular attitude among reviewers about the utility of the handbook as a primer for clients about the administrative organization of the architect's business.

16 In introducing the Tom Thumtack tales on the pages of *Architecture and Building*, the journal editor writes: "These preachments are addressed to architects and builders, of course. To whom else should they be addressed when written for this magazine? Architects' clients and builders' customers— if that is the right word—are also fondly desired as part of the audience. Every one of them will be the better for my medicine if I can only get them to take it—if I can only get them to listen." Theodore Starrett, "[Editorial]," *Architecture and Building* 46, no. 1 (1914): 1.

17 For example, while Vitruvius' dedication of his treatise to Caesar Augustus is understood as a literary convention of the age demonstrating due deference, expertise, and social station, by the time of the Italian Renaissance Leon Battista Alberti clearly intended for his own tome to inform and instruct a future clientele on principles of the art of building. See Joseph Rykwert's introduction to Leon Battista Alberti, *On the Art of Building in Ten Books*, trans. Joseph Rykwert, Neil Leach, and Robert Tavernor (Cambridge, MA: MIT Press, 1988), x.

18 *The Handbook of Architectural Practice*, 13.

19 Thorstein Veblen's works from the turn of the nineteenth to the twentieth century are still informative in this regard. See Thorstein Veblen, *The Theory of the Leisure Class*, Great Mind Series (Amherst, NY: Prometheus Books, 1899 [1998]); *The Theory of Business Enterprise* (Scribner, 1904).

20 James R. Willett, "Glimpses of the Business Side of an Architect's Life," *Inland Architect & News Record* 27, no. 5 (1896): 43.

21 Besides the courtroom complaints of "Client vs. Architect: A Plea," Thumtack offers up "Pot-Pourri," a cautionary tale of weak-willed architect Harold

Lesser and the "architectural aberrations" that enoue from his encounter with the oil-moneyed Pot family, nouveau-riche transplants from the Midwest to New York City. Squires, *Architec-tonics*, 143–53.

22 Ibid., 65–78.

23 Ibid., 43–54.

24 Ibid., 87–96. Thumtack paints his picture with humor, though Squires's own practice partnership with John Wynkoop likely dissolved under the kind of everyday pressures and ideological conflicts that such speculative projects entailed.

25 Some of these permutations have been suggested as precursors to contemporary design-build arrangements. Alfred Willis, "Design-Build and Building Efficiency in the Early Twentieth Century United States" (paper presented at the First International Congress on Construction History, Madrid, 2003), 2119–26.

26 F. W. Fitzpatrick, "The Architects," *Inland Architect & News Record* 39 (1902): 39. Francis W. Fitzpatrick (1863–1931) was an architect active in the Midwest and in the office of the Supervising Architect in the US Treasury Department. He was a frequent essayist in architectural and related trade publications and was a prickly critic of the architecture profession. The most thorough account of Fitzpatrick's professional career is given by Ed Zimmer, a historic preservation planner in Nebraska, in a public talk available here: https://youtu.be/IIeRYvw8g1M.

27 American Institute of Architects, "Proceedings of the Fortieth Annual Convention of the American Institute of Architects" (Washington, DC, 1907), 89–91. Cass Gilbert was reporting as chairman on behalf of the Committee on the Relation of Architects to the Contracting System.

28 Henry Snyder Kissam, "Efficiency of the Architect's Client," *School of Mines Quarterly* 32, no. 4 (1911): 335.

29 T. P. Barnett, "The Business and Art of Architecture: An Address Delivered before the Art League of St. Louis, Mo," *American Architect* 113, no. 2210 (1918): 525.

30 Oswald C. Hering, "The Architect and His Client: Their Relationship in Planning and Building the Home," ibid. 96 (1909): 142–43.

31 *The Handbook* (1st edition) includes AIA membership requirements in Appendices Q, R, S, and T. In addition, the model form of state law for the registration of architects then being promoted by the AIA had obvious exclusionary implications. It is included in Appendix V. At the time of the publication of *The Handbook* in 1920, only twenty states had established such laws.

32 *The Handbook of Architectural Practice*, 14.

33 Ibid.

34 William C. Lengel, "Tall Buildings in Smaller Cities as Investments," *Buildings and Building Management* 13, no. 10 (1913): 19–22. According to its January 1913 masthead, the journal was promoted as "the only magazine in existence dealing with building construction, operation and management from the owners' standpoint." It was published under various titles by the

Patterson Publishing Company in New York and Chicago between 1906 and 1947.

35 "An Architect," *Journal of the American Institute of Architects* 1, no. 11 (1913): 473.

36 F. W. Fitzpatrick, "Tall Buildings in Smaller Cities," *Buildings and Building Management* (1913): 24–25.

37 S. Kruse, "The High Cost of Incompetence," *The Real Estate Magazine* 4, no. 11 (1914): 16. These principles, derived primarily from custom, were continually tested and adjusted through decisions of courts. According to architect and legal scholar T. M. Clark, "As professional men, [architects'] duty is plainly laid down in the text-books, and in many decisions of courts. They are bound to serve their employers with reasonable skill and care, and, of course, with perfect honesty. They are not bound to the utmost skill, such as only a few members of any profession attain to, but they must show what other architects will generally consider to be a reasonable degree of professional intelligence and knowledge. The care and attention, apart from the skill, which they should devote to their employer's affairs, ought to be greater than that which they would bestow upon their own affairs of similar character, in order to satisfy the legal idea of their duty; but the testimony of other architects will be admitted to show whether the care used in a particular instance was all that could reasonably be expected of a conscientious architect under the circumstances." T. M. Clark, *Architect, Owner and Builder before the Law: A Summary of American and English Decisions on the Principal Questions Relating to Building, and the Employment of Architects, with about Eight Hundred References, Including Also Practical Suggestions in Regard to the Drawing of Building Contracts, and Forms of Contract Suited to Various Circumstances* (New York: Macmillan Company, 1894), 28.

38 Kruse, "The High Cost of Incompetence," 18.

39 Ibid., 16–22.

40 "Incompetence among Architects: The Investor Needs Protection [Editorial]," ibid., no. 12: 13.

41 F. W. Fitzpatrick, "More Anent Incompetence: Some Striking Remarks by a Keen Critic upon Mr. Kruse's Recent Article," ibid.: 14–17.

42 For a fuller treatment of Ackerman's professional and intellectual contributions, see my chapter "Drafting Standards: Architecture as a Social Service in the Office of Frederick L. Ackerman," in George Barnett Johnston, *Drafting Culture: A Social History of Architectural Graphic Standards* (Cambridge, MA: MIT Press, 2008), 91–138.

43 Frederick L. Ackerman, "The Architect's Part in the World's Work," *Architectural Record* 37, no. 2 (1915): 149–58.

44 "The Responsibility for Incompetence," *The Real Estate Magazine* 5, no. 1 (1915): 15–20.

45 "Professional and Other Incompetence," *Journal of the American Institute of Architects* 3, no. 2 (1915): 73–75.

46 Frederick Squires, "Tom Thumtack, Client," *Architecture and Building* 46, no. 12 (1914): 457–62.

47 *The Handbook of Architectural Practice*, 14.

48 This sort of practice was discussed at the annual meeting of the American Institute of Architects in 1878. See "The Twelfth Annual Convention A.I.A.," *American Architect and Building News* 5, no. 173 (1879): 124.

49 "Competition for School-House at Washington, DC," *American Architect & Building News* 5, no. 173 (1879): 123.

50 Mrs. Schuyler Van Rensselaer, "Client and Architect," *North American Review* 151, no. 406 (1890): 326. For an insightful account of Van Rensselaer's broader influence, see Alexandra Lange, "Founding Mother: Mariana Griswold Van Rensselaer and the Rise of Architecture Criticism," *Places Journal* (February 2013). https://doi.org/10.22269/130225.

51 "The Supervising Architect's Office Reorganized," *Inland Architect and News Record* 30, no. 1 (1897): 3.

52 Glenn Brown, "The Tarsney Act: Historical Review," *Brickbuilder* 15, no. 5 (1906): 95–98. For a fuller account of this interesting episode of American architecture, see Antoinette J. Lee, *Architects to the Nation: The Rise and Decline of the Supervising Architect's Office* (New York: Oxford University Press, 2000); Darrell Hevenor Smith, *The Office of the Supervising Architect of the Treasury: Its History, Activities, and Organization*, Institute for Government Research Service Monographs of the United States Government No. 23 (Baltimore: Johns Hopkins Press, 1923).

53 "Correspondence regarding Government Competitions," *Inland Architect & News Record* 38 (1901): 7; Brown, "The Tarsney Act: Historical Review," 96–98.

54 Cass Gilbert, "Status of Professional Practice: Address of the President before the 42nd Convention of the American Institute of Architects, December 17, 1908," *Western Architect* 13 (1909): 7.

55 "Matters Relating to Competitions: Extracts from the Reports of 1905–6–7 and 8," in *Frank Miles Day Collection (1861–1918)* (Philadelphia, PA: The Architectural Archives, University of Pennsylvania, 1908), 20.

56 Ibid., 17–25.

57 Frank Miles Day, "Conduct of Competitions A.I.A.," *Architecture* 22 (1910): 151–52. See Appendix C, "Architectural Competitions, a Circular of Advice and Information" in the first edition of the *Handbook of Architectural Practice*.

58 Brown, "The Tarsney Act: Historical Review," 95–98; "Congressional Committee Attacks Tarsney Act," *Western Architect* 18, no. 9 (1912): 92–93; Francis G. Newlands, "The Tarsney Act: The Economy and Efficiency of the Employment of Private Architects on Public Buildings, Report in Part of a Speech Delivered in the United States Senate," *American Architect & Building News* 102 (1912): 73–77; "Tarsney Act," *Journal of the American Institute of Architects* 1, no. 1 (1913): 6–7; John Hall Rankin, "The Repeal of the Tarsney Act," ibid., no. 3: 127–28.

59   F. W. Fitzpatrick, "The 'Tarsney' Act," *Architecture and Building* 44, no. 6 (1912): 20–21. Fitzpatrick had himself been employed in the Office of the Supervising Architect of the Treasury Department at the time when the Tarsney Act was first implemented.

60   Frederick Squires, "Repeal of the Tarsney Act," *Architecture & Building* 47, no. 8 (1915): 281.

61   The comment is attributed to D. Knickerbacker Boyd, Chairman of the AIA's Committee on Public Information. "Fees of an Architect," *The Building Age* 35, no. 7 (1913): 346.

62   The AIA's first schedule of charges was published in 1866. See American Institute of Architects, *The American Institute of Architects Official Guide to the 2007 AIA Contract Documents* (Hoboken, NJ: John Wiley & Sons, 2009), 13–20.

63   In a speech to architecture students at the Art Institute of Chicago, architect James R. Willett offered this advice: "Architects are not free agents, as you will find when you come to practice as such. They are subject to the conditions given by the owner, etc., and if you see what you deem to be mistakes and errors in other architects' work, remember that you do not know all the circumstances; perhaps if you did it might alter your judgment, and you may be quite sure that you will probably make just as many mistakes as anyone else, and then perhaps you will appreciate the injustice of random criticism." Willett, "Glimpses of the Business Side of an Architect's Life," 43.

64   Squires & Wynkoop was swept up in this speculative building boom with their own proposals for 7th Avenue, 16th Street, and 25th Street in Manhattan. "In the Real Estate Field: Loft Building Boom Stimulates Realty Market," *New York Times*, February 16, 1910, 15; "Perspectives of Three New York Loft Buildings Designed by Squires & Wynkoop Architects," *Architecture and Building* 42, no. 12 (1910): 506.

65   Frederick Squires, "Fees–A Reductio Ad Absurdum," ibid. 46, no. 11 (1914): 418.

66   *The Handbook of Architectural Practice*, 14–15.

67   For historical insights about architects' fees in the ante bellum period, see Elliott, *The American Architect from the Colonial Era to the Present*, 45–48; Mary N. Woods, *From Craft to Profession: The Practice of Architecture in Nineteenth Century America* (Berkeley: University of California Press, 1999), 36–38.

68   Woods notes that by 1870, only 140 of the estimated 2,000 architects then active in the United States were AIA members, and the majority of those members (65.5 percent) practiced in the northeast. *From Craft to Profession: The Practice of Architecture in Nineteenth Century America*, 36.

69   These are some of the explanations offered in W. A. Hawley, "The Compensation of the Architect," *Inland Architect & News Record* 6, no. 2 (1885): 17–18.

70   Arne Dehli, "The Present System of Architects' Charges," *Architectural Record* 15 (1904): 545–46. Born and educated in Norway, Arne Dehli (1858–1942) "acquired architectural training and experience in Europe before migrating to [the United States] in the late nineteenth century." Henry F. Withey and Elsie

Rathburn Withey, *Biographical Dictionary of American Architects (Deceased)* (Los Angeles: New Age Publishing Co., 1956), 167.

71 "Latrobe on Architects' Fees, 1798," *American Society of Architectural Historians Journal* 19 (1960): 115–17.

72 "The Compensation of Foreign Architects: The Five Per Cent Commission," *Inland Architect & News Record* 48, no. 4 (1906): 38.

73 "Inadequate Compensation to Architects," *Inland Architect & News Record* 48 (1906): 1.

74 Dehli, "The Present System of Architects' Charges," 546.

75 Glenn Brown, "An Architect's Services and Remuneration," *Inland Architect & News Record* 48, no. 1 (1906): 3–4; "An Architect's Services and Remuneration," *Inland Architect & News Record* 48, no. 2 (1906): 15–18. One supporting note to this analysis, however, can be found in the lectures of French architect Julien Guadet who refers to "le taux uniforme et presque toujours injustifiable de 5%" (the uniform and almost always unjustifiable rate of 5 percent). Guadet condemns application of uniform fee rates as a mere convenience not comporting with the architect's real expense. See the chapter entitled "Honoraires" in Julien Guadet, *Eléments Et Théorie De L'architecture: Cours Professé À L'école Nationale Et Spéciale Des Beaux-Arts*, vol. 4 (Paris: Librarie de la Construction Moderne, 1905), 627–38.

76 American Institute of Architects, "Proceedings of the Forty-Second Annual Convention of the American Institute of Architects," (1908).

77 "The Pecuniary Relation between Architect and Client," *Architectural Record* 26 (1909): 79–83.

78 Squires, "Fees–a Reductio Ad Absurdum," 420.

79 Ibid., 419.

80 "The Architect and the Client: A Banker Speaks on the Subject," *Journal of the American Institute of Architects* 2, no. 12 (1914): 557–59.

81 American Institute of Architects, "Proceedings of the Forty-Ninth Annual Convention of the American Institute of Architects" (Washington, DC, 1915), 14.

82 Ibid., 15.

83 See Appendix G in *The Handbook of Architectural Practice*, 135–36.

84 As Clark S. Davis states in his 2008 handbook article outlining "Architectural Services and Compensation": "Clients are willing to compensate an architect in direct relation to the value they place on that architect's services. Therefore, architects must communicate the full range of their services to their clients as well as the benefits those services provide." Joseph A. Demkin, ed., *The Architect's Handbook of Professional Practice*, 14th ed. (Hoboken, NJ: Wiley, 2008), 469–79.

85 *The Handbook of Architectural Practice*, 15–16.

86 The lecture was delivered to architecture students at the Art Institute of Chicago. Willett, "Glimpses of the Business Side of an Architect's Life," 44.

87 Clark, *Architect, Owner and Builder before the Law*, 12.

88 "Form of Contract Adopted by the Joint Committee of the American Institute of Architects, the Western Association of Architects, and the National

Association of Builders" (Washington, DC: American Institute of Architects Archives, 1888).

89 American Institute of Architects, "Proceedings of the Forty-Ninth Annual Convention of the American Institute of Architects," 92–93.

90 Alternative versions of the schedule of charges published from 1866 through the 1880s are included in *The American Institute of Architects Official Guide to the 2007 AIA Contract Documents*, 13–17. Architect Grosvenor Atterbury's "Schedule of Professional Practice and Charges" is largely modeled upon the AIA's standard form. See folder in Architect Office of Grosvenor Atterbury, "Schedule of Professional Charges," in *AIA, Office Files, Documents: Handbook, Evolution of, 1915–1917* (Washington, DC: The American Institute of Architects Archives, 1914), RG 801 SR 8 Box 1 "Miscellaneous Forms for Handbook."

91 Clark, *Architect, Owner and Builder before the Law*, 86.

92 Frederick Squires, "The Tectarch," *Architecture and Building* 47, no. 2 (1915): 48–50.

93 "Architects and Engineers," *American Architect & Building News* 4 (1878): 54.

94 The rise of the engineering professions is beyond the scope of this work, though the parallels, convergences, and divergences with the field of architecture are informative and relevant. Particularly following the Civil War and the implementation of the Morrill Act of 1862, which established a system of land-grant colleges supporting agricultural and mechanical education and research, the field of engineering moved fully from "shop culture" to "school culture" even more sure-footedly than the field of architecture. Indeed, many of the early academic programs of architecture were founded under the aegis of these engineering colleges. See Ulrich Pfammatter, *The Making of the Modern Architect and Engineer: The Origins and Development of a Scientific and Industrially Oriented Education* (Basel; Boston: Birkhauser-Publishers for Architecture, 2000), 265–92; Andrew Saint, *Architect and Engineer: A Study in Sibling Rivalry* (New Haven, CT; London: Yale University Press, 2007), 171–205.

95 "Architects and Engineers," 54.

96 C. H. Blackall, "The All-Around Architect," *Inland Architect & News Record* 26, no. 3 (1895): 23–24.

97 Reginald Pelham Bolton, "The Engineer, the Architect, and the General Construction Company," *American Architect & Building News* 85, no. 1495 (1904): 59–60.

98 Corydon T. Purdy, "The Relation of the Engineer to the Architect," ibid. 87 (1905): 43–46. (Also published in "The Relation of the Engineer to the Architect (Part 1)," *Inland Architect & News Record* 44, no. 6 (1905): 43–45; "The Relation of the Engineer to the Architect (Part 2)," *Inland Architect & News Record* 45, no. 1 (1905): 4–6.) Purdy was associated with the construction company of George A. Fuller in Chicago before relocating to New York City to found an engineering practice, Purdy and Henderson, involved with the design of steel frame structures for firms such as McKim Mead and White. Saint, *Architect and Engineer: A Study in Sibling Rivalry*, 192–95.

99 Purdy, "The Relation of the Engineer to the Architect," 43–46.

100 Ibid.

101 Ibid.

102 The speaker was Philadelphia architect Edgar V. Seeler, FAIA (1867–1929). American Institute of Architects, "Proceedings of the Thirty-Eighth Annual Convention of the American Institute of Architects" (Washington, DC, 1905), 132–35; Withey and Withey, *Biographical Dictionary of American Architects (Deceased)*, 545.

103 "Cooperation of the Architect and Engineer," *American Architect & Building News* 85, no. 1495 (1904): 60–62.

104 William L. Steele, "The Architect and the Public," *Journal of the American Institute of Architects* 3, no. 11 (1915): 492–93. Steele (1875–1949) was a prominent architect in the Midwest.

105 The "Letter of Transmission and Explanation" of the handbook draft gave credit to four other authors for a handful of handbook sections. "The remainder of the present draft is by the Chairman of the Committee," Frank Miles Day. "An Architect's Handbook of Professional Practice and Business Administration," 1.

106 Ibid., 41.

107 Supportive of Day's call for employing independent consultants, Burt L. Fenner of the firm of McKim, Mead, and White wrote, "I am very glad you recommend the employment of consulting engineers outside of the architect's own organization. ... An expert who is as well qualified in his field as the architect should be in his, is not likely to be found in a salaried position, but will be in independent practice, and will enjoy an income far in excess of that which any architect could pay as a salary." Burt L. Fenner, "Letter to Frank Miles Day Dated 17 October 1917," in *AIA, Office Files, Documents: Handbook, Evolution of, 1915–1917* (Washington, DC: The American Institute of Architects Archives, 1917), RG 801 SR 8 Box 1. Architect John L. Hamilton advised circumspection on the topic of consultants: "As this hand book is intended to reach the owner as well as the architect, it seems to me that the contents of this paragraph should be restated in somewhat different language ...." John L. Hamilton, "Letter to Frank Miles Day Dated 7 February," ibid. (1918).

108 This new text was written by Day's committee vice-chairman Milton B. Medary and utilized a simplified passage suggested by architect John L. Hamilton. "Letter to Frank Miles Day Dated 7 February 1918," RG 801 SR 8 Box 1; Milton B. Medary, "Letter to Frank Miles Day Dated 18 February 1918," in *AIA Board of Directors 1917–1919* (Washington, DC: American Institute of Architects Archives, 1918), RG 509 SR2 Box 2.

109 *The Handbook of Architectural Practice*, 17.

110 Squires, "The Tectarch," 49.

111 *The Handbook of Architectural Practice*, 17–19.

112 Ibid., 17.

113 Bruno Latour differentiates between intermediary and mediator thus: "An *intermediary*, in my vocabulary, is what transports meaning or force

without transformation: defining its inputs is enough to define its outputs. For all practical purposes, an intermediary can be taken not only as a black box, but also as a black box counting for one, even if it is internally made of many parts. *Mediators*, on the other hand, cannot be counted as just one; they might count for one, for nothing, for several, or for infinity. Their input is never a good predictor of their output; their specificity has to be taken into account every time. Mediators transform, translate, distort, and modify the meaning or the elements they are supposed to carry." See Bruno Latour, *Reassembling the Social: An Introduction to Actor-Network-Theory*, Clarendon Lectures in Management Studies (Oxford; New York: Oxford University Press, 2005), 39–40. Where architects intervene as agents or as actors with their representational toolkits—between owners and their desires, between owners and builders, between builders and the contract documents that architects themselves produced—the transformative nature of their interactions ensures that their role is as mediator even when contractually circumscribed as mere intermediary.

114   *The Handbook of Architectural Practice*, 17.

115   American Institute of Architects, "Proceedings of the Twenty-Eighth Annual Convention of the American Institute of Architects," (1894): 132.

116   "Proceedings of the Twenty-Ninth Annual Convention of the American Institute of Architects," (1895): 13–14.

117   The adoption of a code of ethics by the Boston chapter was mentioned at the AIA's national convention in 1895. See ibid., 13. Among Frank Miles Day's papers are copies of the proposed or adopted codes of ethics from AIA chapters in Illinois, New York City, and Boston. See "Code of Ethics," in *Frank Miles Day Collection (1861–1918)* (Philadelphia, PA: The Architectural Archives, University of Pennsylvania, 1908), Box 6.

118   "Proceedings of the Forty-Second Annual Convention of the American Institute of Architects," 10.

119   "Proceedings of the Forty-Third Annual Convention of the American Institute of Architects," (1909): 109.

120   Registering the impact of global events on the field of architecture, C. Stanley Taylor wrote, "The world war has shaken the very foundations of the economic structure of the United States …. Precedents were swept aside by emergency. Unheard-of sums of money have passed in the greatest financial transactions of the ages. Building projects, which in ordinary times would receive weeks of study and take months for construction, have been planned in days and built in weeks. So in the office of the architect history has been made and a future of unlimited possibilities is promised to those of the profession who may wisely combine artistic temperament with practical business administration." C. Stanley Taylor, "The Architect of the Future: Part I," *Architectural Forum* 30, no. 1 (1919): 1.

121   For discussions and debates around the AIA's encouragement of state registration laws, see the "Proceedings of the Fifty-Second, Fifty-Third, and Fifty-Fourth Annual Conventions of the American Institute of Architects" from 1919, 1920, and 1921, respectively.

122 The AIA's model law stated: "Nor shall anything contained in this Act prevent engineers, mechanics or builders from making plans and specifications or supervising the erection, enlargement or alteration of buildings, or any appurtenance thereto for other persons, firms or corporation, or for themselves, provided that the plans and specifications for such construction are signed by the authors thereof with the true appellation of his or her actual occupation in life, such as Engineer', or 'Mechanic', or 'Builder', without the use of any form of the word or title 'Architect' or 'Architects'." *The Handbook of Architectural Practice*, 201.

123 American Institute of Architects, "Proceedings of the Forty-Third Annual Convention of the American Institute of Architects," 109–10.

124 Ibid., 108.

125 Marcus Pollio Vitruvius, *The Ten Books on Architecture*, trans. Morris Hicky Morgan (New York: Dover, 1960), 168–69. Cited in "An Architect's Handbook of Professional Practice and Business Administration," 39.

126 Squires, *Architec-tonics*, 157–63. The chapter was originally published in "Advertising: Reports from the Canon of Ethics," *Architecture and Building* 46, no. 8 (1914): 294–98.

127 "An Architect's Handbook of Professional Practice and Business Administration," 39–40.

128 Chas. C. Wilson, "Letter to Frank Miles Day Dated 29 September 1917," in *AIA, Office Files, Documents: Handbook, Evolution of, 1915–1917* (Washington, DC: The American Institute of Architects Archives, 1917), RG 801 SR 8 Box 1.

129 John L. Hamilton, "Letter to Frank Miles Day Dated 7 February," ibid. (1918), Box 1. Reference to similar points of view may also be found in Cecil Bayless Chapman, "Letter to Frank Miles Day Dated 19 October" ibid. (1917), RG 801 SR 8 Box 1; Edgar A. Mathews and Alexander Wright, "Letter to Frank Miles Day Dated 25 August 1917," ibid.; Dwight H. Perkins, "Letter to Frank Miles Day Undated," ibid.

130 Frank Miles Day, "Letter to M.B. Medary and E.H. Fetterolf Dated 30 November 1917," in *AIA Board of Directors 1917–1919* (Washington, DC: American Institute of Architects Archives 1917), RG 509 SR2 Box 1.

131 American Institute of Architects, "Proceedings of the Fifty-First Annual Convention of the American Institute of Architects" (Washington, DC, 1918), 21.

132 *The Handbook of Architectural Practice*, 108.

133 Paul Goldberger, "Architects Will End Ban on Advertising," *New York Times*, May 25, 1978, 20. This proposed change in the code of ethics, along with the elimination of the prohibition against architects' engagement in building or contracting, was spurred by threats of federal antitrust action against the profession.

134 *The Handbook of Architectural Practice*, 17.

135 Squires, "The Tectarch," 48–50; "Temperament," *Architecture and Building* 47, no. 6 (1915): 206–10.

136 *The Handbook of Architectural Practice*, 18.

137 Hering, "The Architect and His Client: Their Relationship in Planning and Building the Home," 143.

138 T. P. Barnett, "The Business and Art of Architecture: An Address Delivered before the Art League of St. Louis, Mo," ibid. 113, no. 2210 (1918): 525–26.

139 "Topics of the Time: Are We Just to Our Architects?" *The Century Magazine* 37, no. 3 (1889): 473.

140 Van Rensselaer, "Client and Architect," 319–25. A copy of Van Rensselaer's essay can be found in File 059.238 in the Frank Miles Day Collection in the Architectural Archives of the University of Pennsylvania.

141 *The Handbook of Architectural Practice*, 19. These principles were further elaborated in C. Stanley Taylor, "The Owner's Duty to the Architect," *Architectural Forum* 34, no. 2 (1921): 71–74.

142 Charles E. Fox, "Letter to Richard E. Schmidt Dated 4 October 1917," in *AIA, Office Files, Documents: Handbook, Evolution of, 1915–1917* (Washington, DC: The American Institute of Architects Archives, 1917), RG 801 SR 8 Box 1; *The Handbook of Architectural Practice*, 19.

143 Squires, *Architec-tonics*, 17.

144 Architect C. Stanley Taylor, speculating about the future of the architecture profession in the aftermath of the First World War, deployed a suggestive phrase which, as invoked here, is taken as a broader characterization of the profession considered in the spectrum of history. The full context of his comments reads: "First, it must be realized that architecture has passed the stage of merely supplying a demand or satisfying a need. It has reached the point where by constructive reasoning a demand may be created. This function of the office involves imagination, practical knowledge of business procedure and ability to convince a prospective client of the feasibility of a business proposition involving building construction." Taylor, "The Architect of the Future: Part I," 3.

Chapter 4

1 Frederick Squires, "Contractors," *Architecture and Building* 46, no. 3 (1914): 92–96.

2 Ibid.

3 See for example: William H. Sayward, "Sub-Contracts," *American Architect & Building News* 1 (1876): 95–96; Frederick H. Baumann, "Relation of Architect to Contractor and Journeymen," *Inland Architect & News Record* 6 (1885): 60–61; O. P. Hatfield, "The Relation of the Architect to the Builder," *Inland Architect & News Record* 13, no. 2 (1889): 16–17.

4 Alex Black, "Letter from Keokuk, Iowa: An Architect's Death by Violence (Architect Murdered by a Builder)," *American Architect & Building News* 5, no. 173 (1879): 126.

5 For example, at the time of the death of noted architect-engineer William LeBaron Jenney it was commented, "Mr. Jenney despised worse than

anything the grafter, and his manner of dealing with that type of man was effective. Architects have peculiar intimacy with graft because they constantly are running into contact with crooked contractors and builders, and too frequently architects disgrace their profession by dividing with dishonest contractors the fruits of robbery achieved through crooked bidding, or favoritism. Jenney never countenanced this way of doing business." "Architect Jenney and the Contractor," *Western Architect* 10, no. 11 (1907): 117–18.

6   Wilfred Beach, "The Architect," *Architectural Record* 35 (1914); W. W. Beach, "The Problem of the General Contractor," *Architectural Forum* 26 (1917).

7   "Chicago Architects' Business Association," in *Handbook for Architects and Builders*, ed. Emery Stanford Hall (Chicago: Chicago Architects' Business Association; Wm. Johnston Printing Co., 1908).

8   William Bryce Mundie, "The Relations of Architects to the Contracting System," *Western Architect* 13, no. 1 (1909): 9–10.

9   "Form of Contract Adopted by the Joint Committee of the American Institute of Architects, the Western Association of Architects, and the National Association of Builders" (Washington, DC: American Institute of Architects Archives, 1888).

10 Research to date has only scratched the surface in gauging the significance of the emergence of the general contractor in the transformation of the architecture profession. For some notable efforts in addressing that gap, see Mary N. Woods, *From Craft to Profession: The Practice of Architecture in Nineteenth Century America* (Berkeley: University of California Press, 1999), 154–58; Sara E. Wermiel, "Norcross, Fuller, and the Rise of the General Contractor in the United States in the Nineteenth Century," in *Proceedings of the Second International Congress of Construction History* (Cambridge, UK: Construction History Society, 2006), 3297–314; "The Rise of the General Contractor in 19th Century America," *FMI Quarterly*, no. 3 (2008): 117–29; Inge Bertels, "Building Contractors in Late-Nineteenth-Century Belgium: From Craftsmen to Contractors," *Construction History* 26 (2011): 1–18; I. Bertels, K. Verswijver, and I. Wouters, "Under Construction, Building Contractors in Nineteenth Century Belgium," *Transactions on the Built Environment* 118 (2011): 35–44; Elyse Gundersen McBride, "The Changing Role of the Architect in the United States Construction Industry, 1870–1913," *Construction History* 28, no. 1 (2013): 121–40; Jelena Dobbels, Inge Bertels, and Ine Wouters, "The Professionalization of Belgian General Contractors (1877–1914): An Analysis of the Construction Journal *La Chronique Des Travaux Publics, Du Commerce Et De L'industrie*" (paper presented at the Further Studies in the History of Construction: The Proceedings of the Third Annual Conference of the Construction History Society, Queen's College Cambridge University, UK, 2016), 309–20.

11 "The Necessity for Abolishing General Contracting," *Inland Architect & News Record* 33 (1899): 29.

12 "General Contracting a Menace to Architects," *Inland Architect & News Record* 33 (1899): 29–30. The editorial statement in the following month reported: "The stand taken by this journal in regard to the objectionable general contract system has met with marked approval, not only among the material dealers, manufacturers and contractors, to whom it

was fast becoming an unbearable hardship, but the architectural profession as well. In a carefully prepared paper Mr. Dankmar Adler states the architects' and owners' position in a plain and practical manner. As there is no architect of higher professional standing or greater practical experience, and as his arguments all go to show the folly of continuing the general contract system, it would seem that we have conclusively shown that, except in rare and exceptional cases, no one concerned but the general contractor himself ever benefits by that system of letting contracts." "Condemnation of General Contract System Approved," *Inland Architect & News Record* 33 (1899): 37.

13 Dankmar Adler, "The General Contractor from the Standpoint of the Architect," ibid.: 38.
14 Ibid., 38–39.
15 "General Contracts," ibid. 37, no. 3 (1901): 22–23. This paper was excerpted in-full from the *Construction News* of Chicago.
16 "The Place of the General Contractor," *Inland Architect & News Record* 34, no. 6 (1900): 37, 39.
17 American Institute of Architects, "Proceedings of the Fortieth Annual Convention of the American Institute of Architects" (Washington, DC, 1907), 89–92. Though no direct causality is suggested, the report registered the emergence of the general contracting system as an acknowledged force to be roughly contemporaneous with the adoption of the Uniform Contract in 1888. "Some fifteen or twenty years ago, it was the usual custom to get proposals from the heads of various trades and to award a number of separate contracts for the work of one building: one each for the mason, plasterer, carpenter, steam-fitter and so forth. As building construction became more complex there arose a desire to place the work of these various trades under one general contract, and the idea had some advantages to commend it. It was found in practice, that at times, with a number of minor contractors at work in one building there were moments of friction, interference, and delay. Sometimes the minor contracts did not join each other exactly and then an extra bill had to be incurred to complete the structure. Therefore it seemed desirable to put all the work under one general contractor, who would be solely responsible for the whole building and for items which might have been overlooked in minor subdivision. This system appeared to have many advantages, among others, in avoiding the difficulty of telling your client that you were not omniscient and omnipresent. It was not pleasant to tell him that you had forgotten to specify something that would make the plumbing connect with the steam-fitting. You went to him for an extra but you hesitated to do it. So perhaps you were willing to take refuge under the general contract system. But in this respect the alleged advantage was more apparent than real, for as you all know, the general contractor was just as keen to take advantage of any defect in your specification as were the minor contractors, and general clauses intended to bridge the gaps proved to be without binding force." In an invited talk the next year to the Philadelphia Builders' Exchange, Frank Miles Day himself outlined for builders reasons for "the growing distrust of the general contracting system." Frank Miles Day, "Speech at Builders Exchange: Relation of Architect, Builder and Sub Contractor, I.E. Constructor for a Specific Trade," in *Frank Miles Day Collection (1861–1918)* (Philadelphia, PA: The Architectural Archives, University of Pennsylvania, 1908), Box 6.

18 American Institute of Architects, "Proceedings of the Fortieth Annual Convention of the American Institute of Architects," 92. The report as distributed to AIA's membership can be found in "Preliminary Report of the Committee on the Relation of Architects to the Contracting System," in *Frank Miles Day Collection (1861–1918)* (Philadelphia, PA: The Architectural Archives, University of Pennsylvania, 1907), 3.

19 Mundie, "The Relations of Architects to the Contracting System," 9–10.

20 "Remember the Contractor," *Inland Architect & News Record* 49, no. 2 (1907).

21 American Institute of Architects, *The American Institute of Architects Official Guide to the 2007 AIA Contract Documents* (Hoboken, NJ: John Wiley & Sons, 2009), 12–37.

22 "Proceedings of the Thirty-Fifth Annual Convention of the American Institute of Architects" (Washington, DC, 1901), 41–43; "Proceedings of the Thirty-Sixth Annual Convention of the American Institute of Architects" (Washington, DC, 1902), 36.

23 T. M. Clark, *Architect, Owner and Builder before the Law: A Summary of American and English Decisions on the Principal Questions Relating to Building, and the Employment of Architects, with about Eight Hundred References, Including Also Practical Suggestions in Regard to the Drawing of Building Contracts, and Forms of Contract Suited to Various Circumstances* (New York: London, 1894), 81. Theodore Minot Clark (1845–1909) was a prominent figure in Boston serving from the 1880s as professor of architecture at MIT and as editor of the journal *American Architect and Building News*. Henry F. Withey and Elsie Rathburn Withey, "Clark, Theodore Minot. (1845–4/30/1909)," in *Biographical Dictionary of American Architects (Deceased)* (Los Angeles: New Age Publishing Co., 1956), 122.

24 "Report of the Standing Committee on Contracts and Specifications of the American Institute of Architects on Standardization of Documents," in *Frank Miles Day Collection (1861–1918)* (Philadelphia, PA: The Architectural Archives, University of Pennsylvania, 1908), 3–11.

25 Ibid., 7.

26 See file folder FMD 059.239 AIA Report of the Standing Committee on Contracts and Specifications, ibid., Box 6.

27 According to Withey, Andrews was "one of Boston's oldest and most prominent architects at the time of his death, ... an early member of the Boston Society of Architects, AIA, and in 1891 was elected to Institute Fellowship," in *Biographical Dictionary of American Architects (Deceased)* (Los Angeles: New Age Publishing Co., 1956), 21.

28 Robert D. Andrews, "Letter to Frank Miles Day Dated 30 November 1908," in *Frank Miles Day Collection (1861–1918)* (Philadelphia, PA: The Architectural Archives, University of Pennsylvania, 1908), Box 6 FMD 059.238 AIA Committee on Contracts and Specifications.

29 Ibid.

30 For contemporaneous legal considerations applied to the matter of the architect as agent of the owner, see William L. Bowman, "Legal Hints for

Architects," *Brickbuilder* 20 (1911): 237–39; Clinton H. Blake, *The Law of Architecture and Building; a Consideration of the Mutual Rights, Duties and Liabilities of Architect, Owner and Contractor, with Appendices and Forms* (New York: William T. Comstock Co., 1916), 12–35.

31 Robert D. Andrews, "Letter to Frank Miles Day Dated 3 December 1908," in *Frank Miles Day Collection (1861–1918)* (Philadelphia, PA: The Architectural Archives, University of Pennsylvania, 1908), Box 6 FMD 059.238 AIA Committee on Contracts and Specifications.

32 Ibid.

33 See Explanatory Notes to the Fifth Edition in "Report of the Standing Committee on Contracts and Specifications of the American Institute of Architects on the Standardization of Documents," ibid. (1911), Box 6 FMD 059.241 AIA Report of the Standing Committee on Contracts and Specifications 1909–11.

34 "The Standard Documents of the American Institute of Architects" (Washington, DC: American Institute of Architects Archive, 1911).

35 "The Architect and the Builder," *The Building Age* 34, no. 12 (1912): 613–14.

36 Ibid.

37 Architects' perceptions of the alignment of their interests with owners against those of labor are typified by architect Charles Fox's statement: "… in no sense and from no point of view must the American Institute of Architects be regarded as a combination either formed along the lines of a the labor unions or as a combination in restraint of trade or for the purpose of fixing prices, but first, last, and always as a professional society organized and operated for the purpose of elevating the standard of the profession and increasing the efficiency of its members." Charles E. Fox, "Letter to Richard E. Schmidt Dated 4 October 1917," in *AIA, Office Files, Documents: Handbook, Evolution of, 1915–1917* (Washington, DC: The American Institute of Architects Archives, 1917), RG 801 SR 8 Box 1.

38 "Despite the diversity of strikers, some workers have been much more strike-prone than others. By far the largest number of strikes has taken place in the building construction industry, and this has been true since the American Revolution. Aggregate statistics do not exist before the 1880s, but … between 1880 and 1905 construction workers accounted for 26 percent of the strikes, 14 percent of all strikers, and 39 percent of the firms struck." Immanuel Ness, Benjamin Day, and Aaron Brenner, *The Encyclopedia of Strikes in American History* (Armonk, NY: Routledge, 2009), Book, 6.

39 Josephine Lowell, *Industrial Arbitration and Conciliation; Some Chapters from the Industrial History of the Past Thirty Years*, Questions of the Day 76 (New York: G.P. Putnam's sons, 1894), 64–110.

40 W. H. Sayward, "The National Association of Master Builders," *Carpentry and Building* 12 (1890): 135.

41 G. Alexander Wright, *Wright on Arbitration: A Manual for Architects, Students, Contractors and Construction Engineers* (San Francisco: Self-Published by the Author, 1913), 5–7.

42 W. H. Sayward, "Trade Arbitration," *Inland Architect & News Record* 36 (1900): 136.

43 "The National Association of Master Builders," 135.

44 Charles A. Sayward, *The Sayward Family: Being the History and Genealogy of Henry Sayward of York, Maine and His Descendants: With a Brief Account of Other Saywards Who Settled in America*, Variation: Genealogy & Local History (Ipswich, MA: Independent Press, 1890), 141–42, 54–55. Sayward began his career as a contractor in Boston and had represented the Suffolk District in the Massachusetts House of Representatives. According to his family genealogy, "In addition it was noted, he took an active part in the debates on Woman's Suffrage, strongly opposing the measure." ibid., 154–55.

45 Sayward, "Sub-Contracts," 95–96.

46 Ibid.

47 W. H. Sayward, "Builders' Exchanges: Their Advantages & Opportunities," *Inland Architect & News Record* 13, no. 2 (1889): 18–21; "The National Association of Master Builders," 135–38. News was also reported of Sayward's participation in construction organizing efforts in New York City. See "Talking to the Builders," *New York Times*, November 27, 1889, 4; "Mechanics and Traders' Exchange," *New York Times*, April 11, 1893, 9; "The Benefits of Organization," *Inland Architect & News Record* 30, no. 5 (1897): 48–49.

48 "Plan to Prevent Strikes on Buildings," *New York Times*, December 22, 1901, 24. See also: "Trade Arbitration," 32.

49 William H. Sayward, "Labor-Issues in the Building-Trades," *American Architect & Building News* 78, no. 1404 (1902): 59–62. Sayward's speech to the 13th convention of the National Association of Builders held in Washington, DC, was also published in "Labor Issues in the Building Trades," *Building Trades Association Bulletin* 3, no. 12 (1902).

50 Lowell, *Industrial Arbitration and Conciliation; Some Chapters from the Industrial History of the Past Thirty Years*, 95.

51 "Employers' Union Launched," *Building Trades Association Bulletin* 4, no. 6 (1903): 85.

52 "Building Trades Association," *Building Trades Association Bulletin* 2, no. 1 (1901): 5–6; "National Building Trades Employers' Association," *Carpentry and Building* 26, no. 1 (1904): 8–10; "Labor in the Building Trades," *Carpentry and Building* 26, no. 1 (1904): 1. The New York organization withdrew its support from the national organization due to the latter's espousal of explicitly open shop principles: "1. No limit to amount of work a man can do in a day. 2. No restriction to use of machinery and tools. 3. No restriction to use of manufactured materials, except prison made. 4. No person to have the right to interfere with workmen during working hours. 5. The use of apprentices shall not be prohibited. 6. The foreman shall be the agent of the employer. 7. All workmen shall be at liberty to work for whomsoever they see fit. 8. All employers are at liberty to employ and discharge whomsoever they see fit." "National B.T.E. Association," *Building Trades Employers' Association Bulletin* 5, no. 2 (1904): 25.

53 "Proposed Builders' Exchanges Association," *Carpentry and Building* 28, no. 10 (1906): 349; "National Association of Builders' Exchanges," *Carpentry and Building* 29, no. 3 (1907): 93.

54 "Meeting of National Association of Builders," *Carpentry and Building* 28, no. 11 (1906): 361.

55 "National Building Trades & Employers Association of the United States," *Building Age* 34 (1912): 173–77.

56 "Joint Meeting of Boston Architects and Master Builders," *The Building Age* 34, no. 1 (1912): 8–10. A similar event held at the Society of Architects in Columbus, Ohio, featured a speech by a representative of the local builders' exchange who reminded architects of their own "autocratic power" even while asserting that "builders have no grievances against architects." "The Architect from the Builders' Standpoint," *The Building Age* 34, no. 6 (1912): 321–22. A joint meeting of architects and builders in Cleveland similarly appealed for solidarity through reference to amusing and easily recognizable stereotypes and concluding: "Most of the trouble that arises during the erection of buildings is due to misunderstandings. If these could be avoided, we would have little cause for complaint. In closing I wish to suggest that it is of mutual advantage to have owners, architects and builders co-operate with one another in every way, since it is only by co-operation that the best results can be obtained." "Joint Meeting of Cleveland Architects with Members of Builders Exchange," *The Building Age* 34, no. 7 (1912): 385–86.

57 Frank Miles Day, "Letter to A.B. Pond Dated 19 December 1913," in *Frank Miles Day Collection (1861–1918)* (Philadelphia, PA: The Architectural Archives, University of Pennsylvania, 1913), Box 9.

58 "Letter to Clipston Sturgis Dated 13 December 1913," in *Frank Miles Day Collection (1861–1918)* (Philadelphia, PA: The Architectural Archives, University of Pennsylvania, 1913), Box 9.

59 "Letter to S.S. Labouisse Dated 19 December 1913," in *Frank Miles Day Collection (1861–1918)* (Philadelphia, PA: The Architectural Archives, University of Pennsylvania, 1913), Box 9. See also "Letter to Grosvenor Atterbury Dated 19 December 1913," in *Frank Miles Day Collection (1861–1918)* (Philadelphia, PA: The Architectural Archives, University of Pennsylvania, 1913), Box 9.

60 "Ask for Uniformity in Construction Laws," *Evening Star*, March 28, 1913, 3; "Convention of Building Trades and Employers' Association," *Building Age* 35, no. 5 (1913): 247.

61 J. Crow Taylor, "Advantages of a Builders' Exchange," *The Building Age* 36, no. 1 (1914): 31.

62 "Convention of Builders' Exchanges," ibid.: 28.

63 Ibid., 31.

64 Ibid.

65 Ibid., 28.

66 National Building Trades and Employers' Association of America, *Uniform Contract Adopted and Recommended for Temporary Use* ([Place of publication not identified], 1914 circa [No Date]).

67 "Convention of Builders' Exchanges," 28.

68 Frank Miles Day, "Letter to Allen B. Pond Dated 18 February 1914," in *Frank Miles Day Collection (1861–1918)* (Philadelphia, PA: The Architectural Archives, University of Pennsylvania, 1914), Box 9.

69 "Letter to W.H. Sayward Dated 8 January 1914," in *Frank Miles Day Collection (1861–1918)* (Philadelphia, PA: The Architectural Archives, University of Pennsylvania, 1914), Box 9. See also "Letter to Allen B. Pond Dated 18 February 1914," Box 9.

70 "Letter to Allen B. Pond Dated 18 February 1914," Box 9. The criticisms Day had in mind were contained in a "Report of the Joint Advisory Committee of the Boston Society of Architects and the Master Builders' Association of Boston," the latter of which William Sayward served as secretary.

71 "The Philadelphia Conference on Contract Forms," *Journal of the American Institute of Architects* 2, no. 10 (1914): 487–88; American Institute of Architects, "Proceedings of the Forty-Eighth Annual Convention of the American Institute of Architects" (Washington, DC, 1914), 157–59. It should also be noted that the sale and supply of the contract forms had become a lucrative revenue stream for the organization.

72 "The Philadelphia Conference on Contract Forms," 488.

73 "Proceedings of the Forty-Eighth Annual Convention of the American Institute of Architects," 158.

74 "Convention of Builders Exchanges," *Building Age* 37 (1915): 36.

75 A four-day meeting was subsequently held. William Stanley Parker, representing the Boston Society of Architects, negotiated on behalf of the AIA's Standing Committee on Contracts and Specifications; William B. King, Esq., a construction attorney from Washington, DC, negotiated on behalf of the National Association of Builders' Exchanges. "Proceedings of the Forty-Eighth Annual Convention of the American Institute of Architects," 158.

76 Ibid., 159–61.

77 This view, by the way, was supported as well by the Boston Society of Architects who had been tasked by the AIA to negotiate the points with the National Association of Builders' Exchanges. Consensus among architects on the matter of arbitration, however, was far from universal. Ibid., 158, 61. The Boston construction community had long championed arbitration as an alternative to litigation as a means of dispute resolution. Mechanisms for the reconciliation of labor-employer disputes were applied to the relationship between owners and building contractors. This cooperative attitude had been cultivated since the late-nineteenth century, especially through the efforts of William Sayward in his involvement with the National Association of Builders. As was reported in 1891, "The Mason Builders' Association of Boston have been the first to make direct and practical application of the form of arbitration as adopted and recommended by the fifth convention of the National Association." Lowell,

Industrial Arbitration and Conciliation; Some Chapters from the Industrial History of the Past Thirty Years, 99.

78   American Institute of Architects, "Proceedings of the Forty-Eighth Annual Convention of the American Institute of Architects," 158.

79   "Convention of Builders' Exchanges," 231.

80   "Proceedings of the Forty-Eighth Annual Convention of the American Institute of Architects," 161.

81   *The Handbook of Architectural Practice* (Washington, DC: Press of the American Institute of Architects, Inc., 1920), 144. The second edition of the AIA's standard forms published in 1915 actually omitted the architect's authority for aesthetic decisions from Article 10, but the terminology was included in the third edition published in 1918. That is the edition included in the first printing of *The Handbook*.

82   William Stanley Parker, "The New Standard Documents: II," *Journal of the American Institute of Architects* 3, no. 8 (1915): 350–51.

83   "The New Standard Documents," *Journal of the American Institute of Architects* 3, no. 7 (1915): 302.

84   Frederick Squires, *Architec-tonics: The Adventures of Tom Thumtack, Architect* (New York: Comstock, 1914), 57–63; "Contractors," *Architecture and Building* 46, no. 3 (1914): 92–96.

85   American Institute of Architects, "Proceedings of the Forty-Eighth Annual Convention of the American Institute of Architects," 159.

86   Ibid., 163.

87   *The Handbook of Architectural Practice*, 46.

88   Ibid., 49–50.

89   *The Handbook* conveyed "the conviction that direct letting of contracts as compared with subletting through general contractors affords the Architect more certain selection of competent contractors and more efficient control of execution of work and thereby insures a higher standard of work, and, at the same time, serves more equitably the financial interests of both Owner and Contractor." Ibid., 51–53.

Chapter 5

1   Robert Gutman, "The Architect's Handbook of Professional Practice, ed. David Haviland," *Journal of Architectural Education* 45, no. 2 (1992): 122–24. The loose-leaf format pertained from the 9th through the 12th editions. The 13th edition published in 2001 returned to a single-volume bound format.

2   Following Day's sudden death, members of the AIA visited with Day's widow to learn of her wishes. Committee member Milton B. Medary, Day's virtual right hand on the project, reported to AIA President Thomas R. Kimball: "I have visited Mrs. Day at her request and believe she will not be happy about

the Hand Book unless it is at least passed upon in its final form by Mr. Parker and myself. I went over the documents carefully at Mr. Day's house and find that all the early portion of the book, which covered work which Mr. Day and I were working on together, had been practically completed and that within a few days of his death, he had incorporated some final suggestions which I had made as the result of reading his final copy. The latter portions of the book, made up almost entirely of business forms, covers a field which I feel quite incompetent to handle myself and which I believe Mr. Parker would know more about. This part also has been carried pretty far and all of Mr. Day's original material is available. Mr. Fetterolf of Philadelphia, had been working on lettering these standard forms for reproduction in the book. I would therefore suggest that you ask Mr. Parker, Mr. Fetterolf and myself, to put it in final shape for the first edition. It was Mr. Day's thought that naturally the book would pass through future editions from time to time as a result of its use." Milton B. Medary, "Letter to Thomas R. Kimball Dated 12 August 1918," in *AIA Board of Directors 1917–1919* (Washington, DC: American Institute of Architects Archives, 1918).

3   One key device of Day's handbook proposal was a kind of checklist of project procedures that he called the "Agenda for Architects." Respondents to his early draft were divided on the advisability of such a prescriptive form due to worries that it could be misconstrued as a definitive rather than a recommended modus operandi. While the first draft of *The Handbook* included these "Memoranda of Procedure and Practice" as an introduction, the final version incorporated the diary-like notes into an appendix.

4   Douglas E. Gordon, "The Evolution of Architectural Practice as Recorded in 75 Years of the 'Architect's Handbook'," *Architecture: The AIA Journal* 76, no. 12 (1987): 122.

5   See Anthony Giddens, *Capitalism and Modern Social Theory: An Analysis of the Writings of Marx, Durkheim and Max Weber* (Cambridge, England: University Press, 1971).

6   Overviews of sociological approaches to professions can be found in A. Abbott, "Professions, Sociology Of," in *International Encyclopedia of the Social & Behavioral Sciences*, ed. Neil J. Smelser and Paul B. Baltes (Amsterdam; New York: Elsevier, 2001), 12166–69; David Sciulli, *Professions in Civil Society and the State: Invariant Foundations and Consequences*, International Studies in Sociology and Social Anthropology Series (Leiden: Brill, 2009); Hannes Siegrist, "Professions and Professionalization, History Of," in *International Encyclopedia of the Social & Behavioral Sciences*, ed. James D. Wright (Amsterdam; Boston: Elsevier, 2015), 95–100; Tracey L. Adams, "Sociology of Professions: International Divergences and Research Directions," *Work, Employment & Society* 29, no. 1 (2015). Among key references informing the present work are: Andrew Abbott, *The System of Professions: An Essay on the Division of Expert Labor* (Chicago: The University of Chicago Press, 1988); Steven G. Brint, *In an Age of Experts: The Changing Role of Professionals in Politics and Public Life* (Princeton, NJ: Princeton University Press, 1994); Michael Burrage and Rolf Torstendahl, *Professions in Theory and History: Rethinking the Study of the Professions*

(London; Newbury Park: Sage Publications, 1990); Paul J. DiMaggio and Walter W. Powell, "The Iron Cage Revisited: Institutional Isomorphism and Collective Rationality in Organizational Fields," *American Sociological Review* 48, no. 2 (1983); Eliot Freidson, *Professionalism: The Third Logic* (Chicago: University of Chicago Press, 2001); Elliott A. Krause, *Death of the Guilds: Professions, States, and the Advance of Capitalism, 1930 to the Present* (New Haven: Yale University Press, 1996); Magali Sarfatti Larson, *The Rise of Professionalism: A Sociological Analysis* (Berkeley: University of California Press, 1977); Keith M. Macdonald, *The Sociology of the Professions* (London: Sage Publications, 1995).

7   Bruno Latour, *Reassembling the Social: An Introduction to Actor-Network-Theory*, Clarendon Lectures in Management Studies (Oxford; New York: Oxford University Press, 2005), 97. The shift in emphasis in social thought and discourse from structure to agency is signaled, for example, by Bourdieu's notion of *habitus* where individual actions are at least contributory to the ongoing process of producing and reproducing social structures through a kind of "spontaneity without consciousness or will." Pierre Bourdieu, *The Logic of Practice*, trans. Richard Nice (Stanford, CA: Stanford University Press, 1990), 52–64. Giddens' theory of structuration goes a bit further in recognizing the essential reciprocity of structure and agency, that "in and through their activities agents reproduce the conditions that make these activities possible." Anthony Giddens, *The Constitution of Society: Outline of the Theory of Structuration* (Berkeley: University of California Press, 1984), 2. For broad discussions of this discursive shift, see Sherry B. Ortner, "Theory in Anthropology since the Sixties," *Comparative Studies in Society and History* 26, no. 1 (1984): 126–66; Roxana Elena Doncu, "Theories of Agency in Contemporary Social and Cultural Studies: Anthony Giddens, Ulrich Beck and Bruno Latour," *Journal of Romanian Literary Studies* 8 (2016): 1028–36.

8   D. Brain, "Practical Knowledge and Social Control: The Professionalization of Architecture in the United States," *Sociological Forum* 6 (1991): 242. Brain is a professor of both sociology and environmental studies at the New College of Florida, having studied architecture as an undergraduate at Berkeley.

9   Construction law expert Justin Sweet advises: "Agency is a legal concept vital to design professionals. Agency rules, and their application, determine when the acts of one person bind another. In the typical agency problem, there is a principal, an agent and a third party …. The design professional can fit into any of the three positions in the agency relationship. Also the agency concept is basic to understanding the different forms by which persons conduct their business affairs, such as partnerships and corporations." Justin Sweet, *Legal Aspects of Architecture, Engineering and the Construction Process*, 2nd ed. (St. Paul, MN: West Publishing Co., 1977), 45.

10 US cultural historian Alan Trachtenberg has described the "effects of the corporate system on culture, on values and outlooks" of American life that first became manifest in the 1850s. He writes, "By 'incorporation' I mean a more general process of change, the reorganization of perceptions as well as of enterprise and institutions …. By the 'incorporation of America' I mean, then, the emergence of a changed, more tightly structured society with new

hierarchies of control, and also changed conceptions of that society, of America itself." Alan Trachtenberg and Eric Foner, *The Incorporation of America: Culture and Society in the Gilded Age*, 1st ed., American Century Series (New York: Hill and Wang, 1982), 3–4.

11   Following upon Max Weber's thesis about the "iron cage" of bureaucracy articulated in "The Protestant Ethic and the Spirit of Capitalism" (1904–05), Di Maggio and Powell assess what they see as a tendency toward isomorphism or "homogeneity of organizational forms" in which professions are "less and less driven by competition or the need for efficiency" as they are pressed by extrinsic factors to conform to a standard model. DiMaggio and Powell, "The Iron Cage Revisited: Institutional Isomorphism and Collective Rationality in Organizational Fields," 147–60. Similarly, in their speculations about the reconfiguration of professions by the advent of artificial intelligence, the Susskinds have noted the role of standardization of knowledge and processes that is helpful for understanding the underlying impetus of the *Handbook of Architectural Practice*. Richard E. Susskind and Daniel Susskind, *The Future of the Professions: How Technology Will Transform the Work of Human Experts* (Oxford, UK: Oxford University Press, 2015), 200.

12   While the examples that follow arise from the examination of *The Handbook* circumscribed here, early efforts to gauge the significance of some of the conventions of architectural practice can be found in these conference papers: George B. Johnston, "Tradition and Its Interpretation through Architectural Convention" (paper presented at the 78th ACSA Annual Meeting, San Francisco, 1990), 134–40; "Theories of Working Drawings" (paper presented at the 82nd ACSA Annual Meeting, Montréal, Quebec, 1994), 276–79; "Form and Formwork" (paper presented at the 82nd ACSA Annual Meeting, Montréal, Quebec, 1994), 436–41.

13   This schematic narrative is bolstered in part by the work of Arthur Stinchcombe who uses the apt example of architects' blueprints as illustration of his thesis about the process of organizational formalization. Arthur L. Stinchcombe, *When Formality Works: Authority and Abstraction in Law and Organizations* (Chicago, IL: University of Chicago Press, 2001), 3. See also his Chapter 3 where he further develops in greater detail an illustrative argument about how the mediating role of graphical blueprints "make them a good formality to connect a client and its architect to craft contractors."

14   American Institute of Architects, *The Handbook of Architectural Practice* (Washington, DC: Press of the American Institute of Architects, Inc., 1920), 18.

15   See "The General Conditions of the Contract for Construction" (third edition, 1918) in ibid., 143–51.

16   See second clause in "Form of Contract Adopted by the Joint Committee of the American Institute of Architects, the Western Association of Architects, and the National Association of Builders" (Washington, DC: American Institute of Architects Archives, 1888).

17   Frederick Squires, *Architec-tonics: The Adventures of Tom Thumtack, Architect* (New York: Comstock, 1914), 37–38. Andrew L. Drummond was chief of United States Secret Service during the Harrison administration from 1891 to

1894 and head of the Drummond Detective Agency in New York from 1888 to 1919. "Andrew L. Drummond Dies," *New York Times*, February 13, 1921, 22.

18. Chicago J. H., Ill., "A Contractor's Criticism of Architects [Letter to the Editor]," *The Building Age* 32, no. 7 (1910): 308–09; "The Building Contractor vs. The Architect," ibid., 33, no. 11 (1911): 588.

19. William Stanley Parker, "The New Standard Documents: II," *Journal of the American Institute of Architects* 3, no. 8 (1915): 350–51.

20. *The Handbook of Architectural Practice*, 46.

21. Ibid., 68.

22. Attorney Alan B. Stover takes note of this distinction in his history of the AIA's contract documents. American Institute of Architects, *The American Institute of Architects Official Guide to the 2007 AIA Contract Documents* (Hoboken, NJ: John Wiley & Sons, 2009), 20.

23. *The Handbook of Architectural Practice*, 68.

24. Ibid.

25. Ibid., 65–66.

26. See, for example, Kostof's description the models and templates employed in building practices of the ancient world. Spiro Kostof, ed., *The Architect: Chapters in the History of the Profession* (Berkeley: University of California Press, 2000), 12–16, 87–93.

27. Stinchcombe provides an instructive example of this phenomenon, what he calls "informally embedded formality," in the ways, for example, in which an electrical contractor would take responsibility for meeting a host of trade-specific standards and requirements only implied by the architect's general blueprints. Stinchcombe, *When Formality Works: Authority and Abstraction in Law and Organizations*, 6–7.

28. See for example: D. P. Higgins, "The 'Business' of Architecture: Parts I–III," *Architectural Review* 21, no. 9–12 (1916); "The 'Business' of Architecture: Part IV," *Architectural Review* 23, no. 1–3 (1918); Daniel Paul Higgins, "Architectural Office Organization for Post War Conditions," *American Architect* 115, no. 1 (1919).

29. *The Handbook of Architectural Practice*, 144.

30. Ibid., 72.

31. D. Everett Waid, "Letter to Frank Miles Day Dated 8 November 1917," in *AIA, Office Files, Documents: Handbook, Evolution of, 1915–1917* (Washington, DC: The American Institute of Architects Archives, 1917).

32. The field order is a curious aberration within the evolution of the instruments of architectural practice. References to it in the AIA documents only first appear in the 1970s, yet today it has all but disappeared. In its place has been substituted the "Construction Change Directive" plus generic references to the Architect's "authority to order minor changes in the work." The field order, as it was described in the 1970s, was understood as the formalized confirmation of some minor constructional adjustment which had been improvised by the architect and the contractor working together on the spot but for which no extra charges were required.

33 *The Handbook of Architectural Practice*, 72–74.
34 Ibid., 72.
35 Sullivan W. Jones, "The Building Contract of the Future," *Journal of the American Institute of Architects* 7, no. 3 (1919): 119–22.
36 *The Handbook of Architectural Practice*, 45.
37 Ibid.
38 As one contractor asked, "If we go to a lawyer or doctor of our acquaintance for advice we expect to pay for and pay good price too, and we are seldom disappointed. Why, then, should builder be called upon for figures and advice of all kinds and seldom get thanks, let alone money?" Arthur W. Joslin, "Contractors and Builders an Abused Class," *The Building Age* 32, no. 4 (1910): 141.
39 Sullivan W. Jones, "Quantities and Quantity Estimating," ibid., 35, no. 12 (1913): 591.
40 G. Alexander Wright, "The Analogy between Horse-Racing and Estimating," *Journal of the American Institute of Architects* 1, no. 8 (1913): 334–36.
41 Jones, "Quantities and Quantity Estimating," 591.
42 "The Building Contract of the Future," 119.
43 Wright's earliest writings on behalf of quantity surveying include: G. Alexander Wright, "Bills of Quantities and Their Relation to Building Contracts," *The California Architect and Building News* 18, no. 4 (1897): 38–40; "Estimating on Bills of Quantities: The Owner Pays Whether a Contract Be Let or Not," *American Architect & Building News* 55, no. 1100 (1897): 27. For a brief biographical sketch, see George Rushforth, "Obituary: George Alexander Wright," *Journal of the American Institute of Architects* 6, no. 4 (1918): 200.
44 G. Alexander Wright, "Quantity Surveying: A Necessity for Better Estimating Methods," *American Architect* 104, no. 1978 (1913): 200. Wright embarked upon a national speaking tour in 1913 to advocate for the system among architects and builders. He also published a series of journal articles and a booklet outlining the salient issues. George Alexander Wright, *Wright on Quantities: A Plea for a Better System of Estimating Cost of Buildings in the United States* (San Francisco: General Contractors Association, 1913); G. Alexander Wright, "The Quantity System," *Journal of the American Institute of Architects* 3, no. 1 (1915): 38–39; "The Quantity System," *Journal of the American Institute of Architects* 3, no. 4 (1915): 177–79. In addition to quantity surveying, Wright was also an ardent advocate for arbitration as a means of reducing excessive construction litigation. *Wright on Arbitration: A Manual for Architects, Students, Contractors and Construction Engineers* (San Francisco: Self-Published by the Author, 1913).
45 Between 1913 and 1915, discourse on the topic of quantity surveying was especially active in the *Journal of the American Institute of Architects*, *The Building Age*, *Brickbuilder*, and *American Contractor*.
46 American Institute of Architects, "Proceedings of the Forty-Seventh Annual Convention of the American Institute of Architects" (Washington, DC, 1913), 52–55.

47 *The Handbook of Architectural Practice*, 54. The Boston Society of Architects proposed that the chapter on the Quantity System be completely omitted from *The Handbook* expressing the feeling "that it is not likely ever to become in general use in this country ...." Professors of architecture at Cornell University, on the other hand, asserted the inevitability of the Quantity System, "as sure to come as Equal Suffrage and ... Prohibition ...." Ralph Adams Cram, "Transmittal Letter Dated 26 October 1917 from Boston Society of Architects to Frank Miles Day," in *AIA, Office Files, Documents: Handbook, Evolution of, 1915–1917* (Washington, DC: The American Institute of Architects Archives, 1917); Clarence A. Martin, "Letter to Frank Miles Day Dated 15 October 1917," ibid.

48 Edgar A. Mathews and Alexander Wright, "Letter to Frank Miles Day Dated 25 August 1917," ibid.

49 Committee on Elimination of Waste in Industry, *Waste in Industry*, 1st ed. (Washington, DC: Federated American Engineering Societies, 1921). The study had been suggested by the group's first president, mining engineer Herbert Hoover. When Hoover became Secretary of Commerce the following year in the administration of Warren G. Harding, he used the report as a virtual policy blueprint for efforts to streamline and modernize American industrial production. For a more in-depth consideration of impact of Herbert Hoover's policies in the standardization of US building practices, see George Barnett Johnston, *Drafting Culture: A Social History of Architectural Graphic Standards* (Cambridge, MA: MIT Press, 2008), 155–66. For a report of recommendations of the joint committee of architects, engineers, and contractors, see: "Eliminating Waste in Estimating through Quantity Survey," *American Contractor* 42, no. 43 (1921): 27.

50 *The Handbook of Architectural Practice*, 4th ed. (Washington, DC: American Institute of Architects, 1943), 51.

51 Construction historian (and Quantity Surveyor) Brian Bowen has conjectured further about impediments to the embrace of the quantity surveying system in the United States. After the Second World War, he recognizes the growing self-reliance of large construction firms on their own systems of internal cost control and architects' increasing reliance on external cost control consultants. See Brian Bowen, "The Quantity Surveyor: Missing in Action in the USA" (paper presented at the Third International Congress on Construction History, Cottbus, 2009), 227–34.

52 This formulation is suggested by Antony Giddens' description of the recursive, self-producing relation between human actors and their activities. Giddens, *Capitalism and Modern Social Theory: An Analysis of the Writings of Marx, Durkheim and Max Weber*, 2.

53 Frederick Squires, "Contractors," *Architecture and Building* 46, no. 3 (1914): 92–96.

54 In his ruminations on the regular recurrence of the Middle Ages, Umberto Eco has warned "every time one speaks of a dream of the Middle Ages, one should first ask which Middle Ages one is dreaming of." Umberto Eco, *Travels in Hyperreality*, trans. William Weaver (San Diego: Harcourt Brace Jovanovich, 1986), 68. References to medieval precedents, or references to

Ruskin's references to medieval precedents, inexorably seep into contemporary architectural discourse about the potential of digital design and fabrication technologies to contribute to the reconstitution of a craft-based building culture. See, for example, Richard Garber, "Alberti's Paradigm," *Architectural Design* 79, no. 2 (2009): 88–93; Peggy Deamer and Phillip Bernstein, *Building (in) the Future: Recasting Labor in Architecture* (New Haven; New York: Yale School of Architecture; Princeton Architectural Press, 2010), *passim*.

55 Susskind and Susskind, *The Future of the Professions: How Technology Will Transform the Work of Human Experts*, 9–45.

56 Douglas Spencer suggests that the disavowal of labor is a significant characteristic of the architecture of neoliberalism, where "the old question of whether one lives to work, or works to live, is rendered seemingly redundant in the merging of the one into the other." Douglas Spencer, *The Architecture of Neoliberalism: How Contemporary Architecture Became an Instrument of Control and Compliance* (New York: Bloomsbury Academic, 2016), 75–76.

57 Frank Miles Day, "Speech at Builders Exchange: Relation of Architect, Builder and Sub Contractor, I.E. Constructor for a Specific Trade," in *Frank Miles Day Collection (1861–1918)* (Philadelphia, PA: The Architectural Archives, University of Pennsylvania 1908), Box 6.

58 Alfred Willis, "Design-Build and Building Efficiency in the Early Twentieth Century United States" (paper presented at the First International Congress on Construction History, Madrid, 2003), 2119–26; Sara E. Wermiel, "Norcross, Fuller, and the Rise of the General Contractor in the United States in the Nineteenth Century" (paper presented at the Second International Congress of Construction History, Cambridge, England, 2006), 3297–3314.

59 Hoggson Brothers, *Banks: A Description of the Hoggson Method of Building Illustrated with Some Bank Interiors and Exteriors Executed by Hoggson Brothers* (New York: Hoggson Brothers, 1911), 4; *The Hoggson Building Method: Described and Illustrated for the Information of Those Who Contemplate Building, Re-Modeling, Decorating or Furnishing* (New York: Hoggson Brothers, 1910).

60 As the writing of this final chapter progressed, news was reverberating in the press of acquisitions of highly reputable design-oriented architecture firms by large construction companies such as Katerra aiming to re-engineer and streamline the building acquisition process.

61 George T. Heery, "A History of Construction Management, Project Management, and Development Management," (Atlanta: Brookwood Group, 2011) http://www.brookwoodgroup.com/downloads/2011_history_CMPMDM.pdf.," (2011).

62 In the intervening years, construction management was further developed into differentiated modalities of "management on behalf of the Owner of construction procurement and construction." Heery has championed the "bridging" method of project delivery in which architects as owners' agents provide design services through design development at which time project detailing and pricing fall into the hands of architects directly employed by a general contractor. *Time, Cost, and Architecture* (New York: McGraw-Hill, 1975); *Bridging: A Construction Project Delivery Method*, 1st ed. (Atlanta, GA: Brookwood Group, 2010).

63 William G. Blair, "Should Architects Become Builders and Developers?," *New York Times*, August 10, 1980, 246, 55; John Portman, *The Architect as Developer*, ed. Jonathan Barnett (New York: McGraw-Hill, 1976).

64 Judith R. Blau, *Architects and Firms: A Sociological Perspective on Architectural Practice* (Cambridge, MA: MIT Press, 1984); Robert Gutman, *Architectural Practice: A Critical View* (New York: Princeton Architectural Press, 1988); Dana Cuff, *Architecture: The Story of Practice* (Cambridge, MA: MIT Press, 1991); Magali Sarfatti Larson, *Behind the Postmodern Facade: Architectural Change in Late Twentieth-Century America* (Berkeley: University of California Press, 1993).

65 Dana Cuff, "Fragmented Dreams, Flexible Practices," *Architecture* 81, no. 5 (1992): 80–83.

66 *United States of American (Plaintiff) vs. The American Institute of Architects (Defendant)* (1972); David Johnston, "Justice Department Files Antitrust Suit against Architects," *New York Times*, July 6, 1990, 1, 12.

67 "Architects in U.S. Mark Centennial," ibid., February 24, 1957, 1–2; Paul Goldberger, "Institute of Architects Keeps Bans on Advertising and Contracting," ibid., June 9, 1977, 45; "Architects Will End Ban on Advertising," *New York Times*, May 25, 1978, 20; Blair, "Should Architects Become Builders and Developers?," 255.

68 AIA National and AIA California Council, *Integrated Project Delivery: A Guide* (Washington, DC: American Institute of Architects, 2007), 2.

69 Peggy Deamer suggests for example that, at least *in potentia*, "IPD ... is a marker that architects, owners, and builders are capable of devising plans for a new, concrete and symbolic imaginary." Peggy Deamer, "Contracts of Relation," Het Nieuwe Instituut Research & Development, Lecture Transcript (2017), http://www.e-flux.com/architecture/representation/159198/contracts-of-relation/.

70 AIA National and AIA California Council, *Integrated Project Delivery: A Guide*, 10.

71 See construction attorney Howard Ashcroft's essay in Deamer and Bernstein, *Building (in) the Future: Recasting Labor in Architecture*, 145–58. For overviews of BIM functionality and its potential impacts on the field, see Richard Garber, "Optimisation Stories: The Impact of Building Information Modelling on Contemporary Design Practice," in *The Digital Turn in Architecture 1992–2012*, ed. Mario Carpo (Chichester, West Sussex England: Wiley, 2013), 227–39; "Digital Workflows and the Expanded Territory of the Architect," *Architectural Design* 87, no. 3 (2017): 6–13; Scott Marble, *Digital Workflows in Architecture: Designing Design – Designing Assembly – Designing Industry* (Basel: Birkhäuser, 2012).

72 Squires, *Architec-tonics*, 25–33. At the time of this writing, news appears of a university officer allegedly importuning their architects to employ a proprietary "5D BIM" software for which he himself was a paid consultant. Lance Wallace, "Tech Releases Reports Documenting Conflicts of Interest, Ethics Concerns," Georgia Tech Institute Communications Office, https://www.news.gatech.edu/2018/07/26/tech-releases-reports-documenting-conflicts-interest-ethics-concerns; Johnny Edwards, "Audit

Slams High-Living by Officials," *Atlanta Journal-Constitution*, July 28, 2018, A1, 4.

73 Edward Bellamy, *Looking Backward: From 2000 to 1887* (New York: Magnum, 1968 [1888]).

74 Discernable stages in the process of profession-formation are variously suggested in the sociological approaches to professions noted earlier. Within the spectrum of those socio-historical accounts, an additional work is particularly cogent in its consideration of the transformative impacts of new technologies on the structure of expert knowledge. Susskind and Susskind, *The Future of the Professions: How Technology Will Transform the Work of Human Experts*.

75 Robert L. Geddes and Bernard P. Spring, "A Study of Education for Environmental Design Sponsored by the American Institute of Architects" (Princeton University, 1967).

76 See Ernest L. Boyer and Lee D. Mitgang, *Building Community: A New Future for Architecture Education and Practice: A Special Report* (Princeton, NJ: Carnegie Foundation for the Advancement of Teaching, 1996), 63–74.

77 A cogent account of this history along with consideration of emergent parametric possibilities is given in Phillip G. Bernstein, "Parameter Value," in *The Politics of Parametricism: Digital Technologies in Architecture*, ed. Matthew Poole and Manuel Shvartzberg (London: Bloomsbury Academic, 2015), 200–12. For consideration of the "pre-history" of the computational turn in architecture, see Molly Wright Steenson, *Architectural Intelligence: How Designers and Architects Created the Digital Landscape* (Cambridge, MA: MIT Press, 2017).

78 The Susskinds refer to this fourth stage as "externalization." Susskind and Susskind, *The Future of the Professions: How Technology Will Transform the Work of Human Experts*, 202–10.

79 Ibid., 303.

80 See for example: Rakesh Ramchurn, "Everything Is Connected: Architects' Work Is Set to Be Revolutionised by Digital Innovations Such as the Internet of Things, Artificial Intelligence and the Collaborative Economy," *Architects' Journal* 241, no. 13 (2015): 54–55; Rohit Talwar, "Rohit Talwar: As Artificial Intelligence Removes as Many as Half of Jobs in the Future, Architecture's Role and the Use of Space Will Change Fundamentally," *Blueprint (London, England)*, no. 353 (2017): 19.

81 Susskind and Susskind, *The Future of the Professions: How Technology Will Transform the Work of Human Experts*, 303.

82 Architectural historian and theorist of the digital turn in architecture Mario Carpo is both sanguine and circumspect about these prospects. Mario Carpo, "Excessive Resolution: Designers Meet the Second Coming of Artificial Intelligence," *Architectural Record* (2018): 136.

83 See, for example, Dennis Shelden, "Cyber-Physical Systems and the Built Environment," *Technology|Architecture + Design* 2, no. 2 (2018): 137–39; Güvenç Özel, "Toward a Postarchitecture," *Log*, no. 36 (2016): 99–105.

84 Referring to John Turner and Richard Fichter's *Freedom to Build*, Andrew Ross has made a compelling statement about the need for the architecture profession to resist desperation in the face of any perceived existential threats. Deamer and Bernstein, *Building (in) the Future: Recasting Labor in Architecture*, 13.

85 "Mangle of practice" is the provocative term, along with "dance of agency," coined by Andrew Pickering to characterize the tandem trajectory of change driven by the intercourse of science and society. He defines the mangle of practice as "the temporal structuring of practice as a dialectic of resistance and accommodation." Andrew Pickering, *The Mangle of Practice: Time, Agency, and Science*, (Chicago: University of Chicago Press, 2010), xi, 21–24.

86 Such totalizing tendencies may be found among fervent advocates of parametricism as evident in Patrik Schumacher, "The Historical Pertinence of Parametricism and the Prospect of a Free Market Urban Order," in *The Politics of Parametricism: Digital Technologies in Architecture*, ed. Matthew Poole and Manuel Shvartzberg (London; New York: Bloomsbury Academic, 2015), 19–44.

87 This, David Harvey has argued, is the enduring purpose and social contribution of the field of architecture. David Harvey, *Spaces of Hope* (Berkeley; Los Angeles: University of California Press, 2000).

88 Frederick Squires, *The Hollow-Tile House* (New York: The William T. Comstock Co., 1913), 207–08.

89 Blau, *Architects and Firms: A Sociological Perspective on Architectural Practice*, 3. Blau describes a recursive loop of development in which "... particular conditions contain an implicit contradiction that sets into motion processes that unfold to reveal the full implications of the initial contradiction while at the same time they create a resolution that in turn poses a new set of opposing conditions."

90 Squires, *The Hollow-Tile House*, 52–53.

91 *Flooding with Re-Used Water*, Circular/Illinois State Geological Survey (Urbana, IL: Illinois State Geological Survey, 1949), 2.

92 Karen Lang Kummer, "National Register of Historic Places Registration Form: Frederick Squires House" (United States Department of the Interior, National Park Service, 2011).

BIBLIOGRAPHY

Abbott, A. "Professions, Sociology Of." In *International Encyclopedia of the Social & Behavioral Sciences*, edited by Neil J. Smelser and Paul B. Baltes, 12166–69. Amsterdam and New York: Elsevier, 2001.

Abbott, Andrew. *The System of Professions: An Essay on the Division of Expert Labor*. Chicago, IL: The University of Chicago Press, 1988.

"About Alumni: Kenneth M. Murchison." *Columbia Alumni News* 7, no. 23 (March 10, 1916): 707.

Ackerman, Frederick L. "The Architect's Part in the World's Work." *Architectural Record* 37, no. 2 (February 1915): 149–58.

Ackerman, Frederick L. "The Responsibility for Incompetence." *The Real Estate Magazine* 5, no. 1 (January 1915): 15–20.

Adams, Tracey L. "Sociology of Professions: International Divergences and Research Directions." *Work, Employment & Society* 29, no. 1 (2015): 154–65.

Adler, Dankmar. "The General Contractor from the Standpoint of the Architect." *Inland Architect & News Record* 33 (June 1899): 38–39.

AIA National and AIA California Council. *Integrated Project Delivery: A Guide*. Washington, DC: American Institute of Architects, 2007.

Alberti, Leon Battista. *On the Art of Building in Ten Books*. Translated by Joseph Rykwert, Neil Leach, and Robert Tavernor. Cambridge, MA: MIT Press, 1988.

American Institute of Architects. *The American Institute of Architects Official Guide to the 2007 AIA Contract Documents*. Hoboken, NJ: John Wiley & Sons, 2009.

American Institute of Architects. "Preliminary Report of the Committee on the Relation of Architects to the Contracting System." In *Frank Miles Day Collection (1861–1918)*. Philadelphia: The Architectural Archives, University of Pennsylvania 1907.

American Institute of Architects. *Proceedings of the Twenty-Eighth Annual Convention of the American Institute of Architects*. Washington, DC, 1894.

American Institute of Architects. *Proceedings of the Twenty-Ninth Annual Convention of the American Institute of Architects*. Washington, DC, 1895.

American Institute of Architects. *Proceedings of the Thirty-Fifth Annual Convention of the American Institute of Architects*. Washington, DC, 1901.

American Institute of Architects. *Proceedings of the Thirty-Sixth Annual Convention of the American Institute of Architects*. Washington, DC, 1902.

American Institute of Architects. *Proceedings of the Thirty-Eighth Annual Convention of the American Institute of Architects*. Washington, DC, 1905.

American Institute of Architects. *Proceedings of the Fortieth Annual Convention of the American Institute of Architects*. Washington, DC, 1907.

American Institute of Architects. *Proceedings of the Forty-Second Annual Convention of the American Institute of Architects*. Washington, DC, 1908.

American Institute of Architects. *Proceedings of the Forty-Third Annual Convention of the American Institute of Architects."* Washington, DC, 1909.
American Institute of Architects. *Proceedings of the Forty-Seventh Annual Convention of the American Institute of Architects.* Washington, DC, 1913.
American Institute of Architects. *Proceedings of the Forty-Eighth Annual Convention of the American Institute of Architects.* Washington, DC, 1914.
American Institute of Architects. *Proceedings of the Forty-Ninth Annual Convention of the American Institute of Architects.* Washington, DC, 1915.
American Institute of Architects. *Proceedings of the Fifty-First Annual Convention of the American Institute of Architects.* Washington, DC, 1918.
"Andrew L. Drummond Dies." *New York Times*, February 13, 1921, 22.
Andrews, Robert D. "Letter to Frank Miles Day Dated 3 December 1908." In *Frank Miles Day Collection (1861–1918)*. Philadelphia, PA: The Architectural Archives, University of Pennsylvania 1908.
Andrews, Robert D. "Letter to Frank Miles Day Dated 30 November 1908." In *Frank Miles Day Collection (1861–1918)*. Philadelphia, PA: The Architectural Archives, University of Pennsylvania 1908.
"Anthony Comstock Dies in His Crusade." *New York Times*, September 22, 1915, 1, 6.
"An Architect." *Journal of the American Institute of Architects* 1, no. 11 (November 1913): 473.
"The Architect and the Builder." *The Building Age* 34, no. 12 (December 1912): 613–14.
"The Architect and the Client: A Banker Speaks on the Subject." *Journal of the American Institute of Architects* 2, no. 12 (December 1914): 557–59.
"The Architect from the Builders' Standpoint." *The Building Age* 34, no. 6 (June 1912): 321–22.
"Architect Jenney and the Contractor." *Western Architect* 10, no. 11 (November 1907): 117–18.
"The Architect, the Contractor, the Publisher: Not a Fable." *Inland Architect & News Record* 26 (1896): 55.
"Architect's Building New North Wing, New York." *Architecture & Building* 59 (1927): 182.
"An Architect's Handbook of Professional Practice and Business Administration." In *Handbook of Architectural Practice - 1st Ed. Not Published File*. Washington, DC: The American Institute of Architects Archives, 1917.
"Architects and Engineers." *American Architect & Building News* 4 (1878): 54–55.
"Architects as Composers." *The American Contractor* 37 (March 11, 1916): 76b.
"Architects in Costume: Beaux Arts Society Dines and Enjoys a 'Hysterical' Melodrama." *New York Times*, February 8, 1913, 24.
"Architects in U.S. Mark Centennial." *New York Times*, February 24, 1957, 1–2.
"Architects of To-Day." *Architecture* 20 (December 15, 1909): 177–84.
"Art and Architecture: Squires & Wynkoop Dissolve Partnership." *Architecture and Building* 43, no. 9 (June 1911): 22.
"Ask for Uniformity in Construction Laws." *Evening Star*, March 28, 1913, 3.
"Attention Called to Theater Construction (Editorial)." *Inland Architect and News Record* 42, no. 6 (January 1904): 41–42.

Bailyn, Bernard. *The Ideological Origins of the American Revolution.* Cambridge, MA: Harvard University Press, 1992.

"The Ball of the Fine Arts." *New York Times.* 15 February 1914, 59.

"Ball of the Fine Arts: Beaux Arts Architects to Give First Dance at the Astor." *New York Times*, December 22, 1913, 9.

Bannister, William P. "The Practice of Architecture." *American Architect* 129, no. 5 (1926): 40–43.

Barnett, T. P. "The Business and Art of Architecture: An Address Delivered before the Art League of St. Louis, Mo." *American Architect* 113, no. 2210 (May 1, 1918): 525–28.

Baumann, Frederick H. "Relation of Architect to Contractor and Journeymen." *Inland Architect & News Record* 6 (1885): 60–61.

Beach, W. W. "The Problem of the General Contractor." *Architectural Forum* 26 (June 1917): 183.

Beach, Wilfred. "The Architect." *Architectural Record* 35 (1914): 425–34.

Bellamy, Edward. *Looking Backward: From 2000 to 1887.* New York: Magnum, 1968 [1888].

Bennett, Tony. *The Birth of the Museum: History, Theory, Politics.* New York: Routledge, 1995.

Berke, Arnold. "Searching for Palladio: How Did One Italian Architect Shape Some of America's Greatest Houses?" *Preservation* 61, no. 4 (2009): 40–43.

Bernstein, Phillip G. "Parameter Value." In *The Politics of Parametricism: Digital Technologies in Architecture*, edited by Matthew Poole and Manuel Shvartzberg, 200–12. London: Bloomsbury Academic, 2015.

Bertels, I., K. Verswijver, and I. Wouters. "Under Construction, Building Contractors in Nineteenth Century Belgium." *Transactions on the Built Environment* 118 (2011): 35–44.

Bertels, Inge. "Building Contractors in Late-Nineteenth-Century Belgium: From Craftsmen to Contractors." *Construction History* 26 (2011): 1–18.

"Better Care for Women Prisoners in New Jail Which City Will Erect." *The Sun*, March 22, 1914, 2.

Bishir, Catherine W. "Murchison, Kenneth M., Jr. (1872–1938)." In *North Carolina Architects & Builders: A Biographical Dictionary.* Raleigh, NC: Copyright & Digital Scholarship Center, North Carolina State University Libraries, 2015.

Black, Alex. "Letter from Keokuk, Iowa: An Architect's Death by Violence (Architect Murdered by a Builder)." *American Architect & Building News* 5, no. 173 (1879): 126.

Blackall, C. H. "The All-Around Architect." *Inland Architect & News Record* 26, no. 3 (October 1895): 23–25.

Blackall, C. H. "Fifty Years Ago." *American Architect* 129, no. 5 (1926): 7–9.

Blair, William G. "Should Architects Become Builders and Developers?" *New York Times*, August 10, 1980, 246, 55.

Blake, Clinton H. *The Law of Architecture and Building; a Consideration of the Mutual Rights, Duties and Liabilities of Architect, Owner and Contractor, with Appendices and Forms.* New York: William T. Comstock Co., 1916.

Blau, Judith R. *Architects and Firms: A Sociological Perspective on Architectural Practice.* Cambridge, MA: MIT Press, 1984.

Bledstein, Burton J. *The Culture of Professionalism: The Middle Class and the Development of Higher Education in America.* 1st ed. New York: Norton, 1976.

Bolton, Reginald Pelham. "The Engineer, the Architect, and the General Construction Company." *American Architect & Building News* 85, no. 1495 (August 20, 1904).
Bourdieu, Pierre. *The Logic of Practice*. Translated by Richard Nice. Stanford, CA: Stanford University Press, 1990.
Bowen, Brian. "The Quantity Surveyor: Missing in Action in the USA." Paper presented at the Third International Congress on Construction History, Cottbus, 2009.
Bowman, William L. "Legal Hints for Architects." *Brickbuilder* 20 (1911).
Boyer, Ernest L., and Lee D. Mitgang. *Building Community: A New Future for Architecture Education and Practice: A Special Report*. Princeton, NJ: Carnegie Foundation for the Advancement of Teaching, 1996.
Boyington, W. W. "Differences between the Methods of Architectural Practice Prevalent Now and Those of Fifty Years Ago." *Proceedings of the 21st Annual Convention of the American Institute of Architects* (1887): 102–06.
Brain, David. "Practical Knowledge and Social Control: The Professionalization of Architecture in the United States." *Sociological Forum* 6 (1991): 239–68.
Brandeis, Louis D. "Suggestive Form of Contract Printed for the Boston Society of Architects." *American Architect & Building News* 37 (1892): 7.
Bregg, Charles M. "In the Theaters Last Night: 'Come to Bohemia'." *Pittsburgh Gazette Times*, March 28, 1916, 11.
Brint, Steven G. *In an Age of Experts: The Changing Role of Professionals in Politics and Public Life*. Princeton, NJ: Princeton University Press, 1994.
Broun, Heywood, and Margaret Leech. *Anthony Comstock, Roundsman of the Lord*. New York: Albert & Charles Boni, 1927.
Brown, Glenn. "An Architect's Services and Remuneration." *Inland Architect & News Record* 48, no. 1 (August 1906): 3–4.
Brown, Glenn. "An Architect's Services and Remuneration." *Inland Architect & News Record* 48, no. 2 (September 1906): 15–18.
Brown, Glenn. "The Tarsney Act: Historical Review." *Brickbuilder* 15, no. 5 (1906): 95–98.
"The Building Contractor vs. the Architect." *The Building Age* 33, no. 11 (November 1911): 588.
"Building Trades Association." *Building Trades Association Bulletin* 2, no. 1 (June 1901): 5–6.
Burrage, Michael, and Rolf Torstendahl. *Professions in Theory and History: Rethinking the Study of the Professions*. London; Newbury Park: Sage Publications, 1990.
Carpo, Mario. "Excessive Resolution: Designers Meet the Second Coming of Artificial Intelligence." *Architectural Record* (June 2018): 135–36.
Chapman, Cecil Bayless. "Letter to Frank Miles Day Dated 19 October 1917." In *AIA, Office Files, Documents: Handbook, Evolution of, 1915–1917*. Washington, DC: The American Institute of Architects Archives, 1917.
Chappell, George S. "Correspondence to Rockwell Kent Dated 10 April 1915." In *Rockwell Kent Papers, [circa 1840]–1993, bulk 1935–1961*. Washington, DC: Smithsonian Institution Archives of American Art, 1915.
Chappell, George S. "Correspondence to Rockwell Kent Dated 29 January 1919." In *Rockwell Kent Papers, [circa 1840]–1993, bulk 1935–1961*. Washington, DC: Smithsonian Institution Archives of American Art, 1919.

Chappell, George S. *The Cruise of the Kawa Wanderings in the South Seas.* New York and London: G.P. Putnam's Sons, 1921.
Chappell, George S. "Double Lives: Their Interest, Their Advisability and Their Beauty." *Vanity Fair* 19, no. 2 (October 1922): 49, 104.
Chappell, George S. "Lattice – Its Use as an Architectural Embellishment – Part I." *Brickbuilder* 22, no. 5 (May 1913): 105–08.
Chappell, George S. "Lattice – Its Use as an Architectural Embellishment – Part II." *Brickbuilder* 22, no. 9 (September 1913): 201–04.
Chappell, George S. *My Northern Exposure: The Kawa at the Pole.* New York: G.P. Putnam's Sons, 1922.
Chappell, George S. "Paris School Days: How the Student Lives and Works at the Ecole Des Beaux Arts (Part 1)." *Architectural Record* 28 (July 1910): 37–41.
Chappell, George S. "Paris School Days: How the Student Lives and Works at the Ecole Des Beaux Arts (Part 2)." *Architectural Record* 28 (November 1910): 350–55.
Chappell, George S. "Paris School Days: How the Student Lives and Works at the Ecole Des Beaux Arts (Part 3)." *Architectural Record* 29 (February 1911): 139–43.
Chappell, George S. "The Shelton." *New Republic* 38 (March 5, 1924): 43–45.
Chappell, George S. "The South Sea Man Again [Book Review of *Atolls of the Sun* by Frederick O'brien]." *The New York Herald*, November 5, 1922, 7.
Chappell, George S., and Rockwell Kent. "The Nomenclature of the Styles, Adam Style – Greek Freeze: A Humorous Theory Illustrating in Caricature Familiar Schools and Phases of Architecture." *Brickbuilder* 24, no. 1 (January 1915): 23–24.
Chappell, George S., and Rockwell Kent. "The Nomenclature of the Styles, Early Christian – Rococo: A Humorous Theory Illustrating in Caricature Familiar Schools and Phases of Architecture." *Brickbuilder* 24, no. 2 (March 1915): 71–72.
"Chicago Architects' Business Association." In *Handbook for Architects and Builders*, edited by Emery Stanford Hall, 17–21. Chicago, IL: Chicago Architects' Business Association and Wm. Johnston Printing Co., 1908.
Clark, T. M. *Architect, Owner and Builder before the Law: A Summary of American and English Decisions on the Principal Questions Relating to Building, and the Employment of Architects, with about Eight Hundred References, Including Also Practical Suggestions in Regard to the Drawing of Building Contracts, and Forms of Contract Suited to Various Circumstances.* New York: London, 1894.
"Clifford Wendehack, Architect, 62 Is Dead." *New York Times*, May 16, 1948, 68.
"Code of Ethics." In *Frank Miles Day Collection (1861–1918)*. Philadelphia, PA: The Architectural Archives, University of Pennsylvania 1908.
"'Come to Bohemia's' New Haven Tryout Attracts Most of Forty-Second Street Far from Home." *The Sun*, April 27, 1916, 7.
Committee on Elimination of Waste in Industry. *Waste in Industry*. 1st ed. Washington, DC: Federated American Engineering Societies, 1921.
"The Compensation of Foreign Architects: The Five Per Cent Commission." *Inland Architect & News Record* 48, no. 4 (November 1906): 38.
"Competition for School-House at Washington, DC." *American Architect & Building News* 5, no. 173 (April 19, 1879): 122.

Comstock, Cyrus B. *A Comstock Genealogy: Descendants of William Comstock of New London, Conn. Who Died after 1662 – Ten Generations*. New York: The Knickerbocker Press, 1907.

"Condemnation of General Contract System Approved." *Inland Architect & News Record* 33 (1899): 37.

"Congressional Committee Attacks Tarsney Act." *Western Architect* 18, no. 9 (September 1912): 92–93.

"Convention of Builders' Exchanges." *Building Age* 36 (March 1914): 28–33.

"Convention of Builders' Exchanges." *Building Age* 37 (March 1915): 33–37.

"Convention of Building Trades and Employers' Association." *Building Age* 35, no. 5 (May 1913): 247.

"Cooperation of the Architect and Engineer." *American Architect & Building News* 85, no. 1495 (August 20, 1904).

Corbett, Harvey Wiley. *Year Book of the Architectural League of New York and Catalogue of the Twenty-Fourth Annual Exhibition,"* edited by Architectural League of New York. New York: Kalkhoff Company, 1909.

"Correspondence regarding Government Competitions." *Inland Architect & News Record* 38 (1901): 7.

"A Cottage on Oak Road, Tarrytown, N.Y." *American Architect & Building News* 96, no. 1754 (1909): 52.

Cram, Ralph Adams. "Transmittal Letter Dated 26 October 1917 from Boston Society of Architects to Frank Miles Day." In *AIA, Office Files, Documents: Handbook, Evolution of, 1915–1917*. Washington, DC: The American Institute of Architects Archives, 1917.

Cret, Paul. "The Utility of Exhibitions." In *T Square Club Catalogue of the Eleventh Annual Architectural Exhibition 1904–1905*, edited by William S. Vaux and Richard Erskine, 9–12. Philadelphia: T Square Club, 1905.

Croly, Herbert. "The Architect in Recent Fiction." *Architectural Record* 17, no. 2 (February 1905): 137–39.

Crowninshield, Frank. "In Vanity Fair." *Vanity Fair* 2, no. 1 (March 1914): 15.

Cuff, Dana. *Architecture: The Story of Practice*. Cambridge, MA: MIT Press, 1991.

Cuff, Dana. "Fragmented Dreams, Flexible Practices." *Architecture* 81, no. 5 (1992): 80–83.

Day, Frank Miles. "Conduct of Competitions A.I.A." *Architecture* 22 (1910): 151–53.

Day, Frank Miles. "Letter to A.B. Pond Dated 19 December 1913." In *Frank Miles Day Collection (1861–1918)*. Philadelphia, PA: The Architectural Archives, University of Pennsylvania 1913.

Day, Frank Miles. "Letter to Allen B. Pond Dated 18 February 1914." In *Frank Miles Day Collection (1861–1918)*. Philadelphia, PA: The Architectural Archives, University of Pennsylvania 1914.

Day, Frank Miles. "Letter to Clipston Sturgis Dated 13 December 1913." In *Frank Miles Day Collection (1861–1918)*. Philadelphia, PA: The Architectural Archives, University of Pennsylvania 1913.

Day, Frank Miles. "Letter to D. Everett Waid (Undated August 1917)." In *AIA Office Files Autograph: Waid, Dan Everett (1864–1939)*. Washington, DC: American Institute of Architects Archives 1917.

Day, Frank Miles. "Letter to Grosvenor Atterbury Dated 19 December 1913." In *Frank Miles Day Collection (1861–1918)*. Philadelphia, PA: The Architectural Archives, University of Pennsylvania 1913.

Day, Frank Miles. "Letter to J. Lawrence Mauran, Et Al. Dated 6 January 1917." In *AIA Office Files Autograph: Waid, Dan Everett (1864–1919)*. Washington, DC: American Institute of Architects Archives 1917.

Day, Frank Miles. "Letter to M.B. Medary and E.H. Fetterolf Dated 30 November 1917." In *AIA Board of Directors 1917–1919*. Washington, DC: American Institute of Architects Archives 1917.

Day, Frank Miles. "Letter to S.S. Labouisse Dated 19 December 1913." In *Frank Miles Day Collection (1861–1918)*. Philadelphia, PA: The Architectural Archives, University of Pennsylvania 1913.

Day, Frank Miles. "Letter to W.H. Sayward Dated 8 January 1914." In *Frank Miles Day Collection (1861–1918)*. Philadelphia, PA: The Architectural Archives, University of Pennsylvania 1914.

Day, Frank Miles. "Speech at Builders Exchange: Relation of Architect, Builder and Sub Contractor, I.E. Constructor for a Specific Trade." In *Frank Miles Day Collection (1861–1918)*. Philadelphia, PA: The Architectural Archives, University of Pennsylvania 1908.

De Certeau, Michel. *The Practice of Everyday Life*. Translated by Steven F. Rendall. Berkeley: University of California Press, 1984.

Deamer, Peggy. "Contracts of Relation." Het Nieuwe Instituut Research & Development, Lecture Transcript (2017). Published electronically October 19, 2017. http://www.e-flux.com/architecture/representation/159198/contracts-of-relation/.

Deamer, Peggy, and Phillip Bernstein. *Building (in) the Future: Recasting Labor in Architecture*. New Haven, CT and New York: Yale School of Architecture; Princeton Architectural Press, 2010.

Dehli, Arne. "The Present System of Architects' Charges." *Architectural Record* 15 (June 1904): 545–51.

Demkin, Joseph A., ed. *The Architect's Handbook of Professional Practice*. 14th ed. Hoboken, NJ: Wiley, 2008.

DiMaggio, Paul J., and Walter W. Powell. "The Iron Cage Revisited: Institutional Isomorphism and Collective Rationality in Organizational Fields." *American Sociological Review* 48, no. 2 (1983): 147–60.

Dobbels, Jelena, Inge Bertels, and Ine Wouters. "The Professionalization of Belgian General Contractors (1877–1914): An Analysis of the Construction Journal *La Chronique Des Travaux Publics, Du Commerce Et De L'industrie*." Paper presented at the Further Studies in the History of Construction: The Proceedings of the Third Annual Conference of the Construction History Society, Queen's College Cambridge University, 2016.

Doncu, Roxana Elena. "Theories of Agency in Contemporary Social and Cultural Studies: Anthony Giddens, Ulrich Beck and Bruno Latour." *Journal of Romanian Literary Studies* 8 (2016): 1028–36.

Durkheim, Émile. "Progressive Preponderance of Organic Solidarity." In *Émile Durkheim on Morality and Society, Selected Writings*, edited by Robert Neelly Bellah, 63–85. Chicago, IL: University of Chicago Press, 1973.

Eco, Umberto. *Travels in Hyperreality*. Translated by William Weaver. San Diego: Harcourt Brace Jovanovich, 1986.

The Editors of Encyclopedia Brittanica. "Robert Williams Wood." Encyclopedia Brittanica, Inc., https://www.britannica.com/biography/Robert-Williams-Wood.

Edwards, Johnny. "Audit Slams High-Living by Officials." *Atlanta Journal-Constitution*, July 28, 2018, A1, 4.

Edwards-Ficken, H. "The Case of H. Edwards-Ficken, Architect: Against the New York Athletic Club." *American Architect & Building News* 19, no. 528 (February 6, 1886): 69–70.

"Eliminating Waste in Estimating through Quantity Survey." *American Contractor* 42, no. 43 (October 22, 1921): 27.

Elliott, Cecil D. *The American Architect from the Colonial Era to the Present.* Jefferson, NC: McFarland & Co., 2003.

Ely, Henry S., Brian Hooker, and Wells Southworth Hastings. *Yale Fun: A Book of College Humor in Poetry, Pictures and Prose, Chosen with Loving Care from the Yale Record of the Past Eight Years; Conceived in the Sanctum, Founded on Foam, and Dedicated to the Humorous Faculty.* Hartford, CT: R. S. Peck, 1901.

"Employers' Union Launched." *Building Trades Association Bulletin* 4, no. 6 (1903): 85–88.

Ewing, Charles. "Form of Application to Qualify by an Exhibition of Executed Work for Candidature as Associate Member in the American Institute of Architects." In *AIA Historical Directory of American Architects*, edited by American Institute of Architects. Washington, DC: AIA Archives, 1907.

Fajans, Jane. "Practice: An Anthropological Approach." In *International Encyclopedia of the Social & Behavioral Sciences*, edited by James D. Wright, 782–87. Amsterdam and Boston, MA: Elsevier, 2015.

"Fees of an Architect." *Building Age* 35, no. 7 (July 1913): 346.

Fenner, Burt L. "Letter to Frank Miles Day Dated 17 October 1917." In *AIA, Office Files, Documents: Handbook, Evolution of, 1915–1917.* Washington, DC: The American Institute of Architects Archives, 1917.

Fish, Anne Harriet, Dorothy Parker, George S. Chappell, and Frank Crowninshield. *High Society: Advice as to Social Campaigning, and Hints on the Management of Dowagers, Dinners, Debutantes, Dances, and the Thousand and One Diversions of Persons of Quality.* New York: Putnam, 1920.

Fitzpatrick, F. W. "The Architects." *Inland Architect & News Record* 39 (June 1902): 38–39.

Fitzpatrick, F. W. "Lessons of the Baltimore Fire." *Inland Architect & News Record* 43 (March 1904): 10–14.

Fitzpatrick, F. W. "More Anent Incompetence: Some Striking Remarks by a Keen Critic upon Mr. Kruse's Recent Article." *The Real Estate Magazine* 4, no. 12 (December 1914): 14–17.

Fitzpatrick, F. W. "Our Annual Ash-Heap." *American Architect & Building News* 89 (May 5, 1906): 151–52.

Fitzpatrick, F. W. "San Francisco: Notes after a Thorough Investigation of the Results of the San Francisco Disaster." *Inland Architect & News Record* 47 (July 1906): 79–81.

Fitzpatrick, F. W. "Tall Buildings in Smaller Cities." *Buildings and Building Management* (November 1913): 24–25.

Fitzpatrick, F. W. "The 'Tarsney' Act." *Architecture and Building* 44, no. 6 (June 1912): 20–21.

Forde, Kathy Roberts. *Literary Journalism on Trial: Masson V. New Yorker and the First Amendment.* Amherst: University of Massachusetts Press, 2008.

Form of Contract Adopted by the Joint Committee of the American Institute of Architects, the Western Association of Architects, and the National Association of Builders." Washington, DC: American Institute of Architects Archives, 1888.

Foucault, Michel. *Discipline & Punish: The Birth of the Prison*. Translated by Alan Sheridan. 2nd ed. New York: Vintage Books, 1995. 1975.
Fox, Charles E. "Letter to Richard E. Schmidt Dated 4 October 1917." In *AIA, Office Files, Documents: Handbook, Evolution of, 1915–1917*. Washington, DC: The American Institute of Architects Archives, 1917.
Frederick Squires, Architect. "Mercantile Building at N.E. Cor. 24th St. and 7th Ave., New York." *Architecture and Building* 44, no. 5 (May 1912): 222–24.
Freidson, Eliot. *Professionalism: The Third Logic*. Chicago, IL: University of Chicago Press, 2001.
Garber, Richard. "Alberti's Paradigm." *Architectural Design* 79, no. 2 (March/April, 2009): 88–93.
Garber, Richard. "Digital Workflows and the Expanded Territory of the Architect." *Architectural Design* 87, no. 3 (May/June, 2017): 6–13.
Garber, Richard. "Optimisation Stories: The Impact of Building Information Modelling on Contemporary Design Practice." In *The Digital Turn in Architecture 1992–2012*, edited by Mario Carpo, 227–39. Chichester: Wiley, 2013.
"Gargoyle Gate at Weston Field." MIT Libraries DOME, http://hdl.handle.net/1721.3/144989.
Geddes, Robert L., and Bernard P. Spring. *A Study of Education for Environmental Design Sponsored by the American Institute of Architects*. Princeton, NJ: Princeton University, 1967.
Geertz, Clifford. "Thick Description: Toward an Interpretive Theory of Culture." In *The Interpretation of Cultures: Selected Essays*, 3–30. New York: Basic Books, Inc., 2000, 1973.
"General Conctracting a Menace to Architects." *Inland Architect & News Record* 33 (1899): 29–30.
"General Contracts." *Inland Architect & News Record* 37, no. 3 (April 1901): 22–23.
"George Shepard Chappell [Obituary]." In *Obituary Record of Graduates of Yale University Deceased during the Year 1946–1947*, 47–48. New Haven, CT: Yale University Press, 1948.
Giddens, Anthony. *Capitalism and Modern Social Theory: An Analysis of the Writings of Marx, Durkheim and Max Weber*. Cambridge, UK: University Press, 1971.
Giddens, Anthony. *The Constitution of Society: Outline of the Theory of Structuration*. Berkeley: University of California Press, 1984.
Gilbert, Cass. "Status of Professional Practice: Address of the President before the 42nd Convention of the American Institute of Architects, December 17, 1908." *Western Architect* 13 (1909): 5–7.
Gill, Brendan. "The Sky Line: Prospectus." *The New Yorker* (February 23, 1987): 106–09.
Glassie, Henry H. *Pattern in the Material Folk Culture of the Eastern United States*. Philadelphia: University of Pennsylvania Press, 1969.
Goldberger, Paul. "Architects Will End Ban on Advertising." *New York Times*, May 25, 1978, 20.
Goldberger, Paul. "Institute of Architects Keeps Bans on Advertising and Contracting." *New York Times*, June 9, 1977, 45.
Gordon, Douglas E. "The Evolution of Architectural Practice as Recorded in 75 Years of the 'Architect's Handbook'." *Architecture: the AIA Journal* 76, no. 12 (1987): 122–26.

Gordon, Robert J. *The Rise and Fall of American Growth: The U.S. Standard of Living since the Civil War*. The Princeton Economic History of the Western World; Princeton: Princeton University Press, 2016.

Gorman, Herbert S. "Mass Attack on the Censor [Book Review of Nonsenseorship by Heywood Broun, Et Al.]." *New York Times*, September 10, 1922, 35, 39.

Guadet, Julien. *Eléments Et Théorie De L'architecture: Cours Professé À L'école Nationale Et Spéciale Des Beaux-Arts*. Vol. 4, Paris: Librarie de la Construction Moderne, 1905.

Gutman, Robert. "The Architect's Handbook of Professional Practice, Edited by David Haviland." *Journal of Architectural Education* 45, no. 2 (1992): 122–24.

Gutman, Robert. *Architectural Practice: A Critical View*. New York: Princeton Architectural Press, 1988.

Gutman, Robert. "Patrons or Clients?" *Harvard Architecture Review* 6 (1987): 148–59.

Hamilton, John L. "Letter to Frank Miles Day Dated 7 February 1918." In *AIA, Office Files, Documents: Handbook, Evolution of, 1915–1917*. Washington, DC: The American Institute of Architects Archives, 1918.

The Handbook of Architectural Practice. Washington, DC: Press of the American Institute of Architects, Inc., 1920.

The Handbook of Architectural Practice. 4th ed. Washington, DC: American Institute of Architects, 1943.

Harris, Neil. *Cultural Excursions: Marketing Appetites and Cultural Tastes in Modern America*. Chicago, IL: University of Chicago Press, 1990.

Harvey, David. *Spaces of Hope*. Berkeley and Los Angeles: University of California Press, 2000.

Hatch, Anthony P. *Tinder Box: The Iroquois Theatre Disaster, 1903*. Chicago, IL: Academy Chicago Publishers, 2003.

Hatfield, O. P. "The Relation of the Architect to the Builder." *Inland Architect & News Record* 13, no. 2 (1889): 16–17.

Hatfield, O. P., Alfred Stone, and J. H. Windrim. "Report of Special Committee on Uniform Building Contract." *Proceedings of the 22nd Annual Convention of the American Institute of Architects* 22 (1888): 62–65.

Hawley, W. A. "The Compensation of the Architect." *Inland Architect & News Record* 6, no. 2 (September 1885): 17–18.

Hays, William C., ed. *Catalogue of the Annual Architectural Exhibition for 1902–1903*. Philadelphia: T Square Club, 1903.

Heddinger, H. G. "Response Dated 15 September 1917 to Frank Miles Day Letter of 8 August 1917." In *AIA, Office Files, Documents: Handbook, Evolution of, 1915–1917*. Washington, DC: The American Institute of Architects Archives, 1917.

Heery, George T. *Bridging: A Construction Project Delivery Method*. 1st ed. Atlanta, GA: Brookwood Group, 2010.

Heery, George T. "A History of Construction Management, Program Management, and Development Management." Atlanta, GA: Brookwood Group, 2011.

Heery, George T. *Time, Cost, and Architecture*. New York: McGraw-Hill, 1975.

"Herbert Croly Dies at Santa Barbara." *New York Times*, May 18, 1930.

Hering, Oswald C. "The Architect and His Client: Their Relationship in Planning and Building the Home." *American Architect* 96 (1909): 141–48.

Herrick, Robert. *The Common Lot*. New York and London: The Macmillan Company, 1904.
Higgins, Daniel Paul. "Architectural Office Organization for Post War Conditions." *American Architect* 115, no. 1 (1919): 13–16.
Higgins, Daniel Paul. "The 'Business' of Architecture: Parts I–III." *Architectural Review* 21, no. 9–12 (1916).
Higgins, Daniel Paul. "The 'Business' of Architecture: Part IV." *Architectural Review* 23, no. 1–3 (1918).
"The History of NCARB." Washington, DC: National Council of Architectural Registration Boards, 1994.
Hoggson Brothers. *Banks: A Description of the Hoggson Method of Building Illustrated with Some Bank Interiors and Exteriors Executed by Hoggson Brothers*. New York: Hoggson Brothers, 1911.
Hoggson Brothers. *The Hoggson Building Method: Described and Illustrated for the Information of Those Who Contemplate Building, Re-Modeling, Decorating or Furnishing*. New York: Hoggson Brothers, 1910.
"House of Douglas Kent, Esq., Tarrytown, N.Y." *American Architect & Building News* 96, no. 1754 (1909): 52–52.
"House of Mrs. Rockwell Kent, Tarrytown, N.Y." *American Architect & Building News* 96, no. 1773 (December 15, 1909).
"House of Richard E. Forrest, Esq., Cedarhurst, L.I., N.Y." *American Architect & Building News* 95, no. 13 (1909): 15.
"A House on Cobb Lane, Tarrytown, N.Y." *American Architect* 96, no. 1754 (1909): 52.
"Houses of Mrs. James Mcnaught and Mr. E.E. Ling, Tarrytown, N.Y." *American Architect & Building News* 96, no. 1773 (1909).
Hume, Cyril, Thomas Caldecot Chubb, and Francis Woolsey Bronson, eds. *The Yale Record Book of Verse, 1872–1922*. Vol. 106. New Haven, CT: Yale University Press, 1922, 1.
"Important Revision of the Uniform Contract." *Inland Architect & News Record* 40 (November 1902): 25.
"In the Real Estate Field: Loft Building Boom Stimulates Realty Market." *New York Times*. February 16, 1910, 15.
"Inadequate Compensation to Architects." *Inland Architect & News Record* 48 (August 1906): 1.
"Incompetence among Architects: The Investor Needs Protection [Editorial]." *The Real Estate Magazine* 4, no. 12 (December 1914): 13.
Inexpensive Homes of Individuality. New York: McBride, Winston, 1911.
J. H., Chicago, Ill. "A Contractor's Criticism of Architects [Letter to the Editor]." *The Building Age* 32, no. 7 (1910): 308–09.
"John Wynkoop, Architect." *New York Times*, December 14, 1922, 21.
Johnston, David. "Justice Department Files Antitrust Suit against Architects." *New York Times*, July 6, 1990, 1, 12.
Johnston, George B. "Form and Formwork." Paper presented at the 82nd ACSA Annual Meeting, Montréal, Quebec, 1994.
Johnston, George B. "Theories of Working Drawings." Paper presented at the 82nd ACSA Annual Meeting, Montréal, Quebec, 1994.
Johnston, George B. "Tradition and Its Interpretation through Architectural Convention." Paper presented at the 78th ACSA Annual Meeting, San Francisco, 1990.

Johnston, George B. "Traveling Professions: How Local Contingencies Complicate Globalizing Tendencies in the Standardization of Architectural Practice." Paper presented at the Seeking the City: Proceedings of the 96th ACSA Annual Meeting, Houston, TX, 2008.

Johnston, George Barnett. *Drafting Culture: A Social History of Architectural Graphic Standards*. Cambridge, MA: MIT Press, 2008.

"Joint Meeting of Boston Architects and Master Builders." *The Building Age* 34, no. 1 (January 1912): 8–10.

"Joint Meeting of Cleveland Architects with Members of Builders Exchange." *The Building Age* 34, no. 7 (July 1912): 385–86.

Jones, Sullivan W. "The Building Contract of the Future." *Journal of the American Institute of Architects* 7, no. 3 (March 1919): 119–22.

Jones, Sullivan W. "Quantities and Quantity Estimating." *The Building Age* 35, no. 12 (December 1913).

Joslin, Arthur W. "Contractors and Builders an Abused Class." *The Building Age* 32, no. 4 (April 1910): 141.

Kane, James A. "The Hambidge Theory of Symmetry and Proportion in Greek Architecture as Relating to Architectural Design." *American Architect [and] the Architectural Review* 120, no. 2378 (1921): 261–65.

Keebler, Patricia Lawson Heintzelman. "The Life and Work of Frank Miles Day." PhD Diss., University of Delaware, 1980.

Kendall, E. H. "Report of Special Committee on Uniform Building Contract." *Proceedings of the 21st Annual Convention of the American Institute of Architects* 21 (1887): 69.

Kendall, Henry H., George B. Will, and Chester N. Godfrey. "Report [Dated 25 October] of Committee Appointed to Examine and Report on the Draft for an 'Architects' Hand Book of Professional Practice and Business Administration...." In *AIA, Office Files, Documents: Handbook, Evolution of, 1915–1917*. Washington, DC: The American Institute of Architects Archives, 1917.

Kent, Rockwell. "A Conversion." In *Rockwell Kent Papers, ca. 1885–1970*. Columbia University Rare Book & Manuscript Library, 1914.

Kent, Rockwell. *It's Me O Lord: The Autobiography of Rockwell Kent*. New York: Dodd, Mead & Company, 1955.

"Kent Wins." *The Evening World*, February 26, 1916, 12.

Kidder, Frank Eugene. "The Architect as a Builder and as an Engineer." *Inland Architect & News Record* 29 (1897): 22.

King, William B. "Letter to Frank Miles Day Dated 14 September 1917." In *AIA, Office Files, Documents: Handbook, Evolution of, 1915–1917*. Washington, DC: The American Institute of Architects Archives, 1917.

Kissam, Henry Snyder. "Efficiency of the Architect's Client." *School of Mines Quarterly* 32, no. 4 (July 1911): 331–41.

Kissam, H. S. "The Principles of the Business Management of Office Practice of Architects." *American Architect & Building News* 94, no. 1702 (August 5, 1908): 45–47.

Kostof, Spiro, ed. *The Architect: Chapters in the History of the Profession*. Berkeley: University of California Press, 2000.

Krause, Elliott A. *Death of the Guilds: Professions, States, and the Advance of Capitalism, 1930 to the Present*. New Haven, CT: Yale University Press, 1996.

Kruse, S. "The High Cost of Incompetence." *The Real Estate Magazine* 4, no. 11 (November 1914): 16–22.

Kummer, Karen Lang. "National Register of Historic Places Registration Form: Frederick Squires House." 33: United States Department of the Interior, National Park Service, 2011.

"Labor in the Building Trades." *Carpentry and Building* 26, no. 1 (January 1904): 1.

Laird, Warren Powers. "Frank Miles Day: An Appreciation." *American Architect* 114, no. 2219 (July 3, 1918): 15–16.

Laird, Warren Powers. "Letter to Frank Miles Day Dated 8 October 1917." In *AIA, Office Files, Documents: Handbook, Evolution of, 1915–1917*. Washington, DC: The American Institute of Architects Archives, 1917.

Lange, Alexandra. "Founding Mother: Mariana Griswold Van Rensselaer and the Rise of Architecture Criticism." *Places Journal* (February 2013). https://doi.org/10.22269/130225.

Larson, Magali Sarfatti. *Behind the Postmodern Facade: Architectural Change in Late Twentieth-Century America*. Berkeley: University of California Press, 1993.

Larson, Magali Sarfatti. "Emblem and Exception: The Historical Definition of the Architect's Professional Role." In *Professionals and Urban Form*, edited by Judith R. Blau, Mark La Gory, and John Pipkin, 49–86. Albany: State University of New York Press, 1983.

Larson, Magali Sarfatti. *The Rise of Professionalism: A Sociological Analysis*. Berkeley: University of California Press, 1977.

Latour, Bruno. *Reassembling the Social: An Introduction to Actor-Network-Theory*. Clarendon Lectures in Management Studies. Oxford and New York: Oxford University Press, 2005. doi: 9780199256044 (hbk.).

"Latrobe on Architects' Fees, 1798." *American Society of Architectural Historians Journal* 19 (October 1960): 115–17.

Lee, Antoinette J. *Architects to the Nation: The Rise and Decline of the Supervising Architect's Office*. New York: Oxford University Press, 2000.

Lengel, William C. "Tall Buildings in Smaller Cities as Investments." *Buildings and Building Management* 13, no. 10 (October 1913): 19–22.

Lowell, Josephine. *Industrial Arbitration and Conciliation; Some Chapters from the Industrial History of the Past Thirty Years*. Questions of the Day 76. New York [etc]: G.P. Putnam's sons, 1894.

Macdonald, Keith M. *The Sociology of the Professions*. London: Sage Publications, 1995.

Marble, Scott. *Digital Workflows in Architecture: Designing Design – Designing Assembly – Designing Industry*. Basel: Birkhäuser, 2012.

Marshall, Marguerite Mooers. "America's Champion 'Kidders' Make United States a Great Nation; Happy National Trait Saves People in Nerve-Trying Situations." *The Evening World*, June 21, 1922, 3.

Martin, Clarence A. "Letter to Frank Miles Day Dated 15 October 1917." In *AIA, Office Files, Documents: Handbook, Evolution of, 1915–1917*. Washington, DC: The American Institute of Architects Archives, 1917.

Mathews, Edgar A., and Alexander Wright. "Letter to Frank Miles Day Dated 25 August 1917." In *AIA, Office Files, Documents: Handbook, Evolution of,*

1915–1917. Washington, DC: The American Institute of Architects Archives, 1917.

"Matters Relating to Competitions: Extracts from the Reports of 1905–6–7 and 8." In *Frank Miles Day Collection (1861–1918)*. Philadelphia: The Architectural Archives, University of Pennsylvania 1908.

"Mcadoo Building in 32d Street." *New York Times*, September 17, 1911, 103.

McBride, Elyse Gundersen. "The Changing Role of the Architect in the United States Construction Industry, 1870–1913." *Construction History* 28, no. 1 (2013): 121–40.

McDaniel, George W., and Carter C. Hudgins. "Mystery at Drayton Hall: The Surprise Appearance of a 1765 Watercolor Sheds New Light on a Palladian Past." *Magazine Antiques* 177, no. 4 (Summer 2010): 148–51.

"Mechanics and Traders' Exchange." *New York Times*, April 11, 1893, 9.

Medary, Milton B. "Letter to Thomas R. Kimball Dated 12 August 1918." In *AIA Board of Directors 1917–1919*. Washington, DC: American Institute of Architects Archives 1918.

Medary, Milton B. "Letter to Frank Miles Day Dated 18 February 1918." In *AIA Board of Directors 1917–1919*. Washington, DC: American Institute of Architects Archives 1918.

"Meeting of National Association of Builders." *Carpentry and Building* 28, no. 11 (November 1906): 361.

Melhuish, Geoffrey E. "National Register of Historic Places Registration Form: Timber Point House in Biddeford, Maine." 26: United States Department of the Interior, National Park Service, 2013.

"Midtown Building: Remarkable Contrasts Shown on Various Side Streets." *New York Times*, September 1, 1912, X11.

"Monographs on Architectural Renderers. The Work of Rockwell Kent." *Brickbuilder* 23, no. 7 (July 1914): 167–69.

Mundie, William Bryce. "The Relations of Architects to the Contracting System." *Western Architect* 13, no. 1 (January 1909): 9–10.

Murphy, Kevin D. "Cubism and Collegiate Gothic: Raymond Duchamp-Villon at Connecticut College." *Archives of American Art Journal* 32, no. 1 (1992): 16–21.

National Association of Builders of the United States of America. "Official Report of the Ninth Annual Convention" (1895): 38–40.

National Association of Builders of the United States of America. "Official Report of the Third Annual Convention" (1889).

"National Association of Builders' Exchanges." *Carpentry and Building* 29, no. 3 (March 1907): 93.

"National B.T.E. Association." *Building Trades Employers' Association Bulletin* 5, no. 2 (February 1904): 25.

"National Building Trades & Employers Association of the United States." *Building Age* 34 (April 1912): 173–77.

National Building Trades and Employers' Association of America. *Uniform Contract Adopted and Recommended for Temporary Use*. [Place of publication not identified], *c*. 1914 [No Date].

"National Building Trades Employers' Association." *Carpentry and Building* 26, no. 1 (January 1904): 8–10.

"The Necessity for Abolishing General Contracting." *Inland Architect & News Record* 33 (1899): 29.

"Necessity for Fireproofing Schools and Residences (Editorial)." *Inland Architect & News Record* 45, no. 1 (February 1905): 1.

"The Need of Unity." *American Architect and Building News* 1 (January 1, 1876): 2–3.

Ness, Immanuel, Benjamin Day, and Aaron Brenner. *The Encyclopedia of Strikes in American History*. Armonk, NY: Routledge, 2009. Book.

"New Era Dawning for Seventh Avenue." *New York Times*, May 22, 1910, 67.

"New Offices of Adler & Sullivan Architects, Chicago." *Engineering and Building Record* 22, no. 1 (June 7, 1890): 5.

Newlands, Francis G. "The Tarsney Act: The Economy and Efficiency of the Employment of Private Architects on Public Buildings, Report in Part of a Speech Delivered in the United States Senate." *American Architect & Building News* 102 (1912): 73–77.

"News from the Classes: 1885." *The Technology Reivew* 23, no. 4 (November 1921): 631–32.

The Nineteen Hundred & Three Columbian: The Year Book of the Junior Class. Vol. 13, New York: Columbia University, 1901.

The Nineteen Hundred & Four Columbian: The Year Book of the Junior Class. Vol. 14, New York: Columbia University, 1902.

Noffsinger, James Philip. *The Influence of the École Des Beaux-Arts on the Architects of the United States*. Washington, DC: Catholic University of America Press, 1955.

Nonsenseorship: Sundry Observations Concerning Prohibitions, Inhibitions, and Illegalities. Edited by George P. Putnam. New York and London: G.P. Putnam's Sons, 1922.

"'Now Listen Quietly' [Advertisement for Vanity Fair]." *House Beautiful* 46–47 (February 1920): 160.

"Obituary: Frederick Squires." *Williams Alumni Review* (November 1956): 33.

Ockman, Joan, and Rebecca Williamson. *Architecture School: Three Centuries of Educating Architects in North America*. Cambridge, MA; Washington, DC: MIT Press and Association of Collegiate Schools of Architecture, 2012.

"Off with the Mask." *The New York Herald*, January 1, 1922, 7.

"An Office Building for Architects." *The Building Age* 34, no. 8 (August 1912): 428–29.

Office of Grosvenor Atterbury, Architect. "Schedule of Professional Charges." In *AIA, Office Files, Documents: Handbook, Evolution of, 1915–1917*. Washington, DC: The American Institute of Architects Archives, 1914.

"The Organization of an Architects Office: Parts I–IV." *Engineering and Building Record* 21, no. 6, 11–13 (1890): 83–84, 165, 81, 95.

Ortner, Sherry B. *Anthropology and Social Theory: Culture, Power, and the Acting Subject*. Durham, NC, and London: Duke University Press, 2006.

Ortner, Sherry B. "Theory in Anthropology since the Sixties." *Comparative Studies in Society and History* 26, no. 1 (1984): 126–66.

Özel, Güvenç. "Toward a Postarchitecture." *Log*, no. 36 (Winter 2016): 99–105.

Parker, William Stanley. "The New Standard Documents." *Journal of the American Institute of Architects* 3, no. 7 (July 1915): 300–03.

Parker, William Stanley. "The New Standard Documents: II." *Journal of the American Institute of Architects* 3, no. 8 (August 1915): 346–51.

Pasler, Jann. *Writing through Music: Essays on Music, Culture, and Politics.* Oxford and New York: Oxford University Press, 2008.
"The Pecuniary Relation between Architect and Client." *Architectural Record* 26 (August 1909): 79–83.
"Percy Griffin [Obituary]." *New York Times*, March 16, 1921, 9.
Perkins, Dwight H. "Letter to Frank Miles Day Undated." In *AIA, Office Files, Documents: Handbook, Evolution of, 1915–1917.* Washington, DC: The American Institute of Architects Archives, 1917.
"Perspectives of Three New York Loft Buildings Designed by Squires & Wynkoop Architects." *Architecture and Building* 42, no. 12 (September 1910): 506.
Pfammatter, Ulrich. *The Making of the Modern Architect and Engineer: The Origins and Development of a Scientific and Industrially Oriented Education.* Basel and Boston, MA: Birkhauser-Publishers for Architecture, 2000.
"Phi Delta Theta Fraternity House, Williams College." *Architectural Record* 24, no. 3 (September 1908): 242–43.
"The Philadelphia Conference on Contract Forms." *Journal of the American Institute of Architects* 2, no. 10 (October 1914): 487–88.
Pickering, Andrew. *The Mangle of Practice: Time, Agency, and Science.* Chicago, IL: University of Chicago Press, 2010.
"The Place of the General Contractor." *Inland Architect & News Record* 34, no. 6 (January 1900): 37, 39.
"Plan to Prevent Strikes on Buildings." *New York Times*, December 22, 1901, 24.
"Portfolio of Country Residences. Residence of S.B. Lord, Cedarhurst, L.I." *Architectural Record* 28 (1910): 306.
Portman, John. *The Architect as Developer*, edited by Jonathan Barnett. New York: McGraw-Hill, 1976.
"Professional and Other Incompetence." *Journal of the American Institute of Architects* 3, no. 2 (February 1915): 73–75.
"Proposed Builders' Exchanges Association." *Carpentry and Building* 28, no. 10 (October 1906): 349.
Purdy, Corydon T. "The Relation of the Engineer to the Architect." *American Architect & Building News* 87 (January 1905): 43–46.
Purdy, Corydon T. "The Relation of the Engineer to the Architect (Part 1)." *Inland Architect & News Record* 44, no. 6 (January 1905): 43–45.
Purdy, Corydon T. "The Relation of the Engineer to the Architect (Part 2)." *Inland Architect & News Record* 45, no. 1 (February 1905): 4–6.
Ramchurn, Rakesh. "Everything Is Connected: Architects' Work Is Set to Be Revolutionised by Digital Innovations Such as the Internet of Things, Artificial Intelligence and the Collaborative Economy." *Architects' Journal* 241, no. 13 (2015): 54–55.
Rankin, John Hall. "The Repeal of the Tarsney Act." *Journal of the American Institute of Architects* 1, no. 3 (March 1913): 127–28.
"Real Estate Show. To Open at Madison Square Garden This Week – Unique Show." *New York Times*, May 15, 1910, 14.
"Recent Work by Squires and Wynkoop." *International Studio* 37, no. 148 (June 1909): cviii–cix.
"Remember the Contractor." *Inland Architect & News Record* 49, no. 2 (February 1907): 23.

"Report of the Standing Committee on Contracts and Specifications of the American Institute of Architects on Standardization of Documents." In *Frank Miles Day Collection (1861–1918)*. Philadelphia: The Architectural Archives, University of Pennsylvania 1908.

"Report of the Standing Committee on Contracts and Specifications of the American Institute of Architects on the Standardization of Documents." In *Frank Miles Day Collection (1861–1918)*. Philadelphia: The Architectural Archives, University of Pennsylvania 1911.

"A Residence Block, West 74th Street, New York: The Clark Estate Houses." *Architectural Record* 20, no. 5 (November 1906): 404–10.

"Rollo in Society [Advertisement]." *The New York Herald*, September 8, 1922, 32.

"Rollo in Society. By George S. Chappell [Book Review]." *New York Times*, September 10, 1922, 33.

"Rough Writers Start West for Annual Oregon Round-Up: Weaponless, except for Typewriters, They Follow the Advice of Horace Greeley and Hope to Penetrate as Far as the Pacific Coast." *The New York Herald*, September 10, 1922, 2.

Rushforth, George. "Obituary: George Alexander Wright." *Journal of the American Institute of Architects* 6, no. 4 (April 1918): 200.

Said, Edward. "Traveling Theory." In *The World, the Text, and the Critic*, 226–47. Cambridge, MA: Harvard University Press, 1983.

Saint, Andrew. *Architect and Engineer: A Study in Sibling Rivalry*. New Haven, CT and London: Yale University Press, 2007.

"Sanders Chemical Laboratory, Vassar College." *American Architect* 123, no. 17 (1923): 49.

Sayward, Charles A. *The Sayward Family: Being the History and Genealogy of Henry Sayward of York, Maine and His Descendants: With a Brief Account of Other Saywards Who Settled in America*. Ipswich, MA: Independent Press, 1890.

Sayward, W. H. "The Benefits of Organization." *Inland Architect & News Record* 30, no. 5 (December 1897): 48–49.

Sayward, W. H. "Builders' Exchanges: Their Advantages & Opportunities." *Inland Architect & News Record* 13, no. 2 (February 1889): 18–21.

Sayward, William H. "Labor Issues in the Building Trades." *Building Trades Association Bulletin* 3, no. 12 (December 1902): 205–12.

Sayward, William H. "Labor-Issues in the Building-Trades." *American Architect & Building News* 78, no. 1404 (November 22, 1902): 59–62.

Sayward, William H. "Sub-Contracts." *American Architect & Building News* 1 (March 18, 1876): 95–96.

Sayward, W. H. "The National Association of Master Builders." *Carpentry and Building* 12 (June 1890): 135–38.

Sayward, W. H. "Trade Arbitration." *Inland Architect & News Record* 36 (1900): 32.

Schumacher, Patrik. "The Historical Pertinence of Parametricism and the Prospect of a Free Market Urban Order." In *The Politics of Parametricism: Digital Technologies in Architecture*, edited by Matthew Poole and Manuel Shvartzberg, 19–44. London and New York: Bloomsbury Academic, 2015.

Sciulli, David. *Professions in Civil Society and the State: Invariant Foundations and Consequences*. International Studies in Sociology and Social Anthropology Series. Leiden: Brill, 2009.

Seyler, Beverly. "Frederick J. Squires, 1879–1956, Petroleum Engineering." *ISGS History Heritage Memorial* (2006). http://isgs.illinois.edu/frederick-j-squires.

Shackleton, Robert. "Total Factor Productivity Growth in Historical Perspective." Washington, DC: Congressional Budget Office, 2013.

Shelden, Dennis. "Cyber-Physical Systems and the Built Environment." *Technology|Architecture + Design* 2, no. 2 (2018): 137–39.

Siegrist, Hannes. "Professions and Professionalization, History Of." In *International Encyclopedia of the Social & Behavioral Sciences*, edited by James D. Wright, 95–100. Amsterdam and Boston, MA: Elsevier, 2015.

Simmel, Georg. "Exchange." In *On Individuality and Social Forms; Selected Writings*, edited by Donald N. Levine, 43–69. Chicago, IL: University of Chicago Press, 1971.

"Six Publications Run by Columbia Graduates." *New York Times*, January 4, 1903, Magazine Section, 1.

The Sixteenth Annual Architectural Exhibition. Philadelphia, PA: Philadelphia Chapter American Institute of Architects; The T-Square Club, 1910.

"Sixteenth Annual Exhibition of the T-Square Club." *American Architect* 97, pt. 2, no. 1791 (April 20, 1910): 161–63.

Smith, Darrell Hevenor. *The Office of the Supervising Architect of the Treasury: Its History, Activities, and Organization*. Institute for Government Research Service Monographs of the United States Government No. 23. Baltimore, MD: Johns Hopkins Press, 1923.

Society of Independent Artists. *Catalog of the Frist Annual Exhibition of the Society of Independent Artists*." New York: William Edwin Rudge, 1917.

Spencer, Douglas. *The Architecture of Neoliberalism: How Contemporary Architecture Became an Instrument of Control and Compliance*. New York: Bloomsbury Academic, 2016.

Squires and Wynkoop, Architects. "Loft Building at 114–116 E. 16th Street, New York City." *Architecture and Building* 44, no. 7 (July 1912): 305–07.

Squires and Wynkoop, Architects. "The Fire Proof House as the American Type." *Western Architect* 16 (October 1910): 107–08.

Squires, Frederick. "Advertising: Reports from the Canon of Ethics." *Architecture and Building* 46, no. 8 (August 1914): 294–98.

Squires, Frederick. *Architec-tonics: The Adventures of Tom Thumtack, Architect*. New York: Comstock, 1914.

Squires, Frederick. "Contractors." *Architecture and Building* 46, no. 3 (March 1914): 92–96.

Squires, Frederick. "Correspondence to Rockwell Kent Dated 3 February 1914." In *Rockwell Kent Papers, [circa 1840]–1993, bulk 1935–1961*. Washington, DC: Smithsonian Institution Archives of American Art, 1914.

Squires, Frederick. "Correspondence to Rockwell Kent Dated 15 September 1915." In *Rockwell Kent Papers, [circa 1840]–1993, bulk 1935–1961*. Washington, DC: Smithsonian Institution Archives of American Art, 1915.

Squires, Frederick. "Fees—a Reductio Ad Absurdum." *Architecture and Building* 46, no. 11 (November 1914): 418–20.

Squires, Frederick. "Fireproof Houses." *Carpentry and Building* 31, no. 10 (October 1909): 329–31.

Squires, Frederick. "Fireproof Houses." *American Architect & Building News* 96, no. 1755 (1909): 53–55.

Squires, Frederick. *Flooding with Re-Used Water*. Circular / Illinois State Geological Survey. Urbana: Illinois State Geological Survey, 1949.

Squires, Frederick. "The Gargoyle Gate." *Arts and Decoration* 1, no. 1 (January 1911): 130.

Squires, Frederick. *The Hollow-Tile House*. New York: The William T. Comstock Co., 1913.

Squires, Frederick. "Repeal of the Tarsney Act." *Architecture & Building* 47, no. 8 (August 1915): 278–81.

Squires, Frederick. "The Tectarch." *Architecture and Building* 47, no. 2 (February 1915): 48–50.

Squires, Frederick. "Temperament." *Architecture and Building* 47, no. 6 (June 1915): 206–10.

Squires, Frederick. "Tom Thumtack, Client." *Architecture and Building* 46, no. 12 (December 1914): 457–62.

Squires, Frederick, and John Wynkoop. "A Concrete House: A Description of the Constructive Features, Including Reinforcing, Heating, Ventilating and Electric Wiring of a Concrete House." *Cement Age* 11, no. 4 (October 1910): 188, 200–08.

"The Standard Documents of the American Institute of Architects." Washington, DC: American Institute of Architects Archive, 1911.

Starrett, Theodore. "[Editorial]." *Architecture and Building* 46, no. 1 (January 1914): 1–2.

Steele, William L. "The Architect and the Public." *Journal of the American Institute of Architects* 3, no. 11 (November 1915): 492–95.

Steenson, Molly Wright. *Architectural Intelligence: How Designers and Architects Created the Digital Landscape*. Cambridge, MA: MIT Press, 2017.

Stinchcombe, Arthur L. *When Formality Works: Authority and Abstraction in Law and Organizations*. Chicago, IL: University of Chicago Press, 2001.

"A Suit for Architects' Fees." *Inland Architect & News Record* 13, no. 7 (July 1889): 99.

"The Supervising Architect's Office Reorganized." *Inland Architect and News Record* 30, no. 1 (August 1897): 3–5.

"Supreme Court Decision on Architect's Fees." *Inland Architect & News Record* 31 (May 1898): 31.

Susskind, Richard E., and Daniel Susskind. *The Future of the Professions: How Technology Will Transform the Work of Human Experts*. Oxford, UK: Oxford University Press, 2015.

Swartwout, Egerton. *An Architectural Decade: Ten Years with Mckim, Mead & White*. Edited by Jesse Smedley. Seattle, WA: Amazon Digital Services LLC, 2014.

Swartwout, Egerton. "Greek Proportions, Theoretically and Otherwise." *American Architect [and] the Architectural Review* 120, no. 2381 (November 23, 1921): 379–83.

Sweet, Justin. *Legal Aspects of Architecture, Engineering and the Construction Process*. 2nd ed. St. Paul, MN: West Publishing Co., 1977.

T-Square [Pseudonym of George S. Chappell]. "The Sky Line." *The New Yorker*, February 19, 1927, 64–66.

"Talking to the Builders." *New York Times*, November 27, 1889, 4.

Talwar, Rohit. "Rohit Talwar: As Artificial Intelligence Removes as Many as Half of Jobs in the Future, Architecture's Role and the Use of Space Will Change Fundamentally." *Blueprint*, no. 353 (July/August 2017): 19.

"Tarsney Act." *Journal of the American Institute of Architects* 1, no. 1 (January 1913): 6–7.
Taylor, C. Stanley. "The Architect of the Future: Part I." *Architectural Forum* 30, no. 1 (January 1919): 1–4.
Taylor, C. Stanley. "The Owner's Duty to the Architect." *Architectural Forum* 34, no. 2 (February 1921): 71–74.
Taylor, J. Crow. "Advantages of a Builders' Exchange." *The Building Age* 36, no. 1 (January 1914): 31.
"Thirty-Story Bachelor Hotel." *New York Times*, June 11, 1922, 106.
"To Found an Academy of Architecture." *New York Times*, January 23, 1894, 4.
"Topics of the Time: Are We Just to Our Architects?" *The Century Magazine* 37, no. 3 (January 1889): 473–74.
Trachtenberg, Alan, and Eric Foner. *The Incorporation of America: Culture and Society in the Gilded Age*. American Century Series. 1st ed. New York: Hill and Wang, 1982.
Traxel, David. *An American Saga: The Life and Times of Rockwell Kent*. 1st ed. New York: Harper & Row, 1980.
Trumbull, Walter. "Pendleton's Great Roundup Has Savor of Old West: Annual Spectacle, Attended This Year by Rough Writers from the East, a Joyous and Colorful Occasion." *The New York Herald*, October 15, 1922, 2.
"The Twelfth Annual Convention A.I.A." *American Architect and Building News* 5, no. 173 (April 19, 1879): 122–25.
"Two Riding Academies." *Architectural Record* 21 (1907): 229–35.
"Unique Organization Launches Production." *Washington Herald*, April 30, 1916.
United States of American (Plaintiff) vs. The American Institute of Architects (Defendant) (1972).
Upton, Dell. "Pattern Books and Professionalism: Aspects of the Transformation of Domestic Architecture in America, 1800–1860." *Winterthur Portfolio* 19, no. 2–3 (Autumn 1984): 107–50.
Van Rensselaer, Mrs. Schuyler. "Client and Architect." *North American Review* 151, no. 406 (September 1890): 319–28.
"Vanderbilt Gives $100,000: Will Erect Y.M.C.A. Building as Memorial to His Father." *New York Times*, November 7, 1907, 9.
Veblen, Thorstein. *The Theory of Business Enterprise*. New York: Scribner, 1904.
Veblen, Thorstein. *The Theory of the Leisure Class*. Great Mind Series. Amherst, NY: Prometheus Books, 1899 [1998]. New York: Macmillan Company, 1899.
Vitruvius, Marcus Pollio. *The Ten Books on Architecture*. Translated by Morris Hicky Morgan. New York: Dover, 1960.
Waid, D. Everett. "How Architects Work II: Offices of Noted Architects." Brickbuilder 21, no. 1 (January 1912): 7–10.
Waid, D. Everett. "How Architects Work III: Offices of Noted Architects." Brickbuilder 21, no. 2 (February 1912): 35–38.
Waid, D. Everett. "The Business Side of an Architect's Office: The Office of George B. Post and Sons." Brickbuilder 23, no. 2 (February 1914): 47–49.
Waid, D. Everett. "The Business Side of an Architect's Office: The Offices of Mr. Howard Greenley and Messrs. Taylor and Levi." Brickbuilder 23, no. 3 (March 1914): 62–64.
Waid, D. E. "The Business Side of an Architect's Office: The Office of Messrs. Mann and Mcneille, New York." Brickbuilder 23, no. 5 (May 1914): 103–05.

Waid, D. Everett. "The Business Side of an Architect's Office with a Description of the Architects' Building, New York." Brickbuilder 22, no. 8 (August 1913): 179–81.

Waid, D. Everett. "The Business Side of an Architect's Office: The Office of Mr. Donn Barber." Brickbuilder 22, no. 9 (September 1913): 197–200.

Waid, D. Everett. "The Business Side of an Architect's Office: Description of the Offices of Messrs. Henry Bacon; Ford, Butler & Oliver; Ludlow & Peabody; H. Van Buren Magonigle and Kenneth Murchison." Brickbuilder 22, no. 11 (November 1913): 251–54.

Waid, D. Everett. "The Business Side of an Architect's Office: The Office of Messrs. McKim, Mead & White." Brickbuilder 22, no. 12 (December 1913): 267–70.

Waid, D. Everett. "How Architects Work I: Offices of Noted Architects." Brickbuilder 20, no. 12 (December 1911): 249–52.

Waid, D. Everett. "Letter to Frank Miles Day Dated 8 November 1917." In AIA, Office Files, Documents: Handbook, Evolution of, 1915–1917. Washington, DC: The American Institute of Architects Archives, 1917.

Wallace, Lance. "Tech Releases Reports Documenting Conflicts of Interest, Ethics Concerns." Georgia Tech Institute Communications Office, https://www.news.gatech.edu/2018/07/26/tech-releases-reports-documenting-conflicts-interest-ethics-concerns.

Walter E. Traprock [Pseudonym of George S. Chappell]. "My Amazing Discovery: Introducing the Filberts, a New Group of Islands in the South Seas." Vanity Fair (October 1921): 57, 92.

Ward, James. Architects in Practice, New York City, 1900–1940. Union, NJ: J & D Associates, 1989.

Wendehack, Clifford C. "Application for Membership." In AIA Historical Directory of American Architects, edited by American Institute of Architects. Washington, DC: AIA Archives, 1921.

Wendehack, Clifford C. Golf & Country Clubs. New York: W. Helburn, Ind., 1929.

Wermiel, Sara E. The Fireproof Building: Technology and Public Safety in the Nineteenth-Century American City. Baltimore: Johns Hopkins University Press, 2000.

Wermiel, Sara E. "Norcross, Fuller, and the Rise of the General Contractor in the United States in the Nineteenth Century." In Proceedings of the Second International Congress of Construction History, 3297–3314. Cambridge, UK: Construction History Society, 2006.

Wermiel, Sara E. "The Rise of the General Contractor in 19th Century America." FMI Quarterly, no. 3 (2008): 117–29.

Wight, P. B. "Building Contracts." Inland Architect and News Record 9, no. 4 (April 1887): 33–34.

"Will Build for [Christian] Scientists." The Sun, December 31, 1918, 9.

Willett, James R. "Glimpses of the Business Side of an Architect's Life." Inland Architect & News Record 27, no. 5 (1896): 43–45.

"William Tompkins Comstock: July 14, 1842–January 16, 1910." Architecture and Building 42, no. 12 (September 1910): 18 [in advertising section].

Williams, Raymond. Marxism and Literature. Oxford: Oxford University Press, 1977.

Willis, Alfred. "Design-Build and Building Efficiency in the Early Twentieth Century United States." Paper presented at the First International Congress on Construction History, Madrid, 2003.

Wilson, Chas. C. "Letter to Frank Miles Day Dated 29 September 1917." In *AIA, Office Files, Documents: Handbook, Evolution of, 1915–1917*. Washington, DC: The American Institute of Architects Archives, 1917.

Withey, Henry F., and Elsie Rathburn Withey. *Biographical Dictionary of American Architects (Deceased)*. Los Angeles, CA: New Age Publishing Co., 1956.

"Woman's College Buildings Will Be of the Tudor Type: Architects Ewing and Chappell of New York Selected to Design Structures–Bids to Be Asked Soon and the Work Will Be Rushed to Completion." *The Day [New London, CT]*, July 15, 1913.

Wood, Robert Williams. *How to Tell the Birds from the Flowers: A Manual of Flornithology for Beginners*. San Francisco and New York: Paul Elder and Company, 1907.

Woodard, Colin. *American Nations: A History of the Eleven Rival Regional Cultures of North America*. New York: Viking, 2011.

Woods, Mary. "The First American Architectural Journals: The Profession's Voice." *Society of Architectural Historians. Journal* 48, no. 2 (June 1989): 117–38.

Woods, Mary N. *From Craft to Profession: The Practice of Architecture in Nineteenth Century America*. Berkeley: University of California Press, 1999.

Wright, G. Alexander. "The Analogy between Horse-Racing and Estimating." *Journal of the American Institute of Architects* 1, no. 8 (August 1913): 334–36.

Wright, G. Alexander. "Bills of Quantities and Their Relation to Building Contracts." *The California Architect and Building News* 18, no. 4 (April 1897): 38–40.

Wright, G. Alexander. "Estimating on Bills of Quantities: The Owner Pays whether a Contract Be Let or Not." *American Architect & Building News* 55, no. 1100 (January 23, 1897): 27.

Wright, G. Alexander. "Quantity Surveying: A Necessity for Better Estimating Methods." *American Architect* 104, no. 1978 (November 19, 1913): 200–02.

Wright, G. Alexander. "The Quantity System." *Journal of the American Institute of Architects* 3, no. 1 (January 1915): 38–39.

Wright, G. Alexander. "The Quantity System." *Journal of the American Institute of Architects* 3, no. 4 (April 1915): 177–79.

Wright, G. Alexander. *Wright on Arbitration: A Manual for Architects, Students, Contractors and Construction Engineers*. San Francisco: Self-published by the author, 1913.

Wright, George Alexander. *Wright on Quantities; a Plea for a Better System of Estimating Cost of Buildings in the United States*. San Francisco: General Contractors Association, 1913.

"Wrong Methods of Advertising the Architect." *Architecture* 37, no. 4 (April 1918): 104.

Wynkoop, John. "The Design and Construction of a Concrete House: Part 1." *Cement Age* 8, no. 5 (May 1909): 314–20.

Wynkoop, John. "The Design and Construction of a Concrete House: Part 2." *Cement Age* 8, no. 6 (June 1909): 426–41.

Wynkoop, John. "The Design and Construction of a Concrete House: Part 3." *Cement Age* 9, no. 1 (July 1909): 10–19.

"The Yale Record." Wikipedia.org, https://en.wikipedia.org/w/index.php?title=The_Yale_Record&oldid=803048197.

Yarnall, James L. *Newport through Its Architecture: A History of Styles from Postmedieval to Postmodern*. Newport, RI: Salve Regina University Press, 2005.

Young Boswell [pseudonym of Harold Stark]. "Young Boswell Interviews George S. Chappell." *New York Tribune*, November 25, 1922, 11.

INDEX

Ackerman, Frederick L. 109–10
Adler, Dankmar 153, 252–3 n.12
advertising 37, 45, 134–9, 228 n.15, 250 n.133. *See also* ethics
agency relation
   between architect and owner 14–20, 107–10, 123–5, 155–61, 193–4, 245 n.63
   legal aspects of 8, 261 n.9
   sociological approaches to 2, 182–3, 219–20 n.4, 261 n.7, 269 n.85
Alberti, Leon Battista 93, 241 n.17
American Institute of Architects (AIA)
   canon of ethics 94, 104, 116, 133–9, 205–6 (*see also* ethics)
   Committee on Competitions 113–14
   Committee on Contracts and Specifications 20, 124, 157–9, 168–74, 177–8, 240 n.12
   schedule of charges (*see* fee structure)
Andrews, Robert D. 157–60
arbitration
   in construction contracts 17–19, 99, 124–5, 172–7, 258–9 n.77
   in labor relations 161–5
architect
   as artist 11–13, 22–6, 42–9, 58–9, 125–7, 174–5
   as client or developer 4, 9, 13, 35, 204–5
   as master builder 8–11, 14–15, 19–20, 173–4, 199–200, 206–8
   as owner's agent (*see* agency relation)
   selection of (*see under* architect–owner relation)
architect–builder relation 145–79
   conflicts over architect's authority 168–77, 257 n.56
   frictions within 146–51, 251–2 n.5
architect–owner relation 93–143
   architect as owner's agent (*see* agency relation)
   forms of architectural service 96–105 (*see also* project delivery methods)
   owner–architect agreement 122–5
   owner's duties 139–43
   selecting an architect 35, 105–15
   types of clients 99–105
Architects' Building 71–9, 89–90, 212
architects' offices, organization of 35–42, 74–8
architectural competitions 99, 110–15, 134–6, 208
architectural education
   at Ecole des Beaux Arts 61, 67–70, 79–81, 107, 111, 130
   standardization of 7–8, 13–14, 205, 210, 212–13, 239 n.3
architectural exhibitions 42–9
Architectural League of New York 44, 46, 48, 55, 67, 216
architectural practice and profession
   as art and science 22–6, 43–4, 125–34
   as business administration 10–14, 22–6, 35–42, 93–110
   compared to other professions 2, 20, 132–4, 141, 160–1, 211
   conflicts of interest within 14–18, 155–61
   European influences in US 7–10, 118–20, 220 n.1
   formalization of 1–5, 7–8, 13–14, 33–4, 94–6, 181–4, 200–8

INDEX

local tendencies in 7–13, 183–4, 204–5, 209, 212, 240 n.12
models of (*see* project delivery methods)
paternalism of 9, 12–14, 19–20, 105, 116, 133–9
pre-modern formations 1–2, 7–14, 149–52
social aspects (*see* practice, sociology of; professions, sociology of)
standard of care 21–2, 57–9, 93–6, 106–10, 177–9, 243 n.37
state regulation of 13–14, 95, 104, 108–10, 135, 210–13
technological aspects 2–4, 90, 116, 125–32, 181–214
Architecture and Building 61–2, 232 n.54
Armory Show 70–1
artificial intelligence 208–14
Atterbury, Grosvenor 41, 70, 169

Bannister, William P. 13
Barber, Donn 38–41, 52, 70, 73
Blackall, Clarence H. 12
Boston Society of Architects 18, 95, 134, 168, 258–9 n.77
Boyington, William W. 11
Brandeis, Louis D. 18
Brown, Glen 119–20
builders' exchanges 164–79
building information modeling (BIM) 2–3, 199–208

change orders 157–61, 192–4
Chappell, George S. 65–71, 73–91
Chicago Architects' Business Bureau 95, 150
Clark, T. M. 156, 242–3 n.37, 254 n.23
clerk of the works. *See* supervision and superintendence of construction
Columbia *Jester* 50–1
"Come to Bohemia" 79–81
competitions. *See* architectural competitions
competitive bidding, evils of 1, 22, 33, 62, 100, 145–50. *See also* quantity surveyor system

Comstock, Anthony 61, 86–7, 232 n.53
Comstock, William T. 61–2, 66
construction industry
 organization of labor 161–8, 255 nn.37–8, 256 n.52 (*see also* arbitration)
 political economy of 7–10, 99, 207, 261–2 n.10
 technological transformation of 3–4, 24–5, 89–90, 131–2, 199–214, 239 n.4 (*see also under* architectural practice and profession)
consultants 11–12, 115–16, 125–32, 206, 248 n.107, 250 n.122
contractors. *See* general contractors and contracting system; subcontractors
Cram, Ralph Adams 95
Cret, Paul Philippe 42–3
Cuff, Dana 205

Day, Frank Miles. *See also* Frank Miles Day & Brother, Architects
 and *Handbook of Architectural Practice* 20–6, 33–4, 105–6, 181
 as president of AIA 154–6, 225 n.45
 role on Committee on Contracts and Specifications 157–9, 168–74, 177–8
Dehli, Arne 119, 245–6 n.70
drawings and specifications 133, 142, 146, 177–8, 184–9, 194–6
Duchamp, Marcel 70, 234 n.77
Duchamp-Villon, Raymond 70–1

Ecole des Beaux Arts. *See under* architectural education
engineering 247 n.94. *See also* consultants
ethics 13–14, 132–9, 149–50. *See also* advertising
Ewing & Chappell, Architects 47, 49, 65, 67–78
Ewing, Charles 67–8, 73–4

fee structure
 direct cost plus fee basis 118, 121–2, 124

government challenges to 205–6
origins of 118–20, 246 n.75
percentage of construction cost 108–9, 115–21, 151
schedule of charges 113–21, 123–4, 131, 134, 157, 189
field orders 193, 263 n.32
fireproof construction 28, 47, 55–62, 73, 90, 211
Fitzpatrick, F.W. 57–9, 104, 107, 109, 114, 242 n.26
Frank Miles Day & Brother, Architects 47–8

general contractors and contracting system. *See also* project delivery methods
architects' criticisms of 146, 152–5, 252–3 n.12, 259 n.89
rise of 24, 116, 120, 151–2, 177–9, 202, 253 n.17
Gilbert, Cass 41, 104, 113, 120, 134–5, 154–5
Griffin, Percy 60–1, 231 n.46
Gutman, Robert 205, 239 n.1

Hamilton, John L. 23, 137–8
Handbook of Architectural Practice, origin and development of 2–5, 181–2, 241 n.15, 259–60 nn.2–3. *See also* Day, Frank Miles
Heddinger, H.G. 23–4
Heery, George 204, 266 n.62
Hogarth, Jr. *See* Kent, Rockwell
Hoggson Building Method 202–4
hollow-tile construction 28
Hoover, Herbert 209, 265 n.49

Kahn, Ely Jacques 50–1
Kent, Rockwell
as artist and draftsman 47, 49–51, 90–1, 234 n.77
in collaboration with Frederick Squires 30, 64–6
in collaboration with George S. Chappell 67–70, 74–86, 89
Kidder, Frank E. 11–12
King, William B. 23, 178, 258 n.75
Kissam, Henry S. 104

Laird, Warren P. 24
Latour, Bruno 248–9 n.113
Latrobe, Benjamin 119
Lewman, Harry L. 170–1

master builder 8–11, 14–20, 158–9, 161–2, 173–4, 200
Murchison, Kenneth 73, 79

National Association of Builders 14–19, 150, 156, 161–8
National Association of Builders' Exchanges 168–77
The New Yorker 88, 238 nn.114–15

owner–builder relation 8–34, 99. *See also* Uniform Contract of 1888

Parker, Dorothy 82, 86–7
Parker, William Stanley 175–6, 258 n.75, 259–60 n.2
Pond, Allen B. 156–7, 169
Portman, John 204–5
practice, sociology of 3–5, 94, 219–20 n.4, 224 nn.40–1, 260–1 nn.6–7, 269 n.85
professions, sociology of 2, 182–3, 205, 219–20 n.4, 224 nn.40–1, 262 n.11
project delivery methods
construction management 204, 226 n.1, 266 n.62
design–bid–build 206 (*see also* general contractors and contracting system)
design–build 135, 184, 202–6, 242 n.25
integrated project delivery (IPD) 201–8
multiple contract system (*see* pre-modern formations *under* architectural practice and profession)
single contract system (*see* general contractors *and* subcontractors)
Purdy, Corydon T. 127–9, 247 n.98

quantity surveyor system 119–20, 194–9, 265 n.51

Sayward, William H. 15, 17, 158–68, 171–2, 223 n.25, 256 n.44
Sherman Act 205
shop drawings 191–2, 202, 207
"Sky Line, The" 88
Society of Beaux-Arts Architects 68, 79, 233–4 n.70
specifications 186–9. *See also* drawings and specifications
speculative development 101–5, 106–10, 120, 161
Squires, Frederick 26–34, 55–6, 59–64, 226 n.55
Squires & Wendehack, Architects 60–3
Squires & Wynkoop, Architects 28, 47, 49, 51–66
standard of care. *See under* architectural practice and profession
subcontractors, subcontracting 152–3, 161, 164, 173–4, 177–8, 185
supervision and superintendence of construction 15, 119–21, 123, 139, 151–4, 189–91
Swartwout, Egerton 84, 237 n.108, 238–9 n.121

Tarsney Act 111–15
Tom Thumtack. *See* Squires, Frederick
tools of architectural practice 2–3, 7–8, 182–4. *See also specific contractual instruments by name*

Traprock, Walter E. 84–6. *See also* Chappell, George S.
T Square Club of Philadelphia 42, 47–9, 52–3, 55, 67

Uniform Contract of 1888
 architect's authority under 115–16, 123–4, 223 nn.26–9
 dissatisfactions with 17–19
 drafting of 14–20, 150–1, 160–3
 modifications of 145–6, 155–61, 169–77
US Department of Commerce. *See* Hoover, Herbert
US Department of Justice 205–6

Vanity Fair 82–4, 88
Van Rensselaer, Maria Griswold 112, 141
Vitruvius 8, 93–4, 136–8, 241 n.17

Waid, D. Everett 37–42, 71–3, 193, 227 n.5
Ware, William Rotch 10, 221 n.8
Wendehack, Clifford 60–3, 231 n.47
Western Association of Architects 14–20, 161, 222 n.18
Wight, Peter B. 14–15
working drawings 19, 178. *See also* drawings and specifications
Wright, G. Alexander 196–8
Wynkoop, John 28, 51–3, 60–2. *See also* Squires & Wynkoop, Architects